THE LONG SPACE

Cultural Memory

in

the

Present

Mieke Bal and Hent de Vries, Editors

THE LONG SPACE

Transnationalism and Postcolonial Form

Peter Hitchcock

STANFORD UNIVERSITY PRESS

STANFORD, CALIFORNIA

Stanford University Press
Stanford, California

©2010 by the Board of Trustees of the
Leland Stanford Junior University.

Printed in the United States of America on acid-free, archival-quality paper

Library of Congress Cataloging-in-Publication Data

Hitchcock, Peter.
  The long space : transnationalism and postcolonial form / Peter Hitchcock.
      p. cm.—(Cultural memory in the present)
  Includes bibliographical references and index.
   ISBN 978-0-8047-6236-6 (cloth : alk. paper)—ISBN 978-0-8047-6237-3
(pbk. : alk. paper)
    1. Postcolonialism in literature. 2. Transnationalism in literature. 3. Space and time
in literature. 4. Harris, Wilson—Criticism and interpretation. 5. Farah, Nuruddin,
1945—Criticism and interpretation. 6. Toer, Pramoedya Ananta, 1925-2006—
Criticism and interpretation. 7. Djebar, Assia, 1936—Criticism and interpretation.
8. Literature, Modern—History and criticism. I. Title. II. Series: Cultural memory
in the present.
   PN56.C63H58 2010
   809'.933581—dc22   2009032018

Typeset by Classic Typography in 11/13.5 Adobe Garamond

TO THE MEMORY OF MY BROTHER,
DAVID
"Vex not his ghost"

Contents

Acknowledgments

This book began several years ago as a means to understand how postcolonial writing might be thought differently within world literature (and, indeed, how world literature itself would be changed in that relation). I never thought at the time that the *Long Space* as a concept of duration could affect the work of writing the book itself. This extensive engagement has been a lesson for many. First, I would like to thank Emily Apter, who gave me initial encouragement for the idea and the project it precipitated. I am grateful to the Professional Staff Congress at the City University of New York (PSC-CUNY), whose research grants allowed me to work in London, Paris, Cape Town, and Jakarta. I thank Nuruddin Farah for an extraordinary conversation with him in Cape Town, as well as another author and friend, Margie Orford, for helping to facilitate the event. Various conferences and universities hosted talks on aspects of the Long Space. In particular, I would like to thank the organizers of the South and Southeast Asian Association for the Study of Culture and Religion (SSEASR) for letting me speak on Pramoedya in Bangkok, the American Comparative Literature Association (ACLA) for the chance to discuss "the world as concept" in Puebla, and the Museum Moderner Kunst (MUMOK) in Vienna for the keynote I was afforded on the postcolonial chronotope. I have also given lectures at Columbia University, Johns Hopkins University, New York University, the University of Sheffield, and the University of Cape Town on key elements of this research. Thank you all.

Chris GoGwilt has been an important inspiration on the work of Pramoedya, as well as Max Lane, who translated the Buru Quartet. I have not followed all of their advice, but I do hope my efforts here might further the conversation. Hena Maes-Jelinek, whose work on Wilson Harris is exemplary, provided me with important information and answered my queries—however far off the beaten track. Clarisse Zimra and Anne Donadey offered expertise and comment on Djebar, while conversations with Gayatri Chakravorty Spivak elicited clarification on the vexed concept of "world-ing." I thank my students, of course, for usefully questioning every concept at work in my text.

Mieke Bal has given strong support for this project, and I also thank the folks over at Stanford University Press, in particular Emily-Jane Cohen, Sarah Crane Newman, Mariana Raykov, and Elizabeth Forsaith. Thanks, too, to Meechal Hoffman for assistance with the index. This has not been an easy text to write or edit, but I appreciate all of the help I have had in these otherwise lonely processes. That acknowledgment, of course, includes friends and colleagues who, whether living, liminal, or lost, still inspire the words I write and include: Robert Barsky, Tim Brennan, Keya Ganguly, Lawrence Haddad, Isabelle Lorenz, Eric Mendelsohn, Jenny Sharpe, Neil Smith, Larry Venuti, and the inimitable Marco Esposito, "il miglior fabbro."

This book is dedicated to my brother, David, whose untimely death is a constant reminder that my literary understanding of duration is not the equivalent of personal experience or necessarily a window on the fleeting ticktock of time called life. My only hope is that the analysis I provide might lend greater substance to the meaning of duration so no life is wasted by its elision.

Finally, I would like to offer a bow to my wonderful family: to my mother, whose lessons in persistence put mine to shame; to my kids, Molly and Sam, who persist in more ways than I dare to list; and to the love of my life, Amy, who always finds a way to live with these texts while eloquently shaping her own. If this book sometimes challenges me to remember the one I imagined, it is yet ready to come into this world; so, as Djebar would put it, "Enfantement!"

Abbreviations of Frequently Cited Titles of Works

AA   *Art and Answerability* (Mikhail Bakhtin)

ASB   *Anak Semua Bangsa* (Pramoedya Ananta Toer); see also *Child of All Nations*

ATIG   *All That Is Gone* (Pramoedya Ananta Toer)

BM   *Bumi Manusia* (Pramoedya Ananta Toer); see also *This Earth of Mankind*

CAN   *Child of All Nations* (Pramoedya Ananta Toer)

F   *Footsteps* (Pramoedya Ananta Toer)

G   *Gifts* (Nuruddin Farah)

GD   *The Gift of Death* (Jacques Derrida)

GQ   *The Guyana Quartet* (Wilson Harris)

GT   *Given Time* (Jacques Derrida)

HG   *House of Glass* (Pramoedya Ananta Toer)

IC   *Imagined Communities* (Benedict Anderson)

JL   *Jejak Langkah* (Pramoedya Ananta Toer); see also *Footsteps*

LP   *Language and Power* (Benedict Anderson)

M   *Maps* (Nuruddin Farah)

MS   *The Mute's Soliloquy* (Pramoedya Ananta Toer)

OP   *On the Postcolony* (Achilles Mbembe)

PDP   *Problems in Dostoevsky's Poetic* (Mikhail Bakhtin)

PN   *The Philosophy of the Novel* (J.M. Bernstein)

Q   "Quetzalcoatl and the Smoking Mirror: Reflections on Originality and Tradition" (Wilson Harris)

RI   *The Repeating Island* (Antonio Benitez-Rojo)

RK   *Rumah Kaca* (Pramoedya Ananta Toer); see also *House of Glass*
S   *Secrets* (Nuruddin Farah)
TEM   *This Earth of Mankind* (Pramoedya Ananta Toer)
TN   *The Theory of the Novel* (Georg Lukács)
TWS   *Tradition, the Writer, and Society* (Wilson Harris)

THE LONG SPACE

1

The Long Space

Time has more than one writing system.
—Henri Lefebvre

In a poignant sequence in *Jalan Raya Pos* (*The Great Post Road*, 1996),
a documentary about Pramoedya Ananta Toer, the writer lights a *kretek*
cigarette and takes out the trash.[1] It is refuse that contains sheets of manuscript, testimony to the scourge of writer's block. Pramoedya goes into his
backyard and over to a pile of rubbish. He empties out the bin, then deli-
cately arranges the papers before setting light to them. It is another day in
the life of Indonesia's most celebrated writer, then under a form of urban
arrest—a time and place seemingly outside the busy intensity of interpretation and yet a chronotope deeply inscribed in the contemporary world
(of letters, of globalization, of intellectual engagement, of postcoloniality
as an open parenthesis on decolonization). For what is this scene if not
one that passes by while what has passed by has an obtuse purchase on the
present, one that allows this tableau to drift while hermeneutics remains
secure in its operative logic, concrete or abstract, anglophone or at least
European, translating time into space when the former fosters someone
else's agency? The author watches the manuscript burn in the knowledge
that he too has been part of this delenda, but survived.

Such living on (*sur-vivre* in the Derridean sense) offers a vital polemic: it is a measure of persistence, determination, endurance, and the
meaning of a specific time/space in transnational literature. It is out of
place *and* time, perhaps, to invoke time as significant for postcolonial
writing within globalization. Yet however we choose to ground transnational cultural relations, it remains the arena in which one hails writers,

including Pramoedya, within the reach of circulation on "this Earth of mankind" (or what Erich Auerbach once provocatively termed *irdischen Welt*).[2] Asserting that Pramoedya and three other writers—Wilson Harris, Nuruddin Farah, and Assia Djebar, the focus of this study—are largely out of step with a postmodern global episteme is not the point, for they are equally if not more discontinuous with each other, and deliberately so from my perspective. The persistence relates to an alternative understanding of narration, a logic of form not simply outside world literature, the world republic of letters, global comparatism, or normative transnationalism. If this argument partakes of a current time of crisis, it is through a crisis in time, material contradictions embedded in the unfinished business of ending empire. Writing takes time, but in transnational trilogies and tetralogies, duration in dynamic place is a crucial chronotope of decolonization, one that must claim time differently to narrate the fraught space between more obvious signposts like Bretton Woods and Bandung. Reading takes time too, and these extended narratives accentuate time's purchase on their comprehension. All extended narrative does this, but the long space is bound to the concrete predicaments of postcolonial narration as transnational critique.

I locate the long space in the extended novel of postcoloniality beside itself. A relatively narrow approach—and one that often relies on theoretically inspired close reading—it will, however, substantiate some broad materialist claims. If they are not a horizon of the literary and the social, or culture and society, these claims yet form an almacantar by which their current constellation may be judged. The polemic is occasioned primarily by the event of reading inspiring fiction, but also by the manner in which they speak to several key issues of cultural debate: world literature and how it may be determined; the links and breaks between the terms postcolonialism, transnationalism, and globalism; the noncoincidence between literary institutions and the literary; the meaning of form for postcolonialism; the at-once vexed relationship of the novel to nation formation in postcolonial states; postcolonialism as other than the luxury of Western or Westernized cultural elites; critical transnationalism as an interruption of the logic of information retrieval in global circuits of knowledge and power; and the event of colonialism as not historically settled. This is not just a list but an itinerary, and one that cannot rest easy with the mantra that culture is the preeminent form of politics in our time and that when we feel global we participate ineluctably in wresting freedom from the crushing realm of necessity. One cannot negotiate these challenges as if yet another Western critic, by checking off a list, is freed from the privileges of power that produce that subject position. The measure of the itinerary is the polemic it fosters that will deploy the long space as the organizing trope for disputation among them. Indeed, the complex register of the long space is the means to argue beyond the realm of propositional faith that Wilson Harris extravagantly terms "numinous inexactitudes."[3] I cannot leave the long space there, although Harris is most at home in shamanic indeterminacy.

Extended novels are coterminous with the history of the novel, and merely to note extension would require an analysis no less voluminous, a critique that would include the novelization of epic, the consonance of seriality with the commodification of the publishing industry, the related phenomenon of the emergence of the leisured reading class, and an irrepressible will to universalism requiring a dedication to expanded capacity in order to scale its desire. No formula can capture the difference of *Remembrance of Things Past*, *The Lord of the Rings*, *The Pallisers*, *Cities of Salt*, *USA*, *Journey to the West*, *Don Quixote*, *Clarissa*, and so on and so forth, although a few formulas, such as the one which says that narration might cheat the brutish brevity of being human, are as unsurprising as they are insufficient. That the philosophy of the novel so often suspends engagement with the extended narrative form acknowledges such pervasiveness only to underline that elemental persistence is as everyday as it is a bar on substantive theorization.

Because this argument is about a logic of form for which the long space is a shorthand, I wish the following to refract the nature of the extended transnational narration to be discussed later. Provisionally, I offer three propositions gathered by a fourth. These concern institution, world literature, nation, and chronotope. I will explain each one briefly in terms of the itinerary, then in more detail around the meaning of the long space for the project as a whole. While accepting Jameson's admonition to always historicize, that historicity now must face the prospect—also marked by Jameson—of an end to temporality, one that would truncate the continuing work of decolonization.[4] Fortunately, at the macropolitical level the supposed inevitabilities of globalization are being sharply rethought, and important questions are challenging the forms of socialization on offer in the neoliberal world beyond Cold War inertia. None of these oppositional discourses carry guarantees or deadlines, and in that spirit the *long* in my title refers also to future persistence, a mode of engagement more extensive than the exigencies of the present and a level of commitment consonant with the task of facing the enduring facility for exploitation in global integration. The formation of form is that which is most protracted and conjures all kinds of mixed temporalities, aesthetic registers, sharp contradictions, and poignant revisions like this comment by Jameson: "the momentous event of decolonization . . . is a fundamental determinant of postmodernity."[5] To fathom the time of form I offer the following.

First, if we can accept Mikhail Bakhtin's sense that chronotope is the place where the knots of narrative are tied and untied, is this specific to postcolonial writing and how?[6] Chronotope is not any old coordinate of time and space but that figural semantic process allowing narration to proceed to form. In every space of postcoloniality, marked by nation or locale, movement or embeddedness, inscription or orality, culture refracts duration: not just that colonialism was endured, but that its figures of time did not absolutely displace or dismantle local forms of temporality. The transnational chronotope does not contend that time's arrow, a dubious chronologism of "post" as "after" in postcolonialism, confirms the end of colonialism, but rather accentuates the distillation of specific coordinates in its moment (or a process of moments for which I use the term *eventness*).[7] The transnational aspect is a level of interdependency, and indeed in correlating colonialism and postcolonialism the long space is interdependency as extension. Since there is little uniformity in colonialism or decolonization, one should mark this difference by writing chronotopes, a multiplicity more accurately reflecting the contrasts between say, the decolonizing expressions of Somalia and Guyana, Algeria and Indonesia, and indeed between writers and the nations by which they are "tagged" (Farah currently lives in South Africa, Harris in England, Djebar in France and the United States; Pramoedya lived most of his life in Indonesia). Yet it is possible to acknowledge the uniqueness of event that specifies the break from colonial dominion in each instance, while positing a logic of chronotope for all. The weakness of Bakhtin's formulation emerges from the tendency to read "knots" as content markers *sui generis* rather than as abstractions on the means of time/space at stake. The lure of content is unavoidable and I succumb to it without apology. The aim, however, is something more ambitious, which is to take chronotope as a constitutive problem of transnational narration, a knot that is a key to the ways through which postcoloniality can be expressed. While the long space is not exactly a writing system of time in Lefebvre's sense, it nevertheless takes time seriously enough to elaborate its purchase on being in the world.[8] One must be able to imagine history in order to change it.

Second, because this study draws on transnational literature from Guyana, Somalia, Indonesia, and Algeria, I am attempting to ask some questions of the resurgent category of "world literature." The paradigm of the long space indicates unfinished business in decolonization that constitutes a problem in resuscitating Goethe's original declaration to Eckermann in 1827: "National literature is no longer of importance, it is the time for world literature, and all must aid in bringing it about."[9] What concept of time is at stake in world literature's effulgence and, indeed, what sense of "world" that accompanies it? Does not world literature return on the wings of globalization and is it freely interpreted at the very moment when temporality is drained from its inclusive magnanimity? "World" offers the imprimatur of transnationalism as that which is beyond nation and its suffocating prescriptions. It is the passport with copious stamps and extra pages; the ward of book covers with exotic names and palm fronds; the impress of a massive translation machine sufficient to convert there to here in hardback, paperback, or digital download; the substantive component that, once grasped, relieves one from the agony of parochial discernment. And, most important, the *world* in world literature is studiously neutral and requires no further qualification: it is the twenty-first-century ghost of nineteenth-century aestheticism that at once announces the best that has been thought and said. Indeed, for all the assumed neutrality, world literature has the drab hierarchization of petty-bourgeois desire. At the very least it allows one to consume postcolonialism without that nasty taste of social struggle in which a reader's own cosmopolitanism may be at stake. If all of Goethe's pronouncements were mysteriously lost, the term *world literature* would still have to be invented for it is dialectically bound to the inevitabilities of commodification in which all that is solid not only melts into air but is globally circulated.

Franco Moretti has rightly emphasized that "world literature is not an object, it's a *problem*" and one that he has approached, somewhat controversially, through world systems analysis, geometric design, and statistical chunking.[10] He favors a notion of *long* as distance (as in distant reading) rather than as duration, a novel solution to the forbidding difficulty, and quantity, of worlds of difference that tends to suspend the issue of strife in accumulation on a world scale for, well, accumulation on a world scale. This is a simplification of the nuance Moretti provides, although perhaps no more reductive than the tabulations of *Graphs, Maps, and Trees*. The long space is not just "a thorn in the side, a permanent intellectual challenge to national literatures" in the manner of Moretti's world literature, but a specific world of time that does not exclude the strategic value of nation in global endeavors, negatively in nationalism's role in territorial expansion and positively in national delinking from a world of imperial inclusivity.[11] World literature is set as a task not as a statistical formula, a thorn that is the oneiric function of the long space in a transnationalism otherwise eliding postcoloniality.

Our third keyword and corresponding thesis concerns *nation*. Nation seems like the anachronism of anachronisms: it parades its habitual out-of-timeness by raising flags in the face of transnationalism, regionalism, economic and political blocs, and continental integrity. But it does this in both senses of the phrase "raising flags"; it celebrates its longevity in the ritual of nationalistic display while also serving as a warning to all those who believe its fictive assemblage somehow negates the material substance of its collectivity. It is ironic that Renan's 1882 lecture "What Is a Nation?" carries a pointed admonition on the necessity of forgetting to achieve national polity when this amnesia is artfully produced by postnational arguments.[12] Assia Djebar, while wary of any nation idea, particularly as it writes Algerian woman, uses anamnesis to rethink nation rather than fold it back into its prechoate possibility in colonialism.[13] The ambivalence of nation trembles in postcolonial writing, a flag of eventness that must be studied for its unique process and not simply as the failed-state syndrome ideologically serving state dependency or neocolonialism. Rather than jettison the nation idea, it is more useful to consider its ideologies and strategic interests on a case-by-case basis, particularly when specific nation formations have clearly stood for liberation from colonial subjugation. The fictive corollary in Benedict Anderson's "imagined community" thesis is not a measure of truth versus falsehood but imagination's claims on collectivity, whose fungibility is understood from Anderson's readings of Asian politics and literature, through the Philippines and José Rizal, and Indonesia and Pramoedya. In the conceptual oscillation between Anderson's insights on the nation/colonial nexus and the "spectral comparison," a paradigm of transnationalism can be articulated, one whose coordinates trace nation narration as possibility in the trilogies and tetralogies I consider. Literary criticism's major flaw in reading Anderson is to offer him as a literary critic and thereby freely indulge in constructing literary homologies from his grammar of nations. Anderson's facility in languages certainly informs a literariness, but the criticism itself concerns nations and formations of state however deft his choice of literary examples. The result has been an aestheticizing of government structures and histories at some distance from the politics of reading Anderson employs. No doubt I am guilty of this "translation," but on the whole my invocation of nation begins from its fully material manifestation in decolonization and its determinate facility for the long space. The long space says that nations need time ("generations" says Balibar), and even if the novel, or the seriality of novels, cannot tell time in quite the same way, extended postcolonial fiction comes closest to figuring the nation's abstract expression: it is coextensive with nation ontology as an abstraction.[14]

Both world literature and nation are unthinkable outside a logic of institution, a complex matrix of legitimizing mechanisms—from governmental infrastructure, schools, media industries, or "departments" of various kinds, to ideological reflexes that bind worldviews from moment to moment in a manner just cohesive enough to appear a material second nature. David Damrosch signals this institutional aura in world literature by asking "Which literature, whose world?"—questions that consider his own positioning while opening the door to other relations of legitimation.[15] Franco Moretti, however, understands that the febrile connections of institution and legitimation require a declarative reduction in scale that neatly specifies the force of his intervention: "the way we imagine comparative literature is a mirror of how we see the world."[16] It is an answer to Damrosch's questions (even if, chronologically, the questions are an answer to Moretti), but let us think of it briefly as a statement on institution. It is true the way we imagine comparative literature is a mirror of how we see the world, but then how we imagine is a mirror of how we see the world and the reason for comparative literature's necessity is at best qualified. Skepticism traverses the logic from historical contradiction, not opinion. The mirror of comparative literature has not been shattered by declaration but by the social and political upheavals of at least the last fifty years. This is not to announce the eclipse of Comparative Literature (or English) departments but to note that interdependence on a world scale may require *imagining* that possibility. That which coordinates national literature in the imaginary schema of nation is not trumped by world literature; rather, this institutional logic produces world literature as its reflex. It follows that the extant conditions of institution as national legitimation are intrinsic to world literature, and should a world literature develop beyond that legitimizing matrix it will, perhaps, be called literature.

These theses or positions are not in parallel and are as oddly arranged as my literary examples. The galvanizing trope is the chronotope, for it accentuates the coordinates of space *and* time in the otherwise problematic constellation of the other three. Bakhtin only hints that the chronotope could do more work than its prominence in Goethe, Dostoevsky, or Rabelais, but it must do so here for at least two related reasons. First, it is a conduit between the sensuous particularity of the text and philosophical abstraction, a time for'world in both cases that is not anathema to an understanding of institution, institutions of literature, and national institutions of literature. It facilitates a scale of comparative outsideness. One thread that connects the writers and the critical paradigm is, to borrow from Edward Said, a "precarious exilic realm," a condition that does not entail actual exile to fathom its logic but a notion of outsideness, or exotopy, a sometimes literal but more insistently figural border sensibility.[17] Said reads this as an intellectual vocation, a committed engagement in the public sphere; for me this signals a responsibility in scale. If the exilic and exotopic keep coming back in this text, it is to confirm that the intimacy of reading has an extimacy of effects beyond it.

Second, if I push chronotope to transnationalism it is to further discussion on time's claim on that which is presented as its superadequation. The idea that nations require time must be supplemented since this can be deployed to blunt transnationalism's history, one much longer than the term itself. I use postcolonialism within transnationalism to problematize this elision by introducing time/space coordinates into the latter's otherwise slick immediacy. The effect is not just one of catechresis but of slowing down, of marking duration with duration, of saving time by using it. Chronotopic critique, however, is not a means to fight speed and space: its strategy is to insinuate time/space coordinates in transnationalism, the better to specify what is living and dead in their conjunction. In this manner one can read, as Djebar puts it, "the cries of just one second stretched blue as far as the horizon."[18]

We know that colonialism offered a world to be inscribed. Gayatri Spivak calls this process "worlding," whereby Europe, for instance, projects an aura of blankness onto the world, specifically the Third or developing world, to produce a space for subsequent inscription.[19] A complex process of presencing and othering is implied in worlding, and it did not expire with the declarations of independence often interpreted to herald postcoloniality. The problem requires first, a fairly precise elaboration of the concepts of space and time involved, and second, the ramifications of the introduction of literary form onto this terrain. The long space is an abstraction on how the literary concretizes the social as a counter to the historical inscription of the colonial and its attendant meanings. The production of space regulates a logic of state that deludes itself into believing it is the quintessence of development and the pinnacle of civilization. If space as a concept is contaminated by production as projection (the space of worlding), how can the long space resist the worlding of this episteme? The postcolonial writer must continually struggle to de-scribe space as the Other of colonialism. Consciously or not the space of postcolonial writing brings alternative histories to bear on the processes of anticolonial narration. The long in long space is the irruption of local history into the truncated temporalities of globalization and transnationalism in their hegemonic formations. Critiques of postcolonial literature as cultural transnationalism are not possible unless the local comes sharply into view—not simply as content, but as a structural articulation of cultural difference within the narrative. This does not provide a blueprint applicable to every element of postcolonial cultural expression. Yet how irruptions of the local are formulated must be registered within postcolonial criticism, especially to head off repositioning all postcolonial texts as native information.

The long space considers the production of narrative against the destructive effects of the colonial moment, but is not limited to that valence. Just as Fanon attacks Sartre's preface to an anthology edited by Senghor (because Sartre enlists *négritude* for a class struggle defined by Western history), so the long space must problematize the notion that transnational cultural form is reactive to what the West has bequeathed.[20] What the novel, for instance, formalizes can be displaced by the space in which it is engaged. Writers who entertain this challenge may be heralded by primarily Western cosmopolitan literati, yet a different field emerges if one begins with the form and content of the long space as agonistically dialogic. The long space stares Janus-faced into the detritus of colonial aesthetics while glaring wide-eyed at the paradoxes of the postcolonial. Cultural transnationalism does not exclude the contaminated conditions of my time/space, as if that does not contribute to the historical contradictions of cultural "exchange" at this juncture. If Arif Dirlik's point that postcolonialism begins when diasporic "Third World" intellectuals make their way in the West contains a grain of truth, then this is no less true of Western "discoveries" of "Third World" fiction.[21] Nevertheless, the aesthetic may still be used to investigate what remains unassimiliable outside that devoutlywished embrace. And this is also why the challenges of the long space are not simply relevant to a distrusted colonial episteme.

Spatial concepts are common in contemporary cultural critique because the metaphors and materialities of space have become more creatively enmeshed. Space is often enjoined theoretically to do the work of time. The long space, however, invokes time as an aesthetic apparatus for the production of space. This can be elaborated in a number of ways. There are modes of postcolonial writing that challenge the dominance of abstract space over material space within discourses of modernity. It is the latter's concept of the production of space that Lefebvre explicitly challenges in Hegel, enough to construe him dialectically. Interestingly, Lefebvre characterizes his own intervention as "the long history of space" and, while one must remain wary of the speculative and aesthetic reach of Lefebvre's history, it provides a theoretical and political correlative in the current work.[22] Indeed, the significance of transnational trilogies and tetralogies lies in their articulation of the conceived and lived spaces (the representation of space and spaces of representation) of postcoloniality, a critique prompted by Lefebvre's transgression of conventional narratives of space. That *histoire longue* in French oscillates between history and story continues to provide its own provocation.

Another register for the long space as transnational chronotope derives from concepts of culture themselves. The *long* in long space also finds inspiration in Raymond Williams's *The Long Revolution*.[23] This is not an unproblematic association, given the generally Anglocentric and organicist predilections ascribed to Williams's work. Yet in the opening pages to *Orientalism*, Edward Said commends Williams (alongside Gramsci and

Foucault) for demonstrating a central approach in his own work: "We can better understand the persistence and the durability of saturating hegemonic systems like culture when we realize that their internal constraints upon writers and thinkers were productive, not unilaterally inhibiting."[24] Said highlights Williams's readings of nineteenth-century colonialists and imperialists, and he mentions *The Long Revolution* in this regard. Yet this same contrapuntal reading can now be applied to Williams himself.

The genesis for Williams's concept of the long revolution lies in the conclusion to *Culture and Society*: "The forces which have changed and are still changing our world are indeed industry and democracy. Understanding this change, this long revolution, lies at a level of meaning which it is not easy to reach."[25] Williams's approach explores culture as a source of such understanding, as multiple expressions of "a whole way of life." Culture is, paradoxically, profoundly ordinary in that its generality and fecundity dialectically inflect and affect the revolution in industry and democracy. This is one reason why Pramoedya's daily routine should not pass by. Culture thus emerges as the third term in the idea of the long revolution:

Yet there remains a third revolution, perhaps the most difficult of all to interpret. We speak of a cultural revolution, and we must certainly see the aspiration to extend the active process of learning, with the skills of literacy and other advanced communication, to all people rather than to limited groups, as comparable in importance to the growth of democracy and the rise of scientific industry. . . . Of course, this revolution is at a very early stage. . . . This deeper cultural revolution is a large part of our most significant living experience, and is being interpreted and indeed fought out, in very complex ways, in the world of art and ideas. (*The Long Revolution*, 11–12)

These words were published in 1961 and, while we may quibble with how "advanced" is being imagined and how culture may advance, they still resonate today. The level of correspondence is less important than the mode of historicity and the interrelationship of economics, politics, and culture implied. What is long about the revolution is counterintuitive because its processes are drawn out and are difficult to assess. Wars of independence in colonial territories are experienced as an intense rupture with imperialist domain. Yet, whatever the violence and instability of those moments, it is striking that writers ("in the world of art and ideas") have often taken a much more protracted imaginative engagement with the culture and history at stake in such crises. Their structure of feeling, to borrow from Williams again, seeks to articulate not just the promise of the postcolony, but the long and complex sinews of industry, democracy, and culture in which it is precipitate. Although I am less sanguine than Williams that critics and criticism can enjoin this effort, writers are not outside the revolution Williams invokes and such a process, however we might rethink its terms, continues.

The *long* in Williams's *The Long Revolution* usefully posits a project rather than a historical description. Indeed, Williams's procedures require a nuanced imaginative and somatic grasp (a structure of *feeling*?) not always associated with history or sociology. Significantly, one understands what constitutes a methodology in Williams not just by reading the trilogy of works that established his reputation (*Culture and Society, The Long Revolution*, and *Communications*), but through his trilogy of novels: *Border Country, Second Generation*, and *The Fight for Manod*.[26] The abstraction of the "long revolution" is given aesthetic reach by Williams's deeply personal if emotionally edgy fictional exploration of the "knowable communities" and "complex seeing" of his creative fiction. Without laboring the point, the trilogy evolves through the chronotopes articulating a community in Williams's vision. It is long precisely because the nature of that deep structure requires it. The crux is whether the form betrays a level of unknowability in the communities portrayed. For his part, Williams believes that such knowledge depends on duration and the intensity of experience. In the third novel, Robert Lane asks Matthew Price (the central figure) whether his book took a long time to write. Price replies, "It took a long time because it had to be lived" (*Fight*, 38). In effect, the *long* in the long space considers duration and length in fiction by questioning whether the levels of mediation in experience are merely the substance of knowledge and windows on the real of community existence. The long works of fiction at issue are embroiled in similar yet specific historical conditions that do not lend themselves easily to the categories of experience Williams elucidates. I want to draw from the theoretical stimuli of his works without flattening out important changes on the aesthetic terrain. At the very least this means taking account of Gauri Viswanathan's point that even when Williams acknowledges a link between English social formations and matrices of imperialism, his narration of nation typically suppresses the conduit between national and imperial structures.[27] What is transnational about postcolonial fiction often explores the tension in that relationship precisely to figure what is and is not possible under conditions of post-colonial nationhood. From this perspective, the long space interrogates the long revolution, particularly since the industrial, democratic, and cultural progress the latter describes have often proceeded through colonial subjection. That Said, a friend and admirer of Williams, would write *Culture and Imperialism* is a more obvious answer to the significant lacunae in Williams's culturalist mode.[28] Said examines how culture narrates the imperialist project. Said's basic premise, not unique but uniquely nuanced, is that the English novel of the nineteenth century (one of Williams's key interests) contributes to and solidifies continuity in the English imperialist project, at once confirming its reality while projecting a fantasy of its logical consistency in terms of culture and civilization. This "regulatory social presence" (*Culture and Imperialism*, 73) is not just a symptom of the novel's ideological work, but is a subtext of the entire narrative of progress redolent in Eurocentrism and Orientalism. Just as cartography maps out a space for the projection of Western meanings, so the novel can distill this territorial desire as a quintessence of aesthetic practice. Said's readings of the novel, particularly those of Kipling, Forster, and Conrad, foreground European dominion as appropriate to a cultural tradition that, because of the ideological trajectories of imperialist consciousness, still resounds today. Said is at his best in *Culture and Imperialism* when he unpacks the regulatory norms of empire in the great tradition of the English novel as institution. He is on less certain ground, however, when he tracks the ways in which decolonizing and postcolonial writers disturb, destabilize, and attempt to transform imperialist cultural discourses. Said's comments on Achebe and Ngũgĩ, for instance, are always insightful, but do not evince the level of engagement he has extended to Forster or Conrad. This is not to wish that Said had been more of a critic of postcolonial fiction—like Aijaz Ahmad in *In Theory* wanting Said to have been more of a Marxist—because this would miss the actual substance of his intellectual contribution.[29] Said's intervention provides a theoretical link between the massive rethinking of the tradition of the novel in the West and *what could be done* in the formal analysis of the novel of decolonization. Two strategies in particular recommend themselves.

First, Said accentuates the novel's participation in the aesthetic, ideological, and political struggles over space: "The appropriation of history, the historicization of the past, the narrativization of society, all of which give the novel its force, include the differentiation of social space, space to be used for social purposes" (*Culture and Imperialism*, 78). In *The Long Space* specific trilogies and tetralogies deconstruct this space of appropriation. I argue that transnational culture entails a broader, egalitarian, and conflictual novelistic space of negotiation than the hegemonic "worlding" currently imagined. While transnational space can be discussed in a myriad of other cultural forms, the contestable terrain of the novel is particularly acute because of its role in the differentiation of social space to which Said alludes. A significant number of problems emerge from this emphasis, including: the role of the novel in bourgeois social relations, the function of the novel for cosmopolitanism and transnational commerce, and the extent to which what Bakhtin calls "the novelization of discourse" now exceeds the perquisites of what we identify as the novel itself. This is only to acknowledge that cultural comparatism is highly contestable in the social differentiation of space on a world scale. The long space reappropriates the imaginative terrain by literally lengthening the form, but it simultaneously questions the nature of transnational inclusivity by elaborating that cultures take time. Here again, Said provides a pertinent provocation through contrapuntal reading.

Briefly, this draws on Said's considerable acumen in comparatism in which he attempts "to think through and interpret together experiences that are discrepant, each with its particular agenda and pace of development, its own internal formations, its internal coherence and system of external relationships" (*Culture and Imperialism*, 32). The contrapuntal analysis reads the imperial archive against the grain by articulating its sharp disjunctions with and elisions of social space according to other discourses and by exploring how its legitimizing narratives, the novel included, problematize the identitarian modes of, for example, Englishness or Frenchness. Such "new knowledges" are vital and constitute a struggle over structures of feeling in comparative critique. Yet the real challenge for cultural transnationalism is contrapuntal *writing*—the ways in which the artist makes the form her own. The long space refers to a critical mode of engaging transnational fiction and the writing out of postcolonial difference. Contrapuntal writing can, then, be joined to other terms, "de-scribing empire," "un-thinking Eurocentrism," and "decolonizing the mind," to borrow from the titles of works in the field of postcolonial critique. It is a primary mode through which the space of the transnational can be dialogized, rather than recolonized by avatars of West/Rest dichotomies.

Another opening onto persistence is a resolution on the daunting tasks of intellectual engagement hinted by "a precarious exilic realm." Said, in his introduction to a new edition of Auerbach's *Mimesis*, outlines this enduring heritage common among philologists. He suggests even Auerbach's admittedly Eurocentric view emphasized "the possibility of understanding inimical and perhaps even hostile others despite the bellicosity of modern cultures and nationalisms, and the optimism with which one could enter into the inner life of a distant author or historical epoch even with a healthy awareness of one's limitations of perspective and insufficiency of knowledge."[30] This was a comparatism hewed by Said himself "whose underlying and perhaps unrealizable rationale was this vast synthesis of the world's literary production transcending borders and languages but not in any way effacing their individuality and historical concreteness." The drawbacks of such comparatism, however, are legion not least because its tradition (like that of Williams) is so intimately entwined with the great age of European imperialism that shared its desire to transcend borders but tended to efface a good deal more in the process. Philologists were not the well-versed foot soldiers for European expansionism, despite pertinent evidence of collusion in the project. The problem was more infrastructural, in the way institutions of learning were conceived according to national and regional prerogatives, a manner that gave the rapacity of the West a logical consistency. In addition, the prodigious expertise required of philologists (consider, for instance, the range of reference in *Mimesis* and the languages invoked) seemed to exceed the capacity to teach it. As Said points out, Comparative Literature departments sought to develop such expertise but, with a few notable exceptions, the epistemological frisson primarily took place in academies and departments of a different order in France and Germany before the Second World War, for which Comparative Literature has been a vibrant specter. The lesson of persistence, then, with its coordinate in time, speaks to duration in a new temporality with decolonization as a conditional limit. That Said turns in this direction (particularly in *Culture and Imperialism*) deepens his prescience, and in time he may also be read not just as a philologist but as a transitional figure of cultural transnationalism, an interlocutor in a global dialogic more worthy of the term.

I say "transitional" because Said neither completes the project of the European philological tradition nor does he codify or elaborate what a *Weltliteratur* cognizant of a decolonizing caesura might look like. Nevertheless, in addition to his thoughts on space and the contrapuntal, Said offers other elements of a pertinent critical framework. While they must necessarily reconfigure the conditions of Goethe's formulation on *Weltliteratur*, they retain something of its utopian spirit. They are first and foremost conceived within secular humanism of a kind bound to social responsibility unafraid to challenge the creeping fundamentalisms even within its own tradition. This nonconformism (or autodidacticism, a term Said applies to Auerbach) also reminds one of Raymond Williams.[31]

If contrapuntal reading is central to Said's textual practice, the complement to secular humanism is "worldliness." This does not mean the substitution of world for nation but an understanding of specific conditions of their interaction. Postcolonialism is connected to transnationalism in order to emphasize what is exorbitant to each term individually (Said, for his part, will use "extraterritorial," by which he means a specific challenge to the territorial provenance of English).[32] Said's worldliness stands against the homogenizing tendencies of globalization, a lesson learned from reading and translating Auerbach's classic "Philologie die Weltliteratur" in which global standardization shrinks the possibility of *Weltliteratur* in inverse proportion. It also opposes closed interpretation as if a text might exist without its being in the world. Worldliness is a condition of possibility, one that demarcates the world of the text in several senses including: the world it constructs, the world in which it is, the world in which it finds a reader, and the world in which the critic attends to it. Said's point is a very basic one about the text's materiality, a "worldliness that does not come and go" (*World*, 34) even if the principle of worldliness itself is suspended—by the text, by the critic, by circumstantial fiat. Such worldliness, while material, is demonstrably abstract in contrast to the material force of the world as ordinarily construed: a world of nations, peoples, languages, cultures, economic relations. Part of the challenge of cultural transnationalism is to scale up the world of the text while scaling down the eponymous world out there, not in the interest of homology (or simply inflated culturalism), but to bring difference sharply into view. Being in the world means something else again if the text's substantiality is made coterminous with it. Said was never that moved by a sociology of literature (except Auerbach's)—unlike his friend, Williams, who managed to wrest it from Goldmann—but Said does not settle for what Neil Larsen has termed the "textualist fallacy" either and this is a postcolonial critique beside itself.[33] Instead, using the inspiration of an eleventh-century group of Andalusian linguists, the Zahirites, Said argues for a "double perspective" in literary analysis that does not leave the text alone to its devices or indeed to those of the critic:

[W]orldliness, circumstantiality, the text's status as an event having sensuous particularity as well as historical contingency, are considered as being incorporated in the text, an infrangible part of its capacity for conveying and producing meaning. This means that the text has a specific situation, placing restraints upon the interpreter and his interpretation not because the situation is hidden within the text as a mystery, but rather because the situation exists at the same level of surface particularity as the textual object itself. . . . Here is an ambition (which the Zahirites have to an intense degree) on the part of readers and writers to grasp texts as objects whose interpretation—by virtue of the exactness of their situation in the world—*has already commenced* and are objects already constrained by, and constraining their interpretation. Such texts can thereafter be construed as having need at most of complementary, as opposed to supplementary, readings. (*World*, 39)

While the *Welt* in Goethe's *Weltliteratur* tended to mark a schism between German nationalism and the world order in the nineteenth century, Said's worldliness is much conditioned by the event of his text: he invokes the world to give the text and the critic a more expansive vocation. That situation must be respected, but it leads to several qualifications in the concept for which I use the term *eventness*, rather than *event*. Why? It is possible to understand that the text has a specific situation and thus that interpretation has already commenced, but this is not always accessible, at least not as readily as "surface particularity" might indicate. The specificity of the textual event may be lost even though we may assume its conditional worldliness and the pre-history of interpretation. We can adjudicate the event of the text but there the fulcrum of interpretation moves toward the critic and is not simply given in what the text represents. Put another way, Said's use of circumstantiality reminds us of the pitfalls of circumstantial evidence that may not reveal the truth of the event except perhaps in the eye of the beholder. Thus, Said is right to point to the text's being in the world as worldliness, but the line between that event's constraining possibility and the projection of the same by the critic is notoriously thin. Eventness, on the other hand, stresses a logic of event rather than only an assumption about the content of the event. It proffers the paradox that the text has a unique event—and many of them. It also finds the structure of event continually displacing the dialogic interactions of text and critic. In my readings eventness will take several turns to explain hermeneutical necessity as simultaneously a conditional limit on postcoloniality.

The focus on event should not close it to process, one that might outdistance the critic's role in it. The reason for this is also redolent in Said's example. Said finds a model for worldliness among medieval Arab linguists that is then applied to Hopkins, Wilde, and Conrad: he tracks modernity without assuming a European signature. Said's training was primarily in the European tradition; but worldliness is radically inclusive and displacing in its own way. To this we could add that Said challenges the textual fetishism of the literary in the opening of his essay with a discussion of Glenn Gould, whose own event of performance depends on more than Said's ear and expertise in classical music. Yet in both cases what is innovative in Said's approach—Zahirite circumstantiality, a Gould record as a parody of performance—does not interrupt the actual critical exegesis, where the fact that "texts do not speak in the ordinary sense of the word" (*World*, 33) finds them speaking rather well in that mode. The counter-Orientalism disappears in the analysis, as does the text as more than literary. The issue is not to emphasize the provocation over the explication since they are of a piece; but if we take worldliness in all seriousness then it would assess this marked disjunction as itself materially determined and not something in need of correction.

This is an unusual position to take on postcoloniality, which is often read as reclamation of all that colonialism sundered. The heuristic function of postcolonial criticism has been its ability to unsettle the colonial archive by accentuating the real in what has been suppressed: the actual lives and experiences deeply inscribed in the day-to-day processes of colonial adventures, a real that often and critically spoke truth to power against imperialism, and won. Yet it is just as true that postcolonial criticism has been characterized by a discursive overload, one read to be so consonant with high theory that it can be dismissed as ahistorical, textualist in the extreme, and as a careerism far removed from the public intellectual admired in Said. Similarly, while writers who narrate decolonization among other concerns have been justly revered, some are questioned regarding their representative status, as if their very inclusion in the "world republic of letters" is symptomatic of their conspiratorial desire to garner cultural capital above all else. If such worldliness takes on a different name than postcolonialism then so be it, but I do want to relate its prospect as a future conditional to its interest in the long past. The reticular terms of *nation, institution*, and *world literature* catch something of the expanse of the long space by linking extended narratives of transnationalism across different scales of apprehension. The long space as chronotope mediates these interpretive levels but is itself the name for a problem: how can one indicate the time/space of decolonization in a form that is appropriate to its extent? This is a figura at some remove from Auerbach's meticulous critique of Christian texts and their influences and styles and, because I interpret it through noncoincidence, it is also at odds with the teleological impulses of *Mimesis*. Yet for all the timelessness in his appreciation of Dante, Auerbach elaborates figura as "timeful" in its movements, which I take not just as spirit but as an instance of human agency. In an everyday event in Pramoedya's garden such praxis can only be appreciated by connecting destroyed text to that which gloriously survives. How many times was the *Buru Quartet* spoken and written before time found the form of full expression? And how much, indeed, is this form still open, as if the ghost of its substantiation, its figura, also lies before it? The long space is a process of figuration whose chronotope is not bound only to what has been.

I have begun to interrelate duration with extension in narrative, and I have characterized it as a transnational chronotope of postcolonial writing. Several key issues remain including obvious questions about why these writers, why trilogies and tetralogies, and the thematic links between the terms I have invoked and their importance for the case studies. Some of this polemic is presented in the chapters that follow; here, we consider the conceptual specificity of the long space and its organizational substance. This requires returning to *nation* and invoking a critical dialogue between Benedict Anderson and Etienne Balibar where nation itself takes shape in an imaginary dialogic, an "other scene" in Balibar's terms, of novelists who are otherwise "undocumented." We have noted Anderson's work is influential in literary criticism because it builds many of its lessons around literary examples. This is often taken to mean that the imaginary of both literature and nation are synonymous and that writers such as Rizal and Pramoedya are exemplary in narrating nation because they are always coincident with its expression. Anderson does not make this assumption because language first figures the authors' possible expressivity; thus, it is through language that the imagined characteristic of nation can be glimpsed, whether in Prameodya's "national language," bahasa Indonesia, or Rizal's Spanish as anticolonial discourse. The identification of authors is always a shortcut where nation is concerned, and the interest is whether they exceed or resist the identity given in its contours. Nation is not the fixed point against which the writer's affiliation can be measured but rather, like language, is a living substance of identification that moves unevenly with the writer's own dynamism. The state must work very hard to make these points meet because it needs both the cultural imprimatur of writers and the principle of storytelling to suture being from moment to moment. Anderson, then, seizes on particular writers in order to defamiliarize the language of states in formation and especially those negotiated in the arduous processes of decolonization.

Balibar, by contrast, is a philosopher of political structures. This necessitates splitting the nation from the nation form: the former can be read as extant nations and nationalities that produce an identification through reproduction or repetition; the latter, however, is a mode of combination, a social formation whose hegemony is unevenly developed among other formations, dominant or otherwise.[34] Nations can be studied as discrete entities with their own manner of identification and historicity. Nation form, however, is "the concept of a structure capable of producing determinate 'community effects'" (*We*, 20–21) but "is not itself a community." It is a principle that moves across nations and structurally is their absent cause, the constraining concept that paradoxically enables the form to appear. In another essay, more or less contemporaneous with "Homo Nationalis" where this idea is introduced, Balibar spells out the difference with Anderson's model:

Is there, properly speaking, a mode of constitution of individual and collective identity that is specifically national?

We must, I think, study this question at the deepest level: not at the level of the mere discourses of the community (mythical, historical or literary grand narratives), nor even at the level of collective symbols or representations, but at the level of the *production of individuality* itself.[35]

The nation or national form is linked to the production of "homo nation-alis" as a belonging among individuals. In a footnote, Balibar acknowl-edges Anderson's contribution to the second level, but it is a separate proj-ect from the analysis of self to self as a logic of production, a critique even further removed from "mere" discourses like "literary grand narratives." Balibar offers a provocative formulation on individuality as always more than the individual—the "transindividual"—and I interpret this in the same manner I explicate transnational as indicating dynamism "across" rather than "beyond." However problematic the association of the writers I discuss with nations, it is not because they have flown the coop of na-tional identification but because they understand it in ways that consti-tute a transnational perspective on national possibilities. From the notion of transindividual, Balibar then posits three theses. First, there is no given identity only identification (a formulation very close to the methodology at work in the case studies), an idea that respects individuality but only by emphasizing its transindividual process. This places special emphasis on institutions because these are precisely regulative of identification: they attempt to negotiate two impossibilities, the prospect of a single identity and that of its infinite dispersal. If we say that the "we" of nation is only ever given, it is in the interstices of these impossibilities: never only one, never only every one. This will have consequences for the understanding of world literature as an institution. Institutions constrain identification but in a typically contradictory manner: identification oscillates in a "state of unstable equilibrium" (*Politics*, 67), not just between one and every one, but in culture as customary and as belief. In the interests of the for-mer, institutions may cultivate a "fictive ethnicity"; toward the latter, they may promote patriotism as a "common destiny" (*Politics*, 68). In a foot-note Balibar suggests the thrust of *Imagined Communities* does not sepa-rate these elements. Indeed, Anderson argues in practice they are virtually inseparable because together they guarantee one another. Yet by viewing them as poles, as a kind of excessive singularity, one may be able to track how nations move between them. The third thesis states there is no iden-tity as such, just particular hegemonic formations of identification, the most powerful of which are religion and nationalism. Such distinctions help to differentiate aspects of the ideological work of nations. We should, however, emphasize a further oscillation in reading them, which is that even at this "deepest level" a concept of culture is invoked that cannot exclude "mythical, historical or literary grand narratives." Now Balibar's point is to assert the structural significance of the formation; yet perhaps the analysis is itself oscillatory in that culture is never a question of principle alone. Here again we have a framework where three theses are in fact four in which the last, on oscillation, cancels through the first three. It is not the addition of a metalevel that is crucial but an understanding of the structural logic among the components elucidated. Balibar will provide a supplementary concept germane to our study: "historicity itself has a history." In the case of the nation form it underlines, the nation becomes unrecognizable from the point of view of a defining profile. This helps both to differentiate the postcolony from its imperial constellation and to specify one postcolonial state from another. Balibar agrees that "all historical communities are primarily 'imagined communities'" (*We*, 130) but will discuss neither history nor imagination in that formula.

Balibar's structuralism has almost no resonance in Anderson's critique even though he is clearly interested in elaborating the state, institutions, cultures, and languages of nation. Within cultural theory the reasons for this are as obvious as they are troubling. It is at once a staging of a familiar opposition of empirical study and speculative theory, one that Anderson himself addresses but nevertheless reproduces in the polemical frame of *Imagined Communities*, *Specters of Comparison*, and *Language and Power*.[36] Anderson's concept of nation depends on symbolic practices, not just those associated with specific cultural objects, like the newspaper or print culture in general, but those that implicate the workings of consciousness and the unconscious. Having positively invoked the contributions of Williams and Said to the analysis of cultural modes, Anderson's particular acuity is comparable and complementary, especially because he combines a philological interest in intertextuality with a concern for political history. That said, however, not only are there key historical elisions in Anderson's approach to Southeast Asia (as Harry Harootunian has pointed out, the meaning of the Bandung Conference does not register in his reading of nation states), but Anderson's comparatism tends to privilege Western models of the nation state forged through print capitalism.[37] Yet the issue here is a constellation of methodological implications and a politics of reading that seeks not to jettison the literary apprehension of nation as hopelessly contaminated, but instead builds its importance around a formal insistence discrepant with the West as a posited norm.

Anderson's silence on the deep structure of nation form is not produced by beginning from the novel or literary lives as cultural evidence of nation or nationalism, but by his belief that he has discovered this logic in the symbolic. Anderson and Balibar approach the same problem, the nation and exigencies of nationness, through related metaphors: for Balibar, ambiguity, ambivalence, and oscillation; for Anderson, spectral nonequivalence. This permits a dialogue on their institutional critiques: Balibar's from a position that sees hegemony in a fluctuating logic of constraint and multiplicity, Anderson's from an ambivalence about the authentic at either end of his methodological "telescope."

By eschewing structural analysis of the nation form for phenomenological content, however, Anderson misses an opportunity to reveal the shortfalls of the imagined community of nation as serial structure within the artful homogenous time of the now, crossed between Benjamin's *Jetztzeit* and Auerbach's "meanwhile." The solution is not to reconnect the nation form and nation in the silent exchanges of Balibar and Anderson but to understand the logic of separation itself, a critical mode that too often is at one with the institutional reproduction of nation as given. The tension between nation form and nation must be preserved in cultural analysis, and especially postcolonial critique, to register the ambivalence in both as enabling of a seriality that unbinds nation in transnationalism.

Serialization is indeed time's writing system of nation. Anderson permits an understanding of nation formation as a process that is at once institutionally repetitive and inscribed—however we characterize its deep structure. If Balibar's intervention reminds us that the nation form is not itself a community (*We*, 20), then Anderson's thoughts on seriality attend to community practices that are not themselves a form, yet appear to be. Pheng Cheah refers to this as "part of the grammar of every nation" and it may be the absent cause in the process of its narration.[38] In *The Spectre of Comparisons* Anderson argues "the origin of nationalism . . . lives by making comparisons," a brilliant formulation given the spectral aura in which this "living" takes place.[39] Using Rizal's experience of double consciousness as a foil, Anderson argues place asserts a ghostly presence in diaspora, migration, and exile that allows Rizal to understand its meaning as national identification. Because it is a specter, literally a national spirit, it problematizes appeals to origin but also the question of comparison. Cheah has turned spectral nationality into a comparative method by combining

Anderson's ghostly metaphor with philosophical exposition. He also finds an appropriate analogy for Anderson's concept in Pramoedya's *Footsteps* in the phrase "dissatisfied restlessness in the world of comparison" ("gelisah dalam alam perbandingan").[40] As Cheah points out, comparison here is the cause of restlessness but is not just the ward of metropolitan elites or cosmopolitan exiles: it is itself determined by the peripatetic flux of capitalist social relations that, if it sounds like Althusser's absent cause, does not carry the precise structural imperative of causality.

Anderson supplements his thesis on the importance of homogenous, empty time, or calendrical time, for imagining nation with two types of seriality: bound and unbound. The latter maintains the now-time of the newspaper but adds to this the newspaper's condition of worldliness—that its time assumes a world with which it is coterminous—and a degree of standardization in journalistic language. Together these give the impression that the newspaper governs the terms of expression for simultaneity and that their seriality is symptomatic of "new serial thinking" in general that could run "diachronically up and down homogenous, empty time, as well as synchronically, on the newspaper page." Thus: "It was from within this logic of the series that a new grammar of representation came into being, which was also a precondition for imagining the nation" (*Spectres*, 34). In addressing seriality Anderson assumes another precondition in print capitalism that is suppressed here but remains problematic as a form of technological determinism. The other manifestation of seriality is bound because it depends on the categorical assertions and data accumulation processes of the census. The census binds the series by giving an impression of totality girded by the acceptable practice of anonymous counting (while what counts, of course, confirms the self-image of the state). To prove unbound seriality in motion Anderson returns to Pramoedya and translates a passage from his short story "She Who Gave Up," in which the character Is (or Ies) achieves a revolutionary simultaneity through becoming conscious of her serial individuality in modernity.[41] I would want to say, positively, that Anderson's theorization of the imagined community of nation would be impossible without Pramoedya (and Rizal), and more controversially, that it is hard to imagine the extant *Buru Quartet* without Anderson's concept in play. Here the use of a literary example to underline unbound seriality pushes the political economy and history redolent in Anderson's introduction further into the background. The attention to elections as expressions of the will to bound seriality plunges us back into the more familiar territories of political discourse and their institutions, but the reader might be forgiven for thinking that all of the fun in discerning nation accrues to the unbound seriality of fiction. Anderson makes the case that seriality is the complement of simultaneity in national belonging, but it is never clear the logic of seriality is the only or even a primary precondition of nation. One can accept the premise of imaginary identification but still doubt the degree of its force and the shared nature of its categories. Would the logic of seriality be more persuasive in another register, one that did not claim causality so insistently but was imbued with the same ambivalence as its object?

This is the terrain and time of the serial novel. The serial novel is dependent on the historicity of history, so much so that its logic of time/space, the chronotope, cannot be adequately apprehended outside the institutions, literary categories, and imagined communities in which it is conceived. It bears this burden of embeddedness with all of the optimism that socialization infers but this can only problematize its identity, even when it is reedited for a rather different "bound" seriality in the novel between two covers. The topic of the serial novel and its logic of history—forms of time that differ considerably between, let us say, Charles Dickens's *Oliver Twist* and Kou Fumizuki's *Aoi Yori Aoshi*, or the work of Henry James and Stephen King—is one that exceeds the current project. A few characteristics are relevant to the mode of extended fiction that interrogates the seriality of nation, including its connection to print capitalism. In Britain this would find serial fiction filling pages of extra space opened up by newspapers going to a large sheet format intent on avoiding a tax levied on smaller sheets. Newspaper publication inevitably changed the kind of storytelling deployed and the readership. If Anderson is right that the newspaper facilitates an experience of unbound seriality in nation discourse, serial fiction participates in this expansive simultaneity, but this does not secure identification in the name of nation. If fiction projects a community or communities, one task in analyzing serial novels is to understand if this is overdetermined by the exigencies of serialization itself. The main link here is not the newspaper as such (although it is not a coincidence that Pramoedya's *Buru Quartet* is based around the life of Tirto Adi Suryo, a journalist/activist in Indonesia's early nationalist movement) but serial engagement, the process by which narration frames a readership and a desire to involve oneself in its story over an extended period of time.

In the newspaper correlative there are at least two forms of contractual obligation that the writer faces: the more obvious financial bond to the publisher and the expectation that the next installment will be delivered to the reader as scheduled. Yet the fact of serialization does not do justice to the function of time, which considers extension as a determinate link to the experience of time in the narrative. This is the link between serial novels and the novel in series, those that constitute the case studies to follow. The obligation to the regulative interval of publication is minimal but this tends only to intensify the obligation to time and its conflictual modalities. These extend in a variety of ways that redefine seriality and its relation to nation: the historical parameters that identify space as meaningful for the novel; the lived experience of place and distance, a movement we associate with migration, exile, and errantry of various kinds but here are a direct consequence of a specific identification with place (that Anderson characterizes as a "specter of comparison"); the time of writing as shot through not just with Benjaminian memory in a moment of danger but with extant conditions changing in time—shortening, lengthening, causing text to appear and disappear—not simply as a function of editing but by the creative and destructive forces that attend decolonization as lived in different spaces and compositions; and the quandary of closure, how best to enfold narrative when its series is unbound by a logic of time that overreaches it, which for Bakhtin is expressed as novelization but here is more narrowly defined as the open seriality of decolonization. In reading Rizal, Anderson suggests "the novel as literary genre . . . permitted the imagining of 'Las Filipinas' as a bounded sociological reality" (*Spectre*, 251) yet in its extended form what is bound in its collocation of different social markers, of dress, speech, location, everyday practices in profusion is serially undone by elaborating time's process as duration and disjunction. Just as Anderson elucidates the nation at the expense of the structural logic of the nation form so, in his otherwise coruscating critiques of Rizal and Pramoedya, he proffers "bounded sociological reality" without considering seriality as a formal logic of narration (either in Rizal's two novels of Philippine nationalism or Pramoedya's quartet). All of his other themes obtain—translation, circulation, a worldly simultaneity—but time is also the specter *in* comparison and its role in chronotope may be something other than comparative: it is the temporal imperative of persistence against persistence, the struggle to write when that which curtails expression quietly lives on (and can include the nation itself as a condition of subjugation). On this level, the novel in series may find itself in other modes of seriality (re-readings, re-translations, adaptations, canon formations, posthumous additions, and so forth), none of which need provide the content of nation yet may permit it a patina of consistency. This is not the difference between describing a nation and participating in it; seriality is a narrative mode of specific time: first, in the move from the novel's struggle with other forms to the novel's struggle with itself; second, in the elaboration of extended transnational fiction as postcolonial chronotopes. In writing through the moment of decolonization their eventness entails wresting the form from itself. It is not just a question of reclaiming that which the novel has been in its long history, but of articulating *what it could not have been* until the great struggles of national independence and anticolonial revolution in the second half of the twentieth century.

Partha Chatterjee's response to Anderson underlines both the problems of boundedness versus unboundedness in seriality (particularly the diminution of ethnic identity that attends Anderson's critique of the census) and the limits of liberation in the concept of empty, homogenous time.[42] To the extent that we can find generalizing tendencies in the divisions Anderson makes, the introduction of a specific national experience mitigates the political if not the methodological force of the distinctions. But the Eurocentric cynicism that attends the mode of nationalism ("ethics for us, economics for them") is a caricature of Anderson's concern, as if *ratio* only passes through the eye of Hegelian idealism. The more serious issue Chatterjee raises is the "time of capital," which forges its own calendar and abstruse simultaneity. What Benjamin sees as a contradictory chronos, one which provides for messianic moments that break the plodding continuum of capital as stasis, Chatterjee chides as "utopian" because "empty homogeneous time is not located anywhere in real space" (131). Exactly. We can historicize capitalism and one of its complex symptoms, the nation-state, precisely because time's abstraction cannot absolutely suture capital relations from moment to moment. Narratives of progress and linearity might appear as the healing balm for time's abstraction in the now, but this is only ever a monologic alibi for what is actually a real contradiction. Capital cannot revolutionize in timelessness but it cannot revolutionize without timelessness. It is in capital's will to universality that the substance of its history appears.

Setting aside the problematic binaries of bound and unbound serial-ity, of classical nationalism and ethnic nationalism that Chatterjee reads into Anderson's methodology, he nevertheless draws attention to the cen-tral difficulty in the imagined community: the difference between the si-multaneity that enables nationness as lived, the fictive affiliation of the real, and the rather more messy temporal vicissitudes of relative time, where subjective difference may be no less fictive and just as much com-municable. The imagined community of nation measures the time of post-coloniality but it can also be its burden, a seriality that permits the logical extension of dismissing nation and postcoloniality itself as the lived time-space of difference in decolonization. There is good reason to acknowledge Chatterjee's troubling of the national axis in empty, homogenous time, but can that concept be displaced while holding to a utopian function? Antonio Negri offers an answer here that I will read back into the trans-national/postcolonial nexus of chronotope. Unlike Benjamin, Negri casts a jaundiced eye on the revolutionary possibilities of *Jetztzeit* or now-time.

Well, this conception is ruinous. Far from being the destruction of historicism and its perverse political results, the conception of the messianic now-time (*Jetzt-Zeit*) represents the utmost modernization of reactionary thought: it is the conversion of historical, plural, punctual, multiversal materials into the thaumaturgical illu-sion of empty innovation. The conception of the messianic now-time (*Jetzt-Zeit*) reduces the tautology of real subsumption to *mysticism*, and mysticism always stinks of the boss.[43]

Mysticism is all over Benjamin's writing and it is hardly novel to find it in *Jetztzeit* (the same is true of reading Spinoza but, like Benjamin, this has not made him any less of a materialist). What Negri is trying to break is a theological reliance on conceptions of the new, for which *Jetzt-zeit* is a modernist mantra. The classic formula of time's innovation is for him stridently formulaic and a displacement of revolutionary time into a time of unreality—this is in Chatterjee's critique, although the politics is of a different order—where a beleaguered angel stares back into the de-tritus that modernity hath wrought. Just as Anne McClintock has prob-lematized this dubious chronology in postcolonial theory,[44] so Negri seeks to wrest radical thought from a negation of real time to "the conceptual possible more real than the real," a time of revolution. The path from one to the other need not detain us here, but the proposition requires further comment because it implies that no significant social transformation is possible that pivots on now-time, a simultaneity that Anderson claims is indissoluble from nation. In part, Negri is trying to explain how the contaminated logics of modernity hamstring a qualitatively different newness of the new. Yet to recall our discussion of Balibar, this might more easily be brokered through a concept of unevenness, one in which a strategic now-time neither precludes nation nor assumes that it is the quintessence of revolutionary zeal. Thus, geopolitics and transnationalism both, in the manner of catachresis, offer agonistic creativity in a space where hegemony believes there is none. Now-time is not something one chooses but is a determinate instance where a space of agency may be engaged. The nation attempts to regulate this space, but for every time that we can show the prohibitions on what it holds for "community" we can also point to the linchpin in its ultimate ambivalence: that it is also imagined and, as Negri reminds us, "the imagination is the most concrete of temporal powers" (*Time*, 21). Writers often engage the nation's imaginative reach and interrogate its hold on affiliation, on identification, on a community's ability to see itself *as* a community. The chronotope of postcoloniality must take time critically because spatial privilege underestimates time's role in decolonization, the *Jetztzeit* of emergency in emergence (to borrow from Homi Bhabha), a space not just between but across, "trans" as a resource of hope materially inscribed.[45]

Transnationalism of this kind seeks to link writers beyond a spatial and epistemological divide not because their histories are the same but because they speak to a logic of time that remains dissatisfied with "posts" or "eras" or linearity or representing at best through sociological/anthropological content. Anderson is right to see a ghost in this comparatism, and it is not always the white man despite Chatterjee's acute concerns. It is a measure of the shift in the "grounds of comparison" that an absent presence stalks the logic of time in that configuration. Cheah notes that one of Anderson's achievements has been to interrogate what constitutes the basis of area studies not simply by posing some revision in light of the geopolitical shifts of the last fifty years but by offering a powerful comparative methodology that explodes many of its assumptions. If this is more difficult to gauge in the field of literary study, it is because the philological basis for the approach cannot carry the full weight of reinvention against a backdrop of globalization. One lesson for the literary from Anderson is seriality but I have read this back in terms of the novel in series. Jonathan Culler usefully suggests two other provocative implications from Anderson's literary focus that will take us to world literature and untranslatability.[46]

First, the tension between Anderson's analogic claims for the novel and nation and the readings of novels he provides is symptomatic of an impasse in the approach, one where the logic of scale remains undertheorized between these two levels to the point of incommensurability. If the novel is nation-making, or potentially so, one needs another coordinate besides simultaneity to make the case. Anderson does invoke an imperial knowledge system in the novel's founding mythologies deeply inscribed in its function for nation, but this is a matter of historical record, not the process of material constitution itself. The works I discuss, even Pramoedya's, are not national novels because, even when they explicitly address the critical form of nationhood, the primary axis of narration favors a chronotope irreconcilable with the nation that is its putative object. This role for the novel is at once more modest yet decisive. World literature hypostatizes the novel and nationness in one fell swoop; a transnational chronotope defamiliarizes this conjunction by politicizing and not just aestheticizing the time/space of form.

A second substantial problem in the novel's affinity for nation is pursued by Culler with reference to Moretti's argument for the novel as the symbolic form for the nation state.[47] In both Anderson and Moretti the more one reveals the imagined worlds of nation in the novels they choose, the less one can substantiate the particular claim about the novel's organization of time as at one with nation formation. The individual case study shines but the general theory of the novel recedes in direct proportion. This is why, as Culler underlines, it is easier for interpreters of Anderson—if not Anderson himself—to move from the general claim, which is actually about the form of time/space in the novel, to the defining features of subgenres, the sentimental novel or the historical novel. Culler urges the maintenance of a critical "distinction between the novel as a condition of possibility of imagining the nation and the novel as a force in shaping or legitimating the nation" (37), yet this preserves the general principle while de-emphasizing the politics of Anderson's examples. Neither Moretti's claims in *Atlas of the European Novel* nor Anderson's arguments in *Imagined Communities* and *The Specter of Comparisons* hold for the nation-building proclivities of the novel *qua* novel because there is no reason the novel as form-giving cannot just as easily cancel the connection as affirm it. The importance of the correlation is the concretization of possibility not a law of inevitability. The politics of history in Anderson's examples are pertinently directed at the ideological construction of canons and the grounds of comparison themselves.

Does the worlding of empty homogenous time in nation formation also guarantee the effulgence of world literature? Does the specter of comparison that Anderson reads as a formative axis in Rizal's novel narration as nation conjure the ghost of a more general interdependence in global comparatism for which world literature or the world republic of letters have become a shorthand? Pramoedya, Farah, Harris, and Djebar are not outside globality, nor is the current tome immune from a veneration of them within privileged circuits of publication to the detriment of those for whom Heinemann, Penguin, and Albin Michel do not come knocking. From this perspective world literature is even more dubious in its assumptions than national literature, and both maintain an inflated and conspiratorial exclusivity. If the former seems to render obsolete the categorical imperatives of the latter, they yet feed on each other's presence with separate bookshelves in bookstores or distinct courses in literature departments. The business of distinction—in Bourdieu's sense—is very much at work, and cultural capital gives another more questionable dimension to "simultaneity."[48]

Whatever "problem" world literature is seen to represent, the temporality that attends its possibility should not be submerged. The "time for world literature" requires clarification as a relation at once insinuated in the renewed timeliness of Goethe's original formulation. If world literature underlines the force of comparatism in contemporary literary theory, it also reveals some of its complex elisions and displacements. Damrosch has been the most sensitive to the conceptual play in world literature and has offered a keen polemic on how it might usefully be reinscribed in critical practices while holding Goethe's "time" in suspension. First, he reads world literature as a "subset of the plenum of literature" and more specifically "to encompass all literary works that circulate beyond their culture of origin, either in translations or in their original language" (*World*, 4). Damrosch then qualifies the category: "a work only has an *effective* life as world literature whenever, and wherever, it is actively present within a literary system beyond that of its original culture" (*World*, 4). Aware of the criticism that world literature has a penchant for projecting the gaze of

Western desire, Damrosch counters that it can be "properly understood" not as "an infinite, ungraspable canon of works but rather [as] a mode of circulation and of reading, a mode that is as applicable to individual works as to bodies of material, available for reading established classics and new discoveries alike" (*World*, 5). *World*, as we know, is infamously vague in its assignation and can mean everything from one's most immediate context, puffing on a kretek as your papers burn, to an IMF loan through which Indonesia is stapled to a structure of indemnity. Damrosch does not exclude this element of scale (he uses *world* in several senses and deliberately so) but then much falls on "mode" and a methodology adequate to its apprehension.

The value of Damrosch's approach is that, rather than an impermeable edifice of world literature and an equally resolute critical practice, he emphasizes dynamism in the category that permits an investigation of its variability. The anthological imperative attempts to stabilize such flux, and Damrosch has much to say about standardization and standard works, but ultimately once this massive variability is "graspable" then the stabilizing element returns to criticism and the critic. The "mode of circulation, and of reading" places the "available" texts on the same plane ("established classics and new discoveries alike"), and the critic's participation in or production of circulation through reading is a relatively innocuous technique interested only in the common name of world literature. (In Marx and Engels's famous pronouncement in the *Communist Manifesto*, the point of world literature was its "common property," *Gemeingut*, a position earlier taken by Goethe in his conversations with Eckermann.) Damrosch's modal logic is generous and suggestive, and no other work features Menchu, Pavic, Wodehouse, Ngal, Eckermann, and the *Epic of Gilgamesh* arrayed side by side. Indeed, the uniqueness of the event of reading is in part Damrosch's answer to the question in his title and at that level *What Is World Literature?* is an exemplary statement on the category. The stabilizing element, however, is not the reading necessarily but the *eventness* of reading so the critical position can be problematized without affecting the deep structure of the engagement.

As we triangulate between our own present situation and the enormous variety of other cultures around and before us, we won't see works of world literature so fully enshrined within their cultural context as we do when reading those works within their own traditions, but a degree of distance from the home tradition can help us to appreciate the ways in which a literary work reaches out and away from its point of origin. If we then observe ourselves seeing the work's abstraction from its origins, we gain a new vantage point on our own moment. (*World*, 300)

As Damrosch well knows, students of literature are trained to dance all over this "we," but often the politics of positioning engaged is gestural and would miss that here Damrosch is deeply concerned to identify a position of adjudication: that criticism as much as world literature emerges from a "somewhere." The use of triangulation and distance in the formulation is indicative of world literature as mapping, and a cartographic desire conjured from a similar epistemological and imaginative substance. The scopic reflection, to see oneself seeing, obviously requires a category of the other to which *What Is World Literature?* attends but again: just as the literary necessitates a notion of eventness to fathom the processes of identification, so a spatial acknowledgment of the other requires an understanding of outsideness or exotopy, a logic that permits the other to "appear" on the map of theorization or critical appreciation. These two processes, eventness and outsideness, interrupt each other in such complex formations that even when we believe that the "mode of circulation and of reading" is graspable, the triangulation in fact occurs impossibly at a receding horizon (the almacantar once more) rendering world and world literature an effect of reading premised on the suppression of the axis that would interrogate its ground. Better to preserve the precariousness in outsideness as being in process, than the prevarication that marks world literature as being in place. Perhaps this is merely to reiterate Moretti's point that "world literature" is the name for a problem, but his solution often seems to regard critical exegesis as a statistical error in need of refined tabulation.

If Anderson remains fixed by his modular nationalism or the awkward magnification of his reversed telescope, as Chatterjee suggests, Moretti is situated by the distance of comparatism as science and mirror. Just as globalization always tests the politics of relational thinking, so world literature requires categorical largesse to capture its abstruse phenomenological texture. To scale both, simultaneously, is part of what Williams means by *cultural revolution*, although it is something of a leap of faith to imagine the task inexorably falls to Comparative Literature. Moretti understands the basis of Goethe's claims for *Weltliteratur* as an injunction for order, a systematicity that would permit the scaling from nation to world and vice versa. The conversation of cultures that Goethe surveyed does not obtain under contemporary global capitalism, so Moretti uses the world systems theory of Immanuel Wallerstein, with its intricate dynamic of core and periphery, and the diminution of textual reading.[49] Damrosch's deploys close reading to substantiate detached engagement; Moretti marshals systems theory to bolster distant reading.

Distant reading: where distance . . . is a *condition of knowledge*: it allows you to focus on units that are much smaller or much larger than the text: devices, themes, tropes—or genres and systems. And if, between the very small and the very large, the text itself disappears, well, it is one of those cases when one can justifiably say, Less is more. ("Conjectures," 57–58)

Distance is a condition of knowledge, but it is radically particularized by duration; hence my emphasis on the long space. The components of distant reading—devices, themes, tropes, genres, systems—might seem logical companions, conceptual interests bent on analyzing narrative frames. Certainly form is at stake: how best to inscribe the time/space of decolonization? But that may be rather too particular for Moretti, as if Vico with his "new science" or Vico's great admirer Auerbach did not get a little close to text on occasion. The main difference is Moretti's insistence on core/periphery literary relations constituting laws of development with world literature understood as the name for that evolutionary process. Wallerstein has good reason for reading distantly, but literary scholars? (There is plenty of evidence in Moretti's other works that raise this "conjecture" too.)[50] Prendergast, Arac, and Apter have all inveighed against Moretti's formalism as comparatism in part because once one starts to analyze the contexts of concepts the substance of form requires a supplementary specificity.[51] Arac also makes the point that the *primum mobile* of distant reading is really an adherence to the production of theory rather than criticism, but this I think gives too much credence to Moretti's division between concepts and reality.

Distant reading is not formalism but an informationalism that takes the core/periphery nexus as a condition of circulation, then accumulates data as information about such circulation. Despite all the carping about treating books as titles rather than ontal texts Moretti's approach yields interesting patterns and represents something of his desire for "falsifiable" critique. How much we can draw in the way of conclusions depends on variables well beyond the reader's capacity for statistical rigor (Moretti knows that his primary audience does not feature statisticians, which is just as well, according to the statisticians) and would include whether the world of world literature is isomorphic with the world of world systems theory. Similarly, geographers might wonder whether the "atlas" in Moretti's *Atlas of the European Novel* is a metaphor at some remove from, let us say, ordnance survey's origin in George II's desire to defend the Scottish Highlands from "local" rebellion. There are strategic interests in both, but the methodologies and corresponding histories are of a different order. Moretti alludes to the cultural history but not the difference in it, which is precisely what enables the analysis to proceed. "Conjectures," like *Atlas*, is about connections and takes lessons from the analysis of cultural space to make inroads on the reformulation of literary history.[52] The fortunes of the novel are the key to the conceptual breadth of Moretti's world literature, and the novel's now massive quantities preclude the time to which Goethe alludes. Wallerstein's focus on the inequalities of the world system are limned into the formation and comparative dominance of the Euro-literary canon that is simultaneous if not synonymous with its spread, especially but not only when the novel is considered "globally."

There are three main issues that guide my approach in contradistinction to Moretti's passionate embrace of world literature in "Conjectures." First, the imaginary spaces of the literary are fractured by specific experiences of time, so that distance is never privileged over duration as a condition of knowledge. What renders the category of world literature impossible is not quantity per se but the time of its apprehension (the real time of its engagement multiplied by the abstract time of its constellation). Second, while Moretti admits that the complex relationship of novel and nation permits a logical extension to *world* that world literature might not be able to embrace in all of its permutations, he stops short of allowing that world literature itself is the scene of struggle among different modalities, not just genres, but different forms of time/space. The history of world literature is not a reduction of quality to quantity once more, but a contested terrain where the literary strives for worldliness, not world dominance. When we talk of laws of literary evolution we might ponder what modality, other than stagist, might allow their elaboration? Third, the permutations of "system" are vital, but some of the boldest statements on the *world* in world literature might actually be made by writers who are nominally if not consciously participants in it. If the "world" then becomes less formulaic, it is an indication of the hubris that attends a formalism willing to hold at a distance the literary that confounds the category. (Moretti does read the literature he compiles, including Rizal, in order to test the hypothesis of core/periphery in the content of the novels he lists, but then this would require addressing the logic of seriality *that* influence flattens.) The idea that comparative literature, as institution and method, must be a thorn in the side of national literature is a rousing slogan but not much of a politics for something as conflictual as world literature. Scale at this level is also intensity and chronotope is significantly alive to its register.

Postcolonial writers paradoxically remap the unmappable and not in a way that would allow for methodical tabulation or illustration. Farah, for instance, may write of Somalia but Somalia is not the name for that world, at least not in the sense that he assumes Somalia is immediately scriptible as full and self-present identification. He has been accused, and with good reason, of representing Somalia, of speaking for the whole when the social milieu he narrates is but a part of that identification. Such criticism fails to address the logic of identification in Farah's position and how this fluctuates according to both personal exigencies (exile, assassination threats, relocation within Africa) and the often rapidly changing circumstances of what is extant as Somalia. If we hold to the importance of literature for nation, Farah may be deemed "representative," but Somalia has a more significant embeddedness in oral culture that may correspond to what is given "Somalia" in name (and Farah himself is well aware of this). As we will see, the fact that Farah's fiction prefigures the dissolution of the Somali state is not as important as his mode of engagement that questions whether world literature partakes of this problem.

Moretti's is doggedly spatial criticism, and to the extent that the long space invokes theories of space in its formulation, it is guilty of reproducing a certain obsessive spatiality in its practice—although chronotope is deployed to mitigate this reflex. Interestingly, when Bakhtin reads Goethe (who along with Dostoevsky and Rabelais constitute the flourish of novelization) he accentuates his "feeling for time" alongside an ability to "see" space. Bakhtin notes, "in Goethe's world there are no events, plots, or temporal motifs that are not related in an essential way to the particular spatial place of their occurrence, that could occur anywhere or nowhere ('eternal' plots and motifs). Everything in this world is a *time-space*, a true *chronotope*."[53] We are back in the time of the modern, and for the most part the test of world literature is whether its time-space is so fused to modernity that it is its serial manifestation. Bakhtin suggests that the beauty of the modern is almost literally in the eye of Goethe as beholder because what he sees is not just the real before his vision, but history as a dynamic within it. This includes the forces of nature as a movement of time in space and the work of human creation in relation to such processes. Seeing for Goethe, says Bakhtin, was not the beginning of the artistic act but its climax, for "the visible was already enriched and saturated with all the complexity of thought and cognition" (*Speech*, 27). Goethe's is no ordinary eye, for it embodies both vision and the visionary in producing the "living figurative word" (*Speech*, 27).

Like chronotope for Bakhtin, Goethe's "living figurative word" is almost a metaphor but not quite. If Goethe's interest in optics and colors is generally well known, Bakhtin forwards the idea that what he sees is the distillation of time in space, a vision that grants simultaneous perspective on surface and substance. Goethe's *Wilhelm Meister* never quite bears this out because of the profound contradictions of its bourgeois subject, yet his transcription of the observable displaces an obeisance to the romantic idyll that mystifies the present by projecting it back onto a mythical past. The novel of becoming is about the socialization of an individual into the world as a whole that accentuates historicity and privileges the future as a material force. Bakhtin is correct to link this question of insight to Goethe's experiences in *The Italian Journey* rather than to the experience of writing *Wilhelm Meister* itself. More interesting, however, is whether Bakhtin is able to separate being-in-the-world as a process of becoming from the world as a problem for being. In his reading of Goethe, Bakhtin brazenly takes the principle of world literature as a condition of possibility and applies it to Goethe as an established norm: "One of the high points in the visualizing of time in world literature was achieved by Goethe." The process of being is suspended for evaluative typification. The slide from nation to world narration is relayered so that world literature becomes the height from which being-in-process is itself scaled (interestingly, if hardly surprisingly, Bakhtin articulates the same position for Rabelais).[54] Rather than world literature as a site of struggle over the meaning of *world* for global difference, Bakhtin settles for a Goethe who stands in for that contradictory process of cognition. This is a moment of metalepsis, since the more Bakhtin reads Goethe the more he affects the cause he is deemed to identify. This trope surfaces again most easily when literary theory invokes world literature without a constitutive and conditional outside.

The opposite is the case with Moretti's system where world cancels the literary in world literature for an outside of graphs, maps, and trees. Scientific systems can be a lot more cheery and are often literary (the multidimensionality of string theory cannot help but be poetic), but for Moretti represent small experiments with large interpretations. Yet even by invoking Bakhtin's renowned adversary, Shklovsky, Moretti manages to mimic Bakhtin's metalepsis. Moretti begins "Graphs, Maps, Trees" by announcing "a transformation in the study of literature," a transformation that is "delineated" initially by his three articles for *New Left Review* then later in a book that takes the same title, *Graphs, Maps, Trees*. The event of the articles is the transformation but the study of literature, being a rather large edifice, requires qualification, so the opening paragraph that begins with transformation ends with the more modest defense of an approach that "may change the way we work." Like Bakhtin, then, Moretti assumes the object—despite calling it a problem—that his approach is attempting to produce or conjure. The relationship of the novel to world literature is more difficult to think in this way (the evolution of the novel is the effect of constituting world literature as an object), and yet this paradox of reverse engineering is highly appropriate because it disturbs the luxury of linearity on which so much literary history depends. If the process defies conventional orders of time, it is because that which enables the appearance of world literature has a troubled synchronicity far in excess of the novel's temporalities. The novel has the "effect" of world and of literature, but it cannot do all of the work in their combination. Here I return the novel to its rather messy specificity not because Moretti's pattern recognition fails to advance criticism—the example of his approach goes much further than graphs, maps, and trees—but because the form of abstraction in his model lets geopolitics off the hook and fails to account adequately for alternative modes of discontinuous cultural forms within its Braudelesque cycles and waves of data. The *longue durée* remains a valuable conceptual tool because of its logic of time, not the "large mass of facts" ("literary facts" in Moretti's parlance) that it works upon. Its rationale requires engagement that in turn entails a supportive institutional structure, something Moretti recognizes through the Center for the Study of the Novel that he has set up at Stanford. A real transformation will have occurred when the novel is neither an extension of institution nor of the nation state and by itself cannot sustain the literary criticism that feeds on it. While it is not possible to imagine world literature without the novel, analysis of the novel can assist in understanding what would constitute its decline, literally its degeneration. The dominance of the novel may block a greater understanding of the "is" of world literature; it has certainly skewed what we think of postcolonial critique of which the present study is a symptom. Its persistence is also a measure of the politics in which it is caught, just as its expiration would not be the product of cultural fiat. This level of historicity, the life and death of form and genre, is undertheorized in conceptions of world literature.

How might the long space contribute to such debate? This chronotope registers both the abstraction of an emphasis on time in thinking space in contemporary criticism and the specific organization of time/space that writes decolonization. It does not say the seriality of the series unlocks the creative end to all that empire and the colony means, but that working space through time makes strange modernity's purchase on seriality so that the simultaneity of fiction makes time interrogate the story of nations transnationally. By questioning the time/space of and in literature one can appreciate the scale of the local in the global as itself an historical logic. Duration in the long space is a question about a politics of scale that would leave the inequities of time in place. Balibar says Europe is postcolonial, a position that recognizes the vast redrawing of the map by the collapse of communism, the ends of empire, and the new regimes of labor migration, diaspora, and union (as in, European Union). Such recognition is vital, not least because the intimacy of the Other deconstructs any politics of the Same (Eurocentrism cannot hold against the centrifugal forces of globalization and the centripetal conditions of postcoloniality). We should beware, however, of terminological inflation in contemporary critique that tends in its sweep to master contradiction by generalizing its reach. If I hold to a narrow definition of postcolonialism as that which continues the work of decolonization, it is to mark a time that has not been used up by the giddy intensities of circulation on a world scale.

Rather than assume that world literature subsumes the concerns of postcoloniality, the long space questions the possibility of world literature without an adequate account of its temporality. Thus, it is not the reality of globalization that grates with the renewed attention to world literature but its politics of scale. Achilles Mbembe asks, "how does one get from the colony to 'what comes after?'"[55] His approach elaborates "time on the move" burdened by death as negation in colonization. Mbembe's answer is to motivate Heideggerian time to undo Hegelian *Aufhebung*, to find a place of being to negate death as the prohibition on living from the time of the colony. Yet *On the Postcolony* theorizes so close to violence and death that its positive valence, to "exercise existence," remains largely uncoordinated. The works of Djebar and Farah both thematize extremes of violence, but these never occlude the space of possibility in which existence is not only exercised but situated, however problematically, on borders that do not enclose negation. The mark of the series lies there, in the writing of process that gives to the process of writing a task, an enduring public vocation that the last volume does not outlast.

Capital time, or world time, also has a logic of extension and a will to endure although, like the long space, history is at its heels. So dominant is this regime that even its most ardent critics deride autonomy as a dream of authenticity that conspires with the logic of othering capital projects. But world time has not unified history and in that shortfall (how is a universal time unable to universalize a history based on it?) other times, and not simply subjective times, proliferate. That time is a material base of capitalism must be restated since there will be no transformation that does not take time from it. I do not read the long space as time's resurgence or the eternal return but as time's crisis when the differentiation of space cannot account for the passage from nation, across nation, among nations. Is the significance of postcolonial writing that it affects this passage as translation? Could this process obtain even if the text is otherwise untranslated and participates in what Jonathan Arac has described as the "Anglo-Global"?[56]

Because translation simultaneously evokes both relation and institution it lies at the heart of all thought on the national, transnational, postcolonial, and world literature. One is reminded that Goethe's thoughts on world literature were piqued by reading a French translation of a Chinese novel of manners from the Ming Era *Yu jiao li* [The Jade Tender Pear], an experience that, if it did not confirm the quality of Chinese writing (which extended well beyond the convention-ridden example of a genre) taught him that the quality of the everyday was not a German monopoly. For the most part Goethe urged that literature be read as best one could in the original language, a commitment that finds him learning Persian at sixty-five in order to read Hafiz. But the art of translation was not belittled. In fact, Goethe was convinced that every translator was a "prophet in the midst of his own people" because translation promotes intimacy among nations and a capacity for mutual correction. Translation is both a conditional limit and an extension: it is both a hierarchical and hegemonic cultural filter and a paradoxical mark of plenitude of that which translation has excluded. Far from the intricacies of translation technique, its politics is written into exclusion/inclusion and the institutions that facilitate both. It promises a world but can only hint at its extent. This is true even if one restricted one's analysis to European literatures in European languages being included and excluded across Europe (the world of literature on which Goethe focused), with non-European texts as worldly supplements. Translation and circulation are of a different order today with a plethora of languages and literatures on the move within and between nations, but this only accentuates the institutional politics of inclusion/exclusion rather than solves or ameliorates the hegemonies at stake. If Auerbach was overly despondent that "European civilization is approaching the term of its existence," that pall expresses a double bind in both world literature and the prospects of global comparatism. What Goethe viewed as world was often a European extension and what Auerbach saw as global was clearly a European contraction. In this regard, appeals to world literature seem to embody a constitutive oscillation between advancing global inclusion and defending European or Euramerican exceptionalism. Such a conjecture cannot be mediated by modeling, or abstract systems, or institutional enclaves: it is the untranslatable in global relations themselves. The politics of translation are deeply inscribed in the long space not just because it informs how, for instance, the work of Djebar comes to circulate transnationally but because time/space is an instantiation of what Emily Apter calls "translatio," the core of comparatism's very possibility as a literary horizon.[57] This obtains even if the language of the text is of European provenance, Anglophone, Francophone, Lusophone, Hispanophone, and so forth, since whether criticism calls itself "comparative" or "postcolonial" it necessarily reveals the extent to which the language is resituated by chronotopic coordinates, how the writer makes language signify place and time whatever its putative origins.

Where does the politics of postcolonialism stand in all of this? The answer pivots on scale. Why is it that we now believe we have the measure of time and space to rethink a materialist conception of form? The crisis of time hovers at the edge of Moretti's formalism and is acknowledged as a major impetus in his endeavor. Ironically, it only becomes manifest in the theoretical procedures as *content*, so that when he quotes free indirect discourse from Vargas Llosa it is the meaning of content not the position of the speaking subject that interests him most: "From the abode of noise and impropriety, where nobody was in their right place, to the asshole gringos handing him bullshit about sovereignty, democracy, and human rights. This is what comparative literature could be, if it took itself seriously as *world literature*, on the one hand, and as *comparative morphology*, on the other." (*Graphs*, 62). Yes, as simile, *as* world literature. All I offer here is a way to speak to that injunction without giving up on an alternative mode of specificity in difference it might require. If the long space is properly a logic of form that pins time to the space and place of postcolonial narration it is as a measure of extension and engagement not as a prescription for a novel as trilogy or a novel as quartet. The question of seriality with its link to the eventness of decolonization does not explain why some extended fictions are trilogies and others tetralogies. Extension betrays the logic of form; division, however, may be aesthetic, political, practical, or arbitrary. Extension is decisive; division is conjunctural. Even the writers I have chosen to illustrate such difference are subject to a further selection, and the promise of a supplement does not undo the modest scale on offer.[58]

Pramoedya burned his trash out of habit and out of another formation of memory: the author who watched his books being burned while under arrest chooses to trump his inquisitors, real and imagined. One is never sure that the memory from which Pramoedya wrote the *Buru Quartet* permitted him to write in his later years or whether infirmity in time makes it easier to burn text than preserve it. What writing survives in the long space will never equal the narratives that make it. The open seriality of the long space as form-giving can of course be supplemented. This could, for instance, embrace the extraordinary work of Abdelrahmin Munif's *Cities of Salt* "trilogy" (that, true to the notion of division as conjunctural, is at least a quintet) and Leïla Sebbar's narrative of Beur migration, the *Shérazade* trilogy. Since in these tomes Munif wrote of oil and Sebbar of the experience of Africans in Paris, they might represent a topical turn, but it is their tropicality that is of primary interest, as these chrono-tropes are the indices, the imaginary coordinates, of a chronotope that continues the work of decolonization by transnationalizing the time/space of its possibility. When does such writing end? Certainly not with the announcement of a final volume or with the work of an individual author. But if these narratives always mean more than this they remain historical, and it is in that process where a specific mode of seriality may indeed meet closure. I see this as a temporal necessity rather than a teleological aim, an urgency that paradoxically requires attention to extension. It is to that logic of narrative time that this study is dedicated.

The Language of Form

Language is deeper than 'frames,' it transgresses against the frames that would make us prisoners of eternity in the name of one creed or dogma or ideology.
—Wilson Harris, "Letter from Francisco Bone to W. H."

Theory is marked by insufficiency, a failure that is not a sign of hubris but of hope: that its shortfall mimes the logic of truth in language. Take Being, for instance. Whatever the truth in Being, its human axiom, it is not outwardly given in the language that communicates it. The dilemma of the existentialist is precisely the "about" of Being in relation to existence, not the "is" that is its truth. Heidegger writes of the "unconcealment of Being," its *aletheia*, yet it is not a revelation of truth in language, but a sign of what superadequates it.[1] One of the significant tensions in modernity and theories of the modern has been structured by the play of difference between existence and Being, but rather than rehearse what is otherwise a fascinating narrative on philosophies of Being as always philosophies of language, I want to explore the issue paratactically in the writing of Wilson Harris, who reads the history of Being as a "white mythology" and has therefore unconcealed a Being in myth and a language that is spatial and opaque.[2] The latter is a form of Caribbean consciousness that can be traced in other writers, Glissant and Walcott for instance, and remains at the heart of Caribbeanness as currently construed.[3] Harris, however, explores more than the spatial logic of the Caribbean Basin and its mythological mapping in heavily textured language—a measure, in part, of his native Guyana's simultaneous South American cartography. Whatever the inadequacies of theory, the modern for Harris is an opening onto new ways to relate globally. The term that is operative for me is *transnational* but for lexical and even political reasons Harris uses *cross-cultural*.[4] The terms unite around themes of equivalence, excess, sublation, and transcendence. The problem of cross-culturalism has been to find forms adequate to it: a problem of language, certainly, but also one of communication in general.

Harris's writing is vibrantly nonconformist and stands at odds to many trusted theoretical concepts. Narratives are held together by complex symbolisms and mystical correspondences. For some, Harris has become something of a Shaman whose vision reveals the deep structure of human existence, a revelation, revision, or "rehearsal" of sentences that torture and tantalize in equal measure.[5] For others Harris is an obscurantist who, despite capacious erudition and a searing imagination, denies all but the most determined readers from sharing in the alchemy of spirit that his words invoke. Hena Maes-Jelinek, Harris's most rigorous commentator, suggests that Harris's work contradicts many of the precepts of postcolonialism, particularly those that draw from Western theory.[6] Whether one agrees with this position, the challenge in reading Harris is to distinguish his meticulous authorial effacement and antiwriting from a solipsism and obscurity redolent in the afterlife of high modernism. Tracking such influences is not unproductive, especially since Harris's writing leaves tantalizing trails of cultural connection (a basic meaning of "cross-cultural" for Harris). Critics have tended to favor the opposite tendency, however, so that he is often not only split off from the main currents of Western aesthetics and hermeneutics but from any "ism" that might betray a fiercely guarded iconoclasm and originality ("marvelous" or "magical realism" has tended to stick more than any other, despite the fact that Harris has distanced himself from the term).[7] Paradoxically, it is only by reading Harris against the grain that one might be true to the nonconformism that is his passion.[8] This is unconcealment in the space of transnationalism via a code that is counterintuitive, at least from Harris's perspective.

Any discussion of Harris's language of form must come to terms with his particular understanding of the nature of epic and tradition. If Harris provides an imaginative map or spatial imaginary of Guyana, it is predicated on his transformation of "survey" (as a younger man he worked as a surveyor in Guyana on the prospects of hydroelectricity development in the region) into a chronotopic lexicon of memory, place, and journey.[9] The relationship of the epic to the novel is a long and complex one through which Harris plots coordinates of pastness in contradistinction to conventional teleologies of tradition. Historically, the epic is form-gathering and form-giving: it offers specific time/space coordinates that memory weaves between. For Harris, such coordinates are not just mnemonic devices: what is traditional in the form grounds the possibility of tradition itself, cycles that open the form beyond most criticism of the epic. Bakhtin, by contrast, differentiates novel and epic through the former's propensity for open-endedness and polyglossia over the latter's finalized and enclosed quality: "We speak of the epic as a genre that has come down to us already well defined and real. We come upon it when it is almost completely finished, a congealed and half-moribund genre. Its completedness, its consistency and its absolute lack of artistic naivete bespeak its old age as a genre and its lengthy past."[10] Whereas Bakhtin argues for the novel as a genre in the making, Harris claims this as the hallmark of epic: "epic is an *arrival* in an architecture of space that is *original* to our age, an *arrival* in multi-dimensionality that alerts us to some kind of transfiguration of appearances—in parallel with science and architecture—that implies energies akin to extra-human faculties inserted into the fabric of history."[11]

It is possible to reconcile these views once one has identified what is theoretical and artistic in Bakhtin and Harris's formulations. What Bakhtin describes—an academic distinction about epic *as a genre* in terms of its ancient Western formation—seems indisputable. We do not have access to the original aedonic songs on which epic narration would be based. We can imagine them (or intuit them, Harris's preference), but this imagination is more likely founded on the effects of those songs as registered in the epic tradition itself. When Bakhtin emphasizes the finished quality of the epic, it includes the supposition that its generic inspiration is unavailable to the present. Harris will have none of this (in one lecture, he chides one of Iris Murdoch's characters for believing that it is impossible to write an epic today [Q 187]) but that is because he does not start from a generic definition of form. Harris invokes the "rhythms of creative work that give a re-visionary sensation of the life of epic, the transitive chords of epic that bear on many activities" (Q 188). Generic categories are not best described as sensations even if feeling is built into their experience. If we can speak of epic novels it is because the epic has been novelized, not reproduced. Thus, what Bakhtin articulates as novelization is not that far removed from the aesthetic accentuation in Harris's use of "re-visionary" or what he describes in the Carnival

Trilogy as "carnival evolution."[12] On the terrain of genre Harris writes epics *as* novels, not epics.

In Harris's epic novels, what is symbolic in character, time, and place is much more important than what individuates character. The architectonics of Harris's narration is a dream language, a fiction making that pierces the unreality of the real and presents language itself as the form (rather than language as form-giving) of the re-visionary. Harris does not abjure the real, or history, or the Guyana of *The Guyana Quartet*.[13] Epic qualities, however, provide a better window on the world than the realist novel: "we are involved in an orchestration of imageries divine and human, creator and creature, Death and complex liberation from death-dealing regimes that embrace humanity in many areas of the globe. This desire for liberation is instinctive to ancient epic but it needs to be grasped differently, realized differently, it needs re-visionary capacities in our own age" (Q 189–90). To realize epic differently is not just a liberatory desire but a technical imperative. One can believe in epic instincts, but the genre and not the author adjudicates them. Harris understands this all too well. If the promises of epic "remain unfulfilled" (Q 192) this is according to his instincts and sensations as an artist about the epic. Epic for Harris is symbolic, not only an agglomeration of structural components or characteristics. Harris favors the cyclical and the mythical over ends and afters (again, a keyword is "rehearsal"). The "re-birth of epic" offers "a renewed scrutiny of . . . the unfulfilled promises of tradition and of descent and ascent all over again into inequalities, unequal cultures. *It offers in stages a conversion of such inequalities into numinous inexactitudes*" (Q 194, emphasis in original). On this point Harris pulls the epic closer to religious revelation than secular novelization; indeed, it marks a difference with Homer's accentuation of the foibles of gods and humans presented on the same plane of narrative. Harris's epic is less Goethe's "absolute past" and more a genre favoring open-endedness, indecision, and indeterminacy: that is, the novel.[14] This does not foreclose analogizing from the epic, but Harris wants the epic to assume a more forceful presence in the world as the cross-cultural to which all may aspire.

The epic is the medium of the "living open tradition" not the convention-bound tradition that girds, for instance, national identity. To deepen tradition, therefore, is to transgress what is singular about nation and what is specific to character. In his celebrated essay, "Tradition and the West Indian Novel" Harris criticizes George Lamming for consolidating rather than fulfilling characters (the difference is one of conditional limits and universality). This has much to do with Harris's distrust of realism: "there is no necessary difficulty or complexity in Lamming's novels—the necessary difficulty or complexity belonging to strange symbolisms."[15] The latter, of course, is the hallmark of Harris's fiction. Harris continues: "In the epic and revolutionary novel of associations the characters are related within a personal capacity which works in a poetic and serial way so that a strange jigsaw is set in motion like a mysterious unit of animal and other substitutes within the person. Something which is quite different to the over-elaboration of individual character within the conventional novel" (TWS 38). Harris is declaring his dedication to the writing of the "epic and revolutionary novel of associations." His reading of Lamming, however, is misplaced, as C.L.R. James points out.[16] James notes how Lamming writes through the experience of class differentiation in Barbados, and this has a "necessary difficulty or complexity" all of its own. Schisms between the real and false consciousness can be explored in a number of ways that do not resolve themselves into a neat division between realism and the nonrepresentational.

The strength of Harris's sense of epic rests in its associative effects and not in the proof of its "rebirth." Thus, the epic novel demonstrates a certain impossibility: that epic, as epic, might persist in novelization. One could go further and say that the epic novel is neither, that its hybridized interaction is the scene of an abstruse negation of form. Certainly, if we believe Harris's charge that imagination itself must break through its reliance on reason, consciousness, the real, and the material in favor of spirit, numinosity, a universal unconscious, and dream, then the perquisites of genre would seem to offer significant drawbacks. The inadequacy of generic principles spur both rearticulation and withdrawal. Thus, when Francisco Bone in Harris's *Jonestown* speaks of becoming a "vessel of composite epic, imbued with many voices, one is a multitude," he is troping on epic not naming it; indeed, a name is seen to be an inhibiting frame.[17] Perhaps surviving the Jonestown massacre is reason enough for Bone's poeisis (he embodies the voices of those who were lost), but his references to Mayan myth bespeak novelization, not epicalness. Harris favors epic because it is not ensnarled in the time/space fix of realism and there is a postcolonial (and modernist) polemic imbued in that preference. Yet this is an argument principally about varying stylistics in the novel and not about generic (re)composition.

The long space is at odds with formal analysis from that point where criticism attempts to codify the expressive variegations of artistic language. It represents specific symptoms in the problems of form without assuming a formal consistency or generic identity. On one level, the long space is the political unconscious of form in a transnational frame. With respect to the novel as genre, the long space takes seriously the historical specificity of the novel while questioning the limits of its appropriateness. It offers a rhetoric of formal and generic critique highly dependent on utterance context, but sensitive to the pitfalls of content as a window onto the real of postcolonial existence. There are significant overlapping concerns in Harris's sense of what language can do and what forms might shape that action. While his philosophy of the novel is complex, the basic components of Harris's thought are remarkably consistent. He shares with Bakhtin a penchant for the novel as a quintessentially open form but, whereas Bakhtin reads this as an unfinishedness with respect to living language, Harris takes this dialogic as a path to human authenticity by breaking through the impasse of the real and the strictures of the everyday. Bakhtin stresses the active role of the Other in constituting the subject, and Harris too is willing to destabilize and decenter the self-assured "I" in his narratives. Paget Henry suggests Harris's philosophical turn on the ego and consciousness should be separated from the phenomenological interests of Heidegger and the dialectics of Hegel. Henry's point is that Harris's aesthetics develop within Caribbean consciousness, and one that views self-renewal as dependent on a mythopoetic confrontation with the trauma grounding Caribbean being.[18] Thus, Harris defamiliarizes the borders separating consciousness of myth in West/Rest dichotomies and recasts these relations in a dream language of cross-culturalism. Harris's work is transnational because it exceeds the terms and codes of an individual national culture, say that of Guyana, as a primary mode of identification and also because his writing questions the logic of location and identity informing the world system as such.

The long space engages the materialist conditions of postcolonial being. Such a notion of being as agential and constitutive is counter to Harris's intuitions about the role of consciousness. In general, Harris favors an idealism in which consciousness is determinant and world being is racked by obliviousness of the bar it has placed between it and conscious-ness. This is not the philosophical disposition of, say, James, Césaire, or Fanon, but Harris provides a provocative link between a notion of con-sciousness formation and the deep structures of imagination in the Ca-ribbean and South America. Yet, however one characterizes the extreme difficulties of Guyana since independence, it is not for want of imagina-tion or access to consciousness.[19]

For Harris material need and greed lie at the heart of the explora-tion and exploitation of the New World in which Guyana was inscribed. Harris historicizes the origins of Guyana's relationship to the West while simultaneously projecting back before it using the landscape itself as a *temporal* guide. The issue here concerns scale, and few writers have articu-lated its use with such acumen. In "Tradition and the West Indian Novel" Harris invokes scale to calibrate individual artistic response to the "drama of living consciousness" (TWS 34) with a person's connection to "the es-sence of life, to the instinctive grains of life which continue striving and working in the imagination for fulfilment, a visionary character of fulfil-ment" (TWS 34). Scale describes an imaginative experiment "instinctive to the native life and passion of persons known and unknown in a struc-ture of time and space" (TWS 34–35). Note the use of structure alive to the plasticity of imagination. Indeed, the long space of Harris's work fo-cuses on the scales of imagination. The distance, he suggests, between the present and Dante is a function of a specific scale, the ability to perceive a "living open tradition" not closed off to consciousness. Form evolves from scale: language registers shifts in scale.

Relinquishing authorship is a means to give up on the claustropho-bic constraints of the ego's subscription to the real (and for Harris includes the ability of characters like Aunt Alicia to dictate authorial decisions).[20] Receding authorship reveals what is left to being that monadic conscious-ness refuses to concede. This is particularly important in terms of myth and fable and links to "conscience of a space."[21] Place is drenched with nar-ration but not necessarily in the form one expects. Where there is no writ-ing there may be orality; where there is no speech there may be alternative modes of speaking. Landscape, for both Glissant and Harris, "speaks"—it bears witness, it communicates the substance of location. Harris will as-cribe consciousness to rocks and trees as both informative and polemi-cal. His animism gives his fiction a multilayered narration in which every dream permeates not only the consciousness of the dreamer but the space and place in which it occurs with a corresponding scale of apprehension.

In Glissant's writing opacity paradoxically speaks to the popular by limiting the information-retrieval pathology endemic to the Western "I." Spatiotemporal markers and cultural insiderism can resist the tendency to present postcolonial cultures as not only an open book but an easily decipherable one. Whatever the pitfalls of inscrutability, for postcolonial writing opacity remains a necessary risk to problematize the almost inexorable logic of incorporation that girds Euramerican cultural discourse on the South. It should not be read as an either/or strategy, however, as if clarity might not also be creative. In general, critics of Harris point out the challenge his writing represents and, although this still conjures the Western adventurer—say Raleigh—absorbed by the prospect of sudden revelation, it is nevertheless testimony to the profundity of his thought and the deep convictions he holds about the power of writing for Guyana and beyond.

Unlike most interpretations of Harris's oeuvre, I read his tetralogy both with *and* against the author's own models of critique. If there is something provocative in his decentering of conventional authorship, this extends to Harris's position vis-a-vis his work. Just as there is much value to Harris's taste for the oxymoronic and contradictory (found in terms and concepts such as "live fossil," "absent presence," and "slow-motion lightning"), so his subsumption of the individual to universal consciousness paradoxically implies that one can be true to the author by displacing him. Indeed, the process by which Harris infuses the novel as genre with paradox continually doubles or multiplies his departure from conventional models of authorship. It includes the possibility that to think like Harris might cancel the opportunity to read him in any other than a mystical manner.

Rather than offer Guyana as the practiced place of a colonial imaginary, Harris takes a principle of Western ontology, the fantastic projection of the other, and disarticulates it using a cross-cultural imaginary. This constitutes a vital link between the Caribbean and South America in the form of marvelous or magical realism. Without recounting all of the features of magical realism, it has important advantages for Harris's imaginative grasp of Guyana. For one, it eschews anthropological and sociological reportage, the sort of fact finding that Carpentier says leads to a "jungle book": transient experience converted to fictional foray.[22] Benitez-Rojo reads magical realism as a means to undo the logic of "over there" (*Là-bas*), which for him signals the passage from modernity to postmodernity—or rather, the irruption of the postmodern where modernity has ossified into dogma (one tantalizing supposition from this is that the Caribbean founds modernity and prescribes it according to postmodern signifying).[23] The Barthesian *Là-bas* is given particular nuance by Benitez-Rojo when refracted through Caribbeanness but comes with a pertinent impasse. The production of *Là-bas* would seem to be the monopoly of Western consciousness, and one in which the innocuous claims of travel writing drift upward to the aesthetic heights of fictive reflexivity. But Benitez-Rojo is working over concepts of identity and identification as a preface to a discussion of Carpentier and Harris on the myth of El Dorado (redolent in the first volume of Harris's quartet) so a corresponding or analogical reflex is at issue. He says of Carpentier that "With his life's history trapped between Europe and America, he comes to the islands and rain forests in a way that reminds one of Moses and the Promised Land, or, in his last novel, Columbus; that is to say as a 'discoverer' of a world that he has already conceived, that was *his*, and that has been thought up, imagined, and desired ahead of time by Europe" (RI 183). Does Carpentier the Cuban know that he does not know the Other's code, or is the assumption that wherever he goes, including down the Orinoco, he carries the knowledge of the Other within and not before him? Harris may be more intimate with Guyana but the problem of positioning remains: even with the Other's code the result is still text. Thus, Benitez-Rojo arrives at an uncertainty principle from chaos theory and what precedes it: "what the Other means, the total movement of all its meanings—lies always at an unreachable point, at the edge of the infinite *there*, in a space that shifts continually from the possible to the impossible" (RI 182). Harris calls this the "infinite rehearsal of space" and it is to such spatial codes that I now turn. The tradition of map making tells us that in the interests of colonial states being "over there" was not necessarily a precondition. When a border dispute arose between Venezuela and Guyana at the end of the nineteenth century threatening war between the United States and Britain, the solution was not to mount expeditions to explore the borders but, as D. Graham Burnett points out, to repair to the archives in Western capitals.[24] The maps constituted texts of empire arranged side by side in evidentiary zeal without recourse to the space so delineated. While few doubt the violence of maps, much of this has to do with the concept of imagination at stake in map making. The reason Benitez-Rojo links both Carpentier and Harris to the impasse in the Other's code is that they both see that postcolonialism does not make whole the divisions produced by colonialism. They begin a discourse in the Other by assuming identities divide, hybridize, mutate, and recombine in the instant of "I." The task is about the form of combination, creolization, *mestizaje*, and how this unthinks the hegemonic "I" mapping and possessing all it surveys.

In the face of colonial subjugation, oneness is a radical displacement of the underpinnings of imperial inclusion. In Guyana it represents a desire to acknowledge and circumscribe its own diversity as "the land of six peoples" (Amerindian, African, Chinese, East Indian, English, and Portuguese). Whatever the fictive possibilities of its people, for the time being its political economy is structured by a numbers game played principally between the Indo-Guyanese and Afro-Guyanese (who together make up as much as 82 percent of the population). The country's motto, "One people, one nation, one destiny," is no more or less an imaginary resolution for a real contradiction than any other national paradigm. First, the motto, full of the hopes of independence from 1966, announces a stark break from colonial space. It is worth recalling that in British Guiana the colonial seal carried a very different motto, *damus petimusque vicissim*—"we give, and demand in turn." The "we" is the colonial trader, and there can be no doubt to whom the demand was made. One of the meanings of *postcolonial* is the abrogation of this imperative. The second reason connects to the first since Harris reads oneness as multiples that are debilitating if not acknowledged personally and communally. Thus, he begins *The Palace of the Peacock* by dividing the self according to consciousness, temporospatial coordinates, perception/visualization, and an oft-crossed line between life and death. Indeed, the Dreamer, the twin brother and double of Donne who is himself shot and killed in the opening lines, is a "live fossil" whose powers of perception are split, contradictory, and barely approximate to the "I" that describes them: "I dreamt I awoke with one dead seeing eye and one living closed eye" (GQ 19). That both eyes can see is the function of dream, just as are second deaths, which is a vital conceit in the quartet as a whole. In 1960 Harris lays out a challenge: the myth of El Dorado was born of imperial projection, but what if it bears in itself the substance of its own countermyth and this doubling opens the possibility of overcoming myth as deracination for myth as truth?

The language of form is a register of a metaphysical conceit, which at the beginning of *The Palace of the Peacock* is a stunning announcement of the imagination's power to bridge the noncorrespondence of language and dream. Lacan notes that the unconscious is structured "like" a language, which is why the art of simile and metaphor is axiomatic for nonrepresentational correspondence. The brilliance of Harris's dream writing does not lie in the law of fiction but in the form that it takes. The quartet structure as itself form-giving is a subject about which Harris himself has surprisingly little to say (it does not enter his discussion of epic, for instance). In his "Note on the Genesis of *The Guyana Quartet*" Harris speaks of an attempt to prove the truths of nonrealist fiction by bringing the latter "into parallel" ("like", "as") with "profound myth . . . eclipsed in largely forgotten so-called savage cultures" (GQ 7). The eclipse is linked to "haunting" (dream language is also the language of ghosts) and to a highly subjunctive authorial disavowal: "and now across many years when I find I *may* read *The Guyana Quartet as if* it were written by another person, it is *possible* to conceive how the fiction validates itself through buried or hidden curiously live fossils of another age" (GQ 7—my emphasis). The authorial equivocation before "fiction validates itself" is both necessary and symptomatic of the conceit. Harris writes of discarding three novels before starting the *Quartet* and one can only speculate on what represented the failed relationship between author and fiction in that endeavor.

Speculation is also all that is left to Harris's claim in his introduction that he had not seen Michael Swan's *The Marches of El Dorado* (published two years before *Palace*)[25]—a book filled with pertinent narrative including a brief disquisition on the Carib bone flute quoted from Richard Schomburgk's *Travels*—until much later, in 1970 in a library in Toronto.[26] The assertion is important because it highlights the difference between revision and revisionary in Harris's art. Harris does mention that he had heard of Walter Roth's published research *An Enquiry into the Animism and Folklore of the Guiana Indians* which was a key inspiration for Swan (Roth also translated Schomburgk), but again, he did not read the work until later.[27] It is highly unlikely that in his years as the government surveyor for British Guyana Harris did not come across standard ethnographies and cartographies of the very space he was mapping. Roth, for instance, had been the government archivist and curator of the Georgetown Museum of the Royal Agricultural and Commercial Society up until his death in 1933, and surely Roth would not exclude his own work, including the translation of Schomburgk, from that archive.[28] These texts haunt Harris's. The eldest member of Donne's crew on the expedition in *Palace* is Schomburg, and so we must assume that Harris had read Schomburgk—at least the name but perhaps even Roth's translation—in which, as mentioned, Carib cannibalism and the bone flute are discussed. Since Harris knows that the appendix he points to in Swan actually quotes Schomburgk, one might be forgiven for thinking that the denial speaks its opposite. This is the leap of imagination Harris's writing compels and why his archetypal narrator, The Dreamer in *Palace*, is similarly unreliable.[29] If the history in the introduction to *The Guyana Quartet* is remarkable it is because it both accentuates Harris's engagement with the land of his birth and throws into relief its necessary disjunction for Harris's imaginary space to congeal. As with the substance of Alicia's professional advice, the question is not about truth but creative belief. This is what allows him to "play" the bone flute.

The El Dorado myth itself requires a leap of faith, and one driven by the compulsive objectification consonant with the colonizer's gaze. What is the significance of El Dorado for Caribbean and South American identity and how might it serve as a form-giving device in *The Guyana Quartet*? Briefly, in terms of Guyana, the myth owes much of its historical impact to the obsessive fantasies of Walter Raleigh who, on two occasions—1595 and 1617—attempted to gain that golden place for the Crown. The origin of the legend probably lies with the Chibcha Indians, who were said to bathe their king with oil once a year and then powder him with gold dust before he washed off in a sacred lake. Swan reports on the work of J. Acosta (*Descubrimiento de la Nueva Grenada*) that such a ceremony, using turpentine rather than oil, was recorded in the town of Guatavita, near what is now Bogota, some forty years before the arrival of the Spanish. For the Spanish it would become a second, alternative Inca empire and perhaps an even more wealthy one. Schomburgk, in his preface to a new edition (1848) of Raleigh's report on his first attempt, *The Discovery of the Large, Rich and Beautiful Empire of Guiana, with a Relation of the Great and Golden City of Manoa (Which the Spaniards call El Dorado)* offers a spirited rationale for Raleigh's obsession: "Such was the influence of this seducing picture, first sketched by rumour, and then coloured by imagination, that the more victims it drew into its vortex, the more were found to embark in plans for its attainment."[30] Two years before Raleigh's expedition the Spanish again tried to verify what had become an imperialist fetish. Antonio de Berrio led an expedition but to no avail, although it did move the imaginary space of El Dorado further east. Raleigh subsequently captured Berrio, who was persuaded (in no uncertain terms apparently) to reveal all. Schomburgk defends Raleigh's excessive enthusiasm as a ruse of empire; Raleigh did not really believe in the legend but cultivated it to encourage British colonization. Since Schomburgk had been explicitly called upon by the Hakluyt Society to rehabilitate Raleigh, the argument is unsurprising. King James I was less impressed by Raleigh's failure to deliver gold in abundance and, in perhaps another characteristic attempt to appease the Spanish, had Raleigh beheaded in 1618.

Hena Maes-Jelinek and others have discussed how the El Dorado myth has been taken up by writers as diverse as Carpentier, Harris, and V. S. Naipaul.[31] Harris connects El Dorado to his concept of scale (which is also described as a "ladder"—*The Secret Ladder* being the fourth volume of the *Quartet*) because "it has begun to acquire a residual pattern of illuminating correspondences" (TWS 27). This scale takes account of European desire (Raleigh is mentioned), but also of the "black modern pork-knocker and the pork-knocker of all races" (TWS 35--"pork knocker" was a popular English term for itinerant gold and diamond prospectors in the region). Most important, it has a fictive correlative:

> El Dorado, City of Gold, City of God, grotesque, unique coincidence, another window within upon the Universe, another drunken boat, another ocean, another river; in terms of the novel the distribution of a frail moment of illuminating adjustments within a long succession and grotesque series of adventures, past and present, capable *now* of discovering themselves and continuing to discover themselves so that in one sense one relives and reverses the "given" conditions of the past, freeing oneself from catastrophic idolatry and blindness to one's own historical and philosophical conceptions and misconceptions which may bind one within a statuesque present or a false future. (TWS 35–36)

The Palace of the Peacock takes up this challenge admirably. Harris imagines El Dorado to relive and reverse its given conditions. Donne is a quintessential colonizing subject, "cruel and mad" says Mariella who has been beaten by him. If he differs from Raleigh it is by degree not kind. Mariella kills Donne on the first page, yet he is already dead in the world of the *Quartet*, where many are often blind to the past's consciousness of the future as present. Dreamer may be going blind in one eye, but in a world of conquest and gain few people in Harris's novel as epic have eyes to see. Donne says he has to be a devil to survive (GQ 22) and as a universal material instinct he notes, "I'm everything." He is the "last landlord" but over what? "Every boundary line is a myth. No-man's land" (GQ 22). These are also the words of those mapmakers in Europe, but in Donne the trick is that by possessing this land he becomes "no-man" or, like Odysseus, "Nobody." As for the Dreamer, the map of the savannahs is a "dream," yet as part of Donne's split consciousness (and also as his brother) he cherishes the "symbolic map" exceeding the "colonial conventions" of Brazil and Guyana even as the map becomes "a priceless tempting jewel I dreamed I possessed" (GQ 24). A tyrant, Donne has trouble keeping his workforce, and so the journey of *The Palace of the Peacock* is in search both of Mariella and of labor. Donne takes a boat upriver with a crew that is a microcosm of Guyanese cross-culturalism (the consonance between Melville's white whale and El Dorado offers another tale about epic consciousness and nation formation). We are introduced to "upright spiders" (Anancy trickster mythology courses through the narrative) including the Portuguese-descended daSilva twins, the old bowman Schomburg (a mix of German and Arawak American Indian), Vigilance the Indian, his cousin Carroll, "a thick-set young Negro boy," Cameron (of Scottish and slave descent with a "brick-red face"), Jennings the mechanic, and Wishrop the assistant bowman who is yet another double of Donne. The Dreamer sees "the nucleus of that bodily crew of labouring men," but it is not their labor but their soul that is at stake. The crew, like Donne, is already dead, both spiritually and from having the same names as a crew that had previously perished on the identical journey. The other characters on the quest are the jungle, the rivers, the rocks, and the wind. They whisper, speak, dream, and articulate a history that is as much a vessel of Guyana as Donne's boat. Donne heads first for the Mission, Mariella's home and another charged symbol of the colonial adventure. Since the population there believes the crew to be dead and that Donne himself has returned to avenge his death by Mariella, it flees into the jungle. Harris uses the oxymoron "congealed lightning" not just to describe a storm but also in Donne's address to his crew about what to do next ("Meaning was petrified and congealed and then flashing and clear upon his rigid face and brow hanging in his own ultimatum and light" [GQ 49]). He believes himself to be losing all imagination except for an idea that he was a taskmaster involved in "frightful material slavery" (GQ 50). If this smacks of tragic heroism then it is not born out by the rest of the tale.

Donne believes he has a right to the land and its labor. He has wedded into the fabric of Guyana and points to his "dark racial skin" (GQ 51) as a sign of embeddedness. The Dreamer believes otherwise, so Donne mocks him "Is it a mystery of language and address?" The reply is iridescent of the language of form:

"Language, address?" I found it hard to comprehend what he meant. "There is one dreaming language I know of . . . "I rebuked him . . . "which is the same for every man . . . No it's not a language. It's . . . it's" . . . I searched for words with a sudden terrible rage at the difficulty I experienced . . . "it's an inapprehension of substance," I blurted out, "an actual fear . . . fear of life . . . fear of the substance of life, fear of the substance of the folk, a cannibal blind fear in oneself. Put it how you like," I cried, "it's fear of acknowledging the true substance of life. Yes, fear I tell you, the fear that breeds bitterness in the mouth, the haunting sense of fear that poisons us and hangs us and murders us. And somebody," I declared, "must demonstrate the unity of being, and *show* . . . " I had grown violent and emphatic . . . "that fear is nothing but a dream and an appearance . . . even death . . . " I stopped abruptly. (GQ 52)

The dead selves of Donne and his crew are marks of existential inauthenticity. Unlike Heidegger, Harris takes consciousness as also extralinguistic, and the "inapprehension of substance" here is an inability to understand a unity of Being that includes everyone and everything. The insufficiency of language is marked by language, just as language stands in for the dream it can never fully be (it can only provide symptoms, slips, poeisis, and absent/presence). What such pronouncements indicate is epiclike revelation and renewal, and this is the real meaning of an El Dorado. The crew, however, perishes horribly (again) in the service of loftier meaning. Mad Wishrop had worked with thieves and whores in the gold and diamond mines but, on finding his wife in bed with a lover, he murdered the couple (a shot through the eye, naturally) and he was subsequently drowned in the falls, his bones picked clean by hungry *perai*. Their second deaths begin at the point the crew fantasizes the rape and murder of the old Arawak woman that Donne has captured as a guide. The river, anthropomorphized into her dress and demeanor, strikes back by taking Carroll who in his previous life had been driven mad by unrequited love. Vigilance, his stepbrother, takes over at the bow but he is as doomed as any other: "the past returned to him like pure fictions of rock" (GQ 69). Schomburg dies in his sleep, another ghost in the limited way he grasped reality, as Harris puts it. Wishrop goes next, in exactly the same way as the first time although this is also referred to as a "spider transubstantiation," which serves to link Wishrop simultaneously with the Anancy legends and with Christian resurrection theology (interestingly, transubstantiation in reverse is one of the ways that Swan comments on Carib cannibalism, and the term is used by Harris in his "Note on the Genesis"). DaSilva dreams of a time before he was born, back to the "impossible start" where "water start dream, rock and stone start dream, tree trunk and tree root dreaming, bird and beast dreaming" (GQ 87). He hallucinates a parrot who represents the object of his love. In their journey Cameron throws a rock at this bird, wounding it, and by extension, daSilva. For this daSilva stabs him and another crew member is dead again. Harris constantly reminds us of the "fantastic chimera" the narrative represents: even these few details here try to rebuild representation where there is none. By the fourth day of the journey (there will be seven) Jennings muses, "No one could truly discern a reason and a motive and a distinction in anything" (GQ 95), a chaos emphasized through plot and action. In dreams the characters all touch on the essence of their nonbeing and the narrative logic in the story. Vigilance, at the end of Book Three, ("The Second Death" in *Palace*) is described thus: "he rested against the wall and cliff of heaven as against an indestructible mirror and soul in which he saw the blind dream of creation crumble as it was re-enacted" (GQ 96). Here imagination is pushing against the impossibility that denies it consummation.

The closer the crew gets to their prize, the more they effectively disappear: "everyone in the vessel was crumbling into a door into the sun through which one perceived nothing standing—the mirror of absolute nothingness" (GQ 99). Visions multiply and coordinates recede. Rather than remapping Guyana this is a deterritorialization. The narrative dissolves points of reference and de-essentializes space by layering place over place and undermining the merest chronology ("Time had no meaning" [GQ 103]). We think we are climbing a wall by a waterfall with the survivors but no, Donne/Dreamer (they merge) is hallucinating the very moment of creation, "the very nail of moment in the universe" (GQ 101). A room comes into view with a carpenter, "the craftsman of God in the windowpane of his eye" (GQ 102). The carpenter is simultaneously the sign of all creation ("the divine alienation and translation of flesh and blood into everything and anything on earth" (GQ 102) and Death ("with capitals"), a wooden dream as it is described. No one doubts the Christian symbolism that peppers the denouement of *The Palace of the Peacock* (a woman and child also appear) but, like the search for El Dorado, it constitutes only one measure of its symbolic structure. By reversing the seven days of creation through the journey of Guyanese inhabitants, Harris is posing a question about the essence of identity and whether it is universal in what makes up the planet in nature and in humans. Language denies this universal as an absolute because existence and identity are more than the sum of words used to describe them, yet the prose at the end of *Palace* is so blissfully exuberant that in the palace the power of imagination appears to have overcome this shortfall.

In his geographic examination of the function of El Dorado in British imperialism, D. Graham Burnett invokes metalepsis.[32] He is attempting to show how Schomburgk recalls Raleigh as an authority for his exploration yet actually converts that authority, and map, for his own devices. While this is a loose deployment of metalepsis, it nevertheless captures the movement of transformation of causes into effects and effects as causes justifying possession. Schomburgk claims to find the site of Raleigh's El Dorado using an inventive gloss on the hydrographic mapping of the Guianas by Alexander von Humboldt. In the composite identities of the crew, Harris offers an originary glimpse of creation. The tree of life becomes a bird, becomes a palace, becomes a mystical vision of the "fortune of love and the art of victory over death." Here there is something of a similar reversal. El Dorado is a cause of this wondrous soul searching but historically it has functioned as its material, sordid, and brutal effect. Raleigh and Schomburgk, like Donne, embody the banalized substance of human material desire, an authorizing fantasy of imperialism. Harris tropes on this trope not to restore Raleigh or any other apologist for colonization, but to unpick history from both mythic epistemology and originary being. This scene of metalepsis is Guyana. Just as El Dorado is magical, mystical, and imaginary so too is the space where "the palace of the universe and the windows of the soul looked out and in" (GQ 112). For Harris the journey into the interior of Guyana is about the realization that space and its imaginary are *already* possessed. We do not need to claim them materially but imaginatively. In effect, transnationalism is an overreaching of nation by a consciousness of space requiring no nation for primary sustenance.

In the rooms of the palace where we firmly stood--free from the chains of illusion we had made without—the sound that filled us was unlike the link of memory itself. It was the inseparable moment within ourselves of all fulfillment and understanding. Idle now to dwell upon and recall anything one had ever responded to with the sense and sensibility that were our outward manner and vanity and conceit. One was what I am in the music—buoyed and supported above dreams by the undivided soul and anima in the universe from whom the word of dance and creation first came, the command to the starred peacock who was instantly transported to know and to hug to himself his true invisible otherness and opposition, his true alien spiritual love without cruelty and confusion in the blindness and frustration of desire. It was the dance of all fulfillment I now held and knew deeply, canceling my forgotten fear of strangeness and catastrophe in a destitute world. (GQ 116)

The poetry of Harris's language not only displaces the cruel history of Western expansionism and material dogma but destabilizes the legitimizing structures of its expression. Yet all is not well in Harris's mystical fancy. Harris's catechresis wants epic but in a language that denies it. In the 1984 introduction to the *Quartet* he asks, "In what degree, one wonders, is epic rooted in the lost infancy of a people and their need to compensate that loss through various trials, complicated jealousy, guilt, passion, innocence?" (GQ 13). The issue whether epic is a vast displacement for a vanished innocence is complex and vital, but not one that fits easily over Harris's *Quartet*, a group of novellas with structural links at the level of spirit but not necessarily in terms of character, journey, narrative, and hero. One question for the long space is where does the author betray a conviction in the extended chronotopic coordinates of fiction? Andrew Bundy persuasively argues for Harris's dreamwork as a single narration; his oeuvre constitutes a continuing rehearsal of the substance of consciousness and each work is a variation on the intricacy of this theme. Does the *Quartet* work according to its own logic of connection, and does such an alternative rationality write out a new consciousness of space only possible in the sedimented experience of colonization/decolonization?

It is easier to read each volume as a contradictory yet self-contained narrative rather than as a form with greater attributes. Harris notes in his 1985 introduction to the *Quartet* that as a surveyor he was conscious of "the uncertain economic fate of the society, its need to deepen its insights into the soil of place in which ancient masquerades exist to validate the risks a community may take if it is to come abreast of its hidden potential" (GQ 14). It is unclear, however, whether Harris initially envisaged the *Quartet* as the form in which these insights could be best demonstrated, or whether, like Schomburgk's metalepsis, this form is retroactively projected as the cause for such a unity of purpose. Nevertheless, the first volume does elicit structural devices and themes subsequently readdressed, reformed, or revised in the rest of the *Quartet*. Although Harris elaborates a nonlinear conception of time, both the act of writing and the sequence of novels are neither random nor logically juxtaposed. As Gregory Shaw has noted, this progressive modulation has something of the dialectical about it, despite Harris's distrust of history as an Hegelian totality.[33] The elements most relevant to the language of form are allegory, symbolic acts in general, desire, and to borrow from Said, contrapuntal indications.

Allegory remains problematic in Harris's writing because of its relation to postcoloniality and nation. Since Jameson's celebrated essay on "Third World Literature in the Age of Multinational Capital," we are used to separating allegory from any semblance of cognitive aesthetics in the interpretation of postcolonial, Third World, anglophone, or transnational fiction.[34] This is not just in recognition of the spirited attacks on Jameson's essay but because whatever emerges in the interrelation of economic and cultural coordinates does not aspire to a typology of discourse forms in which allegory is key. On the one hand, it merely confirms Aijaz Ahmad's contention that there is no such thing as Third World literature: it does not constitute "an internally coherent object of knowledge."[35] On the other hand, allegory in the "narration of nation" remains axiomatic to the extent it connects the effulgence of the nation idea and the "speaking otherwise" (*allegoria*) of cultural identity. Harris's *Quartet* invokes Guyana in a number of complex ways but its allegorical mode renders the fact of Guyana almost inconsequential. In seeking to elaborate the cross-cultural roots of Guyana's chronotope, Harris's narration pursues a higher unity (paradoxically fragmented) than Guyana itself. But if El Dorado was the phantasm of Eurocentric desire, to what extent is it answered or displaced at the level of myth and allegory? Might these also partake of an inclination to resolve aesthetically what is principally an arena of material contradiction? If the long space deconstructs the binary that shuffles transnational fiction into a philosophy of the Same (redolent in many readings of "world literature"), its formal resolution does not proffer the social practice of the imagination as an end in itself. The contrapuntal indications of national allegory, however, continue to reverberate.

The allegorical and epic quality of the journey in *The Palace of the Peacock* reemerges in the second volume. It shares the Dreamer's symbolic map, although the characters and action differ in tone and point of view. The material coordinates again trace a movement between the coast and interior of Guyana: between the scene of colonization with postcolonial delinking and miscegenation, and a native, sedimented cultural refuge within. The text opens with an epigraph from *The Secret of the Golden Flower*, the edition/translation featuring the collaboration of Richard Wilhelm and Jung.[36] The ancient Chinese text is a key work of Zen Buddhism and, more recently, of New Age spiritualism. *Secret* resonates throughout the *Quartet*, as do Jungian refractions of consciousness. References to alchemy, mandala-like (circular) designs, eye imagery in particular, the fusion of material and spiritual reality, synchronicity, and visions and archetypes are all imaginatively reworked from Daoist and Jungian sources.[37] One can also trace elements of syntax and style from these works through which Harris provides a unique cross-cultural synthesis. In Harris's "Art and Criticism" essay of 1951 (TWS 7–12), Jung is positively invoked and one can only conjecture whether this "writing consciousness" was first attempted in the abandoned novels that precede *The Palace of the Peacock*. (I believe what is cast off is actually revised and "revisioned" for the *Quartet*; there is nothing in Harris's aesthetics excluding such a process, as his reworking and reinterpreting of published texts clearly shows.) "The Far Journey" in *The Far Journey of Oudin* is drawn directly from *The Secret of the Golden Flower*, so one is not surprised by the ethereal quality to the journey described (Harris uses another excerpt from *Secret* for Book Four of *The Whole Armour*). Like the first volume, there is a "spirit-power" to *The Far Journey of Oudin* that is difficult to ascertain. One feels like Beti, Oudin's wife, who struggles hard to become literate in the art of reading Oudin himself. The novel begins with Beti crying on Oudin's death; yet if one reads this after the reversed (and cyclical) tale of creation in *Palace*, one is already prepared to accept the pronouncement with skepticism. Oudin has made a contract with Ram (entailing ownership of Oudin's offspring) and, illiterate, Beti decides to eat the paper scrap on which it is written, as she does with all the written texts coming into the household. Ram has a "conception of empire" (GQ 139) and property drives his relationship with Oudin. Like Donne, Ram's materialism blinds him to the truths of the landscape and the community. Oudin fulfills a need; for Ram he is "a dream, a fantasy and an obedient servant" (GQ 141). If Mariella is both a place and mark of desire in *Palace*, then Beti more obviously embodies this function within a system of patriarchy (her illiteracy, for instance, is a product of this oppression). The other axis in the narrative is the farmer Mohammed's plot with his brothers Hassan and Kaiser and a cousin, Rajah, to murder a half brother, the heir to their father's property. Oudin connects these stories (he looks like the half brother) while simultaneously destabilizing all notions of linear or realist narrative. Oudin's deadlike presence at the beginning of the novel allows us to trace his doubled existence back to this point, and he emerges as a composite of humanity, all races and creeds, who has come from nowhere as a consummate sign of rebirth and hope. The real of property, whether farmland or slave, is undermined by personal and supernatural insecurities. In Harris's world there is always the potential to repent and be reborn (although not in the form that organized religion might wish), and even among the murderous conspirators such light may dawn.

The Secret of the Golden Flower is an appropriate text for Harris's novel in its epic gestures. It places a heavy emphasis on symbolism and the search for a consciousness (and/or the unconscious) that breaks through the deceptions of the material world (Ram's motivations are closest to the latter, while Oudin embodies the desire for the former). The easy passage between life and death recalls the nonbeing in being of Lu's text. Similarly, the "magic spell" recounted in *The Secret* resonates in Harris's text. The notion that "words crystallize the spirit in the place of power" (the countering "spirit power" quoted in Harris's epigraph) is taken as a basic statement about language's ability to undermine the arrogance of material power (although language has a material power all of its own). Beti's perception, on Rajah's death, that he has gone to "a land that is nowhere" (GQ 196) is straight out of *The Secret* but omits Lu's explanation that this is "the true home." It has a powerful appeal to Harris and the kind of Jungian journey to Self that many of his characters pursue. It might also explain the sometimes incidental nature to Guyana in the *Quartet* that can only be a home if it is symbolically "nowhere." A spiritual home motivates a cross-cultural or transnational perception; it symbolizes a gateway culture inextricably linking the ancient and modern through archetypes, the repetition of patterns and forms constituting the deeper, imaginary realm of existence. The spiritual "far journey" must go farther than Guyana but not without registering its imprint on consciousness.

For Harris to trope on *The Secret* is consistent with his aesthetic concerns; although we should note that along with its status as an inspiration to Jung on the nature of psychic processes, it is more generally an occult manuscript giving instructions on an alternative path of imagination to the Promise of God. An attraction remains, but the East that is at the heart of *The Far Journey of Oudin* is Indian, so other Buddhist texts might have been more pointed or poignant. Indeed, the ethnic and racial depictions in the novel have a less than immaterial air to them and show it would be incautious to suppress Guyana wholly from the metaphysics of the narrative. Jeremy Poynting suggests Harris often caricatures the East Indian presence in this novel.[38] He also notes that when critics celebrate Harris's cross-section of Guyanese society aboard the Doradonne in *Palace* they neglect the fact that East Indians are missing from its rich diversity (although one could add that so are the Chinese). Poynting is careful not to infer a nefarious ethnocentrism in Harris's depictions, which is clearly not what Harris is about, but the criticism warrants attention because it highlights a weakness in Harris's imaginative depth.[39] Poynting argues Harris's metaphysical idealism gets in the way of a more fully realized dialectical understanding of Guyanese society, yet this is inconceivable within Harris's notion of the cross-cultural *as* imagination. The more interesting point is that by emphasizing the metaphysical Harris strips his characters of sociological and material complexity. Again, some care is called for since we read a character for her symbolic aura not for some fleshly correspondence.

Harris is hamstrung by exactly the process facilitating his figural universe: referentiality. One could use deconstruction to pry open the signifier in Harris's language (critics have undertaken this labor to good effect), but what happens when nouns, adjectives, and proper names start to ground the symbolic, or the mythic or the mythopoetic?[40] In *Palace* El Dorado was deployed within a primordial myth connecting to the emergence of Guyana itself. But in *The Far Journey* the slight parable of "wicked husbandmen" overlaps with representations of East Indian peasants and budding entrepreneurs who are not quite at one with the "glimmering heaven" of lights beginning the tale. This does not mean Mohammed, Hassan, Kaiser, Rajah, or the scheming moneylender Ram are all too real but, paradoxically, the reality made available to them is constricted by associations that symbolize too much. Since Oudin's insight is forged in the experience of death (he doubles the murdered half brother, just like Donne and Dreamer in *Palace of the Peacock*), the real of the story might appear besides the point; but we are still left with images of the brothers on a less spiritual and ethereal journey, as Poynting also quotes: "a disfiguring and vulgar quest for new ways of making money . . . the acquisition of sordid power" (GQ 162). While Harris does not intend to stigmatize his East Indian characters because of their ethnicity, such associations multiply the more he tries to elaborate their presence. The brothers themselves, particularly Mohammed, harbor racist views of the Afro-Guyanese and believe themselves to be the rightful heirs to plantation capitalism. The difficulty is, as Poynting notes, such antagonism has been misread in Guyanese society at great cost to social and economic stability. At no point does Harris subscribe to ethnic and racial divisiveness, but by drawing on these depictions to structure the morality of the story, he invokes a material reality that punctures rather than proscribes the "rehearsal" of the moral universe in play.

For many, Guyana's national motto, "One People, One Nation, One Destiny" is a postcolonial irony, for the country's modern history has been dominated by the schisms between its East Indian and African constituencies, and its social and economic strife has led it to be called "an outstanding failure story."[41] Despite its metaphysical intonations and however distasteful the race relations depicted in *The Far Journey*, it points to a constitutive real in its representations. If Mohammed and his brothers are no more true or false than any other of Harris's collection of "live fossils" that does not mean they do not refract elements of Being and presence symptomatic of Guyana's predicament before and since independence. The "land of waters" was quickly colonized by the Dutch, who used their expertise in water drainage to cultivate the fertile coastline and their desire for "free" labor to enslave the Amerindian inhabitants. Doubting European benevolence (and, of course, racked by the diseases it brought) the Amerindians retreated to the jungle of the interior. The Dutch then brought in African slaves by the thousand, and the next two

hundred years were dominated by plantation economics and the internecine strife of colonial powers. Slave rebellions and escapes occurred on a
regular basis, and the revolt led by Cuffy in the Berbice region in 1763 is
still celebrated. The British, flaunting their own expertise in slavery, finally
snatched Guiana in 1803 but soon extended the basic principles of the industrial revolution to the colonies: wage slavery was less odious than its
forebear and provided a ready-made market for surpluses. Not that this
in any way reduced the white man's fear of the blacks he had enslaved.
After the British officially outlawed slavery in 1833, the Africans in Guiana quickly moved to run their own farms and take over any abandoned
land. The white planters who remained decided to circumvent dealing
with their former slaves through an open labor market by trusting the
future of the colony to imported indentured labor. Afro-Guyanese, who
had dominated the labor force, quickly found themselves marginalized by
foreign workers—initially Portuguese (upward of thirty thousand), but
then Chinese (at least fourteen thousand), and finally, and most important, 240,000 East Indians.

The story of British Guiana and its transition to Guyana in the twentieth century is only partly about the implosion of the British empire and
the resistance and revolt that precipitated it. It also a narrative about how
the constituencies of a fictional colonial construct segregate or creolize according to self-identity and perceptions of the other. In Harris's treatment
of the crew of the Doradonne there is little that can save these communities: he believes they are equally deluded by the false prophets of materialism and universal bias of various stripes. Their redemption comes through
death and rebirth in a spiritual return to what is primordial and archetypal
among them. If Harris has little truck with normative history on aesthetic
grounds, it is also because Guyana's history flies in the face of his cross-
culturalism. While forces of creolization and assimilation were certainly at
work in post-slave society, initially at least the Africans and East Indians
formed two very distinct groups, culturally, politically, and economically.
This legacy is written into postcolonial Guyana. Harris believes creoleness
is a "saving nemesis" because "it implies recuperative powers and vision
within a scale of violence that is dismembering societies around the globe"
but such a "nemesis" has not defused the racial antagonisms of the country
of his birth.[42] Oudin dreams hard in *The Far Journey*, but even in his "ge-
nius of space" he cannot cancel the racism and ethnocentrism informing

the political unconscious of the society in which he mysteriously appears. Is his journey wasted?

The language of form articulates a space in which a truer human potential becomes possible (true not necessarily to a specific place, hence the "trans" for the nation of Guyana) in a shared unconscious. The difficulty of *The Guyana Quartet* is that, like Harris himself and many of his putative characters, the reader has intuitions, but these may contradict or hold in suspicion the truth claims of Harris's language. Perhaps what distinguishes Harris the artist from Harris the politician is he cannot imagine a process beyond the adjudication of the artist himself through which such differences might be resolved. If this is not always strictly idealist, it often feels utopian, as if language not only compensates the material derogation of Self but also stands as its productive alternative. The rebirths in *The Far Journey* want to write out or sublate the imperfections of the materialist soul haunting its major characters: the "rightful heir" is not contracted to the material, but to spirit, and the ego in Harris's tale, which is most often a version of the authorial "I," seeks redemption in writing, "the ink of spirit" (GQ 222).

Just as the seven days of creation are reversed in *Palace*, so *The Far Journey* works its way back to Oudin's death that is its beginning. These reversals are rehearsals to the extent they play out Harris's concern for the life/death cycles constantly moving the human beyond the "partial truths" of the everyday. In "The Writer and Society" Harris suggests that "We may be closer than we think to the Hermetic arts of [Giordano] Bruno and of the alchemical imagination where the filter of the mind was as much part of the process of experiment as the material itself under scrutiny" (TWS 57). Stephanos Stephanides avers this logic implies Harris's embrace of the "dialogical novel," yet qualification and extension is required.[43] The dialogic rests on the perception of audience within and without the narrative, an expectation of reply internally organizing writing. Elaboration is necessary if we are to understand more fully the imbrication of Harris's cyclical or mandala-like patterns in the long space with the Bakhtinian notion of novelization, or the various ways in which storytelling dialogizes. Harris is closer to Martin Buber on "dialogue" and "dialectic" and views these possibilities as release from the manichean binaries typical of the "novel of persuasion" (TWS 29).[44] Thus, while Oudin's death at the beginning of *The Far Journey* may leave him, spiritually, in a circle (the "end of his labor

of death" [GQ 124])—that Stephanides links to *shakti*, the female symbol, "the primordial womb"—the dialogic aspects of what follows seem to
question the "wholeness of the inner self" this implies.

The tension is forged by what Maes-Jelinek calls a "duality of existence."[45] Harris does not narrate on the evidence of consciousness *sui
generis*: the question remains whether the inner self limits the effulgence
of consciousness at all? We are free to liberate ourselves from time in
dreams, but for the materially oppressed in Guyana's history more urgent
freedoms present themselves. If *The Far Journey* evokes the duality of existence, readers may be forgiven for thinking that one of them is barely cog-
nized. Yet, Oudin's journey is significant on a number of levels. For one, it
symbolizes the disinherited peasant's resistance to the machinations of the
greedy. Oudin makes a pact with the devil in Ram, but his "journey," as
an escape and as a spiritual revelation, brings him to another place beyond
death and extinction. His decision to elope with Beti and thwart Ram's
plans has an air of heroism to it, but it is important to Harris's vision that
Oudin's physical movement does not occlude the voyage within, which
both aids in Beti's freedom and in Ram's reformed outlook by the novel's
end. Travel to the interior (of Guyana) is never innocent, but on this occasion facilitates less a conception of the epic hero and more a notion of
rhythmic renewal even in the very human emotions of love and devotion.
Every map implying property or ownership in *The Far Journey* is redrawn
by the paths Oudin symbolically treads. But these journeys are cycles, and
there is no guarantee Mohammed's desire, or Ram's, might return once
more to enclose space in the name of commerce and transaction. Individual change in the novel is literally and figuratively circumscribed, and language remains the measure of this inconstancy.

Just like Oudin's decentered heroism in the story (with Beti's own
heroism as a contrast), the language of the novel is demythified. For all the
mystical allusion and death-in-life reversals, much of *The Far Journey* rests
on everyday dialogue and, paradoxically, realistic reproductions of Guyanese dialect. While the opening of the novel is consistent with the dreamy
denouement of volume one, from Beti's first cry, "Oudin dead. Oudin
dead" (GQ 124) we are also in the presence of conversational speech alive
to regional and multilingual possibilities. This novel stands in stark contrast to the archaic explorer/discoverer tones of *Palace* and confirms that if
the space of language can be expanded by spirit, it can be simultaneously

contracted and localized by the materiality of extant speech. Certainly, even in Beti's outburst, the missing verb poetically reverberates Oudin's ghostly presence (and Kurtz as another colonial fantasist), but in general Harris delights in transcribing the lilt and cadence of conversational English in Guyana. One could read this negatively, as if the ascription of the barely articulate to the brothers, for instance, is a further stereotypic representation of South Asian Guyanese, but then such speech, even at its most stuttering, conveys their worldviews as individuals. Mohammed, ironically the most outspoken, understands well the pitfalls of diaspora and deracination for language:

He [his father] come in this country with he daddy—we grand daddy that dead before we born—from India. And we got to forgive he for the strict unfathomable way he got of looking at we like if he grieving for a language. Is ancient scorn and habit at the hard careless words we does use. But is who fault if the only language we got is a breaking-up or a making-up language? At least nobody pretending they is anybody high-schooled and polite 'cept they got hard cash to rule. Is a parable we meaning all the time every time we can't help twisting we tongue when we speak the truth. (155)

Rather than condescending, I read the author's relationship to this speech as resonant of what Harris calls elsewhere the "creoleness of the chasm," part of the "make-up language" inhabiting the space between cultures, between discrete identities.[46] The father "grieves" for a language when he hears his sons speak theirs, but their journey necessitates precisely the "break-up" Mohammed remarks upon. And while a transcription, it does not exclude the artist's eye and ear. The word "unfathomable" is a Harris trademark, and as for "parable," it is perhaps a mistake speaking the truth of the brothers' story. The "strange jigsaw" of the epic and revolutionary novel here includes speech refusing individuation while resolutely locating it. Rajah exclaims "Let me mek me story plain-plain" (GQ 156), which could indicate a willingness to conspire with his brothers but also signifies the text's own desire to break through its synthetic and synesthetic surfaces. Similarly, while such outbursts might show the extended family as barely literate, the issue of literacy itself is never far from the politics of decolonization, especially in a colony that specifically tied democratic and property rights to the language of empire.

The nexus of creolized English and property in British Guiana is highly relevant to one "present" in the novel, the year 1951. The People's

Progressive Party (PPP) would hold its first congress in April 1951; indeed, this would mark the beginning of the long-standing friction between the politicians Forbes Burnham and Cheddi Jagan and by extension the post-colonial positioning of Africans and South Asians in Guyana. The PPP quickly sought universal suffrage and an end to British dependency. Given the Cold War context and the scientific socialism of the PPP's party plat-form, the British government sent over a Royal Commission led by Sir E. J. Waddington to defuse the situation. Initially, the British took quite seri-ously the claims of the landed elite to enforce a literacy (in English) and a property requirement for the vote, but when the Colonial Office offered its final decision on Waddington's report in October 1951, only the liter-acy clause remained. Independence was bracketed but at least the PPP's push for universal suffrage had borne fruit. As for the question of prop-erty (a key theme in *The Far Journey*), the PPP was committed to destabi-lizing the power of the great sugar estates (protected by the British under the auspices of the governor) and redistributing land to workers of much smaller means. The problem of land use and ownership fueled social un-rest right up to independence and beyond. Its ties to democratic constit-uency and the use of English were pronounced, and it meant education could no longer be the ward of the colonial elite.

Interestingly, in their "charcoal" death and rebirth, both Kaiser and Hassan link language to perceived economic and racial hierarchies. Has-san dreams of a return to India in order to spread his ashes, but Kaiser curtly reminds him he would be viewed as an outcast and "untouchable ghost." He asks, "What language had he save the darkest and frailest out-line of an ancient style and tongue?" (GQ 181). Kaiser, on the other hand, views his "charred skin" as a new opportunity: "I can pass as a negro pork-knocker and I shall take a passage to the goldfields of Cuyuni and Mazaruni. I shall steal into Venezuela, and swim across oil" (GQ 181). Yet Kaiser's ambition is equally delusional, a fact underscored by his recollec-tion of an exchange with a German mining engineer whom he had driven to Georgetown. After Kaiser signs his passenger's voucher, the German notes "I thought you were *Kayser*, he said, but I see you have written *Kiser*, K-a-i-s-e-r" (GQ 182). Told that he signs with the name of an emperor, Kaiser responds, "I have heard of black emperors whose signature alone will rule the world" (GQ 182). What is signed is Kaiser's ignorance of the name if not the principle. These exchanges situate Kaiser and Hassan within the extent of their literacy: they cannot return to India without "language," without "custom."

Beti's predicament is compounded by patriarchal assumptions. In his essay, "Literacy and the Imagination," Harris devotes some attention to Beti's plight, and especially her coming to literacy, her capacity to "*read* the world, to *write* something within herself, *through* herself" (emphasis in original).[47] This notion of literacy is closer to Gayatri Spivak's on "transnational literacy" than it is to reading and writing through a specific language.[48] For Harris, it has vital implications for Beti's freedom and for the production of the text itself. Beti may eat the convenant Oudin has made with Ram, but her understanding of Oudin's doubleness—the heroic rescuer yet deceitful trader—is a form of textual production and possibility. In Harris's view, Beti not only consumes text, but becomes the author of it by doing so. Harris equates the realist author with a kind of authoritarian axiom, preferring instead self-effacement as textual agency. But what does Beti's literacy mean to the form of this fiction?

Certainly it is a knowledge consuming, quite literally, the "partial truths" of contractual obligation. Identified as little more than chattel, Beti eats language as a false guarantee, then vomits as a mark of catharsis and collective truth. To recall Swan's comment on Richard Schomburgk's description of Carib cannibalism once more, Beti herself enacts a kind of "reverse transubstantiation" through a literacy that, like the *timehri* engravings seen on Guyanese rocks, preexists the colonization of English. I do not subscribe to Stephanides's view that Beti's knowledge is akin to some Mother Goddess and is "the eternal womb of regeneration who receives Oudin's creative seed" (GQ 135), although there is symbolic weight to support this reification through deification. If her presence is mythical, she differs from Mariella in *Palace*. Her illiteracy before the script of empire emboldens Beti to provide meanings for Guyanese existence. Whether these exceed or erase Harris's authorship is another matter. Whenever the subaltern cannot read or write the language of state, she yet speaks the spirit of its contradictions. If the novel is still Oudin's journey, it is Beti's consciousness that traces it.

If the mythopoesis of *The Far Journey* is grounded by the vernacular (what Maryse Condé, in another context, calls "creolité without the creole language"), then the third novel, *The Whole Armour*, is—despite its heavy Christological symbolism—rooted by plot.[49] The relatively confined geography, close to the mouth of the Pomeroon River, tightens the exigencies of Harris's story. True, there is Cristo's sojourn into the jungle (forty days and forty nights), but the life of spirit and coming to consciousness is primarily directed at a small coastal community. The novel's title comes from Paul's Epistle to the Ephesians and refers to an armour of truth, righteousness, peace, faith, and salvation augmented by the sword of Spirit. With epigraphs throughout the subsections of the novel from the *Bible* as well as from Gerald Manley Hopkins, Goethe, Blake, and *The Secret of the Golden Flower*, the life of the spirit is very much to the fore even if the Christian allegory is subject to Harris's idiosyncrasy. Much of the poetry of the novel derives from symbolic death and rebirth, with the individual acting as a conduit for more purposeful modes of existence and community. We begin with Abram's dream of falling.[50] Abram is an outsider, an old man who seeks rebirth in innocence from the Blakean travails of guilt and misspent experience. While the Biblical Abram is renewed by the birth of Christ, Harris's character will accrue a measure of salvation in helping Cristo, Magda's son who has been falsely accused of murder. The bond of Abram and Magda here is made from mutual outsideness, underlined by the pointed references to their mixed race, "half-caste" heritage (Magda is black and Chinese). As in *Far Journey*, Harris tends to use "race" expansively, although it is a dangerous gambit precisely because of the strained race histories of Guyana. To this degree, "cross-cultural" is cross-racial, and Harris reads miscegenation as a dynamic principle of de- and refamiliarization. Racial multiplicity is paradoxically pure to the extent that it de-emphasizes racial exceptionalism as a social force. This is less the privilege of Harris's own mixed-blood genealogy and more a reflection on the problematic real of Guyanese identity.

Abram does hide Cristo, but before Cristo can be smuggled out on his uncle's boat, Abram dies of a heart attack, a time of transubstantiation: "the ultimate moment to leap had come, he knew, and to abandon a grotesque imitation of life for the spirit of universal dust and the innocence of a phantasm of pollen" (GQ 251). He sees his reflection in Cristo's eyes and then falls to the ground, "wanting to say something ghostly and utterly reassuring but the confirmation of innocence froze on his lips in the self-reflection of ancient horror and reluctant fibre and dread of the unknown" (GQ 251). Cristo tries to explain to Magda what happened but she convinces herself, and him, that he had run from guilt. Returning to

Abram's hut, all they find is a ripped and bloody shirt. Thus begins the invocation of the tiger (as the jaguar is referred to by Guyanese) and a myriad of associations. The tiger will return again and again in the novel and corresponds to the tiger made famous by Blake (whose poem is quoted). The novel turns on "fearful symmetry" as humans face nature and the nature in themselves. Cristo embodies both the attributes of the tiger and the lamblike innocence of its counterweight in Blake's schema. The subsumption of one in the other informs Cristo's sacrifice: he will eventually submit to the community's desire for vengeance for a crime he did not commit. Yet, for all the correlations between Harris's novel and its sources, his voice, particularly in its form-founding of Guyana, is utterly unique. The tightness of the plot throws the language of form into stark relief and finds Harris's cosmology less obtuse and paratactic on its own terms.

In this "rehearsal," Harris's cyclical and self-canceling language comes close to a dialectical negation of character for plot. Yet Harris subjects the plot to an inner consciousness that has no direct object in his narrative. Just as many of his characters experience an almost rote double negation (they die to live to die again), so *The Whole Armour* proceeds by an intricate emptying out of meaning sequestered by an objective world. Adorno suggests in his reading of Hegel that dialectic seeks to speak the nonidentity of the world without becoming it and this is an apt if ironic way to describe the formal motions of Harris's language.[51] But, as Adorno points out, the Hegelian dialectic does not dwell sufficiently on the intervention of language itself in sublation, and perhaps this symptom too is the undecidable working against Harris's otherwise strenuous dematerialization of Guyana. Thus, the replaying of Christian allegory reinforces its spiritual armor only to find what Adorno calls "semblance" displacing it at the level of language.[52] The seemingness of Guyana gets in the way of Harris's mythopoesis of deobjectification, but language, as its vessel, articulates this impasse much better than the object to which it refers. Harris's project is not snared merely by the materiality of language; the struggle of the text is to refract the dialectic of imagination without negating its powers of communication.

If Harris's language emphasizes process over objecthood, we should not be surprised that the outward appearances of his characters are so interchangeable. Once Magda and Cristo find Abram's rotting body, his deathly appearance becomes an appropriate alibi for Cristo's transubstantiation. Clothes are exchanged to signify Cristo's death rather than Abram's and Magda conspires to make this semblance truth. "Realism weds us to death" so Harris answers with death's unreality.[53] Abram disappears while his body is buried as Cristo. The plot spins around this focus on death's metonymy. Ultimately, however, the plot is held together by Harris's tiger, and more should be said about its "symmetry" in the dialectic of negated opposites.

The tiger propels the narrative forward by "explaining" Cristo's death and Abram's "disappearance" (he is thought to be chasing a tiger). Emblematic not just of experience, but of violence, its contradictory presence is redolent in Harris's defamiliarization of nature and human by freely crossing its divisions. One character, Peet, dreams of "Abram's tiger" attacking him, but as an image beginning in sound: "a breaking sea on a jagged coast at Abram's doorstep. It assailed him, full of pounding threatening sibilance, a striding breath of grandeur, whispering and overlapping and rising notes in a hushed vagrant roar that suddenly grew and became so deafening he was transported to see the flecks of tigerish foam on a dark-fluid body, striped by the animal light of the moon" (GQ 281). The menace of the tiger is its form, but the principle of its form is manifest in everything (the moon also has a resonance—Maes Jelinek suggests in conjunction with the sea and the earth it offers its own "tigerishness").[54] Like the peacock in *Palace*, the tiger functions as an *objet a*; for Peet it emerges as the displaced desire for Magda and, as desire's cause, allows him to replenish his fantasy of her. The semblance of the tiger does not require its cognate: its substantiation lies precisely in the way it is split off from the certainties of subjecthood. "Tigerishness" is appropriate: it always exceeds its objecthood in nature. Peet is born again from his experience "out of the jaws of Abram's tiger" but then, again characteristically, views his own newborn hallucination, the image of Cristo, "burnt by the fumes of hell and reality. . . . However much he tried to mend a carnival conceit and glory it remained a basket and a sieve—crippled by the compulsive perception of the bizarre womb of Abram—out of which Cristo had been reborn and spilt" (GQ 283–84). Peet had earlier accused Magda of staring at him as if he were a ghost and here, with his fantasy of Abram begetting Cristo, a trinity is enjoined.

The trinity of plot—what R. S. Crane elaborates as character, action, and thought—is, in Harris, almost always dominated by the latter.[55] This does not imply the imposition of authorship, but instead its scrupulous suspension for the agent of consciousness itself. Indeed, the symbolic deaths and rebirths, and the more problematic trope of the womb, are together reflective consciousness at work. The tiger imagery is the plot working out the paths of consciousness as redemption ("The beast lived everywhere at once, in every breast, on every breath. Mankind itself was the tiger" [GQ 299]). Mattias reports that the tiger has been seen standing on its hind legs and he is at once drawn into its aura: "It was the birth of a universal discontent and the shadow of the death of the past, the presentiment of an apparition combining the serial features of archaeological and racial mystery" (GQ 290, to which we might add Blake's question: "Did he who made the lamb make thee?"). In love with Sharon, Peet's daughter, Mattias views Peet at the wake as his future father-in-law. Meanwhile, Sharon herself is visiting Magda, who reveals Cristo is alive and wants to see her (much to Magda's chagrin, Cristo prefers Sharon!). Despite the melodrama, tiger consciousness (in the section "Time of the Tiger") predominates.

Reminiscent of cinematic cross-cutting, the plot flashes forward to Sharon and Cristo making love, then back, through Sharon's memory, to the night of the wake. According to fable, Cristo had killed the tiger that had mauled Abram and now wore the tiger's skin as a trophy to his own wake (thus, "the tiger on its hind legs"). Cristo's return will provide the novel a finale even as each character's incompleteness is a product of an unfulfilled connection with a shared ancestry: the people *and* the land of Guyana. The association is mythical, like the omnipresence of the tiger. The myth is not about formal consistency but how language might break through frames of reference. Consciousness is immanent in the form to the extent language can fathom the ethereal as successfully as the objective world. Because language is the medium and not just the message, the narrative cleaves to plot but in the process creates fantastic excess—like the tiger intended, paradoxically, to register fusion, oneness, in spirit. In the long space of Harris's writing, such immaterial objects of consciousness suture the cycles and repetitions of narration. They are the products of an imagination revealing the soul of form in a language coextensive with it. If the parables are not altogether biblical, they remain in their visionary transubstantiation, numinous.

Mattias dies accidentally (although, in the crispness of plot, Peet comes close to being accused of the death before exoneration by the dying Mattias himself). The tiger is an appropriate symbol to link the characters for several reasons: the Blakean contrast with the lamb and all that is innocent; the commingling of beauty and violence that epitomizes life in the community; the extravagant association of the tiger's stripes with everything from the chiaroscuro cast by moonbeams to the coexistence of races in the same being; and finally, as in Cristo's coat, the tiger represents the "whole armour," the medium of triumph over ambivalence and self-doubt. In the fourth and final part of the novel Harris claims such spiritual victory will be elusive or transient unless it is acknowledged as the substance of unity between humans and their universe.

This is explored through the prejudice directed at Sharon: she is portrayed as a veritable witch for the desire she inspires in men. Cristo wants her to understand his story, but he also wants to comprehend her feelings. (In a moment of rare humor she reveals that she liked Mattias a great deal and that he was a big fan of Beckett's *Waiting for Godot*! Mattias, we are told, had gone to Cambridge.) Reminded of their respective parents, Cristo bursts out: "I wish with all my life . . . one could show them they're *our* problem child after all, that we're *hundreds of years* older than they dream to be. And why? Because we have begun to see ourselves in the earliest grass-roots, in the first tiny seed of spring—the ancestral tide and spring of Jigsaw Bay, I swear, and that's why we're so different. We're reborn into the oldest native and into our oldest nature, while they're still Guyana's first aliens and arrivals" (GQ 333). The belief stems from Cristo's forty days in the jungle, an experience resembling Harris's since it results in direct contact with Amerindians. Cristo wanders in search of work to pay for safe passage into Venezuela. Scarred, tatooed, "decapitated" from razor grass, and caked in mud from negotiating a bog, he alights upon some similarly "painted" Caribs who take him for their own. Cristo is almost convinced himself until he sees his reflection in the water and returns, once more, to his identity as "a black man from Africa." Yet this is not the end of his strange sojourn. He "dies" once again in a dream of the gallows, which snaps him into a self-realization as everyman: "every guilty body rolled into one. Vanquished as well as slave, rapist, Carib, monster, anything you want to think" (GQ 345). Cristo is put back together by "white priests and magicians," but his renewal does not protect him from rumor and revenge since Mattias's father has implicated him in crime. Cristo cannot escape the community's everyday fears, and the novel ends both with Peet's death and with the promise of Cristo's to follow. Will Cristo's death save Sharon from wrath, his mother, or even the people of Pomeroon as a whole? The issues are open but the novel suggests Cristo's understanding of himself as multiple and one is neither general nor "universal." Thought itself emerges as the "immortal diamond" (from the Hopkins epigraph), but even this is refracted through a second crystal to which it is not reducible: language. The plot has its melodrama, but the real drama of the narrative is how Harris strives to rescue thought from the platitudes of the real. There appears to be no armor that will save Guyana the signifier from its signified. In the final volume of the quartet, Harris will write out the deracination of Guyana by a scrupulous return to the self as fictive possibility. The cycles of life/death/life will continue but this time in the form of a Harrisian doppelganger.

The Secret Ladder is at once a contradictory text. In the last volume of the *Quartet* Harris disappears as an author only to be reinscribed, biographically, in the figure of Russell Fenwick, the government surveyor. From an aesthetic position of realism and the social as an inveterate trick of conventional imagination, Harris's narrative yet articulates a fully fledged arena of Guyanese community, however dysfunctional one might view its contours and contents. True to the quartet's mythic proportions, Fenwick's antagonist is Poseidon, a fisherman and farmer who wants to protect the descendants of runaway slaves from the ravages represented by the government's plan to provide irrigation for the coastal lovwlands. Yet again, however, the narrative flies in the face of the logic originally presented in *Palace* of a nation looking to its interior to discover the true coordinates of its being. In *The Secret Ladder* the people of the riverhead are seen as recalcitrant and backward, unable to understand the progress represented by Fenwick's expedition. The African Guyanese are not vessels of history as the previous novels had advanced, but psychologically scarred by the legacy of slavery itself and ill-equipped to comprehend the embeddedness determined by their environment. Fenwick's mission, far from marginalizing the influence of Poseidon and his people, draws them further into the revelatory spirit that Fenwick experiences, so that each contradictory omen the text advances ultimately folds back into the complex surfaces of the *Quartet* as a whole. The measured tenor of chaos is signaled in the end by the seventh day, which is where the tetralogy began.

As if to remind the reader of the journey she or he has made, Harris sprinkles the opening of the novel with tantalizing connections to the others.

Fenwick's crew is detailed as if a mirror image of Donne's (although two Chinese are added). A savannah is referred to as Oudin, and Fenwick has named his dinghy *Palace of the Peacock* after the city of God or gold that lends structure to the "inchoate Amazon basin" (GQ 358). So far so good. If all of the *Quartet* is about scales of apprehension of Guyanese space and identification, the last volume is the most explicit about how Guyana's enigma of origins confounds normative socialization and narration. The territory, like the story, is laddered by paradoxically incalculable measures, like the Canje "in the ladder of ascending purgatorial rivers" (GQ 367), whose rising and falling waters Fenwick is trying to assess. Poseidon, the grandson of a runaway African slave and a symbol of rebellious marronage, is seen as "the black king of history whose sovereignty over the past was a fluid crown of possession and dispossession" (GQ 369). For Fenwick, "Poseidon had been hooked and nailed to a secret ladder of conscience, however crumbling and extreme the image was" (GQ 371). Harris seeks a metaphor to bind the tale together only to find such a bond insufficient to the deep structures in which metaphor is enmeshed. Just as the water catchment capabilities of the Canje are undermined by erosion and a fecundity that cheats prediction, so the complex trajectories of Guyanese being subtend any formula or hierarchy (ladder) that might stand in for the immeasurable in relating them. *The Secret Ladder* is thus true to the *Quartet* in general while upending the certitude the fourth corner of Harris's text might provide. The language of form is a scale that confounds calibration.

Robert Carr has suggested Fenwick's water gauge is a symbol of "the inheritance of Western administrative procedures" and it is criticized as such.[56] That Fenwick's government-sponsored expedition is bent on calculating how well the interior might irrigate the coastal plains is a register of colonial rationalization and administration. The gauge is destroyed by Poseidon and his supporters and typifies the schisms existing between the jungle inhabitants and those of the coast. We should add, however, that while Harris would be quick to question the reliability of the gauge in understanding the terrain of Guyana (he, after all, was a trained expert of such instruments) its Western provenance does not encapsulate the division between Fenwick and Poseidon. Furthermore, Harris is less interested in objectifying difference than in assessing how the object world might provide a window through which the imagination can realize a mutual embeddedness in consciousness. On this level, Poseidon is just as trapped by *ratio* as Fenwick.

In Fenwick, "the secret ladder of conscience" is destabilized by duty, which constantly seeks to legitimize his perceptions. This would not be an impediment were his sense of duty consistent with his sense of self. In fact, the action of *The Secret Ladder* is driven by the difference between the discovery of self and land in Fenwick's vision. Such revelation begins with Fenwick's first impressions of Poseidon, but then is deepened by his subsequent reflections on his relationship to Guyana. Here the novel is both an allegory and an autobiography of authorial presence, a ghostly figure for the artist's relationship to fiction that methodically emerges in the *Quartet* as a whole. In his essay "Interior of the Novel," Harris claims the author "is the complex ghost of his own landscape of history or work. To put it another way, his poem or novel is subsistence of memory."[57] It is not a memory *of* discovery that is important vis-à-vis the self, but memory *as* discovery that constitutes the *Quartet*. Think once more of Raleigh or the Schomburgks in the exploration of Guyana, or the various mutations of Donne and Fenwick, daSilva and Magda in Harris's fiction: they do not bring to life the "is" of Guyana. Instead, the complex play of indigenous and exogenous, the incessant hybridizing from conquest and migration, creates forms that offer the revelation of memory as a trace of what paradoxically has not been: the unified spirit with a land common to all impeded by false interpretations of the principle of profusion itself. As Fenwick ponders Poseidon before him, one comes to understand why the novel as form must fall short of containing a memory guaranteeing understanding.

Fenwick adjusted his eyes. He could no longer evade a reality that had always escaped him. The strangest figure he had ever seen had appeared in the opening of the bush. . . . Fenwick could not help fastening his eyes greedily upon him as if he saw down a bottomless gauge and river of reflection. . . . He did not trust his own eyes like a curious fisherman, playing for time, unable to accept his own catch, trying to strip from the creature who stood before him—the spirit with which he himself had involuntarily invested it. . . .

Poseidon addressed Fenwick at last. His mouth moved and made frames which did not correspond to the words he actually uttered. It was like the tragic lips of an actor, moving but soundless as a picture, galvanized into comical association with a foreign dubbing and tongue which uttered a mechanical version and translation out of accord with the visible features of original expression. . . .

He listened, no longer with a sense of contempt, to the agitated crooked voice of the creature he had caught, trying at the same time to follow the silent accents of an ageless dumb spirit. It was as if he (Fenwick) however much he protested within himself at the ceaseless ruse of cruel nature and sentimentality, could never, any more, rid himself of the daemon of freedom and imagination and responsibility. (GQ 370–71)

Fenwick believes himself to be a man of order and rationality, in command of a "plain job" (GQ 381) suffused with utilitarian concern, not power or exploitation. Presented with Poseidon as his Other, Fenwick objectifies his strangeness but just as quickly doubts his transcription of this realm of difference. Fenwick's curiosity is piqued by the prospect of "gauging," yet this lure clearly contradicts the forms of his apprehension. The spirit of Harris's formal concerns are closer to Poseidon's expressive conundrum than to Fenwick's reflection: he "made frames which did not correspond to the words he actually uttered." Language is deeper than "frames" indeed. But the language of form is only partly the "silent accents of an ageless dumb spirit" because it questions the capacity of form itself. This is the way that freedom, imagination, and responsibility become devilish for they know what is lost in translation cannot be discovered in form *per se*. In "Profiles of Myth and the New World" (1966) Harris argues spirit cannot be spoken as is but may be "ventriloquized" by "rhythm, gesture, sound signifying priorities that are beyond exact representation or seizure."[58] He notes he became aware of "variables within the language of Imagination" while he worked in the savannahs and rain forests of Guyana. Like Fenwick, this experience provokes reflection on what is ageless and otherwise unspoken but no character (or form) is adequate to its "numinous inexactitudes." There is only the ghost or trace of the imagination in Being, not the substance of its presence or the certitude of its actualization as an axiom of apprehension.

The drama of *The Secret Ladder* is the confrontation of Fenwick and Poseidon and whether this empties the nation, Guyana, as a philosophical possibility for form. While Guyana is often incidental to the mythical imprimatur of the *Quartet* it nevertheless represents the initial conditions in which the relationship of I and Other is manifest. Ostensibly, the nation and the novel provide a form for Being, but Harris finds language transgressing such forms when archetypes are particularized. Let us triangulate the epigraphs that begin the novel. From a man who himself has visions, it is perhaps unsurprising that Harris would quote Blake, here from Blake's paean to his favorite poet, Milton (there are epigraphs from Blake in each volume of the *Quartet*): "With our vegetable eyes we view . . . visions" (GQ 354). Blake's poem portrays Milton as a Christ-like figure who returns to Earth one hundred years after his death to "justify the ways of God to man" by overturning the constraining reason of Urizen and the corrupt practices of Satan. Milton's charge is prepared by Los, who is a symbol of creativity and inspiration. Harris's use of quotation here simplifies the vision conveyed in Blake's poem:

> These are the Children of Los; thou seest the Trees on mountains
> The wind blows heavy. Loud they thunder thro' the darksom sky
> Uttering prophecies & speaking instructive words to the sons/Of men:
>   These are the Sons of Los! These the Visions of Eternity
> But we see only as it were the hem of their garments.
> When with our vegetable eyes we view these wond'rous Visions.

In Harris's quotation the identification is with the human whose natural eyes see visions, but in Blake's poem this perception is partial ("the hem of their garments") and falls short of apprehending "Visions of Eternity." There are counterindications in the *Quartet* where Harris himself is a son of Los "uttering prophecies & speaking instructive words to the sons of men." If we juxtapose Harris's quotation with the others, however, another possibility emerges. The Mayer quote, for instance, testifies to a common thread in Harris's *Weltanschauung*, the permanence of constants within conditions of flux: "There is in nature, a specific dimension of immaterial constitution which preserves its value in all changes, whereas its form of appearance alters in the most manifold ways" (GQ 354). This is a theory of the archetype once more.[59] "Immaterial constitution" has religious overtones (St. Augustine, for instance, uses it to designate the soul), but its pertinence to Blake lies more in the revelation implied; the apprehension of specific dimensions depends on the ability to see beyond what is available to "vegetable [natural] eyes." The Blake and the Mayer quotations provide an expansive spiritual engagement with nature that does not exclude principles of scientificity; after all, the world of objects has always been more than the sum of its appearance. The question is what might furnish an appropriate form for such an articulation? Blake struggled mightily to correlate the moment of vision with a language that served its description: there are many explanations for his illustrative zeal but one would include the shortfall represented by language itself. The problem of form also presupposes an authorial logic in which "visions" are not compromised by language yet remain communicable. This is the confrontation of movement and stasis, technology and nature, civilization and the primitive—all of which are subthemes in *The Secret Ladder*. Harris is less concerned with the obstinate binaries these represent but with a deeper aesthetic echelon of inquiry, a coordinate supplied in the quote from Macmurray.

John Macmurray's moral philosophy, particularly on the realm of Self and Other, stands at odds with conventional rationalist modes of Western thought. Harris quotes from Macmurray's two-volume magnum opus, *The Form of the Personal*, in which Macmurray lays out his critique of egocentric philosophy while forwarding an alternative logic of action-based interrelation: "It is indeed an integration of the movements of the [A]gent with the movements of the Other, so that in action the [S]elf and the Other form a unity."[60] The form of action is architectonic: a logic of building wholes from Self and Other (Maes-Jelinek notes Harris's fascination with an "architectonic self").[61] Fenwick's relationship to Poseidon is a practical demonstration of the principle in which the unity involved is both a category of being in the world and an architectonic element of literary form: Guyana can only be realized in the active negotiations of Self and Other in which its eventness is narrated. The action of Fenwick and Poseidon together does not constitute the unity of the text (for his part, Fenwick relies too heavily on the confines of *cogito*) but is symptomatic of a cross-cultural engagement at the heart of Harris's explorations. Macmurray's text concludes with an appeal to natural theology in the realm of a "personal universe" whose constants are also those implied in Harris's reference to Mayer. Harris's three epigraphs suggest what is extant in Guyana's present; and history stages a more general principle of action founded on spiritual rebirth rather than material gain, but ultimately there is no consistent logic binding them.[62] What is true for Blake in his mythic representation of Milton does not reproduce the logical coordinates of either Mayer or Macmurray. They are paradoxical framing devices shaping the form of a narrative that exceeds them. They are alibis for form, not by offering false substance to Harris's approach to fiction, but by continually drawing the opacity of his narrative into a unity located elsewhere, in a *geist* rather than in a Guyana.

In Macmurray's argument for "the world as one action" one sees why Harris might interpret this as a philosophical correlative for the constants of "immaterial constitution."

This integration *is* the action and its unity is intentional. It would be impossible unless the process of the Other, independently of the agent's intention, were itself systematic; for if not there would be no ground for any expectation that the movement initiated by the agent would be continued by natural processes, in one way rather than another. If we could not rely upon the world outside us, we could not act in it. We can act only through knowledge of the Other; and only what is a determinable unity can be known. It does not follow, as we have seen, that its future can be completely determined in advance; only that whatever occurs must be systematically related to what has gone before, so that through its changes the world remains one world. (*The Self as Agent*, 220)

Harris attempts this unity in a number of ways: for instance, by eschewing realism for a kind of simultaneity between past and present, by elaborating life cycles in which rebirth allows for personal change in the "self as agent" without contradicting a fundamental unity in the world, and by underlining that any confrontation with nature is simultaneously a desire for a knowledge of the Other constitutive of the Self (a process initiated for Harris by his survey work in the interior). Most important, Harris refuses to countenance a dualism of body and soul, material and immaterial, and this informs his ethereal prose. Work like Macmurray's is not the key to Harris's reflections on self and other but accentuates the apprehension of Guyana as multilayered contact zones, "an emergent fiction of truth" (GQ 12) in which the action of the *Quartet* confounds putative plot, and characters exist in a constant tension with Others who remain their possibility.

Fenwick sets out the importance of his encounter with Poseidon in a letter to his mother. Poseidon, a hundred years old, is the grandson of a runaway slave who as legend would have it, "had turned into a wild cannibal man of the swamps, devouring melting white cocerite flesh wherever he spied the mirage of high baking land" (GQ 369). Fenwick, a hybrid of African, European, and Amerindian heritage (with "unique vagaries and fictions" [GQ 383]) is struck by Poseidon's affinity with a jungle that has meant both constant hardship and independence. Fenwick wonders if he sees something of his father in Poseidon, also of African descent but who had died shortly after Fenwick's birth. The meeting is a reminder of

Fenwick's Black identity and the role of such heritage in what Guyana can become. The *Quartet* is finished just before the final push for independence in Guyana, but the political divisions Fenwick alludes to in his letter continue in the friction between Forbes Burnham and Cheddi Jagan going back some years before (differences already registered in *The Far Journey*). Fenwick believes the East Indians will win out over the Africans in the next general election but that the African not be "misconceived" (GQ 385). Fenwick has just scratched out a reference to birth and rebirth in his confrontation with Poseidon ("it's a question of going in unashamed to come out of the womb again" [GQ 384]), and there is enough in this double-voiced discourse to register the disjunctive community ethos pervading the novel.

Community factionalism is intensified by Fenwick's newfound consciousness: his warning against misconceiving does not guard him from misapprehending. The mistrust that he registers for his surveying crew is a foretaste of the suspicions characterizing its relationship to the "interior." Fenwick cannot assuage the fear of the local population that once they are surveyed they will be exploited. Bryant, the African, would come closest to realizing the importance of Poseidon's embeddedness although, because Poseidon attacks Catalena (Bryant's lover) Bryant ends up killing the man he reveres as his spiritual grandfather, an "epic stratagem" of unintended consequences. In a more serendipitous turn of fate, the "wild twins" who had set out to cheat Fenwick of some money find Chiung instead (since he has borrowed some of Fenwick's clothing). Chiung promptly insults them and they return later to kill him—punishment is swift and violent in Harris's portrayals. On hearing this, the people of the Canje no longer think they have the law on their side and flee, and this saves Catalena from rape (if not assault) and both Catalena and Bryant from death and a "communal" burial with Poseidon. Whether good or bad intentions are emphasized, law does not adjudicate the suffering Fenwick's expedition precipitates. Indeed, the references to law in the novel undermine its status in securing property and all manner of rights in favor of an "immaterial constitution" that "dismantl[es] a prison of appearance" (GQ 417). Thus, the seven days of creation are reversed to leave the reader where *Palace* will begin.

Like Césaire, Harris despises "civilization" calculating dispossession as an inevitable consequence of its civilizing mission. That Harris was in the employ of this machine does not make the figure of Fenwick an object of self-loathing, but is another measure of the contradictions between the inquisitive and acquisition, desire and enrichment, knowledge and possession. Such relations are not simply plot devices or intricate narrative exigencies: the principle of negation as sublation recalls the issue of formal unity, the binding of Self and Other exceeding their binary. While Harris is suspicious of the dialectic as a form of calculation, the imagination neither excludes the dialectic nor the dialogic in the full range of their possibilities. The neatness of Harris's conclusion to the *Quartet*—Fenwick awakes at the dawn of the "seventh day"—states the paradox that language is the medium of the measureless but is nevertheless measured in that signification. If, as Paget Henry contends, Harris articulates consciousness beyond the ego, language itself hangs onto just enough ego to allow other egos to inspect it.[63]

Thus, when Harris uses the word "measureless" to describe either the moving landscapes, the ever-changing mobility of the earth, or his own labor in the "unfinished genesis of the imagination," the language of form elaborates an absence of measure, a dynamic supersyncretism denying subordination to the real as formal reflection. The "unfinished genesis" is a long space where form finds a language continually and eloquently overreaching it. Harris does not begin with the quartet as a conditional limit on the organization of his novels; rather, he intuits an organic elaboration of language around themes that crisscross and meld each book in the tetralogy. *The Guyana Quartet* stitches together a logic for thinking the enormity of Harris's project. Guyana is not incidental to this process: it is a harrowing template of historical violence and imaginative possibility. But everywhere Harris looks the state's governing logic elides the more complex conditions of embeddedness that would allow greater mutual understanding and the full flowering of human endeavor. The *Quartet* situates the writer in relation to an aesthetic and existential project: to begin and expand a taxonomy of spiritual relation and to come to terms with Harris's outsideness with respect to his "homeland." Just as no character fully corresponds to Harris's position in the *Quartet* so no composite of these figures adds up to the outsideness overdetermining their array.

The noncorrespondence between author and character, even within the figure of Fenwick, is another mark of Harris's idiosyncratic modernism. Consider, for instance, how the *Secret Ladder* ends with references to an incidental plot displaced by the organizational agency of time, time *as* a character, as a motivated element of the chronotope expanding and contracting the long space of Harris's Guyana:

Time no longer stood to allow them to dig a hole in which to let their prisoners down beyond anyone's reckoning; and then time too was required to seal it up so that no one would dream it had ever been opened. Time not only to seal the earth so that it would look as if it had never been touched but to open it again, in broad daylight, before formal witnesses—as if for the first time . . .

[. . .]Time for Bryant and Catalena to appear to run and make swift love on every trail across the earth; while Fenwick grew to believe they had put their foot and escaped upon another in the secret ladder. The land was a mystery in which he would never chart where they had vanished. . . .

Let the foolish lovers fly into nothingness while time stopped to bring witnesses to the burial of God enclosing the instruments his disciples had vainly possessed—the apparatus of the law they once honoured . . . No one could force a void in the spirit of the law even with an act of humility or the surrender of one's land and property. Least of all by damming the ghost of responsibility. Time should have known better but it always seemed so ignorant of its own nativity or asylum or prison-house. And yet it would have prided itself on knowing *now* (if in stopping to read it had successfully executed) what no one else could dream to know. . . . God's grave over emptiness, over the unacknowledged wedding of man and woman, the unacknowledged burial of man and woman. . . . Time was prepared to bind its possessions above these unknown relics and over no other origin and abyss of itself. . . . It was an unendurable sentence which had been entertained, and which needed universal strength in execution that neither the dead nor the living possessed. . . . The instant the prison of the void was self-created, a breath of spirit knew how to open a single unconditional link in a chain of circumstance. (GQ 464–65)

For Harris narrative is a philosophical form and not only a novelistic one. If, following Macmurray, we hold time is the form of action, then here the traditional denouement of the novel's chronotope is suspended in favor of time's agency in the sublation of plot. This is a very god-like move, but the spirit invoked is not altogether of the artist's choosing. The law it figures is not to be possessed but remains essentially immaterial. What is being buried in this moment of time's action is a form of natural law; it is being buried by material appropriation. Poseidon's people, the community of escaped slaves and indigenous folk are ceding embeddedness, the law of action in their specific place, for integration in a modernizing machine.

The water will be measured and harnessed, and industry and farming will light up along the coast. This is a veritable "prison of the void" but its emptiness can be breached for "a breath of spirit knew how to open a single unconditional link in a chain of circumstance." It is hard, even now, with the insistent imagining of such a spirit in Harris's oeuvre, to seize this unconditional link as that which paradoxically breaks the normative chain of the novel as form. Language must seek a form for which there is no circumstantial referent other than the time of form-giving itself.

The *Quartet* is a long space of both dialogical and dialectical elements. The former emphasizes a vernacular of space in which the six peoples of Guyana speak to one another across the time of their emergence. This speech is informed by the rapaciousness of "discovery" and Harris decenters this revelation because it elides, through violence and exploitation, the foundations of cross-cultural or transnational understanding. Harris believes this dialogic to be the substance of a rebirth of epic, yet it is precisely the quality of the dialogic that undoes the time of the epic in the present. Harris's engagement with epic provocatively disturbs the doxa of the postcolonial novel by eschewing the real as a guarantee of transformation. This would be an idealism but for a further interrogation of the form by dialectics, an interpretation in part drawn from Macmurray's position on time as action. A key difference would be that time is not simply *an* actor—it exists in multiples in Harris's fiction; it is the multiplicity of time that marks Harris's fiction as both idiosyncratic and quintessentially Caribbean, a palimpsest of times wrought by the struggle over modernity as deracination. A variety of times—indigenous, exploratory, national, gnostic—both fracture and suture Harris's text. They preserve the openness of the form while dialectically synthesizing diverse and sometimes incompatible elements. Harris's long space narrates these times dialectically but the difficulty remains in tracing their connections to Caribbean and South American chronotopes in general. Such a labor of dialectics is especially pronounced in reading Harris and leads one to suspect the exotopic relation that makes Harris "British" (a British writer of Guyanese descent is the usual mantra) is also one which finds Guyana a mystery. According to this supposition, the invocation of epic is a displacement of active engagement; the narration of epic time is maintained precisely because it is inaccessible from the present. Harris contradicts Bakhtin's elaboration of novelization over epic by taking epic as blocked by a novelization unable to address the deep structure of community identifications. If novelization is only a sedimentation of Western formations of Self and Other, then it fails in its sweep to articulate the *longue durée* of alternative transnational propinquity and personhood. But novelization for Bakhtin was only ever a process of "selving," a general principle of narration, not an iron law of a particular Self or the defence of a specific location. The challenge is whether the form can sustain Harris's mythopoeisis as a condition of selving, or the self as agent in Macmurray's parlance, or whether this dialectic reverts to a particular self, the author as epic hero. That Harris leaves this question unresolved is not surprising,[64] but Harris continually confronts what the novel itself seems to deny, a form, as Buber puts it, "that wants to become a work through him."[65]

In Harris this precipitates a serial reflexivity: the long space of the unfinished genesis of the imagination overlaps the formal exigencies of the novel so single works or groups interrogate the grounds of expressivity. They talk to one another. Thus, one could begin again by arguing the conceptual clarification to the *Quartet* is heard in *The Carnival Trilogy* rather than in the flourish of *The Secret Ladder* that sends the reader spiraling from the seventh day to the first once more. The serial, engaged process of reading may be more daunting, but this is an affirmative manifestation of exotopy: the outsideness of the later extended fiction refigures the conceptual frame of the former without negating its Guyanese roots and cadences. The *Quartet* does not preserve otherness as a projection of European inquisition as acquisition, but as a dream with an interpretation elsewhere, in another consciousness if not another state of mind.

The Exotopy of Place

Nuruddin Farah's fiction subsumes form to character as metaphor. Even if Farah had not invoked the substance of metaphor in talking of his fiction, critics have consistently revealed metaphoricity at the heart of his endeavors. Whether exploring the fate of Misra's vexed affiliation in *Maps* (1986), the first novel in Farah's *Blood in the Sun* trilogy, or Soyaan's search for an explanation of the death of his twin brother in *Sweet and Sour Milk* (1979), the first novel in his trilogy *Variations on the Theme of an African Dictatorship*, one finds characters who are at one with the agon of Africa in general or the conflictual emergence of Somalia as a postcolony.[1] Such correspondences, however, are problematic. Despite the heartfelt nuances in Farah's representations of women, for instance, metaphorizing their condition can easily be misread as reproducing the very masculinist discourse their characterization is meant to question.[2] Similarly, while certainly not apologizing for the violence of colonialism, Farah's searing investigations of family dysfunction can appear like blaming the victims in colonialism's aftermath. One can correlate these excesses of characterization with the ambiguities of national identity itself. Certainly, Farah's formal engagement with the postcolonial predicaments of the nation state is profound. Yet we should qualify this connection, not just to allow for Farah's capacious imagination, but also to track the complex logic of identification and disavowal structuring exile in the long space. What is striking about Farah's language are the numerous ways in which he stretches it as a measure of the outsideness that is its very possibility. Such a postcolonial exotopy not only confounds the obligatory narratives of exile trumpeted by world literature, but also questions compulsive metaphoricity.[3]

Outsideness and metaphoricity are further complicated by otherwise laudable attempts to describe Farah as postmodern.[4] Certainly, abrupt movements in time and space, multiple and disjunct identities, and fantastic elements that defy the norms of realism are not beyond the borders of postmodern narration. The postmodern label circumscribes any and all unreflexive categorizations of Farah as a postcolonial, anglophone, diasporic, exilic writer of the "Third World." Perhaps this is only to remark the effulgence of the postmodern is coterminous with the global, and what is revealed in transnational writing bears the imprimatur of cosmopolitan identification. If my critique of Farah does not deny such affiliation (my reading, after all, may be deemed its very effect), he figures this in a more agonistic manner and—by articulating his identification with Somalia—Farah's fiction effectively cancels a seamless continuity between the novel and the global life of nations, just as Somalia has effectively nullified the form-giving prescriptions of the Berlin Conference (1884–85) and the attendant "scramble for Africa."

Outsideness here is informed by two competing notions of I and Other. In the work of Mikhail Bakhtin *vnenakhodimost'* (outsideness, outsidedness, or what Tsvetan Todorov terms *exotopy*) operates in several registers.[5] The monadic self is for Bakhtin a sign of absolute death, an outside with no border. The border of self is ripe with being; indeed, it is its reason. If exotopy is a posited border, then its spatial coordinates are highly suggestive: "A person has no internal sovereign territory, he is wholly and always on the boundary; looking inside himself, he looks *into the eyes of another* or *with the eyes of another*" (PDP 287). At this level, exotopy is a philosophy of the outside understandable only at the border, one with a corollary in cultural space:

. . . a domain of culture should not be thought of as some kind of spatial whole, possessing not only boundaries but an inner territory. A cultural domain has no inner territory. It is located entirely upon boundaries, boundaries intersect it everywhere, passing through each of its constituent features. The systematic unity of culture passes into the atoms of cultural life—like the sun, it is reflected in every drop of this life. Every cultural act lives essentially on the boundaries, and it derives its seriousness and significance from this fact. Separated by abstraction from these boundaries, it loses the ground of its being and becomes vacuous, arrogant; it degenerates and dies. (AA 275)

The borders of the individual and that of a culture are less the sign of exclusion but of socialization itself. But it is not enough to suggest that an author opens perspective on a discreet cultural domain or bounded space; rather, the author's constitutive outsideness figures a taxonomy of space, or what Bakhtin describes as "an intense axiological atmosphere of responsible interdetermination" (AA 275). This grounds not just the answerability to nation, but also articulates the *trans* in *transnational*. Responsible interdetermination has the authors of the long space question the boundaries of nation in decolonization even as nations are made by such responsibility.

This is one way to assess the difference between Farah's exile and the principle of the exilic immanent to his narration. It also counters both the suggestion that Farah seeks to stabilize identities vis-à-vis his imaginary state (Somalia, or what he has called the "country of my imagination") and an unequivocal postmodernism.[6] The space of negotiation between the individual and the state does not reside in the shifting of pronouns (as in *Maps*), or in the structural ambivalence of giving (as in *Gifts*), or even in allusive shape-shifting (as in *Secrets*); it is intrinsic to the logic of outsideness binding the author to the substance of form. Characters are less metaphors for such form-giving complexity but symptoms of a constitutive impasse in the imagination of nation itself.

Farah figures this difficulty in a number ways, most prominently in the imbrication of sexuality and desire as a deep conscience of the nation. One could read this primarily as authorial compensation for the conditions of exile itself: a tenacious redress for living beyond home. (Having been identified as an ardent critic of Somali dictators, chief among them Siyad Barre, Farah could hardly be blamed for his exile; he eventually visited Somalia in 1996, after twenty-two years of absence.) Farah rarely refers to his outsideness as exile, preferring instead a writer "living and working abroad," which now is technically accurate since he may return as he chooses.[7] Because of Farah's insistence on the psychic taxonomy of this relation, criticism of his writing tends to evoke a postcolonial analysand for whom Somalia is "a new country and a new logic, another reality, born of psychic necessity."[8] Yet the exilic has all manner of manifestations, as Kwame Anthony Appiah notes in his appreciation of Farah: "Writing is always more about identification than identity: the work of the imagination is never simply to express our selves."[9] The exotopic function does not return meaning to the author as ultimate arbiter, but pinpoints the logic of relation in the form-giving properties of specific writing. Just as novel-ization defamiliarizes the terms and conditions of the epic and lays claim to writing the Other as an African in the modern era, so Somali cultural practices work to fashion the novel as it cannot fashion itself, a process of identification that stretches boundaries (sexual, national, political, and cultural) in provocative and necessarily problematic ways.[10]

The *Blood in the Sun* trilogy is at once the sign of postcolonial dis-tress, Somalia as a kind of archetypal failed state, and a site of struggle over the lived relations of sexuality and sexual identification. Farah's gam-bit has clearly sought a link between these levels of social being as an index of what must change for Somalia to be at home in the world.[11] In *Maps*, the first novel of the trilogy, this connection is explored through Askar, a Somali boy who grows up in the Ogaden, itself a space of contesta-tion ethnically Somali but politically Ethiopian. In a versatile critique of the novel, Rhonda Cobham suggests that in the three forms of pronoun (I, you, and he) used to relate Askar's relationship to the Oromo servant Misra, we can trace the kernel of crisis in Somalia's sense of self as divided, as "misgendered": "The inability of the narrative voices that define Askar to differentiate between Askar and Misra, between maleness and female-ness, and between age and youth or accuser and accused works also as a metaphor for the shifting status of the signifier 'nation' within the Oga-den and for Somalia as a whole" (Cobham, 52). The term misgendering comes from a discussion in the novel (M 168) about how nonnative speak-ers of Somali, and people like Askar who are at the edge of Somalia's eth-nic reach, replace the masculine third person singular with the feminine third person singular. Misgendering usefully characterizes the unstable nature of national and sexual identities in the novel as these challenge eth-nographic essentialisms accentuating clannish incommensurability. What happens, however, if we read them as symptoms rather than metaphors, as signs of material and mental flux less secured by the marvels of linguistic competence or authorial intent?

The central relationship of Askar and Misra is entwined with an eth-nicist assessment of Somalia's postcolonial statehood, as if the border dis-putes over the Ogaden (the story is set around the Ethiopia-Somalia War of 1977 over this territory) might be resolved through the erotic and the adoptive.[12] Askar's mother dies as a result of giving birth to him, and his father dies in the nationalist struggle the day before Askar's birth. Misra, a servant in the extended family, takes up the charge of Askar's care, and there follows several sequences in which Askar's selves dissolve into an identification with Misra as his surrogate mother. They become blood relatives from consanguine intimacy. Blood would not be spilled nationally, these scenes say, if blood were shared, as it were, incestuously. Derek Wright notes, Askar as "the human analogue of Ogaden" is subject to a sexual "confusion" about his origins, just as the parenting of Somalia as nation has been riddled by the coupling of warring imperialist states (Britain, Italy, France), Cold War geopolitics, and postcolonial feuding.[13] In this biological fantasy as political fiction, Askar's identification bleeds into Misra's, not just in assuming an outsider relationship to the being of Somalia, but by internalizing the bodily feminine. Identification here is prosthetic and supplementary: at one point Askar believes he is menstruating and this is later linked to a constant taste of blood in his mouth. Yet Askar also projects masculinity onto Misra, assuming the position of a "third leg" between hers in bed, as if this might guarantee his own. In attaching himself to Misra as a phallus Askar effectively claims the space of her femininity. But by making Misra male and by seeing himself as the logical extension of that maleness, Askar constructs a kind of autoerotic Oedipal dynamic in which he can simultaneously desire to kill the father in her while claiming the mother for himself and as himself. Askar tells her one day that if she did not continue to look like a corpse he would have to kill her (M 38) so she would remain like his deceased mother, a telling displacement (and perhaps premonition, as the story unfolds) forged by untimely absence. At one point, Misra suggests Askar imagine he is a blind man and that she is his "stick" (M 16), a statement more about his imagination than hers.

A phallic economy extends to Aw-Adan, one of Misra's lovers, who removes his wooden leg before climbing into bed with her. Askar recalls the prosthesis when Misra is explaining how the body turns stiff after death, which serves to remind Misra of Aw-Adan's visits and to equate phallic certitude with lifelessness and virility at the same time. Askar then remembers or fantasizes watching Aw-Adan gain his erection, after having "lost" his leg, a metonymic moment punctuated by Misra's cries of "my man, my man, my man" (M 32). Whatever "secrets" Misra and Askar share beneath the sheets (their "games" are only suggested) the reader is left in no doubt that femininity and masculinity are critically in play in the novel and to understand the body's signifiers, one connects its blood to the flow of nation, the blood and guts of affiliation.

The problem for Farah's novel is not that these terms do not work in terms of sexuality and nation but that they work too well, as if the connection between the erotic reverie of Askar and Misra to the fate of Somalia is only one of scale: trope on their bodies and one has a logic for nation and its dysfunction. There are advantages to scaling, not least of which is that bodies make nations so it behooves us to examine how nations are made in the body image of their participants. Yet there is a particular danger for the postcolonial nation, whose failures and corrupt excesses assume the form of a pathology for Western observers. Farah wants to save Somalia from itself, not prepare it for neocolonial cures. The danger of unproblematic scaling is that one loses the nuance of what Askar calls "notional truth" (M 228) in relation to a national one. The problem of *Maps* is in differentiating these imaginary spaces, these sexually charged bodies of correspondence. In what ways might we hold to Farah's acute observations of male and female desire without reconstructing a masculinism anchoring the state with phallic sutures?

Farah reads Somalia as a literary experiment—he goes as far as saying it is a badly written play by Siyad Barre—and for criticism this is an appropriate endeavor.[14] Hilarie Kelly, for instance, describes *Maps* as "a Somali tragedy of political and sexual confusion" and finds a fatal flaw or two in Askar's waywardness.[15] The invocation of the tragic itself confirms not just a literary distance but the logic of narration afforded by transnational commentary. The text permits the logic of scale foregrounding the notional as national. Again, the inevitable tendency is to read off the minutiae of character as the notional truth of nation or, still more controversially, as the fateful compulsion of the African male. If indeed Farah creatively valorizes the narrative strategy of mapping the truth of form it is in its centrifugal logic vis-à-vis Somalia, a poetics of transgression, rather than by tinkering with borders established by colonial fiat.

Even Derek Wright, who is one of Farah's most astute commentators, interrogates the scale of *Maps*, the personal and the national, only to confirm that such a relation sets the stage for the subversion by the former of the latter ("Parenting," 172). Wright correctly pinpoints Farah's own analogical insistence that questions who is appropriately Somali Ogaden.

(Askar believes it to be himself, but the truth of the hybridized territory actually favors the Oromo-Amhara Misra who, nevertheless, has her affiliation pinned to Ethiopia.) Askar represents not so much a dream of nation deferred but an ethnicist identification violently exotopic to the substance of difference in the Horn of Africa. Those in the novel who embrace purity in Somali identity—Uncle Hilaal for instance—ironically accentuate the conditions for dispersal and fragmentation. Itemizing what constitutes a Somali undermines the ethnicist claims to territory; and this *méconnaissance*, a pattern of blood as the space of nation, permits a reversion to tribe, to specific traditions, to a desperately centripetal sense of masculinist conviction. The critic will favor Farah's scaling because of its contrasting ambiguity and allusion (interestingly, Wright will use the same analysis in one essay to argue for Farah on parenting the postcolony as he will forward in another on Farah as postmodernist).[16] Such destabilizing tendencies must be appreciated; but when Farah suggests of the colonial maps of Africa that "we should redraw [them] according to our economic and psychological and social needs, and not accept the nonsensical frontiers carved out of our regions," the "we" falls less on Somalis or Africans but on the outsideness of the imaginative writer whose capacity for troubling borders solves the riddle before transnational eyes: Africa's propensity for "failed nations."[17]

The idea is to maintain perspective on the political efficacy of the exotopic imagination without taking analogy as diagnostic doxa. Nobody doubts the intriguing possibilities suggested by Askar's sexual identifications, but these might work better to question the logic of analogy itself rather than the failings of this nation or that. Certainly Farah has insistently argued against formations of patriarchal masculinity in his fiction; from his first novel *From a Crooked Rib* (1970) to *Knots* (2007), there is an unflinching dedication to unmasking the complex ideological and practical political constraints on Somali women. Yet this feminist solidarity often works within the terms of analogy even as it questions the image of the victimized woman as emblematic of nation. Analogically, the novel as form also tends to stand in for the narrative of nation and for the epic orality of African traditions that only compounds the wariness at issue. In the figuring, rather than figures, of Askar and Misra the status of masculinity is radically particularized while the form of exotopy spatializes this specificity. Farah thus offers the perplexing formula that Somalia is outside or beside itself while the propensity for exorbitance is actually found in assigned gender and sexual roles. The invitation to analogy is in fact the affirmation of noncoincidence, which lies at the root of Farah's opacity.

Askar exudes a masculine capacity for self-misrecognition, so much so that he is willing to affirm Misra's sense that he has made himself (M 23), and that he was the midwife at his own birth. In general, however, there is a lack of self assurance in contrast to Misra's conviction and resolute understanding. But each doubt in Askar's self-identity facilitates a corresponding condition of objecthood in Misra. An aura of doubt surrounds the text, from the Aristotle epigraph, Hilaal's letter ("all is doubt"), the Conrad epigraph that begins Part Two of the novel ("Every image floats vaguely in a sea of doubt") to the issue of Askar's involvement in Misra's death. Such fundamental ambivalence questions identities and borders so that, despite the split in forms of narration—judge, audience, and witness—the parameters of adjudication shift beyond them. The objectification of Misra continues unabated, intensifying to the point where her life and body are ripped apart. Whatever the doubt in the meaning of Askar, and by analogical extension, Somalia, there seems much less vacillation on the question of Misra's womanhood and affiliation.

Farah does not favor victimhood but, given the agency one sees in many of his other women characters (Margaritta, Medina, Ubax, and Sagal in the *Variations on the Theme of an African Dictatorship* trilogy, Duniya in *Gifts*, Sholoongo in *Secrets*), one feels Misra's character is more sharply constrained. She may well have been operative in the Ethiopia-Somalia War, providing intelligence that led Ethiopian security forces to a hiding place of the Western Somali Liberation Front, but the lure is to read her as a parable of Somali possession, since Misra's name is explained as coming from the Ethiopian *Misrat*, meaning "foundation of the earth." Here is woman as territory once more, "taken" by force, raped by colonialism and now by postcolonial border disputes. Metaphors of violent attachment abound in *Maps*, but their patriarchal logic complicates Askar's passage from a culturally ambiguous boy to a nationalist Somali man. However Misra is associated with earth (and it is important to note that her dead body is fished from the sea), her foil to Askar's becoming Somali conjures a myriad set of cultural ascriptions. Misra, Askar explains to Uncle Hilaal, as an Oromo belongs to "a peripheral people" (M 170), a prejudice that calms Hilaal's disappointment with Askar's desire to append Misra's identity to his. Yet

Misra's exotopic function is linked to Askar's selfhood not just by her foreignness but by how this outsideness is culturally articulated. Two points are salient here.

First, if nations are indelibly the space of languages, which languages are used bear witness to specific trajectories of nation formation? While Misra might define herself as Ethiopian, Ethiopia's written culture does not think much of her Oromo oral traditions and she is possessed by Amharic. As Wright points out, Misra's Ethiopian association may place her at odds with the Somali, but her Oromo identity shares with the Somali an oral heritage patronized by Ethiopian literacy.[18] Individuals can choose languages but in terms of the state languages choose you (that Farah knows some five languages and writes in English places him closer to Misra than Askar regarding Somali identity). According to Uncle Hilaal, a Somali is a man or woman whose "mother tongue" is Somali: "no matter how many borders may divide them, no matter what flag flies in the skies above them or what the bureaucratic language of the country is" (M 174). Since Misra speaks Somali, Askar wonders whether she—like him—can acquire Somali identity papers? Hilaal answers in the affirmative but adds that she might need two male witnesses to sign an affidavit that she is Somali (even Hilaal's progressive views on women's rights are compromised by masculinist cultural traditions).

Second, Askar knows Somali, Amharic, and Arabic. His tutor in Mogadiscio, Cusmaan, also encourages him in English as part of the knowledge he must use to liberate his people from colonialism (M 175). But this does not mean that the "master's tools" are the royal road to independence, particularly now that Somali has an official orthography. The issue of Askar's language acquisition is also underlined by Cusmaan's proclivity for pornography so that Askar's first sentence in English, "This is a pen" is connected to English by Cusmaan's phallic complement to the lesson, a *Playboy* centerfold. If the joke is on Askar, Farah's criticism is pronounced. Askar relates these words to those dictated by the Archangel Gabriel to Mohammed, the Prophet: "Read, read in the name of Allah who created you out of clots of blood, read!" (M 176–77), and to a Koranic verse, "The Pen" that exhorts, "By the pen and what it writes, you are not mad" (M 177). When told of these experiences Hilaal suggests that both the "pen" and the "book" are indices of power, "metaphors of material and spiritual power" (M 178) flaunted both by Arab imperialism and by the

Europeans in the form of technology. Few doubt the power of inscription, but what can this mean for Askar's identification when the erotic and the spiritual are so obviously juxtaposed and where Arabic, the language of the Koran, is described as "an alien language with its alien concepts and thoughts imposed forcefully on the mind of a child"? (M 88).

Aw-Adan is both Askar's Koran teacher and Misra's lover. Because Aw-Adan beats Askar for mispronouncing the Word and because Askar also has to listen to Aw-Adan's lovemaking with Misra, Askar develops an ambivalence about Arabic and Islam. The scale of identification, however, skews the question of Somali affiliation at stake not because a secular view is forbidden but because the equation of pornography and English in Askar's learning does not extend to the language in which the story is told. The problem here is specifically about the responsibility of scale, not realist objectivity. If Misra, already of the "earth," enables Askar (whose name means "soldier" or the "bearer of arms") to distinguish the land from the sky, she also symbolizes a more deadly separation permitting Somali to emerge as a violent signifier. This is the danger of any metaphorization of woman in the discourse of man but it has a particular valence in providing a topography on which the nation can be drawn. Aw-Adan comments that from a very early age Misra for Askar was a "space" (M 12), something to be traversed, explored. For Misra, Askar seemed both space and time, offering up a chronotopic presence. Askar territorializes Misra, annexes her being to his under the guise of adding himself to her (a "third leg," a "third breast"). Yet the cost of this self-presencing is not addition, or surplus, but all too literal subtraction and extraction. Even before Misra "adopts" Askar, her story embodies the sexist cartography of virgin earth to be penetrated and possessed. Although this is sifted through the uneven fabric of Askar's memory and Misra's rationalizations, her tale is one of incessant masculine machination.

Misra's very conception was contractual: her mother, an Oromo, agreed to provide procreative services to an Amhara nobleman seeking male issue. Since Misra was the result, both mother and child were abandoned. Later, Misra was abducted by a warrior who claimed her in a skirmish with Ethiopians but who then fled south with her to avoid recriminations. They are taken in by a wealthy family, but the warrior dies soon after and Misra is adopted—but quickly is moved from daughter to lover, then wife by the man of the household. Misra eventually kills the man in "an excessive orgy of copulation" (M 72). The vexed theme of sex and death, however, does not end there. Misra is taken in by another wealthy family and again eventually becomes a wife. She divorces the man but not before two miscarriages and the birth of a baby, who dies at eighteen months. And all this before she meets Askar!

Perhaps Misra is guilty of giving too much rather than just being taken, but the weight of her victimization displaces both her foibles and her resistance. Thanks to Qorrax Misra is pregnant but she has an abortion. Once she has nurtured Askar in his manliness ("Somaliness"?) and he is imbued with that Fanonian spirit to always question, Misra herself is subsumed by Askar's subjectivity. When he moves to Mogadiscio to live with Uncle Hilaal and Auntie Salaado, he not only enters the maelstrom of Somali urban life but learns that mapping necessitates division, borders, and separation. Askar believes he has killed his mother in order to live and by suggestion he repeats the process with Misra. And, just as Misra first points out Somalia on a map, so Askar will come to define his Somali identification by realizing this being, as separate from Misra. In part this is underlined by his circumcision: "Now he was at last a man . . . totally detached from his mother-figure Misra, and weaned. In the process of looking for a substitute, he had found another—Somalia, his mother country . . . a generous mother, a many-breasted mother, a many-nippled mother, a mother who gave plenty of herself and demanded loyalty of one, loyalty to an ideal, allegiance to an idea, the notion of a nationhood" (M 100). Fostered by Misra's outsideness, Askar's Somali identity congeals into national allegiance, and from here Misra is not only detached but the space of her being for Askar begins to disintegrate.

If Farah's "psychic topography" threatens to overwhelm the plot as well as its Somali correlative, it serves to articulate Askar's gendered self-identification in and as Somalia. Thus, when Misra comes to Mogadiscio in search of Askar, he believes her to be half her original size and he wants this missing half to reassert itself. Misra fled the Ogaden because she was suspected of being a traitor, but not before her house was burned down and she was raped. Hilaal and Salaado have no sooner registered Misra as a family member than she is diagnosed with cancer and has her left breast removed. Misra fights the disease with a passion "lodged in the center of her heart—the passion to live!" so it is significant that when she is murdered she is also mutilated, her heart cut out. Misra is thus reduced to the kind of carcass she often prepared. This is the tragedy of metaphoricity, and to some extent its melodrama. The instances of Misra's oppression are part of the materialization of patriarchy: she is not oppressed as a metaphor but as a woman. Yet the psychic schema of the novel insists, albeit through misplaced and misremembered instances, that the narratives of the maimed and mutilated are the condition of Somalia's becoming: "Stories with fragmented bodies!/Bodies which told fragmented stories!/Tales about broken hearts and fractured souls!" (M 161). Farah does not endorse the idea that woman's signification is struck through by a masculinist national allegory. But is an alternative posed to the process by which Askar's self-questioning necessitates, by gender and national affiliation, the evisceration of all that Misra can be?

Farah's feminist critique in *Maps* scales up the metaphor of Misra's miserable life as a comment on the Somali national idea rather than bringing this mapping down to size, to the scale of difference that is the country's very possibility. Farah is precisely aware of the difficulty in negotiating the scale of nation in his work that must, because of his transnational interpellation, impact the way Somalia is read.

Years ago, whenever I was asked what country I came from and I responded, "Somalia," most of my interlocutors would then rejoin rather dryly, "Oh, Siyad Barre," a linkage which irritated me no end. I used to harangue anyone who made the metonymy, anyone who mistook the part for the whole. Nowadays, with pity on their faces, my interlocutors first recite a string of warlords' names, then talk about the Somali refugee communities in their respective countries. So that is how Somalia is seen: refugees on the run, starving babies with drones of flies gathered around their eyes, and gun-toting gangsters on a technico-battlewagon creating havoc. Somalia has become synonymous with strife. (*Yesterday*, 191–92)

There can be no doubt many Western images of Somalia satisfy the guilty conscience cast by the long shadow of the colonial episteme. The issue here is the responsibility of forms in which the space of nation becomes imaginable, a space that might, in the historical concreteness of *Aufhebung*, come to sublate what is extant in nation itself. It is here that Misra is not only "outside" but exorbitant; she exceeds in her specificity the general demand, the patriarchs' generic demand, that the earth is theirs, for the taking, for instating.

Maps foregrounds noncoincidence via the Western epigraphs on doubt dotting the text (Socrates, Dickens, Kierkegaard, Conrad, and the

Bible) that are reflexively undermined by the parts they divide.[19] Spatially, the narrative pivots on the appropriateness of thirds and, while this is not a subject position where either Misra or Somalia might rest easy, it throws some light on Farah's alternative postcolonial cartography. Askar asks, "Misra, where precisely is Somalia?" (M 116). In all the blurring of their gender and sexual energies, the relationship of Askar and Misra problematizes what is extant as Somalia. If you cannot place your country how can you seek solace in national identification? Maps are an alibi, an excuse for noncoincidence in the being of a nation. We think of them as settling border disputes, but the substance of cartography is what grounds such disagreements in the first place. As we follow Askar's growing attachment to maps he becomes more secure in his Somaliness. Eventually, however, with the experience of the war over the Ogaden and with his greater understanding of cartographic history, his convictions dissolve. Askar's maps may copy a "given reality" but their "notional truth" renders them relatively inconsequential. Who is more important, Hilaal asks, "the truth or its finder?" (M 228). This is where the substance of Somalia, like the trace of Misra's being, exists on different scales.

The schism between Ethiopia and Somalia produces the Ogaden as a third space: it is a zone of otherness that must be claimed and kept separate simultaneously. There is an actual land at stake, but the nation idea is its reality as abstraction and this determines its claims on national subjecthood. As a logical component of Farah's narrative, the Ogaden is an exotopic zone where I and Other negotiate, sometimes violently, national being. The problem of scale suggests the map of Somalia is always its people and never its people: the subject is itself the bar on its abstraction and the very product of the nation idea. We psychologize and anthropomorphize the nation not out of mistaken identity but because it is a spatial extension of our relationship to the Other. When Askar receives his Somali identity papers, his solemn assurance of their content quickly becomes a grudging acceptance of their implication: "I did think that I was expected, from that moment onwards, to perceive myself in the identity created for me" (M 173). All identity papers are forgeries to some degree. The otherness that enables Somalia is not just about its comparative ethnic homogeneity in contradistinction to Ethiopian heterogeneity but its relationship to its own signification. Since Benedict Anderson's *Imagined Communities* we are used to reading this nationness as already read, so Somalia is predicated on a print culture that dutifully supplies Somali identity papers. Here again the question of scale is vital because the nation idea in Somalia is not just the fact of its eventual orthography but the chronotopic ensemble of its vast and intricate oral traditions (particularly in poetry) with the cultural archetypes of colonialism and imperialism.[20] The answer to the patronizing logic of failed nations lies in broadening cartography to the scale of history and politics, not by collapsing it into the national subject.

Hilaal, the intellectual conscience of the novel, asks Askar, "Where is *the third*, where is *the other*?" (M 144) and the answer depends precisely upon exotopic scale. Thirdness for Askar is the mutually determining outsideness of him and Misra, a zone of engagement that touchingly supplants his lost triangulation of mother and father. (Hilaal, in promoting Askar's separation from Misra, also means to conjure the prescience of Askar's adoptive family in the form of his Aunt and Uncle.) This spatial embrace, with its references to third breasts and third legs has a body map all of its own in which Askar figures himself as woman, freeing him, he believes, from the masculinism of Uncle Qorrax. Askar's body mapping, delivered in an ambivalent trio of voices (first, second, and third person) projects onto Misra while idealistically believing that he is her extension. Note the hesitancy in the following declaration where the reader herself is asked to conspire in this supposition: "I was part of the shadow she [Misra] cast—in a sense, I was her extended self. I was, you might even say, the space surrounding the geography of her body" (M 78). The doubt is not necessarily a ruse of aesthetics; the premise is integral to Farah's understanding of human identification. What happens, however, if we mistake this geography for the Horn of Africa? If Misra is nominally Ethiopian, then does Askar the Somali surround her? Is Somalia the extended self of Ethiopia? Askar's personal geography speaks to geopolitics but one should resist making it its substance.

In fact, while *Maps* is suffused with all manner of tropological thirdness, Farah motivates doubt to circumscribe the conditions of exotopy in play. In a culture with long traditions of pastoral nomadism and an adherence to tribal genealogy, a national border is always outside itself. In the riverine south of Somalia, cultivation historically has led to a tribal concern for land as property, but even these borders do not provide the rationalized edge of extant Somaliness. Commentators have enlisted Farah himself among the ranks of the nomadic since this largely romantic version of

rootlessness is in accord with postcolonial cosmopolitanism. Exile, however, is not nomadism: it is conditioned by an outsideness dependent on
borders, not their absence. If nomadism is useful in understanding Farah,
it is perhaps as a more volatile feature of *noncoincidence*; it does not square
with the traditional binary between the subject as nation and a nation subject. Thus, as Farah points out, "Although one often links a person in exile
to a faraway locality, the fact is I felt joined more to my writing than to
any country with a specific territoriality."[21] Farah often tropes on Somalia
as a creative impetus in *his* imagination rather than begin with the concept of the imaginary state, the very idea of nation itself. Here the space
of form betrays an exotopy in which Farah can believe he is not in exile
precisely because that would mean referencing "specific territoriality," a
necessary displacement in the face of social upheaval defying the form of
nation Somalia would otherwise fit.

Bakhtin believed that aesthetic creation could only begin when the
author returns to her- or himself: the axiological character of the other
could be engaged first by "sympathetic co-experiencing" but then, necessarily, by a return to a constitutive outside.[22] In one version of exotopy
Bakhtin argued for outsideness within an aesthetics of unfinalizability,
not in the service of metaphysics but conjoined to an understanding of the
aesthetic act as dynamic as the social. It urges the culpability of the author
in writing and produces a map more doubtful about its own capacity to
represent. Both Farah's postmodern and postcolonial predilections are implicated in this exotopic openendedness that is as cogently articulated as
it is politically obtuse. What works at the level of signifier cannot anchor
reason's interest in the state. What are the implications of this aesthetics of
noncoincidence for gender in *Maps*? Is Misra, for instance, bound by the
externality of masculine certitude or does the phallus as signifier float so
that even in death the hole where the heart should be, a quintessential lack
of lack, decenters patriarchy for nation? Farah, as much as Bakhtin, knows
that aesthetic outsideness is a luxury compared to the outside requisite of
oppressive hierarchization. The majority of his women protagonists fight
this malevolent othering at every turn. All we have been considering here
is whether the critique of Somali identification disables or displaces the
analysis of gender hierarchy at play in *Maps*. The problem of scale is not
solved by slippery metaphors or shifting pronouns. Similarly, if feminism
rightly challenges governing assumptions of the state, Farah's belief in the

connection of authoritarianism and the oppression of women still requires clarification in terms of writing and exile.

What is given to the form of the state through colonialism and imperialism cannot be expunged in the moment of independence. The failed state of Somalia is not a failure of imagination of Somalis despite the fact that individual Somalis, Siyad Barre for instance, imagined creative cohesion as coercion. Yet the fact of cartographic machination on the part of Western powers in itself cannot fully explain the lived relations of the "post" in postcoloniality either. Its function as a caesura in the *longue durée* of Somali traditions of association and community represents a massive reordering of identification on any number of levels (economic, political, and cultural), but these effects do not constitute a checklist by which success or failure is guaranteed. Farah believes that he might save his country by representation, keep it alive by novelizing it. There is much to recommend this endeavor, but its value lies in the form-giving properties of Farah's narration rather than on whether Farah's intricate characterizations are true or not to Somali identity.

One axiom of postcolonial writing lies in the writer's ability to disengage the colonial episteme—the power of knowledge intrinsic to colonial rule—or what Mbembe calls *commandement*.[23] Mbembe argues that the colonizer had to maintain a specific imaginary of state sovereignty, one that both established right and countenanced violence. But, the violence of *commandement* comes with a supplementary duty—reason's obligation—so that the fundamental violence of colonization also wears the face of care directed at those uncivilized minions who apparently cannot take care of themselves. What is taken from the colonized by force is paradoxically presented as colonialism's gift; the right of dominion is the grant of civilization, statehood, and freedom from the barbarism of yore. The substance of this doublethink in colonialism is fairly well established, but its portent for postcolonialism is more difficult to fathom. Delinking from a particular colonial state can be measured simply by the colonizer's departure, but its systems of right and violence, the state apparatus of *commandement*, did not take flight in the same way. Postcolonial history has investigated such systemic remains and whether the progress offered by colonialism could be had without maintaining or reproducing deleterious powers of subjection themselves. Postcolonial study has also been dedicated to what might undermine independence in the guise of trying to secure it. Perhaps this latter remains colonial debris, even if the organizations that promote such aid strongly disavow connections of this kind. The problem of the gift is postcoloniality's "fix" and it is central to Farah's thoughts on what makes Somalia.

In an acknowledgment in *Gifts*, the second volume of the *Blood in the Sun* trilogy, Farah notes, "In writing this novel I have incurred many debts, the most important of which is owed to Marcel Mauss, author of *The Gift*" (G i). Farah understands the nature of the gift, for it is precisely in its relationship to debt that it can be freely given and received. Mauss did not make of his book a gift to Farah because the latter's acknowledgment of the gift annuls the possibility of giving. Yet Farah points to the debt involved, not the status of the gift, so the nature of the gift has in fact been affirmed. In *Maps* Farah confronts Somali identification as a conundrum of desire and separation. In *Gifts*, however, a postcolonial unconscious is figured in the acknowledgment of the gift that overdetermines not just the nature of relationships (particularly the love of Duniya and Bosaaso) but the formation of Somali state identification. The logic of the gift suggests that the Somali state is under erasure: it has been canceled in advance by the gift of statehood.[24]

Farah's narrative argues that international aid is, philosophically speaking, a gift, and one so tied to indebtedness that it is more than colonialism's echo: it is the logic that suspends the "post" in postcoloniality. Farah will insinuate this logic in the story by juxtaposing everyday life in Mogadiscio (Mogadishu) with newspaper reports of international debt servicing cast against a backdrop of social and economic crisis. This allows Farah to contrast traditional giving with modernity's version and also pose narration itself as a gift, the unspoken transaction of the exotopic author with his postcolonial state. The gift, like the map, is open to a politics of scale since it may be used to describe both micro- and macrological transactions. Farah's story on the art of symbolic exchange, however, reveals a whole series of provocations on the logic of form in his writing.

Derrida picks up on Mauss's theorization of the gift to examine its constitutive aporia. Derrida's basic point is thus: "For there to be a gift, there must be no reciprocity, return, exchange, countergift, or debt. If the other *gives* me *back* or *owes* me or has to give me back what I give him or her, there will not have been a gift, whether this restitution is immediate or whether it is programmed by a complex calculation of a long-term deferral or différance."[25] The difficulty of thinking the gift starts where no reciprocity exists, since even if no actual exchange or countergift occurs, what was offered may have been done with the expectation of return; the gesture itself may imply debt. The notion of the gift is made doubly strange for what is freely given must not be freely accepted as such: the gift appears in its nonrecognition; the substance of the exchange may not be revealed as a gift, at least not as a present in its present (one aim of Derrida's investigation is time's present, the gift of time, which will be connected to eventness and the oughtness of the I in exotopy). As Mauss shows, the gift is enormously important to social interaction; its symbolic mode signifies the language of the interpersonal in general and this is why its philosophical disposition is so intriguing. If the rationality of the map never actually corresponds to the borders it draws, the gift is summarily erased by the light of cognition. For the postcolonial nation to exist beyond colonialism it must not give back, it must not owe, it must not acknowledge debt for that which is given. This does not cancel gratitude but it cannot be shown in relation to the gift *per se*. The function of the gift exists properly for time, not acknowledgment, and this is the coordinate that links *Gifts* to *Maps*.

The central "gift" of Farah's novel is the foundling, an abandoned baby boy "discovered" by Nasiiba, Duniya's daughter. Duniya, who since Bosaaso's initial flirtation has been considering the meaning of signs, wonders what this appearance might signify. Was this a test, like Khadr in Islamic mythology becoming a cow to measure human endurance? Was this baby Khadr in disguise? The baby is named, although nobody recalls exactly who did the naming, *Magaclaawe*, the "nameless one" as if by naming without a name acknowledgment itself might be deferred. Like Askar, Magaclaawe enters the narrative apparently parentless and in this manner supports Wright's thesis that Farah is concerned to show Somali national identification is dependent on the making of appropriate parents. Bosaaso is immediately inspired to make a gift, specifically the clothing that had once belonged to his now dead son, but refrains for fear he might offend Duniya. The gift remains in desire, a trope that will emerge time and time again in the text. Duniya, a midwife and the story's main voice, imagines the foundling as the offspring of jinns, *ilmo jinni*, a thought conjuring both mystery and fear. Magaclaawe clearly unites a family. Bosaaso undertakes the bureaucratic establishment of the Nameless One's "existence" with great relish, and Mataan, Nasiiba's twin brother, warms to the endeavor of the father figure by also braving officialdom. Registering the child's existence, like recognizing the familial bonds of legal guardians, strikes Farah as a typically absurd act at odds with the humanness of his characters. In terms of the gift, the imprimatur of official "existence" presents the child with a time to mark its being: it literally confirms the foundling's presence in the present and therefore offers a displaced annulment of its status as gift for Duniya, Bosaaso, and the twins. Such official discourse contrasts sharply with tradition, but perhaps the Nameless One is external to both. Duniya treats his infected navel and notes he lacked the first potlatch of newborn baby boys, hair from the tale of a she-camel (described as a "gift camel") used to tie both ends of the umbilical cord.

Deprived of this founding gift, Magaclaawe is nevertheless not bereft of the gift's allegorical purchase on the conditions of exchange in Somali society. Indeed, to settle down the restless child Mataan relates a pertinent Arab folktale in which a man borrows a large pot and then, unprompted, returns it with a smaller one inside. After the man's neighbor reminds him that he only loaned him one pot, the man, Juxaa, tells him the large pot gave birth to the small one overnight and that both are his to keep. Is this a gift? To the extent that the extra pot was neither asked for nor expected and that Juxaa disavows his largesse, the aura of the gift is invoked. But this is not the end of the story. Juxaa borrows the big pot again and when he does not return it his neighbor comes to visit. The pot died, Juxaa explains, so he buried it. When the neighbor expresses incredulity Juxaa retorts that it is no more fanciful than one pot giving birth to another. What is the purpose of Mataan's parable? When the neighbor finally accepts the little pot he might believe he has received a gift but Juxaa has in fact repaid his initial kindness by enlisting him in a different transaction, an exchange. Perhaps Juxaa has surmised his neighbor believes he has incurred a debt by borrowing the pot and Juxaa therefore repays him in kind. Given his neighbor's acceptance of the surplus Juxaa decides the neighbor will expect this surplus the next time and therefore when he borrows the pot again Juxaa cancels the obligation by keeping ("burying") the pot. While it is possible that Mataan merely means to tell a story, any story, to placate the child, its meaning has an important resonance both to the child's appearance and to the larger theme of international aid that informs the novel. If the "Nameless One" is God's gift and is not reclaimed by his biological parents then the obligation is to him not the provider, whose event of giving is confirmed by nonreciprocity. But if there is a debt involved, and one Nasiiba has not yet revealed, then this is no gift and a burden of exchange is operative. The second lesson of the tale emerges only when figured alongside the statements on aid. To understand this connection requires elaboration of the notion of the gift both as content and as a formal interruption of Duniya and Bosaaso's love story.

The moment of *Gifts* is after the war between Ethiopia and Somalia when Farah's country plunges deeper and deeper into crisis. Farah believes this is the time when the Somali government effectively lost control over Somalia, and important decisions over food distribution and financial security were turned over to international aid organizations (OXFAM and the like), the World Bank, and the International Monetary Fund (IMF). One expects criticism of the IMF and the World Bank, whose very dependence on capital exchange extinguishes any trace of giving without return (the South's periodic defaults on debt reintroduce this trace only to have other obligations conferred in the guise of "restructuring").[26] It is less common to view famine relief this way, but Farah's novel disabuses the reader of any idealism about international aid. Do not bother adding the little pot, his narrative suggests, unless one is prepared to keep the big one eventually. Giving, Duniya's giving in particular, is bound to seem more humane in comparison to gifts measured by acronyms or the grace of a military intervention tagged, with no sense of irony, as Operation Restore Hope. Structurally, however, this critique presents Farah with a problem: how are these heady matters of international machination entwined with the love story at the novel's heart?

In *Gifts*, the fix of the gift for postcoloniality is not rendered as an effect: it is the logic of form that is its very possibility. Sometimes, however, the statements on aid are tacked on to the end of chapters as newspaper clippings or news agency reports. They mediate the tenor of official discourse through fictive approximations (without dates or copyright they yet mime the veracity of the world press). Two of the lengthiest interruptions are written by Duniya's second husband, Taariq Axmad, a journalist. The first report is a prologue, in this case to the appearance of the "Nameless One" and therefore, in Farah's use of the parabola of parables, is a complement to Mataan's tale of the pot. Taariq's "Story of a Cow" begins with a simultaneous nod to Askar's "notional truth" and to Somali oral traditions: "This is a true story." Set during a period of severe drought and famine it tells of two families headed by males "coincidentally" named Musa and Harun (after two Muslim prophets and brothers), who remain in their community when most everybody else has left for "an organized UNICEF feeding place" (G 57). Harun has an emaciated cow from which the two families obtain milk. Musa wants to stay less because of the cow but because he is suspicious of foreign handouts, especially non-Muslim ones, and he believes the land will soon once again offer up its bounties. As the cow's milk yield decreases Musa prays for divine intervention to save his baby daughter and then strange things happen. The cow migrates to Musa's compound and only seems capable of yielding milk to him—and in increasing quantities. Musa renames the cow twice (Marwa, then Safa, after the two sacred mountains of Mecca) and the yield increases beyond its prefamine capacity. The two neighbors continue to share the milk according to their original agreement. Later, when some travelers pass by and comment on the abundance of milk, Harun cannot help boasting about his cow while Musa remains silent. The following day the cow disappears and the travelers claim that all they saw leave was a saintly looking man. The famine breaks and the other families return. When Musa is asked if Khadr, the saint and miracle maker, had turned himself into a cow to test them, he remains silent and this is how the story ends. Here the nature of the gift is in the grace of God, and there is enough hesitation in Taariq's "true story" that the reader wonders whether Somalis can depend on such good fortune. Indeed, when Duniya reads Taariq's tale she immediately sets about searching her home, her faith in her own unselfishness having been shaken. She finds money that she had given Nasiiba to pay the family's monthly debts. In this way, debt and its restitution appear as a countermand to belief and represent the other tension in the aura of the gift: is it in the happenstance of its own time, the device of the unexpected, or is it an effulgence of God's plan, the divine in the unexpected? Taariq seems to favor Musa's religious observance over Harun's ego, as if his resistance to foreign aid is justly rewarded by God, yet this is only by comparison to the alternative narrative of wishful thinking provided by the reports on aid. The "baby in a rubbish bin" and "the story of a cow" are tests of self-reliance in a world where the innocence of the gift is chimerical.

Taariq's second report, "Giving and Receiving: The Notion of Donations," provides a gloss on the function of the gift in Somalia. Like the first story, it is read by Duniya, and the readers of the novel must measure their reactions in relation to hers. The question of address here is crucial for a number of reasons. First, *Gifts* was Farah's first book to be printed and published in Africa (Baobab Books of Harare) and so, even with the important qualifications regarding anglophone literacy, using an essay within the novel on the "notion of donations" may help to legitimize the "real world" concern of the narrative's themes. Second, Taariq's essay has a double-voiced manner in which he takes up the position of the African for an international audience, and this inevitably invites a comparison to Farah's status as a Somali writer. Third, the position of the report for the novel's form is crucial: its effectiveness is sharpened by the thesis of the gift that runs through it. Thus, Farah poses a solution to the dilemma of voicing in *Maps*: the value of outsideness lies not in the shifting from first to second to third person, but in measuring this ambivalence simultaneously in *the same address*. Taariq's sweeping indictment of foreign aid is not just an event in decolonization but stages the function of eventness itself for the postcolonial state as time's gift for narrative.

Taariq begins by identifying giving as a human instinct, but historically specific: "We" give for a number of reasons, he says, but the "we" in use is fundamentally the adopted first person plural of the dominant and the necessarily nefarious (the first example is of the serpent "giving" the apple to Eve). In giving "naturally" the "we" yet gives in a sociopolitical manner: "We give hoping to receive something corresponding to what we've offered"; "We give to meet the demands of a contract"; "We give in order to feel superior to those whose receiving hands are placed below ours"; "We give to corrupt"; "We give to dominate" (G 194). Taariq takes up the position of this global "we" in order to interject with an African "I" concerned to understand the gifts of Europe, North America, and Japan to starving Africans. The image of the emaciated African child with her hands extended, pleading for food, is not some innocent shorthand in donor rhetoric: it is integral to the afterlife of imperial logic that now, in the brave new world of transnational capital and mobile hegemonies, says we give that you may give back in the only way you know how, in helplessness.

The events of giving that Taariq has in mind are charity runs organized to raise money for starving Africans. Meanwhile, "Africa waited in the wings, out of the camera's reach, with an empty bowl in hand, seeking alms" (G 195). Taariq notes laconically, "To starve is to be of media interest these days" (G 195). Yet Taariq's double voicing is only partly directed at that magnanimous "we" that gives so freely. He wants the African "I" to address its own participation in this parade of potlatch. Foreign governments have often aided money-grubbing dictators who filch from their own people and then use starvation to get still more. Now the "we" of the report is problematized by an alternative agency: "Can we conclude that if foreign governments stop aiding the African dictators with food hand-outs, then their people will rise up against them?" (G 195). There is no definitive answer either within Taariq's article or in Farah's novel in part because food aid itself is only one element of a complex equation that includes the struggles of powerful states (at that time the Cold War maneuvering of the Soviet Union and the United States), regional strife, dependency, tribalism, and forms of resource subsistence. Taariq notes that Somalis are used to periodic droughts and famine and adjust their consumption accordingly: "They held their heads high, allowing no one to humiliate them, letting no one know that their hearths had remained unlit the previous night" (G 195). But this works only if the famine is seen as an act of nature and not of governmental dysfunction.

Much of Taariq's article appeals for its bluntness and common sense: "Famines awake a people from an economic, social or political lethargy"; "Foreign food donations also sabotage the African's ability to survive with dignity" (G 196). Other statements have the air of social critique tinged with philosophy: "Empty brass bowls make excellent photographs" (G 195); "Every gift has a personality--that of its giver" (G 197). This last is connected to what is printed on bags of donated grain, usually identifying an organization or a country or sometimes both. Images of flags are often deployed since, if the donor cannot count on literacy, it can depend on the circulation of images. One wonders the extent to which the donor's imprint matters to the starving individual? Are images of bags piled high in warehouses meant to wend their way home? Taariq's discourse questions the gift's role in international exchange. When it wears the giver's character it suppresses eventness in favor of gesture: it is less about the redistribution of wealth or surplus and more about the affirmation of power and control. The pride in the label effectively nullifies the contents of the bag as gift and instead those suffering famine are presented with a bill, a contract of debt signed at the moment they open their mouths for rice.

Although Somalis expect food to be shared, says Taariq, this is not the substance of the foreign donation.

Finally, Taariq's report turns to the staging of the gift and to the brief appearance of the African on the world stage. Referring to Africa's one-liner in Conrad's *Heart of Darkness*, "Mistah Kurtz, he dead," Taariq finds a similarly truncated voice in current affairs. Another reference is *Out of Africa*, both the book and the film, which are roundly criticized for exchange based on extraction not reciprocity.[27] Taariq notes the film features "Somalia's most famous daughter," Iman, who, naturally, has a nonspeaking role. The phrase "out of Africa" evokes a fatuous engagement with the continent in which Africans themselves become notational devices. Dinesen invokes an experience "based on" (out of) Africa, but the pleasure of the text exists in its outsideness as an absolute where the Other is granted presence only to be subsequently disengaged (with the "I" relieved to have left the place). This too is the substance of African famine as an event: to be "out of Africa" is to have used up one's capacity to give to it, and the moment closes with the luxury of "donor fatigue." In the difference of donor fatigue and systemic famine lies the tragedy of inequality on a world scale repeated as the farce of event, as that which sustains the time of suffering. Like the poor soul in Conrad's novel, Taariq retreats into a "skeletal silence" broken only by the permissible "thank-you."

The gift presents Farah with a difficult issue: like the map, the gift measures the impossible link between national identification and individual desire. On the one hand, this may underline Farah's understanding of a failed nationalist dream; on the other, it registers a discursive limit in the novel's understanding of the state. To the politics of scale we add another conceptual key: the abruption of the postcolonial state asks for form and the novel replies with the gift of narrative as disjunction. It is an unequal exchange but, what if this impasse is neither a failure of the state nor of the imaginary state conjured by the novelist and is instead the very logic of the state's nonexistence as a national form? This does not disavow extant states or postcolonial nations but understands the writing of their formation as a challenge to what is given to nation. Thus, the novel does not mime the perquisites of nation formation as they are often construed; it traces the logic of alternative constituencies that do not depend on the *ratio* of subject to nation state where the debt crisis of one is the begging bowl of the other. The abruption of form is the event rather than that which examines the process of giving itself, its eventness. To make this distinction Farah falls back on a steadfast emotive standby: love.

Duniya is a much more complicated and engaging character than Misra, whose textual effects depend altogether too much on Askar's scattered and masculinist piecings. Like Misra, Duniya has been through a lot: an arranged marriage to a much older and blind man, Zubair (from which she has the gifts of Mataan and Nasiiba); a second loveless marriage (to Taariq) that produces a third child, Yarey; and a demanding low-paying job as a nurse in a maternity hospital. Duniya dreams of a restless butterfly in danger of being swatted by a cat, and it is with this reverie still dancing in her mind that she meets Bosaaso. Bosaaso is driving a taxi and Duniya gets in, pleased to rest her tired limbs. The ride is Bosaaso's gift: rather than accept money he proposes a trip to the cinema with her children. Without paying Duniya feels the weight of obligation; an exchange is in play, and so the gift is written over by a sense of contract. This cancels the gift in the incident but it reemerges in love itself that seeks no restitution from its giving. Farah understands that even love may garner a philosophy of exchange, but because giving in love is juxtaposed so starkly with reports that Duniya happens upon about the effects on Somalia of international giving it operates as the gift's real relation.

Mauss saw potlatch as community defining despite the introduction of debt and circulation on which it depends.[28] Love is largely incidental to what is simultaneously archaic and axiomatic in the gift: its meaning for power and collective obligation. Farah's debt to Mauss produces the reports on international aid (as an indictment of false giving), but the love story is Farah's own philosophy of the gift about what the heart bestows that is never a synonym of the collective. Nationalism might force this equation, so *Maps* suggests, but if people were given a choice they would love each other rather than a nation. Yet *Gifts* has its moments of sacrifice for nation. Dr. Mire, Duniya's boss and a friend of Bosaaso, came back to Somalia after twenty years to donate his services "to the government and people of his country" (G 17). Bosaaso, an economist of some repute, also freely offered his expertise at the Ministry of Economic Planning so it is not as if collective obligation excludes national identification. But Taariq's questions, "Who gets what, gives what to whom?" (G 199) resonate in acts such as these. With corrupt officials syphoning off money from aid packages, it would seem that Mire and Bosaaso give in vain when it comes to the stability of the state. Does personal emotional attachment compensate for what is squandered nationally?

The same question can also be asked of both *Maps* and *Secrets* where the personal must do double duty as character and symbol. If we learn from Duniya and Bosaaso's relationship, or from Duniya's extended family, however, what binds them together communally does not govern the forms of the political nationally or internationally. The more Farah has his characters discuss such connections, the less likely they seem to obtain. Indeed, turning everyday conversations into philosophical reflections on the issue sometimes closes off love's possible impact on macrological concerns. When Mire invites Bosaaso and Duniya over for dinner, the catalyst for their exchange is a discussion about the meaning of Duniya's name. (Bosaaso suggests "world," but Mire points out that the word comes from the Arabic "Dunya" for cosmos.) The aura of giving saturates the conversation. Europeans and Arabs may wander Africa making gifts of their deities, but Duniya wants to know what is in it for the Arabs specifically to "give" in this way? Even the benevolence of belief is predicated on exchange. Mire takes this as a fundamental difference between Judeo-Christian and Muslim practices and that of Somalis. For Somalis, he points out, life is a preface to death and death is respected for the termination it represents. These other beliefs, Mire argues, depend on the gift of life being exchanged for the gift of an afterlife (with an obvious touch of irony, Mire's woman friend is a German named Claudia Christ). "God gives, man gives" jokes Bosaaso (G 97), but one gives with the expectation of reward. Mire and Bosaaso then discuss the foundling and the contrast seems clear, but the baby boy's status as gift is complicated by his function in Duniya and Bosaaso's relationship. They are keeping him, Bosaaso opines, but he is really keeping them by providing a bond through which they can strengthen their love. One implication, therefore, is their care for the child is less than altruistic: he gives back a space of intimacy. At one point Duniya thinks of the Somali cosmos, balanced on the horns of a bull whose head is secured by staring at a cow. Thus the text teeters under all the weight given it.

Whatever the impositions of foreign culture and finance, Magaclaawe offers an alternative logic: his eventness is described as a "happening" (G 110), and there is enough uncertainty in Duniya's interpretation of it that the reader too is left to doubt its significance. If the Nameless One is, like Askar, "a question to himself" as an orphan and outsider, he is not granted the privilege of asking. His death halfway through the novel is left largely unexplained (one possibility is that he is killed by Qaasim, Duniya's brother-in-law and landlord, who is the last person to see him alive and is his biological father, having had an affair with Fariida, a friend of Nasiiba's). This stands in contrast to his effect on Duniya and Bosaaso, who now know they can give together and to each other. But the foundling's life and death is also the cause of storytelling around which narratives congeal. The first part of the novel is titled "a story is born" and describes both Duniya's telling and the time of the foundling's life. The gift of the story is the time in which it unfolds, but its actual inscription partakes of exchange that, unlike the foundling, is a gift of a different order. This is something of the phenomenological distinction that Bakhtin uses regarding Being-as-event.[29] I use it to maintain a sense of given time for narration to take place. For Being, selfhood is a project (*zadanie*) that depends on a process in which what is given (*dan*) lives in tension with what is set as a task, with what must be conceived (*zadan*). While theory cannot present Being-as-event in itself (it is a principle not a recorded content), it can at least reflect upon the process in which Being is held together. For Derrida, time's gift is decisive: the gift gives, demands, and takes time (GT 41) and this gift only arrives in narrative. It is not an auxiliary or complement to the gift, an "external archive" (GT 44), but is immanent to its action; yet it is not synonymous, otherwise narrative itself would be superfluous.

The foundling always marks a crisis in legitimacy, not just for itself but for the society that ponders its oughtness, its obligations to its appearance. This is why the foundling or orphan features prominently in all three volumes of the trilogy: it tests not just the power of personal relations but the tenor of legitimacy in the state. Making the foundling "nameless" in *Gifts* only accentuates what is set as a task for the community in which it finds itself. The community must learn to narrate itself not simply to make sense of the foundling to itself. It is appropriate that at the foundling's wake the participants trade stories about death and creation myths, for these mark Magaclaawe's event in Being without assuming its uniqueness. Mire recounts the story of the six-year-old taken from this world who tries to get an explanation from God. God explains that "We knew you to be a sinner" and thus he spared him from actually offending God. The boy prostrates himself saying "God gives, He is All-Knowing and Merciful" (G 129). Mire is questioning legitimacy, although no further comment is made. Taariq offers an alternative story, this time featuring a God who wishes to create man not in His image but in the image of an Ethiopian. The creations are fired in clay, but at first they are too dark (consigned to some nether region of Africa) or too light (and packed off to Scandinavia). Finally, perfection is achieved and this man is Ethiopian. The creation myth sets about securing legitimacy. Thus, to the questions "Who gets what, gives what to whom?" we must add "Who is the teller, and tells what to whom?" or as Duniya puts it, "at the center of every myth is another: that of the people who created it" (G 130). The foundling has provided a semantic horizon and lives on, as Duniya suggests, in people's telling but also, and crucially, in her relationship with Bosaaso (the next section of the novel is called "Duniya loves").

The event of the foundling tells Duniya that, if she cannot completely throw off her suspicion of gifts (she offers her possible epitaph, "Here lies Duniya who distrusted givers"), to love creates greater acceptance and confidence. Duniya is worried people will think she only wants Bosaaso for his wealth, but in the end her self-conviction frees her to love (and, by and by, to drive and to swim). The last part of the novel, "Duniya gives," features a more literal consummation of her relationship with Bosaaso. Bosaaso also proposes marriage and the narrative curves in that direction. Abshir, her brother living in Italy, comes home to visit, a party ensues, and all seems well in the world. Yet the end of the novel also attends to storytelling in contradistinction to giving in international aid. Indeed, it is typical of Farah that he subverts a degree of expectation so that the narrative itself be considered for what it gives.

For Duniya, the moment of narration is pronounced: "Her own epiphanic instant had occurred at a moment, on a morning, when a story chose to tell itself to her, through her, a story whose clarity was contained in the creative utterance, *Let there be a man*, and there was a story" (G 245). The religious and patriarchal overtones of this revelation are expected given the discussions of belief elsewhere, but as love blooms Duniya keeps her feminist inclinations. Additionally, in traditional oral narrative, the teller of the story is merely its vessel and what gets told is more than the speaker's vision in telling. Whether this is true for the omniscient narrator is more difficult to assess, although at the end of the book the narrator withdraws in a flourish: "The world was an audience, ready to be given Duniya's story

from the beginning" (G 246). It is an injunction on the international public sphere, but since the story is given it is worth considering the statement
in terms of the gift.

The affective embrace of the gift depends on the utterance context
of the novel. This is emphasized not just by the characters, but by Farah's
attempt to connect or contrast these with the perquisites of the donor
machine. Farah forces the issue via Duniya's numerous chance encounters with newspaper and radio reports on the subject of international aid.
Yet these examples do not elucidate the problems of giving that complicate Somali communal forms of self. If we consider the utterance context
of the novel in its form-giving capacity, we might yet understand Farah's
novel as a gift itself in its process, in its logic, that challenges the pious pre-
tensions of Northern donors who may well read African fiction the way
they write checks, courteously but not without the expectation of return.

What does the novel give that Farah might give to Somalia? If we understand the consanguine ties between nation and narration, the "blood
in the sun" of his trilogy (written in the Somali son's blood), then Farah's
tale of love and donation presents a special problem because he begins
from what the novel cannot give freely on its own accord: the traditions
of oral poetry in Somali identification. *Gifts* is replete with storytelling,
excerpts from Somali folklore and everyday life, but however we valorize
novelization, it is not clear the form of the novel gives to Somalia any more
innocently than those sacks of rice. How does Farah make *Gifts* answerable to the novel as inexorably colonialism's success, a narrative form writ
large in modernity's reach?

For Derrida, the oral is the problem; specifically, the prioritization of
speech in Western metaphysics. From this point of view the novel writes
difference into the idealism of presence and can destabilize an ontologi-
cal fixity that speaks for the other and not with it. In his Neustadt lecture, Farah opens by intimating just this power of writing for the art of
decolonization: "I was born into a difference at a time in my continent's
history when the power of speech lay elsewhere, in other people's tongues.
In those days, we, as colonials and as Somalia, existed more in reference
to whom we were made into as colonial subjects than whom we presumed
ourselves to be, or who we ought to have been."[30] The novel has also made
colonial subjects but it can critique the elsewhere of speech, the space of
enunciation usurped and annexed. Although the postcolonial novel has

engaged this process, it remains profoundly ambivalent about its claims to cultural representability—especially when "the world was an audience, ready to be given Duniya's story from the beginning." The power of the postcolonial is in its promise of the caesura as interrogative, in its tenacious reinscription of the intersubjective, as Bhabha avers.[31] Bhabha borrows the notion of a "temporal break" in language from Lacan to argue for the intersubjective directed toward a "rediscovery of truth . . . in the order of symbols." Form, however, is not the condensation of this agonistic will to truth in the symbolic power of language as language. Yet it may be a logical manifestation of the temporal break forcing the novel to give differently from its contribution to cultural colonization. Rather than account for this only as a measure of style or content, *Gifts* considers this as a problem of utterance in context.

Within six months of the establishment of a Somali orthography (Latinized in 1973), Farah was serializing a novel in Somali for a local newspaper, a rediscovery of truth in the order of symbols that quickly ran afoul of the country's censorship board and for which Farah was detained on several occasions.[32] The connection between this utterance context and that of the publication of *Gifts* in Africa almost twenty years later is not just Farah's unyielding critique of Somali politics, but his attempt to construct a more intimate space for his story-giving, a context in which he might be read to speak directly to Africans.[33] Thus, the form of the novel inflects serialization as a public discourse, as if the text is broken up according to the time of readers. Each chapter features an epigrammatic summary, a bond that allows the story to be followed in shorthand or long. Here the gift is a lure, a promise of story repaid by further reading. The summaries speak to both a sense of loss reimagined (including the lost public space of a Somali newspaper) and to how the novel gives differently, despite its debts to the West. The echo of serialization is an index of the novel's political unconscious: a context for an imagined Somali dialogicity. But surely the actual number of Somali readers of a novel published in English outside Somalia is going to be relatively small? Dialogicity refers to implied address so that utterance context also means imaginary relations, possibilities of address that keep a form open to eventness and not closed by its status as cultural event. The novel is not simply the gift that keeps on giving; rather, its formal markers may find a context in which it gives most prodigiously and without need of return. Perhaps this is the pathos of Farah as an outsider, and the immediate context for *Gifts* (it was drafted in Khartoum, Sudan) further marks this exotopy. The novel offers another context whereby the interaction of inner and outer speech situates the addressed as the addressor and in this way a world as audience is interpellated.[34]

How does the form of address affect the issue of the novel as gift? Abshir, like Farah an ex-patriot, offers two more versions of storytelling for Duniya's family and friends to consider. First, "all stories are one story, whose principal theme is love. And if the stories feel different, it is only because the journeys the characters are to undertake take different routes to get to their final destination." Second, "all stories celebrate in elegiac terms, the untapped sources of energy, of the humanness of women and men" (G 246). These are wonderful sentiments but do not sufficiently describe this novel. Magaclaawe reaches his final destination too quickly for love to be his story's principal theme. Similarly, when Bosaaso's first wife throws herself out of the window clutching their child, she betrays a "humanness" that one feels uncomfortable celebrating. Perhaps Farah felt that Abshir should have some summary statements on storytelling since his visit was desired by Duniya, but there are so many good storytellers in the room (including Taariq, Mire, and Nasiiba) one feels cheated they have no chance to disabuse Abshir. Farah could be baiting a foreign anglophone audience who may believe that no matter where a novel comes from, it thankfully does not have a different story to tell after all. Or the address may invoke an African reader who will see enough in the mingling of folklore, oral tales, media reports, and the like to doubt whether the get-together at the end of the novel constitutes a rendezvous of victory. Here the form of the novel double voices because it gives the lie to what has been given in the time of its passage.

While Bakhtin tends to favor the novel for verification, he spends less time on its form-giving logic than Lukacs, although both recognize the form of the novel is premised on becoming.[35] The openness of the novel as form marks this logic of becoming. Form-giving at a basic level transcribes experience but in the novel its fictiveness can only be maintained by the dialectical tension between what is true to the form and what resists representation in representation, or what J. M. Bernstein, theorizing from Lukacs, calls form-giving and mimesis.[36] To the extent the novel gives form in the process of its eventness it is already a gift: it cannot give a totality of reality but gives form in its stead as an index of narrative's relationship to temporality. The novel suspends disbelief in its form-giving capacity. It must forget what it gives in form or time cannot give in temporality. The principle of form-giving cannot itself be represented and thus the novel forms in light of a certain impossibility in the concept of form. Freed from this debt in representation it parades an exuberance in every other direction, which is its second characteristic vis-à-vis the gift.

The novel's special claims on giving still require clarification on its uniqueness within a philosophy of forms since the logic of form-giving is not revealed by a novel that thematizes giving. The issue of exuberance bears crucially on the emergence of the postcolonial novel but how? For a theory of exuberance that is itself exuberant one might turn to Georges Bataille, whose notion of general economy attempts to turn economics on its head by identifying luxury rather than scarcity as its most acute problem.[37] The kernel of wealth, he argues, is gift-giving, "squandering without reciprocation" (38). The principle of exuberance in gift-giving interrogates the difference between international aid and what is given in the postcolonial state. According to Bataille, potlatch exists to sign the fundamental problem of the dissipation of wealth. Like Derrida, Bataille builds on Mauss's study to indicate a logic in the gift and finds it demonstrates luxury's lie, the meaning attached to rank by wealth. Derrida will go on to examine the gift's double bind in relation to time as that which does not belong, the gift itself as the sign of what cannot be possessed, time. At a very basic level, international aid in *Gifts* points to giving as rank (in at least two senses); it freely gives to confirm its belief in a state of excess (individual donors, to be sure, may well be mired in debt), an exuberance that returns in the form of a favor or promise of subsequent value extraction. One of the "reports" Farah attaches explains the Italian government has presented an aid package including help for rice farming *and* a further influx of Italian professors at the National University of Somalia. They are proud of an institution that is the only university outside Italy where all the subjects are taught in Italian and, naturally, want to maintain this colonial excess. Like the rice bags, every donation is signed by hegemony or its will.

The postcolonial state, however, is not just the passive recipient of exuberance. As Mbembe makes clear, the postcolony has taken to highly developed systems of exuberance itself. The *commandement* he describes disrupts the tidy binary of donor and recipient between First World and

Third and focuses instead on issues of excess and the creativity of abuse.[38] Farah too, has dedicated much time to articulating the dirty secrets of the postcolony and in *Gifts* this includes the squandering of donations by the government and enthusiastic displays of giving (either to themselves or foreign dignitaries). Under the rubric of "an aesthetics of vulgarity" Mbembe examines excess in the postcolony as a chaos of signs where rulers and ruled constantly attempt to "rewrite the mythologies of power" (OP 108). This extravagance produces "a regime of unreality" defying state order. Yet, he points out, the conditions of international aid as debt reproduce themselves in the postcolony: first, by nurturing a salaried bureaucracy to whom a gift of employment is also an indebtedness that maintains the state apparatus; and second, in the staging of generous festivals of food distribution (to the chosen few) that enthrall precisely because of food scarcity in general. Particular forms of gift giving, like the *Qaaraan* that Taariq describes, certainly produce and sustain community identification but they do not, in themselves, pose a solution to state dysfunction. This is a primary contradiction of the postcolony: its forms of association are not given in the state that is supposedly their quintessence.

Although Bataille's views of economy are suitably hallucinogenic, they do not quite apply to postcolonial narration. The Nameless One, however, is almost an "accursed share" for he gives his presence without expectation, without claiming reciprocation as a bond among lovers. He remains nameless because naming constitutes a possession that would annul the gift. He dies to preserve this principle in giving. This is only one aspect of giving for Farah, who juxtaposes the generosity born of family ties as a cultural expression of the Somali nation with the state typified in the image of outstretched hands. To the extent that the novel gives form to the experience of this culture it also conveys the eventness of Somali identification. Yet this is not the form in which the state has emerged so the novel measures not just the vibrant practices of giving in everyday life but the failure of *its* approximation. Thus, Magaclaawe lives on in Duniya and Bosaaso but remains dead according to the dictates of state temporality.

The foundling in *Gifts* dies "nameless," but Kalaman, the protagonist of *Secrets*, has the gift of a name with no obvious origin, although Nonno, his "chosen" paternal grandfather, says it was the cry of a crow made at his birth. Kalaman sets about unraveling the mystery of his name (literally, "split mind") and birth and *Secrets* revolves around this quest.

Because the first two volumes of the trilogy weave abstract symbols between individual and nation—maps are the contours of the mind, the nation is a gift of conscience, and so forth—the final novel has precipitated
criticism poised on the belief that its secret is the third term of such correlatives, that secrecy splits families and destroys nations in equal measure. Neal Ascherson suggests, "Unstated, there are allegories prowling
through this story. Kalaman, trying to discover whose son he is, is following the journey of his own people but—unlike Somalia—reaches the
truth without being obliged to hate or kill those whose son he is not."[39]
Anne Ursu says simply "In *Secrets*, the nation is personified by a family
whose own past tears apart their lives."[40] In a more provocative reading
Ngaboh-Smart nevertheless opines, "Notwithstanding its preoccupation
with a domestic theme, *Secrets* is nonetheless a sequel especially to the
last two novels [*Maps* and *Gifts*] before it in that, like them, it deals with
conflicts and movement of signs depicting the problematic of Somali nationhood."[41] Maybe a secret is not much of one if it is so easily revealed?
Given the preponderance of references to secrets in Farah's novel perhaps
the revelation of Somalia is just as obvious: the more you see it, the less it
appears to exist. This would not be a surprising inversion on Farah's part,
although it is one that has infuriated readers who, offered the lure of the
Other as a secret, find in the end that there is not one. When this desire for
the secret of the Other is frustrated is the author "translated" or discarded?
What if transnationalism was not just the name for this "translation" but
the living-on of an opacity that transgresses both nation and translation
by refusing to give up all of its meanings as postcolonial, as the ward of a
newly formed state?

To list the secrets in *Secrets* is to provide a litany of obviousness despite the fact that most of them remain unexplained. The secrets are not
content markers of secrets but a form of abrogation since they often resist
explanatory context. Here a notion of literacy is at stake, closer to what
Gayatri Chakravorty Spivak calls "transnational literacy," than either a
facility with language or set of motifs.[42] Such literacy is a measure of the
unknown in the "trans" of transnationalism; it is an invitation to think
the unassimiliable under current regimes of otherness on a world scale. It
is not a text that merely needs to be read for revelation but necessitates a
logic of answerability or responsibility to its inscription, conditions of literacy beyond the publication and distribution of "Third World" novels.

That Farah writes in English underlines the failure of normative literacy because he presents opacity as an injunction *to* literacy, to a kind of unlearning rather than a demonstration of its effect. *Gifts* ends with a paradox of the gift and thus it seems appropriate to critique *Secrets* as that gift's disruption, as a dissolution of form-giving in whose name secrets are to be revealed.

It would be a neat closure to the trilogy if the secret of *Secrets* was simply there was no secret. The truth of identification cannot be secreted: it stands as an indictment of the clandestine, the clans and their patriarchs, and the condescension of the international community. How does *Secrets* follow *Gifts* and by turn *Maps* but refuse the trilogy's obvious pact in linearity? The gift depends on a cancellation of the exchange function that Bataille tracks in the aura of excess, in luxury's luxury. In potlatch this annulment is an alibi because what is freely given returns in the form of power: dispensing with luxury is performed in the service of accumulation. The form-giving qualities of the novel complicate the model significantly because it attempts not simply to narrate the event but to embody the principle of eventness itself. The novel may freeze time, may provide legible coordinates of time's frame, but what it gives is temporality, time's process in which events become meaningful. The form-giving capacities of the novel are connected to a desire in giving but that gift alone does not sustain eventness. Context is an active participant in temporality, not simply an imaginative option. It is also a measure, however, of the gift's double bind in terms of the unconscious: the gift of love is predicated on a corresponding gift of life and fateful gift of death. This aporia is given in *Gifts* by the story of Magaclaawe.

The death of the foundling is a structural pivot in the trilogy. We have three novels but the *Blood in the Sun* narrative is split in two by the passing of the "Nameless One." On one side of the death there is the war over the Ogaden and the crisis of a declining state worn down by dictatorial hubris and the function of postcoloniality for the Cold War. On the other side of Magaclaawe's demise are the effects of this interweaving of the political and personal optimistically, in the renewal of certain family ties, and cynically, in state paroxysm and the degenerative themes of bestiality, incest, rape, and fantastic compensations. Yet despite this linearity Farah's trilogy maintains an interest in parabola and metalepsis folding the narrative back on itself so at the end of both *Gifts* and *Secrets* the reader is asked to begin again or consider the end in the beginning. *Secrets* ends with the same line with which it begins but its answer to *Gifts* is more pronounced: it explains what the gift of Magaclaawe's death might mean to the narrative's form-giving possibilities. The secret of Duniya's love flowers from the "Nameless One" and constitutes the unspoken in the gift, the injunction to respond to death. *Gifts* is also haunted by the "Nameless One" whose gift of death remains, lives on, in the detritus of Somali identification. But Farah is not particularly interested in the negative capability of death as the annulment of being Somali. Instead, *Secrets* figures death as that which nurtures the Other's knowledge of the "I" by sustaining a secret securing its possibility. In *Secrets*, Kalaman's existential maneuvering is bent on asserting a deathly supplement, one that gives solace neither to the protagonist nor to the reader. Death does not provide catharsis, a remark again on Somali folk traditions where beliefs do not view death as a prelude to a glorious and eternal afterlife.

In an investigation of religion and a reading of the Czech philosopher Jan Patocka, Derrida explores the secret truth of faith as a gift of death, one requiring a demonic presence to fathom the terms of salvation and responsibility.[43] Several critics have discussed Islam in Farah's writing but here I am interested in how the novel as form might secularize and sacralize in the space of I and Other. Derrida pursues the possibility of a religion without a religion in the function and forms of the gift of death, and this has implications for the passage from *Gifts* to *Secrets* and the *Blood in the Sun* more broadly construed. When Derrida states "A secret always *makes* you tremble" he invokes God as cause, the *mysterium tremendum*, whose "gift of infinite love" produces a radical dissymmetry between this gift and human finitude with its correlative and largely Christian characteristics of "responsibility as culpability, sin, salvation, repentance, and sacrifice" (GD 56). Allah also gives infinitely and is merciful in the giving but it is the associated dissymmetry and trembling that are crucial here. The infinite gift is the essence of gift, that which cannot be absolutely reciprocated or bettered in life (thus, *The Gift of Death* responds to the aporetic structure of *Given Time*). The same dissymmetry exists for the imagination: it can create infinity but not live in it. The secret of God's infinite gift of love is at the core of trembling before God (it instantiates guilt). As Derrida puts it, "We fear and tremble before the inaccessible secret of a God who decides for us although we remain responsible, that is, free to decide, to work, to assume our life and our death" (GD 56). Yet this does not exhaust how secrets make you shiver and its relationship to the gift. Just as *Given Time* is about temporality, so *The Gift of Death* turns to responsibility in identification.

How can another see into me, into my most secret self, without my being able to see in there myself and without my being able to see him in me? And if my secret self, that which can be revealed only to the other, to the wholly other, to God if you wish, is a secret that I will never reflect on, that I will never know or experience or possess as my own, then what sense is there in saying that it is "my" secret, or in saying more generally that a secret belongs, that it is proper to or belongs to some "one," or to some other who remains someone? It is perhaps there that we find the secret of secrecy, namely, that it is not a matter of knowing and that it is there for no-one. A secret doesn't belong, it can never be said to be at home or in its place [*chez soi*] . . . The question of the self: "who am I?" not in the sense of "who am I" but "who is this 'I'" that can say "who"? What is the "I," and what becomes of responsibility once the identity of the "I" trembles *in secret*?" (GD 92)

The scale of reason in Farah's *Secrets* is caught on the barbs of the subject's relationship to secrecy and responsibility. Kalaman is a hero of his quest for self-identity but he is not a hero who has a secret; he trembles in the realization that secrecy itself is ostensibly given in the knowledge of others but actually inscribed in an injunction of responsibility never wholly his, the Other's, nor indeed the author's to both. This is, for instance, the foundling's "secret" in *Gifts*: "Everybody had turned the foundling into what they thought they wanted, or lacked" (G 128). They think he has a secret but he is that principle of secrecy and cannot be "had." In *Secrets* by contrast, the revelation of secrecy is so tied to a place, a home, that a lack of knowledge becomes dispossession and the lack of answers becomes the disintegration of the place itself, Somalia. "How can another see into me," asks Derrida, "into my most secret self, without my being able to see in there myself and without my being able to see him in me?"

Secrets is Farah's most difficult work to date but the one with the least satisfying complexity, perhaps because of the circumstances of its writing. The novel is begun in Uganda. A first draft is completed in Berlin. Farah's mother dies while he is finishing a second draft. He then moves to Ethiopia where he completes a third draft just as Siyad Barre is being driven from power. The following year Farah moves to Nigeria but it would be another six years before *Secrets* was published (during which time his father dies, in Mombasa, Operation Restore Hope does not, and Farah visits Somalia for the first time in many years). So far the process of *Secrets'* writing remains a secret but between migration and the death of the parents an existential riddle is being drawn that questions the capacity of language itself (one of the earlier titles for the novel was "Words").[44] Certainly, elements of history appear to write the story from within, as if what delays the text is the instability of frames that postdate the scene of its action. The difficulty resides not just in the dense multiplicity of "I" narrators (and the close proximity of a third-person storyteller) but in deciding whether the peripatetic surfaces of the text are emblematic of individual and national dissolution or of a kind of trembling in narration itself that increasingly doubts its act of salvation.

The "Prologue" in *Secrets* announces this restlessness in Kalaman's self-questioning, warning us against an "easy answer to a difficult riddle," which is not just his name but "One corpse, three secrets!" The novel ends with the same words but punctuated thus: "One corpse. Three secrets." The difference in punctuation is that between reflection and resignation, between Kalaman thinking back on Nonno's death and its exact moment. The comma allows for a certain continuity between the death and secrets, while the full stop suggests secrets now have their own existence; they live on without Nonno's adjudication or secrecy. Initially, we are plunged into Kalaman's childhood memories and his early friendship with Sholoongo who is several years older and is described by Nonno as a *duugan*, an unnatural baby who should have been buried soon after birth. Nonno himself is quite the storyteller (he is reported to speak to birds in their own languages) and freely embellishes his narratives, adding secrets here and mythical details there. Part of the prologue is focused on storytelling as hyperbole, and part on the significance of names and naming. Nonno's choice of "Kalaman" is about individuality but also secrecy for it is a name that can stand apart both from his father and from Nonno himself, as if the bloodline did not exist. When Kalaman suggests adding his mother's name Nonno objects, saying it might imply he was illegitimate, a possibility meant to linger. Kalaman's first-person narration is the most unstable in the trilogy although at this stage it can be read as boyish naivete. He recalls that at the age of eight he was engaging in sex with Sholoongo, who makes fun of his small penis yet makes use of it at every opportunity. Sholoongo herself is described in supernatural terms, a young woman who is not only lustful but magical and can emerge in the dreams of Kalaman's mother as a shape-shifting wraith. Sholoongo's father, Madoobe ("Blackie" or "the Black"), is also the object of speculation, since Kalaman saw him speak in tongues to a heifer one night before having sex with the animal. When he tells Sholoongo of this adventure she explains that her Dad was domesticating the beast before taking it as his wife and indeed later Madoobe appears with a young bride. The prologue ends with a folktale whose point is to deter the listener from divulging secrets, a tantalizing warning since to this point the narrative has been speculative not clandestine, ribald rather than sinister, sacrilegious rather than secretive, and playful rather than purposeful. When Said S. Samatar faults Farah for stylistic and narrative excesses he misreads their import.[45] As the prologue underlines, this story is a folktale, as truthful as imaginative minds like Kalaman's and Sholoongo's will allow it to be. It is a service to point out that the word for *scorpion* in Somali is "hangaraloo" not "hangaroole" (although a language with a recent orthography might foster all kinds of variations), but Samatar wants *Secrets* to be authentic whereas Farah sees that guarantee as a trap. In the end Samatar describes *Secrets* as a "fiercely non-Somali novel," which from a countryman might seem the worst of criticisms, but from the point of identification, with its secret that cannot be possessed, is a fair assessment of its centrifugal restlessness.

But *Secrets'* riotous surfaces belie the logic of its formal structure, a narrative gathered between a prologue and epilogue with two parts themselves separated by a third described as an interlude. This frame is part of the paradox of the novel and indeed the trilogy, both of which strive to harness the force of novelization when that impetus itself is characterized by convention. (*Maps* also gestures toward a tripartite structure but includes an interlude separating Part One from Two and Three that contains a typical warning: "no depth, just surface" [M 138]). There is no secret in the novel's fiction but there is much secreted in the novel's fictive frame. Just like the Dickensian gestures in *Gifts*, *Secrets* carnivalizes its formal markers so that the whole is much greater than the sum of its parts. The long space is not simply an abrogation of genre (since this is axiomatic to the novel *as* genre) but is an interrogation of the terms of subjecthood inscribed by the past as a kind of formal interregnum, the space of colonization, that stands between the now of nation and its precolonial possibilities. The trilogy does not mime a continuum torn by imperial caesura (as if the final volume is the restitution of truth in writing), but the extended narrative cannot find community sustenance in the immediacy and brevity of the present: it must seek an identificatory logic in duration, in an architectonic of time and space that, if it does not ground nation, examines the structure of embeddedness itself. What makes the *Blood in the Sun* a trilogy is implicit in what makes *Secrets* "a fiercely non-Somali novel": its formal outside, like Farah's outsidedness, cannot assume an equation in "Somali novel." That every nation should have a novel is precisely the problem of nation and novel, an alignment that the long space seeks to tremble. The long space constitutes a symbolic form that questions "the calm passion" (as Franco Moretti calls it) of the Golden Age of the European novel while yet introjecting its understanding as interregnum, the chronotope of bourgeois and colonial coincidence.[46] Indeed, by considering postcoloniality as a genre one is confronted by its historically specific significance in the genealogy of genre, a secret as Derrida describes it that is responsible to the meaning of form in the great wake of colonial subjugation (GD 10). Secrets may well propel the narrative of Farah's *Secrets*, but their history of responsibility lies elsewhere in the extant conditions of novelization, the process through which Farah "gives" Somalia.

Even when *Secrets* purports to explain Somalia's recent chaos, it is no more an answer to national turmoil than the belief in Sholoongo's shape-shifting. Its narrative point of view does not place itself outside of superstition or magic, as if a little reason might stave off some descent into tribal conflagration. "My eyes have happened," says Nonno at the point of death, but the lesson is in his eventness of seeing, not in what is seen itself. A different way of seeing begets a different "way of the world" and this is why the ordered structure of Farah's novel is so insistently beside itself before the logic of secrets to be revealed.

Like *Maps*, *Secrets* foregrounds masculine voyeurism in its main character. There is trickery in seeing the characters seeing what some critics mistake as an obsessiveness bordering on the puerile: Kalaman and the others view or indulge in masturbation, bestiality, the size of male members (Nonno's, in particular), and a host of genital intimacies and biological functions (Askar believes he menstruates, Kalaman drinks menstrual blood). In *Maps* Uncle Hilaal states simply, "Sooner or later, sex" (M 234).

He explains that no story can be considered complete without sex, but nothing quite prepares the reader for this in *Secrets*, where sex is always sooner and in prodigious supply. Indeed, if one were to take Hilaal's remark as a topos then the climax of *Secrets*, Sholoongo fucking Nonno almost to death (he dies soon after), would seem to make such heady subjects as the fate of a nation a matter of life-affirming copulation. Sex is also the ground of secrets and, however literal the text may become, it is never free from symbolism where family and nation are concerned.[47] Voyeurism accentuates the significance of desire but if what is seen jars the conscience of the prudish this is only by way of focusing on the real issue. As the narrator puts it in the pivotal interlude: "Our challenge is to locate the metaphor for the collapse of the collective, following that of the individual" (S 191). The text refuses that location, even in sex, and thus Kalaman's search for his beginning, an origin forged by multiple rape, provides only problematic metaphors for its metadiscursive heart, the nation that Nonno continually confuses with Kalaman's character.

Secrets are everywhere in *Secrets*—in wells, attached to the legs of homing pigeons—but the principle of the secret is not about to locate anything as luxurious as a meaning for social disintegration. What it rehearses is the necessity for responsibility, an indirect connection to the restoration of Somalia delivered only by clues and gestures in the novel's content and form. And even this level of hermeneutical possibility is questioned. As Nonno notes, "secrets sabotage the very purpose for which they are being withheld, they give away the very thing one wishes to protect" (S 114). Like maps and gifts (and to some extent words), secrets enact their own displacement and annulment; they continually subvert truth's reason in their conditional stability. Thus, the secret as metaphor extends Farah's rhetoric of the imaginary state, one that warns all against symbolic equivalence in the literary act. Nonno, who is often Farah's intellectual conscience in the novel (like Hilaal in *Maps* and Bosaaso in *Gifts*), tempts the reader with symbolic equivalence but no more than that. He makes the most connections between what is happening within the family and the deepening crisis of the state that will, in the years immediately following the action of the novel, precipitate the departure of Siyad Barre, then clan battles and warlordism. The secret of connection is not revealed and all that is sabotaged is social realism as an explanation. Secrets, then, are deflections and so is Kalaman's search since the main protagonist is Sholoongo.

There is an appropriateness to Sholoongo's importance and a central paradox; namely, the "blood in the sun" is not the "blood in the son" (say, Askar or Kalaman) but the blood in the daughter, or Somali woman. "Fathers matter not" the saying goes in *Secrets*, "mothers matter a lot." Sholoongo thus joins Duniya and Misra as a positive resource of hope in Somali society. The mere assertion does not wrest either women or Somalia from the throes of subjection, objectification, and victimhood. Certainly mothers challenge the prescriptions of male authoritarianism, but in the end what is feminist about Farah's narration is that women are primarily not the secret to be revealed; they may, on occasion, embody a specific answer to the excesses of masculinism but they do not stand as the light in some preternatural postcolonial darkness. That Sholoongo is a shape-shifter is the closest the text comes to stating a formal homology between woman and state and the form of the trilogy. Like the mark that appears on Kalaman's hand, Sholoongo only seems like the key to the narrative's disquiet.

Structurally, Sholoongo functions like Misra's extracted heart and Magaclaawe: her absent presence promises meaning (even Nonno offers this formulation [S 200]) but delivers a lack in lack that thwarts the logic of othering. Sholoongo's shamanism precipitates all sorts of speculative reason and tempting rumors. She has returned from the United States (where she leads the New York branch of the All-American Shape-shifters' Union!) to conceive a child with Kalaman whose bloodline she knows to be of radically unstable paternity. Her half brother, Timir, has returned with her and is also in search of a child for him and his partner. Together these two question anything resembling normative or heterosexist family values in the trilogy, but they never assume a pure ground of negativity, the foil that restores faith in a patriarchal nuclear family or an unadulterated genealogy. If the form of the novel gestures at stability, Sholoongo's influence is nothing short of anarchic, and her lust alone blasts the vitality and virility of the men in the novel. To underline that Sholoongo's selfhood is more than other people's portrayals, Farah has her casually leave some autobiographical notes in Kalaman's apartment that reveal Kalaman himself as a lusty child who often initiated their sexual encounters. Nevertheless, Sholoongo is represented as both a human and an animal who tests the powers of reason. If she is not the substance of Somalia, she overreaches the filial and the essential in clannish bloodlines.

Sholoongo's outsider status mirrors Kalaman's in Somali self-defini-
tion. Kalaman, a computer geek, finds professionalism in Somali society
does not free him from the values attached to blood, and any prestige he
might garner through work is overdetermined by the sanctity of descent.
Jacqueline Bardolph argues that Farah's first two trilogies challenge traditional family structures by exploring "horizontal" formations among
brothers and sisters and, despite my emphasis on the orphan, there is
much to recommend this reading.[48] Kalaman is intimidated by Sholoongo's ability to see him more clearly than he can and inspire his partner,
Talaado, to do the same. Through Sholoongo's visit, Kalaman is made to
understand that his self-doubt does not promise rectitude even in moments of apparently appropriate resolve before his mother: "I suppose it is
high time I married Talaado and gave you a grandchild, and made Yaqut
another Nonno" (S 265). Coming after all of the taboo breaking in the rest
of the novel Kalaman's statement hardly answers the narrative's secrets,
three or otherwise.

The secret as a trope confounds the contours of identity for identification. It may be true, as some readers have argued, this is what makes
Farah a global humanist who articulates a universal disposition. According to this view, Somalia itself is the notational device and its failings are
due to its inability to account for the many variations that make up the
extended family requisite of the modern nation state. It is an intriguing
idea, not just because of Farah's humanist leanings, but because it underlines the fictional effect of nation where postcoloniality is concerned. The
more one attempts to narrate the existential substance of postcoloniality,
the more its national predicate fades; the greater its narratological duration, the shorter its time for political subsistence. On one level, the given
time of the postcolonial state is also its gift of death; in the *Pharmakon* of
Western desire the cure of nation is simultaneously postcolonial poison.
Stylistically, *Secrets*, like *Maps* and *Gifts*, employs aspects of folk culture
to intimate continuity in everyday life, despite the implosion of the state
and outbreaks of looting and violence following Siyad Barre's escape from
Somalia in 1991. Farah does not view such cultural practices as innocent;
the grotesquery of *Secrets* depends in part on its code breaking, on its hyperbolic incredulity where rumor and superstition are concerned. These
elements are often interpreted as exotic. The folkloric in Farah's work is
a challenge to anyone who wants to read beyond objectification. It is the

agon of the long space that such concerns do not secrete blueprints for
being otherwise in the postcolony yet, for Farah in particular, one cannot
imagine any sustainable community could emerge without the *durée* embedded in place.

One example in *Secrets* is the discussion of *nabsi* and *nuuro*.
Sholoongo has temporally moved into Kalaman's home and so he asks his
father whether he should throw her out. *Nabsi* is explained as a mystical
notion that cautions against outright rejection. It is a mediating influence
that protects humans from rashness of every kind based, more or less, on
precedent. To overlook *nabsi* in his treatment of Sholoongo would be to
court calamity of a different kind. When Kalaman seeks Nonno's advice
on the issue his counsel is basically the same, but he suggests that Kalaman
take heed of *nabsi*'s complement, *nuuro*. *Nuuro* is tantamount to instinct,
intuitions (Nonno, of course, describes them as secrets) that allow animals and humans alike to survive in conditions of peril. Kalaman, Nonno
believes, does not have *nuuro* because his "working faculties require no
supplementation": his actions are governed by reason, and *nabsi* ensures
that in reason's realm the unreasonable do not go unpunished, by god or
by duty.

"You can't walk away from this *nabsi*," he said. "It's like walking away from a civic responsibility. *Nabsi* raises its head, puts a stop to unfair treatment of persons
weaker than oneself. *Nabsi* brings the torturer to his senses, *nabsi* makes sure that
massacres of animals, wasteful murders are brought to a retributive end. I would
hypothesize that if *nuuro* led the elephant to Fidow's door, it was *nabsi* which
killed him." (S 103)

While the trilogy offers no formula for the restoration of Somalia, it
continually folds back on itself in the belief that narration maintains life
in the absence of more general civic responsibility. Farah's writing does not
simply wait out horrors, however—nor does Djebar's in a different context—but conjures *nabsi*'s prescience when so much else seems to vanquish
answerability's purchase on socialization. The rawness of *nuuro* presents its
own dangers (the animalistic associations with Sholoongo, her wild and
primitive desires, are often demeaning effects of *nabsi*). If it is not the key
then neither is *nabsi*, which sees life as an endless revenge tragedy where
fate or God must sort things out. It is Nonno's tragedy that he holds fast
to the play of *nuuro* and *nabsi* as he careens toward death: he wants *nabsi*
to give him peace even as *nuuro* intercedes through Sholoongo's amorous

advances. If *nuuro* helps him speak to the birds, *nabsi* takes him into the cul-de-sac of numerology. Nonno has combined these spirits in Sufi mysticism yet in the Epilogue, when close to death, he seeks further guidance by praying to Allah. Kalaman, ever the convenient voyeur, observes this moment and channels a conscience that is irrepressible in Farah's narration:

As I take in the significance of what is happening, I recall Nonno saying not long ago that it is in the nature of knots to come undone, and in the nature of buried things to be dug up by Time. Are we to deduce from these dicta that it is in the nature of humans to countenance humility in worshipful self-expression in moments of personal and national crisis, when we are on the verge of death, our nation is on the precipice of collapse, the country is in turmoil, and the entire continent being taken to a land of virtual ruin, a land without memories. Do we prostrate ourselves before our Creator in a tardy expectation of being pardoned, saved, our lives put right, when for years we have spoken in the periphrastics of self-delusion, speaking of family allegiances while advancing our personal interests? (S 287)

Whether the phrasing exists in Somali or not, there is something crucially apposite in "the periphrastics of self-delusion," circumlocution that ties Somalia's disintegration not just to the hot-aired bureaucrats of the international public sphere but to the wasted words of the literate in Somalia. Words have betrayed the country's communality: they have stood in the way of direct reproach, perhaps for fear that anything other than the periphrastic might raise the ire of the "Mayor of Mogadiscio," Siyad Barre, who knew that when words speak truth to power an assassination plot (against Farah, for instance) is in order. If colonization, as Aimé Césaire argues, leads not to civilization but to "progressive dehumanization" then postcoloniality, according to Kalaman, is dogged by regressive complacency.[49] Language must always offer secrets, feints, and alibis because that is one of the meanings of language. Kalaman here is also self-deluding so that when he adopts an apocalyptic tone ("land of virtual ruin, a land without memories"), we are meant to ponder his own periphrastic compulsions. Nevertheless, memory is at stake in Farah's fiction: what is left to being if memory does not function? Memory remains unreliable, and Farah's alternation of narrative points of view accentuates this truism as does his suspicion of any descent into pure nostalgia. Time and again in Farah's storytelling Somalia is bracketed by memory lapses or the excision of instructive remembrance.

After Nonno's lesson on *nabsi* and *nuuro* Kalaman understands why he must show patience toward Sholoongo. But what of her secret? Nonno argues through parables to underline that "nothing is unknowable so long as another human being has knowledge of it . . . when a secret is known to two humans, such a secret will be known before the death of both parties" (S 104). Our own secrets are impossibly hermetic; the taxonomy of secrecy begins in the realm of the other which both ensures the notion and guarantees that the secret will out. Nonno therefore suggests that Sholoongo's secret—betrayed more by conjecture than whispered intimacy—is her mythical stature, one which conjoins the animal and human. She embodies *nabsi* and *nuuro* and this lies at the heart of her shamanism. Sholoongo's secret reminds Kalaman that his remains unarticulated, a source of pain that he can assuage, for the moment, only by silence. This "parenthesis of quiet," gives way to Nonno's recollections of the same scene (the Rashomon effect) in which Kalaman recounts the tale of Sholoongo's arrival and stresses, as his father had done, the role of *nabsi*. The use of parenthesis is a remark alongside the discourse on *nabsi* and *nuuro* but suggests a complementary trope alongside parataxis, parabola, and the periphrastic in organizing the trilogy.

In *Secrets* the secret functions as a parenthetical device but does not follow Nonno's ascriptions. His voice may tremble as he recounts the secret of Sholoongo, but the secret that makes him shiver is that which cannot be had, that which does not belong, as Derrida suggests. The secret of the secret exists in its aphoristic frame, in its potential to comment on the subject and, in *Secrets*, to orchestrate the substance of social relations. Here then, the secret occupies the position of interclusion since none of the many secrets in the novel actually open up beyond the promise of self-revelation (they belong where they should not belong). Because "secret" is used so liberally in *Secrets* one loses its link to responsibility and its profusion comes close to digression. Where it could be a parenthetical force it is often a distraction that does not fathom whether Kalaman's tribulations are symptoms of state disintegration. The secret expresses the negative capability of parentheses, as commentary that mystifies. Farah can preserve the right to opacity without necessarily ceding the narrative to escapism or solipsism. But even at its most literal the novel still tends to muddy its thesis with secretive asides.

If the secrets diverge from the importance of secrets for parenthesis, the question of responsibility for the "I" looks very different when *Secrets* is placed alongside *Maps* and *Gifts*. Nonno's evasions about his relation to Kalaman recede into the background as the aura of secrets themselves enclose and emphasize the Nameless One, Magaclaawe, whose poignant existence takes on the substance of aphorism in the center of the trilogy. His being does not need authenticating for him to galvanize the relationship of Duniya and Bosaaso. Indeed, the space opened up by the parentheses of volumes one and three gives a new sense to "immediate family," to responsibility unfettered by the codicils attached to either state dictate or clan protocol. Perhaps the orphan has always worked to conjure answerability in this way, but one is struck by its organizing principle here: a nameless, speechless one who disturbs the field of understanding itself. On the other side of *Gifts* stands *Maps* where an identification suturing communities to imperial borders provides a deeply problematic interclusion, a hideous space of violence. Caught between two conflicting chronotopes of Somalia, the remains of imperial division and the displacements of postcolonial intrigue, Magaclaawe lives on as the space of possibility beyond death (thus: one corpse, three [volumes of] secrets).

We can be certain that for Farah this formal enclosure—Magaclaawe clasped between the tremulous lunalae of Maps and Secrets—is altogether too neat, and yet the trilogy in the extended time/space of postcoloniality affords a narratological precision otherwise absent in the material uncertainties of Somali statehood. If his first trilogy provides a critique, "variations" on the false promises of authoritarian rule, then the second ceaselessly attempts to figure what is left to being that is to a great extent unauthorized, inauthentic before presumed dictates. Secrets in the final volume make a good deal tremble, including the relationship of the author to the imaginative space of home so that Farah's narrative itself cannot pretend to be an authentication of some true Somali identity, like Askar's papers once more, that would roll back the conditions of multiplicity the trilogy solemnly records. Thus, in addition to the sense of parentheses as both a blocking off and a position from which to give shape or argue from within the trilogy, we should account for the contextual bracketing of the trilogy as a whole, for the notion that despite the formal intricacy of Farah's imaginary state his writing itself is bracketed in what Somalia can become.

If exotopy accounts for the writer's relationship to the text and the lived outsideness of exile, the long space is overdetermined by form-giving elements beyond biography and enters into a dialogue with the material constraints of scale at specific moments in history. It does not absolve the writer from the "responsible interdetermination" invoked earlier but clarifies the conditions in which it can be figured. Wilson Harris contends that the form-giving elements of the literary are distilled in tradition as an active presence and, to the extent that *The Guyana Quartet* dialogizes the trajectories of tradition, a responsibility is enacted and enjoined. He then considers this injunction in terms of scale:

A scale of distinctions emerges, distinctions which give the imagination room to perceive the shifting border line between original substance and vicarious hollow, the much advertised rich and the hackneyed caricature of the poor, the over-fed body of illusion and the underfed stomach of reality—room to perceive also overlapping areas of invention and creation, the hair-spring experiment of crucial illumination which divides the original spiritual germ of an idea from its musing plastic development and mature body of expression. It is this kind of scale which is vital to the life of the growing person in society. And this scale exists in a capacity for imagination.[50]

Such scale is crucial to the form-giving of the long space. Although Farah refers to Somalia as the "country of my imagination" it is only partly a measure of the "shifting borders" to which Harris refers. Scale is introjected, according to Harris, when "a work begins to write itself" (TWS 47), a point at which determination is intradetermination. We have already suggested Farah's exotopy complicates the function of scale in the trilogy. But what else might bracket it and contribute to a chronotope of Somalia, envoiced?

At least three sets of coordinates inform Farah's intense consciousness of space. One could track Farah's responsible interdetermination of Somali orality, not just in the direct quotations of or allusions to poets and folklore but in the way he is answerable to the primary speech genres of everyday life. Whether such "a work begins to write itself" *in English* must remain a vital question, but how this language is abrogated by untranslated Somali might provide a key. Responsible interdetermination can also be read in the intertextuality of Farah's fiction that maintains a dialogue with other African writers, as well as those beyond the continent who speak to exile in particular.[51] This is a register of Farah's understanding of the moment of his fiction, of its role in histories of writing. Such specificity connects Farah's work to postcolonialism, modernism, and postmodernism, an interest where the first term creatively explores the difference between the last two. The scales of distinction here mark more than an echo of traditions but the manner in which the writer is prepared to rewrite them, to struggle creatively with their prescriptions. The agon of the long space exists in its protracted engagement with the supposed inevitabilities of the form, but it no longer expects history to guarantee the truths of narration.

The second set of coordinates focus on the writer's reception, on the extant conditions of readership and the marketing of the author. Language and form are not marginal but, given the immense difficulty of African writers securing a living from their craft, cynical finger wagging about self-promotion is not helpful. The ideologies of form, with their concomitant refraction in the "choice" of language, are insinuated in the niche marketing of race and ethnicity as textual tourism, in the representation of "world literature" as itself intercluded from great national traditions and their pretenders. If cultural imperialism now fails to resonate that is not to say culture is not a hegemonic transnational force with nationalist designs. Farah has been relatively neglected for the majority of his career; although there has been significant concern within African Studies, and interest has generally burgeoned since he won the Neustadt Prize in 1998. This situation is reflected in the publishing field. *Gifts*, for instance, did not originally attain an American publisher; indeed, it was first published in Finnish two years before it appeared in English in Zimbabwe in 1992. Transnational, on this level, refers to the uneven flows of globalism.

A third set of positions connects to chronotope and to a responsibility regarding the material conditions of narrative that creatively engages the givenness of social being. This is the most paradoxical because conscience of space may well be underwritten by a political unconscious not coincident with an author's self-identification. It is, rather, a narratological code too often interpreted as the author's revelation and active consciousness. The chronotope does not guarantee the suture of text to context, or indeed form to content, but the logic of connection itself is axiomatic in the substance of narrative. The difficulty in reading Farah's second trilogy, *Blood in the Sun*, and especially the last volume, *Secrets*, is that Farah wants to return the prescience of his Ur-family, the unofficial family of adoption and informal relations, to the realm of mystery, but his most prominent characters wish this family to correspond to the nation and the affairs of state. More than one reader of *Secrets* has noticed that there are few comments on the actual crisis of the state in the novel's present (the period leading up to the fall of Siyad Barre), but these are all read retroactively as the realistic kernel of the text, and may be termed the "periphrastics of delusion" in the international public sphere. Farah prods this interpretation so the irony intensifies when the Neustadt follows *Secrets* and Farah's country of the imagination is described as "indelible." Surely the temporality of the novel, its chronotopic situatedness, is marked by the temporary, by the fleeting, by that which escapes author/nation norms? Its scales of distinction finally settle on dissolution, and *Secrets* does not close the parentheses of either nation or trilogy even as Farah's authorial outsideness seems to guarantee authenticity before an urgent international audience.

4

Meanwhile, on Buru

In Benedict Anderson's *Imagined Communities* nation is imagined through language as a primordial connection, lived synchronically in homogenous, empty time.[1] Initially, he notes that national anthems "provide occasions for unisonality, for the echoed physical realization of the imagined community" (IC 144). But then Anderson provides some literary instances that accentuate a more nuanced fatality in such communities, in which language expresses the sharp and barely translatable specificity of national belonging. The crux of the argument falls to a final example drawn from Pramoedya Ananta Toer's short story "Things Vanished," originally published in the collection *Stories from Blora* (*Cerita dari Blora*, 1952). Anderson wants us to listen to the words although the lines "are most likely closed" (IC 146). One can detect a sonality in reading Pramoedya's Bahasa Indonesia aloud, but the reason the lines are closed in the context of Anderson's book is they are untranslated (that Anderson could have translated them and that Pramoedya's work is available in over thirty languages serve to emphasize the polemic).[2] Language difference is the aporia of nation formation. If it gives to nation an imagined sense of what is held in unison, in unisonality, it troubles the very same community when its uniqueness is placed alongside the anxious plenitude of linguistic difference that threatens, at every instant, to bleed into its unifying cause. The impossibility of language difference is the underbelly of transnationalism and a reminder that even if, as I have argued elsewhere, translators are the unacknowledged legislators of the world, comparatism's capaciousness will never be identical with that world.[3]

"Things Vanished" is an autobiographical story in which Pramoedya evokes his upbringing in Blora, his birthplace in Java.[4] It is a touching tale remarkable for the innocent tenderness the narrator recalls in his childhood relationship with his mother (Pramoedya's mother died when he was seventeen). The mother sings to him, tells him stories, and on hikes talks to him about the ways of the world. His father's increasing absences are a cause for anxiety in the boy, but Pramoedya leaves the narrative content at the level of the boy's naivete. A collection of memories, the tale employs a standard of the great stories of antiquity, the refrain. Within a short story the refrain has the power of a poetic device, rhythmically sounding on the tenuous fibers of memory itself. In "Things Vanished" (also translated by Willem Samuels as "All That Is Gone") the refrain is based on the Lusi River that flows through Blora, a river that during the rainy season reaches flood stage and destroys its own banks. As each memory is recalled it reminds the boy that the moment itself is lost to eventness, to the uniqueness of the river banks before each flood. Thus, "But all that is gone now, vanished from sensory perception to live forever in memory" (ATIG 7); or, "But that too is gone now, carried away long ago, leaving with me only memories and feelings of wonder" (ATIG 14). And finally, in the passage that Anderson leaves untranslated:

How long does it take to speak a sentence? The sound of his [father's] voice was but for a few moments. A momentary tremble of sound waves, and then it was gone, not to be repeated. Yet, like the Lusi that constantly skirts the city of Blora, like the waters of that river, the remembered sound of that voice, coursing through memory, will continue to flow—forever, toward its estuary and the boundless sea. And not one person knows when the sea will be dry and lose its tide.
But all that is gone, gone from the grasp of the senses. (ATIG 30)

The length of time required to speak a sentence depends on many factors, not just the length of the sentence, its language, but the time that is given to speak it. This is the submerged dimension in nation narration, one that comes to rest in principles of duration and one that the long space embraces. Postcolonial nations composed in the decolonizing era following the Second World War are relatively young, and many have been rearticulated in the wake of the Cold War. The problem for narration is not that of recalling the moment of independence and autonomy but is rather its very proximity. The writer often measures the triumph of national independence against its aftermath *in living memory*. Conjuring mythological origins remains a possibility, but the moment of revolutionary innocence is lost to history, gone from the grasp of the senses. Like the Lusi, the tale in the process of telling is transformed and its survival rests in the faculty of memory, not purely in extant content.

James Siegel, whose understanding of traditional Java helped shape Anderson's reading, published an English translation of "Things Vanished" in 1977, and offers a further gloss on what has vanished that Pramoedya otherwise inscribes. Part of the tenacity that Pramoedya displays in Bahasa Indonesia is its ongoing recollection and displacement of Javanese. Siegel comments, "The erasure or emptying of the past has two dimensions. It is a process of active neglect or turning away from it, and it is one of being rid of it for purposes of one's own. In this sense, it spells out two meanings of the Javanese word for "vanish." This word, practically the same as the Indonesian (*ilang* versus *hilang*), has two compounds that the Indonesian lacks. One of these is "to be remiss." . . . The other is "to cause to vanish" as in to make an illness vanish, thus "to cure."[5] Coupling memory with vanish in this way, Pramoedya is preserving Javanese synchronically while ensuring its disappearance historically, a paradox with easy parallels in deconstruction but underdeveloped vis-à-vis postcolonial writing.[6] He is also displaying the storytelling art attributed to the mother and the servant woman Nyi Kin, who both repeat their tales almost daily so repetition itself figures in the stories' impact, in their memorization.

There are at least four lessons from Anderson's strategy that can usefully be applied to Pramoedya's *Buru Quartet*, the focus of this chapter. First, the national narrative in the *Quartet* is based on shaping a language sufficient to absorb colonial history by retelling it, otherwise. The language is translatable but the shape of its struggle remains abstract, indicated only for nonspeakers by its sonality. Yet the deep structure of nation narration is overdetermined by a second dimension that relates the language of its expression to a specific genealogy of storytelling, one that has thrived in Indonesia but collides with the form whose plasticity is at one with the revolutionizing rhetoric of modernity: the novel. Pramoedya discovers himself in an almost axiomatic fix for postcolonial writing: he is a storyteller for whom the novel is intricately appropriate for narrating nation and yet it is the very form that displaces memory in the storyteller's art. We might restate Anderson's thesis on unisonality to argue a third point: while the sound of language indicates a resonant placement, the struggle for the postcolonial nation provides not an image of unisonance but dissonance. It must interrogate colonial languages, both that of the colonizer and that of the local population that did its bidding. The problem is that dissonance not only displaces the colonial but is itself caught in a process of displacement; it is iterative rather than foundational and partakes of a precariousness in expression that can only be translated provisionally. This might be read as an advantage because the authority of the translator and translation is theoretically diminished, but it might also buttress the exoticizing of postcolonial texts as charming peripatiea rather than serial pronouncements on the formation of an alternative belonging. This is the untranslatable of Anderson's untranslated passage. The fourth point exists as a challenge and builds on the other three. How will Pramoedya elaborate a form for nation telling that neither engulfs storytelling nor extinguishes the epic faculty on which the language depends?[7] Is that which makes memory palpable also that which makes history for the nation "vanish," like the banks of the Lusi? The long space of the postcolonial nation that is also the substance of its profound transnationalism cannot find solace in the simultaneity of the "meanwhile." It must fight its prescriptions at every turn as Pramoedya indicates at the end of the first two volumes of the *Buru Quartet*: "Buru. Spoken 1973. Written 1975."[8]

The concept of nation requires a narrative mode but narration itself is prescribed by the nation as form.[9] Form here is an idea that imaginatively projects a means to narrate, a medium that would render its subject discernible. But any form that exists first as an idea is circumscribed not just by putative borders but by the limits of idealism and ideology. However much we conveniently match those notions to the form of nation, narration destabilizes the logic of nation form, calling into question every manifestation of narrative appropriateness. It is a living demonstration of the struggle in sign as a process of language *and* identity. Social struggle is form-giving but not necessarily form-completing at any one moment of history. Ernest Renan suggested that "Forgetting, I would even go as far as to say historical error, is a crucial factor in the creation of a nation."[10] Yet forgetting is overdetermined by psychic displacement, by the machinations of a state that must render its origin heroic if not benign, and by the aforementioned waywardness in narration itself that cannot guarantee the integrity of the nation form.

Taking as its signal the simultaneity of modernity with the nation state and print culture, the postcolonial novel refashions the detritus of the colonial into a national identity that partakes in what colonialism and imperialism denied: expressing what is sedimented in the actually existing culture of place through the new possibilities presaged by anticolonialism and decolonization. But the postcolonial novel is riddled by contradictions for which no amount of aesthetic hubris can help it escape. If the "novel narrates nation" its postcolonial form casts a pall over all three words in that statement: the novel is always already contaminated by its colonial emergence; print culture does not exactly exhaust the realities of narrating place; and the nation is just as much a block on independence as it is its tried and tested conduit. If the novel is the effulgence of print culture—aesthetics raised to the level of fiction in European bourgeois identity—the argument goes, then the appearance of the novel in postcolonial states questions the claims of autonomous nationhood and liberation from what European dominion bequeathed. Such criticism not only misreads the complexity of national liberation movements in the colonies but freezes the potential of the novel as form. There is a constitutive compulsion that links the novel, the nation, and the postcolonial that must be desacralized. This would not negate the association of the novel with a class structured in dominance, the nation with a European penchant for annexation and possession, and the postcolonial with "Third World" elites who speak for that which they do not know. Instead, the supposition is that novel, nation, and postcolonial are names for specific problems intensified or dissipated by their concrete relationships on a case-by-case basis. If the long space is a means to open up a more antagonistic dialogue between these locales, it is because the narration of nation in the postcolonial novel has already prompted just this mode of possibility. Geopolitically we wish to believe that the postcolonial is not fixed in the headlights of Western modernity. Yet the postcolonial as delinked has led to peremptory explanations of failed states and nations. Too Western, comprador; unWestern, incompetent. In the main, analogizing between nation and novel does justice to the problems or possibilities of neither but, more to the point, fails to understand the formal interruption provided by the extended postcolonial novel, the serial, the novel of duration, in the art of an otherwise impossible narration: articulating the "ing" in being, what might actually mark the "post" in postcolonial. What the long space puts in play is a symptomatic allegiance and disavowal in novel and nation. Novels should not be expected to solve the riddles of nations (and neither should nations for that matter).[11] They can, however, say a good deal about the temporalities that gird and scale nationness in the material specificities of the postcolony.

The *Buru Quartet* is perhaps the closest to the long space as nation narration. Indeed, the consonance is so intimate that for anyone wishing to understand the parameters of postcolonial literary theory's relationship to nation, Pramoedya's quartet of national awakening in Indonesia provides an archetype. Every facet of the will to nation as contravention of imperial and colonial domain is elaborated: whether one tracks the imbrication of personal *Bildung* with nation formation (chiefly through the tetralogy's main protagonist, Minke, a Dutch-educated Javanese aristocrat and writer, who is steeped in both Western and Javanese culture); the importance of print culture to the nation idea (Minke's story is loosely based on the life of Tirto Adi Suryo (1880–1918), a journalist and activist in the budding nationalist movement);[12] the articulation of nationalism as an ideology and as a consciousness; the historical embeddedness of nation narration (the first chronotopic frame of the tetralogy is the increasing desire to delink from Dutch colonialism from 1890 to about 1920); and finally, and most important, the extent to which the nation idea is indissoluble from the power of its community as imagined.

The elaboration of nation as an imagined community is one of Benedict Anderson's key contributions to postcolonial analysis, but some critical applications of this idea show a striking incompatibility not just with each other but with the actual polemic in Anderson's work.[13] Sometimes interpreters stop reading *Imagined Communities* after the following pronouncement: "I propose the following definition of the nation: it is an imagined political community—and imagined as both inherently limited and sovereign" (IC 5–6). I am interested in the inspiration for Anderson's formulation, bound as it is to his vital contribution to Southeast Asian Studies. It is only relatively recently that criticism has turned its attention to the case studies that inform the "imagined community" idea, especially since Anderson's subsequent theorization in *Specters of Comparison*.[14] The rearticulation provides a ghostly return not just to the meanings of the *Buru Quartet* but also to the entire discourse of nation.

Anderson's acknowledged influences are Victor Turner (on "journeys" of multiple kinds), Eric Auerbach (chiefly from *Mimesis* and the changed historical conditions of early modernity that permit comparatism), and Walter Benjamin (his discourse on Messianic time, in particular, the kind of simultaneity found in what Benjamin calls "homogenous, empty time"). Anderson's criticism includes some short but ingenious examples of literary analysis, chief among them his discussion of José Rizal (the "father" of Filipino nationalism and the celebrated author of *Noli Me Tangere* is invoked directly in the second volume of Pramoedya's tetralogy).[15] Pramoedya is also considered in *Imagined Communities* (more so in the second edition and in greater detail still in *Specters of Comparison*—Anderson has also reviewed Pramoedya's writing and written an introduction to the English translation of *Tales from Djakarta*)[16] but it is his long article, "*Sembah-Sumpah*: The Politics of Language and Javanese Culture" written contemporaneously with *Imagined Communities* that is the most resonant of the effect of reading Pramoedya on Anderson's "Nation" idea.[17] In the introduction to *Language and Power* Anderson recalls how he was piqued to study Javanese and Indonesian literature in detail and in the 1970s began a long correspondence with Pramoedya on the issues that concerned their interrelation: "More broadly, Pramoedya gave me an inkling of how one might fruitfully link the shapes of literature with the political imagination . . . the convergence of all these fortuities came in 1982. . . . I began writing the manuscript that in 1983 was published as *Imagined Communities*" (LP 10).

Pramoedya lived long enough to witness an Indonesian archipelago rocked by national awakening, anticolonial struggle (against the Dutch, a war in which he was a combatant), imperialism (Japanese), the threat of reoccupation (by the Dutch but also with the support of the British), the socialist postcolonialism of Sukarno, the machinations of the Untung coup (September, 1965) followed by a long dictatorship (Suharto's), and the effulgence of democratic institutional reform and of an Indonesia newly-inscribed in the complex discourses of globalization.[18] He had the distinction of being imprisoned and persecuted by multiple camps: by the Dutch (1947–49); by the Sukarno regime (1960, principally for Pramoedya's support of Chinese Indonesians); and most brutally, by Suharto's New Order (who permitted him to watch the burning of his books and manuscripts before packing him off to jail from 1965–79, almost ten years of which he spent on the notorious Indonesian "gulag" island of Buru where torture, beatings, and death remained close at hand). After his return from Buru he remained under city arrest until the fall of Suharto in 1998 and, with a newfound freedom, traveled outside Indonesia in 1999 to promote his memoir, translated as *The Mute's Soliloquy*. If Harris, Farah, and Djebar construct their imagined communities from the exilic outsideness of distance then Pramoedya's exotopy, literal and aesthetic, is simultaneously proximate and marginal, as if his experience of Indonesian space is historically precipitated by juxtapositions of consciousness and detention, by intimacy and exclusion. Farah's lesson on maps includes a commentary on the cartographic scales of modernity that promise education and the fully fledged *Bildung* of national belonging and instead deliver civil war and neocolonial incursions. The *Buru Quartet* is also about *Bildung* but finds Indonesia decentering its prescriptions. Indeed, what is anxiously imagined is mapped by the sharp contrast between Minke's embrace of modernity under Dutch colonialism and the lived reality of its recall from Buru Island. The moment of danger will not permit Pramoedya to engage the present directly and so he remembers it as a past to which it can only problematically correspond. If the nation is composed in "homogenous, empty time" its "meanwhile" is yet radically disjunct.

Although Pramoedya was briefly a purveyor of tobacco, he spent most of his life writing (the later years, as I note in Chapter One, were often marred by a specific form of writer's block). His short stories in particular, because they often draw on Indonesian oral tale conventions, work even better when they are read aloud. In this respect, they remind one of Kamau Brathwaite's understanding of "nation language": an interpellation of a specific linguistic community—in this case, Javanese speakers of Bahasa Indonesia.[19] Pramoedya interrogates traces of Javanese cultural and economic arrogance as well as colonial collaboration. Anderson, steeped in both the cultural and linguistic history of Indonesia, offers a crucial understanding of this position. He argues it is the burden of Javanese culture and traditions that compel Javanese writers like Pramoedya to embrace Bahasa Indonesia, which fulfills a kind of centrifugal function in the life of the nation, yet places them in a veritable "internal exile" (LP 199) vis-à-vis the Javanese elite. Anderson points to the irony in such struggle since the Dutch had clearly encouraged the dissemination of Bahasa Indonesia as a surrogate for its own expanding power in the region (its Malay roots and routes could link the islands in a way that Javanese or Dutch could not). In Pramoedya's case linguistic difference is accentuated by actual "internal exile" so that his exotopy is defiantly involuted: the more he makes Indonesia greater than the aspirations of Javanese, the more he falls victim to the sinuous manifestations of Java's hegemony in the archipelago. The kernel of the essay "*Sembah-Sumpah*" finds this process symptomatic: "In this sense, the whole literary and paraliterary tradition with which the body of this essay deals can be thought of as *karya pulau Buru*, a 'product of Buru'" (LP 199). Buru, the New Order's prison island, is here read as central to the literary struggle that the *Buru Quartet* enacts (the *Quartet* itself sits, ghostlike, in parentheses following this very quote). Suharto's regime consolidated itself through murder (at least one hundred thousand sympathizers or members of the Communist Party of Indonesia, the PKI, were killed) or expulsion (Indonesia had thousands of political detainees, many of whom died in captivity, as Pramoedya records in a gruesome table in *The Mute's Soliloquy*). Significantly, Anderson tracks the connections between language development and specific crises of power that neither the Dutch nor the New Order could adjudicate in constructing Indonesia. The nation is a product of Buru, its "meanwhile": in a stunning metalepsis the *Quartet* is not the nation's effect, a symptom of its being, but stands as its very possibility, the material condition in which it is imagined. While in Bukit Duri prison twenty years earlier Pramoedya discovers a means to interrogate the space between the nation and narration, to allow the creative possibilities in Bahasa Indonesia to flourish against the island inhibitions and prejudices of Javanese. Just as Dutch colonialism had presaged the possibility of a community broader than Java, so even the vernacularization of Javanese could not—because of its feudal, dynastic, generational, and collaborationist proclivities—assume the multifaceted burden of imagining a community greater than itself. In this linguistic struggle Pramoedya finds Bahasa Indonesia a narratological touchstone. Its very appearance is a symptom of the weakening of literary Javanese. Pramoedya's perspicacity is not conjured out of air: it is bound to the materiality of a moment that finds him writing in jail in his twenties of the absurd weight that the dead represent for the living, in the assumed hierarchies that make humans servile and his fellow Javanese prostrate. And for his Javanese audience, the immediate one in the prison and the interpellated one beyond its walls, language is portrayed as a viable means to pry open the deadening reach of time's continuum.

This is only a glimpse of Pramoedya's biography meant to thematize his relationship to nation narration. An impossibility remains because the specificity of Pramoedya's defamiliarization of Javanese through Bahasa

Indonesia trumps the possibility of adequately translating the tetralogy so that, for the most part, the translation relies on periphrasis rather than on a more complex engagement with its linguistic struggle. Only Pheng Cheah has attempted to take these lessons to the *Buru Quartet* as a whole and, with acknowledged translation assistance from Anderson, has provided incisive interpretations of individual passages.[20] Contextual specificity defies translation: what might be apparent to Javanese listeners and readers cannot be made understandable to other interpreters as the text stands. Word for word translation is often rendered opaque because of Pramoedya's sideward glance, a desire to prod the conscience if not the consciousness of those for whom servility has become doxa within Javanese. Bahasa Indonesia is a lingua franca, a means to traverse some three hundred languages in Indonesia, and it is a second language for most Indonesians. Translation efforts are qualified by the fact that Bahasa Indonesia is comparatively young (adopted by the republican movement in 1928, but an official state- sanctioned language only since 1945) and its spelling systems are very much in flux. Whatever is said here of nation formation, it is critically mediated by the specific conundrum of a life and language.

The *Buru Quartet* existed first not as oral stories that Pramoedya told other prisoners on Buru Island before he finally got the chance to inscribe them, but in his sustained engagement in the early 1960s with reclaiming the history of Indonesia's anticolonial nationalism. Indeed, *This Earth of Mankind* (*Bumi manusia* 1980), the first volume of the tetralogy, is dedicated to G. J. Resink, a friend who was crucially involved in the displacement of Dutch historiography in Indonesia. Pramoedya preserves the memory of his research by retelling it as stories that focus on a fictional recreation of the life of Tirto Adi Suryo. Storytelling becomes a mnemonic device for history *in the absence of the printed word* (the actual research was burned with Pramoedya's other manuscripts). If the novel performs modernity's project and if print capitalism is at the heart of nation formation, here we have a classic work of *Bildung* that is yet structured around what novelization is meant to sublate, the spoken word. Small wonder that it questions the ever handy isomorphism of nation and novel. Pramoedya tells a story of Indonesia's history to preserve it orally against the prospect that he, one of Indonesia's most famous writers, would not survive the camp in which he was detained. The importance of the long space is that its time/space is determined to an extent by the moment of colonialism and its effect on the experience of place in the postcolony. The specificity of the form arises from the concrete conditions of its possibility. Anderson notes that "It is the magic of nationalism to turn chance into destiny" (IC 12). Here the magic of the postcolonial nation turns history to ashes, turns memory into storytelling and, by chance, turns those stories to writing that will extend to four volumes not of history, but of novels. Nationalism might well become destiny but meanwhile on Buru Island Pramoedya was more concerned for his immediate fate. The nationalist history was not poured into the form of the novel; rather, the novel was absorbed into these oral stories told to prisoners. Temporal coincidence, as Anderson describes modernity's "meanwhile," is here indissoluble from a moment of danger that is also a struggle over form. "Buru. Spoken 1973. Written 1975." The presumed teleologies of postcoloniality are reconfigured in that space. "Novel" may not be the best way to describe the *Buru Quartet*, a transcription of a memory of historical texts edited by a friend for publication (and here translated).

Because of the details in the *Quartet* one might assume it is a historical novel, but its genealogy is complex. During the 1950s Pramoedya became associated with Sukarno's leftism and in 1958 he became a member of Lekra, the Institute of People's Culture. By 1962 he was the editor of *Lentera*, a weekly supplement to the paper *Bintang Timur*, itself a key organ of socialist nationalism. Pramoedya's tremendous literary and journalistic output during these years was tied to his belief that the writer was not an adjunct to national identification but was a significant agent in its realization. Pramoedya was also an educator and helped to found the Multatuli Literature Academy (named after the nineteenth-century Dutch anticolonial writer, whose *Max Havelaar* is a key influence on Pramoedya—Multatuli is discussed in the third volume of the tetralogy).[21] The didactic quality of many passages in the *Quartet* springs from this belief: literature raises nationalist consciousness and consolidates the cultural life of the postcolony. While one can connect the *Buru Quartet* with the eight novels he wrote during this period, the instinct for seriality in Pramoedya's storytelling comes as much from his journalism and the power of regular publication in Java's public sphere. Thus, if the *Buru Quartet* inherits the wisdom of the collective and an ability for populism from the genre of the historical novel, it is tempered by a cultural vanguardism in which writers do the people's work on behalf of the nation.

There is much controversy about Pramoedya's Lekra years. Clifford Geertz, for instance, describes Pramoedya as "Indonesia's Zhdanov," a cultural commissar who in 1963 led a campaign denouncing a group of writers and painters who dissented from the Lekra line and actively participated in the suppression of their work.[22] Anderson, on the other hand, believes that if you read Pramoedya's pronouncements in *Lentera* during this period (Anderson himself has helped arrange for their indexing and republication) a different picture emerges that, while it does not excuse Pramoedya's activities, demythologizes the authoritarianism he is believed to wield. The controversy was revived in the mid-1990s when Pramoedya received the prestigious Magsaysay Award in the Philippines. In his piece "My Apologies" Pramoedya directly addresses his critics without naming them and flatly denies ordering the suppression of anything.[23] For Geertz, however, the facts are clear: "[I]t is a matter of record that, amid the increasing hysteria of the Party's massive, near-miss surge toward power (*Lekra* alone claimed a half million members), he [Pramoedya] called for 'smashing,' 'crushing,' 'devouring' and 'eliminating' non-communist writers."[24] There is a deeper ideological struggle here that organizes the material of the *Buru Quartet*.

On the one hand, we have Pramoedya reconstructing the historiographic project sundered by the burning of his manuscripts, the act of incarceration, and the prohibition on writing. On the other, we have Pramoedya continuing his nationalist work by undermining the New Order's claims to legitimacy, a situation in which it is better to articulate the past than it is to engage a present that threatens one's immediate survival. Yet neither of these desires coincide to make history, for the *Quartet* is not out to reflect reality but produce one. It answers the stifling cultural criteria of the New Order with literature's capacity for defamiliarization and for deploying what is immanent to reality as an internal distanciation of ruling ideology. It is most assuredly *not* propaganda because however much the tetralogy typifies characters, its formal polemic exists beyond them and it engages with constraints that it cannot write off through arch pronouncements.

In *This Earth of Mankind* Minke begins his notes as an act of mourning and so two themes, self-discovery and romance, are enjoined on the first page. There is also a nod to Multatuli: "Mankind too often claps with only one hand" (BM 1, TEM 15). But then Minke's rationale is immediately up for revision: he claims to have merged the notes, some thirteen years later, with "dreams and imaginings" so that "Of course, the writing became different from the original" (BM 1, TEM 15) and one cannot but think of the materiality of Pramoedya's framing once more, except that in his case the original research itself has been destroyed. With the luxury of his notes—and indeed an available archive of letters, newspapers, court testimony and the like—Minke might make more of versimilitude, but when he talks of "compiling" ("setelah kususun," "after having been compiled by me" BM 62, TEM 74) it is patently subject to dreamy predilections. (Fiction's effect on the archive is a constant theme and functions as an epithet in the tetralogy. In *Child of All Nations*, for instance, Minke reminds the reader, "In this manner, the story was compiled by me" [ASB 38, CAN 47].) Minke's note taking is a mark of his embrace of the modern, his "European training"; it is as if inscription itself trammels the science and technology that fascinated him, as if writing will be the truth of progress (and, one might add, as if he were writing the preamble to *Imagined Communities*: "One of the results of scientific knowledge that continually amazed me was the printing house" [BM 2, TEM 17]). The early pages of *This Earth of Mankind* are full of the wonders of the modern, so full in fact that Minke's cloying earnestness invokes the modern enlightened soul too well, and begs for contravention. Even the title of the novel is a modern awareness signaled in Minke's cosmopolitanism. Minke's story begins in 1898 in Surabaya, a key Java port for Dutch colonialism and its interest in the extraction of spices, and a notable place for modernity since trade routes require all kinds of commercial and cultural infrastructure. This includes the conditions of time, a "temporal coincidence" in homogenous, empty time "measured by clock and calendar": Minke refers to the ascension to the throne of Queen Wilhemina, differentiated only by time zones, "7 September 1898. Friday (Legi in Javanese). This was in the Indies. There in the Netherlands: 6 September 1898, Thursday (Kliwon in Javanese)" (BM 6, TEM 20). Thus, the crowning is celebrated by a "meanwhile" in the colonies.

Minke is a Native, the only one studying in a prestigious Dutch-language school, and much of his self-awareness comes through his understanding of the importance of blood, not just for the Dutch but for the Javanese in particular whose aristocratic genealogies (from which Minke has issued) reach into the contemporary elite. Robert Suurhof introduces him to Annalies, the daughter of a Dutch businessman and his Javanese concubine, (a Nyai) Ontosoroh. As types the stage is set. Will modernity change the inevitabilities of blood and at what cost to identification, not just Minke's, but that of Indonesia itself? A key interest is the figure of Nyai Ontosoroh herself who consistently defies Minke's assumptions while drawing attention to blood's ally in social hierarchy: names (Minke's name alludes to a racist remark by one of his Dutch schoolteachers, Mr. Rooseboom, who means to invoke "monkey" as a rank for his young Javanese student).

The *nyai*'s presence confuses Minke about the protocols that might apply. Nyai Ontosoroh, who wishes to be addressed by that name, speaks Dutch and shakes his hand. What should he do before a Javanese concubine who is "European," and one who is said to run the Boerderiji Buitenzorg, an agricultural company whose name alludes to the first governor-general of the Dutch East Indies? She calls Minke "Sinyo" in acknowledgment of his European education and speculates that he is either the son of a *bupati*, a Javanese aristocrat appointed by the Dutch to run a slice of their colony, or a *patih*, next in line to a *bupati*. Minke is neither but he is flummoxed by the anomalous decorum of the meeting and thus Nyai Ontosoroh suggests that he call her Mama, as if he were her son. He will become her son-in-law but one is struck, once again, by the significance of the adoptive or surrogate mother in the formation of national identification. Johannes Resink claims that Ontosoroh (her name is Sanikem, but Ontosoroh is a Javanese substitute for Buitenzorg [TEM 24]) is the central character of the tetralogy.[25] The case can be made because the didactic quality of many of the exchanges in the quartet are intended to inspire, and in her actions and her words Ontosoroh is just this agent of change. Here the politics of naming underlines the fateful imbrication of two ideologies: Dutch colonial distinction, and a desire on the part of an otherwise effete Javanese elite to maintain a semblance of status by any means necessary. Nyai Ontosoroh is the punctum in this hypostatized image of Dutch colonialism, her ability to run the company and do it well has the aura of utopia about it (pointedly, she employs women workers on the farm). Again, we might write off this proto-revolutionary figure as an idealized anticolonialist, but her example is not just a function of the doubled remembering of Pramoedya and Minke but a redoubt for the storyteller before other prisoners. Did a concubine change her name, her status, her meaning for an Indonesia to emerge as separate from the colonial adventure so that we might languish in jail at the behest of the New Order, whose order is but colonialism's logic, renamed?

The device of writing is the alibi of storytelling within the novel so the reader is presented with a succession of micronarratives, followed by explanation of how they are written up, which is actually the text before us: rewritten (compiled and, as I have suggested, subsequently transcribed and edited). The conceit is apposite for two reasons. First, Minke's Europeanized, forward-looking love of writing will extend beyond composing advertisements and auction copy to inscribing personal experience as the telling of nation. Second, Minke's note taking permits the serial transcription of individual stories, the effects of which constitute the structure of Minke's development. The episodic quality of the tetralogy derives in part from the piling up of these micronarratives that may themselves spring from the exigencies of oral presentation on Buru. In an interview Pramoedya suggests the storytelling on Buru preserved only the outline of his narrative and that, when eventually given the opportunity to write, he poured in the details.[26] The tetralogy continually reproduces the aura of mnemonic seriality in details using Minke's emergent nationalism as its formative outline. Obviously, the articulation of episodic linearity is at the heart of the novel's seasoned plot-giving propensities, and Pramoedya's writing does not escape the anachronistic and the formulaic. Nevertheless, the eventness of orality undermines normative notions of the novel *precisely* when they are required to perform their most form-giving conventions, the suturing of a nation idea. Is this the substance of time in postcoloniality as chronotope?

Pramoedya believes novelization is a solution to death's presence in the prison camp, but it is not an adequate answer to the faculty of memory the stories in the tetralogy embrace. There, time stretches along an axis of intimate finitude; in writing time is bound by a kind of posterity in waiting, not for the writer's end but for a future that comes to it. "Dan bakal kutulis," says Minke, "And I would write about it" (BM 61, TEM 73), and "after compiling," there are the words before us. Minke's focus on the Mellema family is predicated on love, fascination, and understanding the logics of colonialism, but Pramoedya knows that Minke needs more than curiosity to come to terms with the latter and thus, to fight the deleterious effects of his reordering, other characters take up the position of narrator. In *This Earth of Mankind* Nyai Ontosoroh's recollections, impossibly framed by the crisscrossing of time between orality and novelization, Minke and Pramoedya (and the extra dimension provided by the possibility that prisoners on Buru recounted elements of stories that he may have forgotten or misremembered), provide a cutting example of Dutch colonialism but also of the local conventions on which they played. To further complicate the issue of truth in telling, Nyai Ontosoroh's story is revealed first to her daughter Annalies as an explanation of her past and is subsequently related by Annalies to Minke (a necessary narrative conceit because Ontosoroh would have little reason to tell Minke of her background directly). As she tells it, Sanikem had a father who was literate and ambitious and wanted more in life than being a factory clerk. Unfortunately, this meant wanting to be the factory paymaster, hardly a job with wide horizons but one that would provide, he believed, connections and social status. To pave the way Sanikem's father lavished his servility on the Dutch *tuans* (masters), eventually offering Sanikem to one for twenty-five guilders and a promise of promotion. So Sanikem becomes the nyai of Herman Mellema. She learns Mellema's business to the point that she can and does take over much of its daily operations. She reads Dutch newspapers, books, and magazines that arrive each month (Mellema liked to read but he liked to be read to even more). When they had children Mellema was the legal guardian since Dutch law did not recognize Nyai Ontosoroh's parental rights as a Native, but still she counted herself more fortunate than when she was sold by her father. Indeed, she is resolute on one point: "Let all of what's been done be cut off from now" (BM 82, TEM 94), a sentiment not unlike the historiography promulgated by the New Order in Pramoedya's present on Buru Island. Much of Nyai Ontosoroh's story comes down to legitimacy, particularly when Maurits Mellema arrives in Java (he is Herman's son from his Dutch marriage). Whatever Ontosoroh has done for Herman, Maurits had more rights as a legal offspring. The tone is melodramatic but the basic point is polemical: the dubious ethical base of Dutch colonial practices cannot be overcome by accepting their presence as legitimate.

Family legitimacy is not the same as national legitimacy, but nevertheless Minke struggles to correlate these themes when the social outlaws in the narrative emerge as the legitimate voices of nationalist yearning. Minke could take Annalies's version of Nyai Ontosoroh's monologue and make a short story of it but instead he writes one from his own imaginings, publishing it in Dutch in the *Surabaya Daily News* under the none-too-subtle pseudonym "Max Tovelaar." Thus, to the legitimacy of blood we must add the legitimacy of narration which, because it is about the right of inscription (the story is "compiled" by Pramoedya without the right to write) acts as a bridge between the story's micro- and macrological concerns. Sonality invokes the storyteller without translation; legitimacy conveys the imagined community as always already translated, "Buru. Spoken 1973. Written 1975." Significantly, on reading Minke's tale, Nyai Ontosoroh tells him to read more Malay. Minke is dumbfounded: "What did she know about the world of narrative? Moreover, why did she like to read stories and try to interfere in the affairs of the writers' imaginary characters, even the language that they used . . . ?" (BM 97, TEM 110); or "I felt her views were attacking my rights as a storyteller" (BM 98, TEM 112). This is the naivete of the hero of a *Bildungsroman* who will lose his innocence to the wisdom of humanity. But Minke is no Wilhelm Meister because the historical rupture informing postcoloniality does not issue from the same point of address as the crisis of revolutionary Enlightenment in Europe. Minke's comment "At the beginning of growth . . . everyone copies" (BM 101, TEM 114) is meant to be ironic. The fact of asynchronicity is not simply an acknowledgment of multiple Enlightenments but is a structural disjuncture in the manner that stories can be told.

"This earth of mankind" (bumi manusia) is Minke's refrain and marks his worldliness. It is the ground upon which national belonging emerges: a centrifugal openness to the other that overcomes insularity or what Pramoedya will often refer to as *kampung*, the parochial. All of Minke's cosmopolitan skills, his notetaking about international affairs, his newspaper, magazine, and book reading, his awe before the juggernaut of technological advances—all of this prescient simultaneity bears on the "meanwhile" of the Dutch East Indies. The nation predicates a destiny, one that in fact describes a metalepsis in nation narration (the nation must invent one as its cause), but in the first volume of the tetralogy Minke's thoughts are about a substitution of a different kind. Instead of conjuring indigenous destiny he ponders colonial exchange: "Why wasn't England in charge of all this? Why the Netherlands? And Japan? How about Japan?" (BM 106, TEM 119). England rushed in to "manage" the colony at the end of the Second World War after Japan was defeated. Among the culturally specific references that Pramoedya builds into the tetralogy the most obvious is the stretching of Indonesia's "meanwhile" to include not only the coincidences of Minke's pronouncements but a long space that begins paradoxically from displacement, from an internal exile that is also about this earth of mankind. Minke, and to some extent Pramoedya, may reorder the narrative with suitable imaginings to produce the linear plod of the modern and its arrow of time, but the "meanwhile" of modernity takes a somewhat more circuitous route in Indonesia's nation formation so its place in the world describes a "meanwhile" as interregnum, as suspension of conventions about the grammar of nations.

The central action of the first volume is dominated by Minke's refrain, a repetition through which he hopes to persuade himself—or Pramoedya his readers—that the consciousness of "this earth of mankind" cannot be stopped. Yet the assertion registers an ambivalence because it represents a thesis that Minke's experience necessarily contradicts. His parents remind him nobility is nobility no matter how circumscribed by Dutch power but Minke's refrain is invoked like a mantra or a talisman to protect him, ironically, from the vagaries of aristocratic convention: "Flog me with your whip, king, you who do not know how science and knowledge opened a new round on this earth of mankind!"; "The world of *priyayi* was not my world. My world was not about position, rank, pay and deceit. My world was the problems of this earth of mankind" (BM 110–11, TEM 124–25). Just as Nyai Ontosoroh breaks from the feudal practices of her parents ("You should not follow your feelings. Our world is about profit and loss" [BM 77, TEM 90]), so Minke must disavow his family as something that would otherwise block modernity's flourish in East Indies' history. Yet, it is not his parents who constitute the impediment to the realization of nation but persistence in general (and thus the paradox of the long space) that includes and does not simply suspend the storyteller's art. And this is the pathos too of Pramoedya, meanwhile on Buru.

There are other characters who, like Nyai Ontosoroh, measure both the prospect of change and the obdurate stasis that colonialism also reveals. Minke's teacher, Magda Peters, is spurred to confront what we might otherwise call "real relations" and pointedly so in light of reading one of Minke's stories. (In a deft touch, Minke notes that the title had been changed and that the editor had made textual alterations with which he disagreed, as if Minke's "compiling," and Pramoedya's, and indeed the work of Pramoedya's lifelong editor Yusuf Isak, did not also participate in this art.) Peters asks her class to critique the story and Robert Suurhof,

Minke's classmate and competitor for Annalies's affections, blasts the tale as a product of delirium. Because the story is based on Minke's notes about the Mellema family, Robert knows who the author is and proceeds to berate him (in Dutch via Malay): "The person, Miss," Suurhof continued, "is not even an Indo. He is lower than an Indo unacknowledged by his father. The person is an Inlander, a Native [pribumi] who has smuggled himself through the cracks in European civilization" (BM 193–94, TEM 213). When Minke is revealed as the author, Peters defends him because it allows her to challenge the Orientalist assumptions of Suurhof and the rest of the class. The confrontation is overly contrived, as is Peters's later melodramatic embrace of Minke ("And she kissed me until I was breathless. Breathless!" [BM 197, TEM 217]), but Pramoedya is seeking a way to link Minke's development to Dutch sympathizers like Peters, whose understanding of colonialism, including the collaborationist agenda of "association" theory, is drawn to indigenous people who challenge its prescriptions. After meeting Nyai Ontosoroh, Peters comments, "If there were just a thousand Natives like her in these Indies, these Dutch Indies, Minke, these Dutch Indies might yet close down" (BM 210, TEM 233). This is Pramoedya using the art of memory to address the present from a future signaled in Indonesia's possibility in the past.

Minke's pronouncements evoke the nationalist aspirations of Java's urban intelligentsia, an educated stratum caught between aristocratic tradition and capitalist modernization. Nyai Ontosoroh is self-educated, and if opposing colonialism is an imperative, it sometimes seems that it extends only to the point where like-minded Javanese businesspeople can assume ownership of the means of production and right the wrongs of the Dutch using indigenous wage oppression. As a member of the celebrated Generation of '45 Pramoedya understands the political force of cultural workers and intellectuals, yet as we have noted he himself has been accused of suppressing the very same constituency.

The form of the tetralogy appears in the commingling of novelistic genres, and by including letters in the story Prameodya conveys ideas in dispute without reducing the main narrative to panoptic railing. The story is not beyond soap opera (a genre of seriality) and melodrama, which peaks in *This Earth of Mankind* around the murder of Herman Mellema. He is poisoned by a pimp, Ah Tjong (Zhong), possibly in cahoots with Mellema's son, Robert, and a seedy character called Fatty (Jan Tantang). No reader cares about Herman enough to worry about who killed him but it does allow for a trial in which the issues of property, propinquity, and legitimacy are debated. Minke has to defend himself for reporting on the misguided rumors and racist assumptions that precede the trial, and Nyai Ontosoroh too, speaking in Dutch, bravely fends off the condescension of the court. The plot emphasizes that no matter what the humanitarian principles of the Dutch, colonial law is fatally compromised by prejudice in advance of judgment. As Mr. de La Croix puts it earlier, "Europeans cannot do anything to help them [the Javanese]. It is the Natives themselves who must begin to do this" (BM 133, TEM 148).

Minke's desire to compile and arrange this awakening is analogous to Pramoedya's attempt to bring together multiple narratives into a recognizable whole. If the orality in the prison allows the story to be told in "outline," then the transciption of Minke's tale in detail encourages sequence as itself a mnemonic device. Time and again Minke's compositional logic allows for Pramoedya's writerly reassemblage: for instance, "So that this story of mine is somewhat orderly [chronological]" (BM 140, TEM 157); and "Because I also give priority to the order of time" (BM 151, TEM 169). This is a formal constraint born of emergency in which Pramoedya seizes hold of memory, in Benjaminian fashion, to cut the continuum inscribed in colonialism's project.[27] The author wants to dialectically resolve sequence with the explosive force of *Jetztzeit*, a present that erupts from the "meanwhile" of Buru; but since the synthesis that would make nation exists as a narrative condition returning from the future, the collocation of Minke's notes, letters, reportage, court testimony, interviews, and conversations bears the impossible weight of formal disruption. One cannot fault Minke for his enthusiasm: "To socialize openly with all my friends. To be free [Bebas]. To get new, limitless knowledge. And: to take in everything from this earth of mankind, from the past, present and future" (BM 170, TEM 188–89). Yet the tension in the narrative exists between accumulation and duration, and the now that scintillates in the latter works to disorder the sequence privileged by the former. Here the tetralogy is a thesis novel in which its time and space are themselves more didactic than the radical rhetoric the text foregrounds.[28] But if its chronotope is its polemical key, why is the text divided as such? Why four volumes, not one, and so forth?

Not much is made of the breaks in Pramoedya's *Quartet*, except perhaps for the one between volumes three and four when the narrative voice switches from Minke to Pangemanann, the Native intelligence officer working for the Dutch. Indeed, if the first three volumes offer Minke's story of nationalist awakening then the final volume is a bleak counterpoint, suggesting a correspondence between the Dutch culture of colonial surveillance and the New Order's control of Pramocdya and his fellow prisoners. The division, while structurally critical, is unwieldy in practice: a two-volume publication would make the latter seem like an epilogue (which may not be far from the truth) but would push it beyond Minke's recollections. Another argument for a two-volume work would place the division between volumes two and three, whose separation works both at the level of plot and the publishing history of the tetralogy. Although we are told the entire tetralogy was written at a feverish pace in 1975, the first two volumes appeared in 1980—the year after Pramoedya's release, and the final two volumes in 1985 and 1988, respectively. The writing emergency changes dramatically, not least because of the ban that was placed on the first two volumes in 1981. Does new prohibition turn transcription into revision? Even under city arrest, the availability of an archive beyond the oral on Buru provided Pramoedya with means to shape the long space of his imagined community, especially his day-to-day observations of New Order practices in the 1980s and the influence of his other reading during the period. Interestingly, the first British and Australian editions of volumes one and two were published together as *Awakenings* (1982). If the narrative was conceived as a tetralogy Penguin hedged its bets on whether the whole would actually appear. In his interview with Chris GoGwilt, Pramoedya says only: "It is not my title, but I don't mind Penguin using it. That's their business; and, in marketing the book, presumably there is a reason for the title."[29] While Max Lane, the quartet's English translator, offers little in the way of explanation for the division in volumes, he nevertheless reminds the reader that Minke claims to have written the novels *This Earth of Mankind* and *Child of All Nations* while in Surabaya before going to school in Batavia (now Jakarta). The third volume, *Footsteps*, is then offered as a "new beginning" detailing Minke's more intimate involvement in nationalism. If *Awakenings* cleaves much closer to a conventional sense of *Bildungsroman*, then the third volume finds Minke a more active presence in the historical texture of Indonesia's possibility. This "new beginning" is vital, particularly since volume three is published in the same year as Pramoedya's nonfiction work on Tirto Adi Suryo, *Sang Pemula* ("The Pioneer," "The Beginner," or "The Originator") which is both a biography and an arrangement of resource documents on the man who provides the historical basis for Minke. In an essay on *Sang Pemula*, Takashi Shiraishi suggests that Pramoedya's long introduction to the book "place[s] the documents in a proper historical context," an ordering that Minke (and Tirto perhaps) would have appreciated, and one wonders whether the tome is not just a supplement to the memorization on Buru Island but is immanent to a text that is published contemporaneously?[30] One lesson is clear: in theorizing a tetralogy one must come to terms with the formal projection in relation to the exigencies of publication. This is necessarily part of any extended narrative since serialization permits publication while the work is still in progress but it has specific importance for understanding Pramoedya's achievement, which is not only about writing from memory in conditions of extreme hardship, but is about the nation as simultaneously sequentially narrated and retrospectively created either side of the event of decolonization (that itself is ongoing in *both* directions).

This Earth of Mankind ends as it begins, in *media res*, in the midst of mourning. Just after graduation Minke marries Annalies but it is not long before Dutch law, with the help of the unscrupulous Maurits Mellema, intervenes. Maurits, as the "Pure Blood" heir of his father's estate, is awarded two-thirds of it. In addition, he applies for guardianship of Annalies who is legally recognized as Herman's daughter and, according to Dutch law, is underage and unmarried (because Minke is a Native). Maurits wins a decision to bring Annalies to the Netherlands to complete her education and neither Minke nor Nyai Ontosoroh are allowed to follow. Annalies sinks into a deep depression and no amount of writing or storytelling by Minke can prevent her being taken away. The volume ends with Minke admitting defeat but Nyai Ontosoroh adding that at least they fought back honorably. This is the ending of a novel in series, a novel that brings the action to a crisis but does not attempt to resolve it through traditional denouement. Will Minke get his beloved Annalies back? Just as important, the thesis of the novel, bound as it is to Minke's consciousness of Native identification, is underdeveloped. Education and events have clearly shaped Minke's worldview but it is unclear if he will turn such consciousness into a complex anticolonial discourse. This, in turn, underlines the force of the novel's most pressing unfinished business, the persistence of Dutch colonialism itself. The reader is left with a tale in need of resumption, one that *Child of All Nations* immediately supplies: "Annalies has sailed" (ASB 1, CAN 13).

There is an obviousness to the division between volumes one and two, marking a break between Minke's innocence and experience, his warm embrace of developments in science and technology that modernity confers interrupted by the machinations of colonialism that accompany it. It is ambiguous, however, whether the decision to divide the text was based on its whole or on the peculiarities of serialization: to get a portion of the manuscript out while another was being prepared, or to make each part manageable in itself yet complementary. When the novels were released in 1980 they enjoyed immediate success, and Indonesian readers welcomed the return of one of their foremost writers. That they were banned the year after for promoting Marxist-Leninism and communism was a clumsy way of connecting them to Sukarno rather than referring to the actual content of the texts. Branding the two volumes in this manner turned them into *samizdat* literature irrespective of whether Indonesian readers sought a sympathetic ear for Marxism. Not surprisingly, identifying the texts as surreptitious promoted the search for precisely this quality and encouraged readings that would pitch Pramoedya's memory against the official discourse of amnesia dear to Suharto's New Order. There are certainly elements of socialist thinking in these books both because socialism plays a part in the emergence of nationalism in the archipelago and because Pramoedya's main idea in novelization is *not* a chronicle but the articulation of a kind of socialist answerability.

Child of All Nations maintains Minke's structural vision of reordering notes into narrative while promising an openness to the future: "People say that what is in front of humanity is only distance. And its limit is the horizon. As one crosses this distance the horizon moves away" (ASB 1, CAN 13–14). Yet this horizon also stands in the past because the truth of memory cannot make time and space synonyms of progression. What Minke fights as a future conditional, Pramoedya narrates as a subjunctive past; but both question official mythology, whether colonial or postcolonial, and this is symptomatic of the tetralogy's dynamism. Minke himself juxtaposes "horizons" between two competing discourses, one which refers to a Javanese god Batara Kala, the other to what the Dutch call the "Teeth of Time." This onward march reduces all to nothing, and in that nothingness rebirth becomes possible, according to Minke.

The removal of Annalies to the Netherlands inspires Minke to new levels of activism against the injustices of Dutch order (order and ordering, or compiling as we have suggested, link the archipelago's history at the beginning of the twentieth century to the [New] Order and ordering at its end). Panji Darman, a Native and classmate, accompanies Annalies to Europe and his letters (presented by Minke: "They are in sequence according to the date written" [ASB 19, CAN 29]) reveal both the protests at her departure and the circumstances of her arrival in Amsterdam. Annalies's health worsens and before long the same cables that Minke extols in the first volume bring him a telegram announcing her death. Colonial law kills Annalies and Minke's revenge is to seek and exploit its contradictions. Thus his mourning (announced in the first page of the tetralogy) is marked by reading (as Pheng Cheah astutely comments, many scenes in the quartet are "events of reading"), and the more Minke reads the more he understands the eventness of his own being.[31] The narrative foregrounds eventness as the process of being, not only in postcolonial identification but in the long space, the logic of form in its inscription. The writing is coded according to memory and provides a unity to eventness that cannot be adjudicated by writing *sui generis*. We might think of Minke's obsessive compiling as a version of Pramoedya's relationship to memory that struggles to shape the past before it, and its storyteller, are extinguished. On the work of memory Paul Ricoeur notes:

It is as though recollection inverted the so-called natural order of time. By reading the end in the beginning and the beginning in the end, we learn also to read time itself backward, as the recapitulating of the initial condition of a course of action in its terminal consequences. In this way, a plot establishes human action not only within time . . . but within memory. Memory, accordingly, *repeats* the course of events according to an order that is the counterpart of time as "stretching along" between a beginning and an end.[32]

Minke wonders, "I truly don't know if the beginning of my notes is exact. In any case, everything must have a beginning. And this is the earliest of my notes" (ASB 2, CAN 14). His reading brings meaning to the "beginning" he begins again, this time tempered by a desire to use the eventness of his being to struggle against the inevitability fostered by Dutch colonialism.

The tone of the second volume changes significantly from the charming enthusiasm that Minke applies to his learning in *This Earth of Mankind*. In part this follows the teleological leanings of *Bildung* development, but it also measures a fateful correspondence between Minke's personal misfortune and an intensification of sociopolitical crisis. Chapter Three begins, for instance, with a précis of observations on changing geopolitics in Asia that is as much a tribute to Pramoedya's historicism as Minke's thin rationalization, "Perhaps in all of the Indies I am the only Native who has notes like these. [Is anyone else interested in other nations?]" (ASB 40, CAN 49). Minke remarks on a correlation between the ascendancy of Japan, particularly in its incursions into China, and the fact that the Dutch elevated the status of Japanese in the East Indies to that of the Dutch themselves (Indies State Decision No. 202). The Dutch sought to preserve their colony against Japanese predations while remaining neutral on Japanese imperial adventures elsewhere. The wonders of hindsight are not lost on such passages, but they indicate a trajectory in which the past meets the future and these ironies render the political themes of the tetralogy substantial.

Minke consolidates his worldview by using the comments of friends and associates in his notes as a sounding board. Thus we get the opinions of Jean Marais, Minke's old landlord, Telinga, and the journalist Maarten Nijman in quick succession, with their positions suggesting historical movements in Asia were concretely refracted through Natives and that neither they nor the Dutch could avoid these currents. Minke mingles "other voices" into these statements and we hear Pramoedya too saying, "Ah, can we forget the Chinese War, 1741–1743, that removed the control of the Dutch East Indies Company along the north Javanese coast?" (ASB 43, CAN 52). The storytelling mode takes Pramoedya's skill in oral traditions and integrates it into the novel via individual characters recounting their tales (mediated by Minke's notes as well as other go-betweens in the telling). The historiographic passages do not follow this logic, however; they are the charred remains of Pramoedya's research burned at the time of his arrest in 1965 that construct the tetralogy from stories of characters spoken to his fellow prisoners, even as this is displaced onto Minke's powers of assembly.

What is an appropriate language of resistance? Minke has published his articles in Dutch which, while directly addressing the colonizer, has a more circumscribed effect on Native readers. The majority of these would be educated and/or part of the Dutch colonial elite, but there is much discussion over whether anticolonialism might best be served by writing in Javanese, or even English. Minke's friend, Nijman, suggests the latter in order to gain access to the publishing world of Singapore and Hong Kong. In the meantime he arranges an interview, in English, with

Khouw Ah Soe, a Chinese nationalist who wants to unseat the Ching Dynasty and make China a republic. Like Minke, this desire is framed in terms of a modernity pitched against aristocracy: "True, but that was when the Older Generation was the Younger Generation. Now it is the modern epoch. Any country and people that cannot absorb European strength and rise up by using it will be devoured by Europe" (ASB 59–60, CAN 68). Part of the inspiration comes from the Japanese (and it appears Khouw Ah Soe has studied in Japan even if he does not admit it), although they will maintain the monarchy through modernization and, again with hindsight, their tactic to prevent being "swallowed up" would become imperialism. But there is a quaint irony to this scene of a Dutch-speaking Javanese noting the English conversation of a Chinese nationalist for publication in a Dutch colonial paper. Of course, Anderson's point about the power of print culture includes translation between languages, which is intrinsic to circulation in modernity. There is also the question of editing since, to Minke's dismay, his notes are turned into an antirepublican outburst that places Khouw Ah Soe's security in jeopardy. The appropriateness of language is overdetermined by other ideological considerations and Minke is left to wonder again about his Europeanness. Nyai Ontosoroh, who still refers to Minke as "Child" (the child in the volume's title) says this is his weakness: "You have just one shortfall. You do not know yet what colonial means" (ASB 76, CAN 83).

Minke's continuing education proceeds by Khouw Ah Soe providing the function of a talking book or pamphlet. I do not find these passages as forced as some commentators because they have a history not just within Indonesian letters but within the subgenres of the novel. Social problem novelists like Disraeli, Gaskell, Eliot, or Dickens are not derided in English literary history for placing a soap box or two within their narratives. In Pramoedya's case there is a conscious attempt to render each pronouncement critical to Minke's ongoing engagement with existence. Much of the politics is bound to form: the nation narrative demands this content to substantiate its historicity, the time/space of its genesis (on this level, at least, Farah, Djebar, and Pramoedya are nation narrators, while Harris is not). Pointedly, Khouw Ah Soe tells Minke of the experience of the Philippines, which had sought to found Asia's first republic but was thwarted by the geopolitical struggles of Spain and the United States. Minke is maddened by his ignorance of Filipino nationalism, but connects this to the absence of reporting on the fight and the generally obsequious nature of East Indians under colonial rule: "With my inner eyes I spread my sight around me. There was complete stillness. They [the Javanese] were fast asleep in dreams. And I myself was confused, furious, aware of my powerlessness . . . " (ASB 76, CAN 93).

The melodramatic subplot that follows the travails of Minke's adopted family provides relief from didacticism, but Pramoedya often blends these two elements so a fictional representation of a historical figure (Minke for Tirto) is never extracted from the maelstrom of the time. As Razif Bahari points out, Pramoedya's interest in the history covered by Tirto's life is not revisited to get the history right, but to bolster the thesis that Indonesians in the present must come to grips with their participation in Indonesian becoming. (Ironically, as Miriam points out to Minke in a letter, the archive of that eventness is detailed elsewhere, in the colonial collections of the Netherlands.)[33] The sources may be different but they are not opposed in Pramoedya's long space. Thus, as Minke pastes in letters to the novelization of his development, it is not history that is authorized but the subject's participation in its formation, then *and* now.

Raden Adjeng Kartini is as inspirational for Prameodya as Tirto; indeed, prior to his arrest Pramoedya had already published two volumes on the life of this Western-educated Javanese nationalist and feminist (the manuscripts of the final two volumes were destroyed by the New Order, as were a collection of her works that he had edited and a draft of a book on women's lives before Kartini). So much of Pramoedya's writing pivots on the plight of Javanese women because of his reading of Kartini and, if she is not a central figure in the tetralogy, she remains a significant presence in the kind of consciousness conveyed by Nyai Ontosoroh.[34] Certainly there is a feminist strain in the *Quartet* that works against the often brutal excesses of patriarchy and masculinism, and its nationalism is fed by opposition to what is portrayed as feudal thinking. As postcolonial history shows, however, the promises of nationalism leave much unfinished business in the wake of independence, and this often includes the liberation of women.

The theme of language is never separated from the politics of recollection; how Pramoedya inscribes memory is precisely linked to Minke's discovery of Malay's utility. He is encouraged by Kommer who, like Minke/Tirto, is a journalist and novelist.[35] It is not necessary to agree with the polemic advanced in Minke's exchanges with Kommer to appreciate how it might alter Minke's perspective on the role of language in national identification. Writing in one's own language begs the philosophical issues that bear on writing and the "ownership" of language, questions that are acute in postcolonialism not just because of the imposition of language afforded by colonial invasion but because the geopolitical borders of the colonial state often cover or smother a stark multiplicity of languages (to hold this difference in check the Dutch maintained some 280 native states in the region from precolonial days—as long as their leaders observed Dutch hegemony). We have already mentioned the deployment of Malay as a lingua franca but the extent to which this can be one's own is questionable, even if the philosophical problems are set aside. Minke notes: "What can be written in Malay? A poor language like that? A patchwork of words from all nations [semua bangsa] around the world?" (ASB 102, CAN 109). The plot in *Child of All Nations* keeps folding back into the appropriateness of language and means Minke must supplement his proficiency in Dutch, the kind of supplement that brings unisonality to crisis when a nation language assumes itself as undivided and indivisible.

At the center of *Child of All Nations* are two tales symptomatic of the form-giving of storytelling and are critical to Minke's developing political voice. The first is about Surati, and is by now a familiar one of the young girl whose father wants to ingratiate himself with the colonizer by selling her to a *tuan*. The father is Paiman or Sastro Kassier, Nyai Onto-soroh's brother, who wants to follow in the grand tradition of Sastrotomo by trading Surati to the new *Tuan Besar Kuasa* factory manager, Mijnheer Frits Homerus Vlekkenbaaij, affectionately known as *Plikemboh*, or "Ugly Penis"! As always, Minke prefaces his story with his version of "Once upon a time": "These were the notes I made about Surati's experiences, overseen, improved and supplemented by me" (ASB 125, CAN 131). The story includes Minke's emerging talent for internal polemic so that the social problem addressed carries with it a general critique of the plight of the colonized. This is what will link it to the second story, but with an important twist. The sugar mill in Tulangan is the economic engine of the town and a symbol of its obeisance to Dutch authority. As paymaster, Sastro Kassier only added to the immiseration of the workers by taking a cut of their pay for himself and his coconspirators, the foremen. When Plikemboh asks for his virgin daughter, Sastro Kassier resists at first but in the end decides that Plikemboh is a European and his power must be respected. Unfortunately, he tarries too long and Plikemboh plots to have Sastro Kassier accused of stealing wages. Cornered, Sastro Kassier signs an agreement to hand over his daughter. The point of the story is not the specter of concubinage but Surati's novel resistance to it. On her way to Plikemboh she takes a fifteen-mile detour to a village quarantined by the Dutch army because of smallpox. She would rather die from smallpox than suffer the indignities of Plikemboh. Surati's journey to the village on a moonlit night features some of the most lyrical passages in the entire tetralogy. It is as if Minke's burgeoning humanism and Surati's quiet determination fuse to illuminate her difficult decision.

Surati is in the village for three days, long enough to contract the disease, but then she leaves because she wants to use her death to ensure Plikemboh's. Surati travels on to Tulangan and presents herself to Plikemboh who sates his desire for the virgin but succumbs to smallpox a few days later. It is an extraordinary sequence because it combines the agency of a young woman otherwise denied it with a storyteller's art for measured detail and revelation. Tulangan itself becomes "infected" with Surati's agency and colonialism appears miraculously suspended: "The sugar cane fields were no longer maintained. The steam powered electricity plant was mute. The factory whistle was silent. Tulangan was in darkness. The chimneys lost their glory, peering over Tulangan as though curious about what was happening, then nodding sadly for no eyes were willing to gaze back at them" (ASB 151, CAN 156). Except for the eyes of the storyteller who marvels at this caesura. In a final flourish Surati survives and so does the sugar mill: "An important sugar mill may not be destroyed by smallpox. Capital must continue to develop and grow. But people may die" (ASB 151, CAN 156). Thus, "And the sugar factory of Tulangan remained grand as it supervised and governed all of Tulangan: humans, animals and plants" (ASB 152, CAN 157). Minke weighs the glory of modernity against the oppression it confers. A romantic plea against the domination of technology over nature is discernible but the young nationalist also imagines a less destructive synergy between the two. It is a classic petty bourgeois antimony Minke hopes that nationalist autonomy can avoid. The story of modernity's meaning for postcolonial liberation is precisely drawn by this antimony, which is not evident in Minke's narration but in Pramoedya's memory of the twentieth century.

The second story is deftly tied to the first by having Minke tread the same path as Surati in the environs of Tulangan, among the sugar cane fields, "Making Java become the second biggest nation in world sugar production" (ASB 154, CAN 160). Minke is obsessed with modernity but, piqued by friends' criticism of his language and abstractions, he wants to learn from the countryside. Pramoedya knows the land and the peasantry from experience, and the tension in the tale is measured between Pramoedya's understanding and Minke's discovery. Minke meets a farmer who eyes him with suspicion as a *priyayi* from the mill. Minke is initially disturbed by his roughness then by his insolence in switching from low to high Javanese (honorifics are meant to maintain social hierarchy), yet he is determined to "know his people." What he learns is that the peasant, Trunodongso, is being exploited by the sugar cane factory. He is underpaid for the use of his land and what remains barely provides subsistence for himself and his family. The mill owners cut off water supplies for the paddy fields, which prepares them for sugar cane cultivation, but they also ensure the peasants do not make extra money from sugar cane by digging up the roots once the contract for the land expires. Minke is reminded once more the colonizer has learned of the peasants in a way he has not; yet on this occasion he pushes his assumptions on education further, seeing his cosmopolitanism as a form of universalism derived from modernity (that may or may not be a wolf in this interpretation but certainly owes its mythology to Romulus and Remus):

I have been suckled from the breasts of this modern time: from the Natives themselves, from Japan, China, America, India, Arabia, from all peoples of this earth. They were the mother wolves that supported me as a builder of Rome! Is it true you will build a Rome? Yes, I replied to myself. How will it happen? I did not know. In humility I acknowledged: I was the child of all nations, of all epochs, past and present. Place and time of birth, parents, all are just by chance, something entirely not sacred. (ASB 125, CAN 169)

The production of a desacralized Everyman is certainly one idealism provided by modernity but few can match Minke here in the power of his attachment to it. There is a common denominator in nation building, and Minke believes its essence is not only transnational but transhistorical. The primal scene of peasant identification, then, concretizes what were previously formal abstractions and technocentric blather. The cause of the local becomes a means to express the global, linking the Netherlands to the East Indies. One still feels Pramoedya chiding Minke for his naivete and aristocratic snobbery; however, his experience, and the story of Surati, mark a new engagement with colonialism: "All who have fallen, I began my story regarding Trunodongso, have been accommodated, awakened and restored by farmers" (ASB 187, CAN 190).

The stories of Trunodongso and Nyai Surati represent Minke's first attempt to integrate the social protest of his reportage with fiction's eye on the real. While Nyai Ontosoroh continues to prod with her insights ("Isn't existence itself more real than people's opinions about reality?" [ASB 176, CAN 180]) and Kommer presses the issue of using Malay, Minke is exploring a new rhetoric. If this proves the efficacy of print culture in modernity's sway, its politics of discourse is more about Pramoedya's historiography. Memory fabricates an archive, and this one must be made Indonesian over and against the rigorous historiography made in the name of Dutch colonization or the conveniently forgetful compulsions of the New Order. Here the use of storytelling, relatively autonomous tales rendered in sequence—"overseen, improved and supplemented"—constitutes the plotting of the long space, extension in what J. M. Bernstein in *The Philosophy of the Novel* calls "the double time of narrative."[36] Memory derives a purpose to action confirmed by plotting but this retrospection cannot fully account for action as multilayered in time, the simultaneous hither and thither that does not follow a consequence desired in the ordering of memory. Bernstein uses the *Odyssey* as an example of a narrative repeating what occurs in memory. Memory provides a sequence but as an infinite series structured more or less by chance. Bernstein suggests that "a recollection may be the very process by which the present comes to self-identity, so that the recollecting is the recognition and recovery of lost (forgotten) potentialities whose narrative relating is (the condition for) their realization" (PN 134). This is the realm of Proust but also the Messianic memory of Benjamin, to which we have already alluded. The stretching of time is its doubling so Minke's storytelling series questions the present that recalls it. The memory that ties Minke to Pramoedya (and Tirto) underlines a double time of narrative that wants historicity to live even in the absence of its teller. Not only does this explain Minke's eventual disappearance, but also the precarious position of Pramoedya's remembering. Minke learns Malay to establish an "intimacy" with facts not given in Dutch. The paradox of the accuracy of Dutch facts on the East Indies is not their falsity but that they are not proximate. The value of experience is overdetermined by the relative forces of language (literacy, circulation, state authority) that may find Malay strategically advantageous in some contexts but not in others. In a novel written in Bahasa Indonesia, the Chinese nationalist, Khouw Ah Soe, sends a letter to Nyai Ontosoroh in English so that Minke may translate it into Dutch for his Javanese "Mama." He also sends one to Minke, and there is a third letter, in Chinese, that remains untranslated. Does Javanese here guarantee a truth in mediating or not the others? If so, it has to work double time. The plot in *Child of All Nations* also has to work double time as the narrative struggles to make Minke's consciousness evolve through other characters' accounts. This is most effective in the interaction of Minke with Nyai Ontosoroh, Mama, who counters his idealism with world-weary understanding. It is a symbiotic relationship, however, that reveals how Minke's storytelling jogs Ontosoroh into reading her own complicity in the exploitation of peasant farmers. She vows to pay back the farmers ("The figure was the same amount of capital we used to begin our enterprise" [ASB 224, CAN 225]) and build schools to teach them Dutch and arithmetic, as if this will quickly undo a systemic logic. What she sees as the languages of modernity do not convey neutral knowledge and, while her gesture offers communist redistribution, the "tragedy of living" as she calls it includes the possibility that education about exploitation can become education in exploitation.

Even without the publication of Trunodongso's story, the socioeconomic contradictions described in working the land drive the narrative, fighting back the inertia of colonial quietude: "Evidently the book could still not be closed. One event after another kept trailing us" (ASB 226, CAN 227). What appears as adventure time is displaced by the chronotope of postcoloniality which, in recalling its promise, limits its eventness by concretizing historicity.[37] You cannot have as many hours and days as you want: you may not even have pens or paper to record them. As Pramoedya remembers, then writes, he frames a dialogical relationship with his protagonist. The importance of Tirto is greater in his representation *as* Minke than what is extant in the historical record precisely because of his function as fiction in producing the long space (*Sang Pemula* is itself structured around this acknowledgment). Pramoedya both interprets Tirto and interpellates him, hails him as an ideological ward who might stave off amnesia about the early nationalist struggles against the Dutch *and* the inevitability of the death of writing on Buru. Yet Tirto as Minke remains necessarily incomplete: he forms a constitutive outside speaking back to Pramoedya across the space of history. The sharp contingency of telling must be engaged as an active presence in the now that permits a future conditional to be imagined. One of the misinterpretations of Anderson's thesis is that "imagined" is conceived as a completed action in the present but the nation is shot through with futurity: it will have been imagined. Minke notes, "Trunodongso, I have failed badly in this. Another time you will be one of my characters—you, who does not know about the modern age" (ASB 234, CAN 235). And there again is the story before us, but the condition of erasure in Minke's composition *persists* at the moment of recollection because there is no guarantee on Buru that the character who has become, will not become a destroyed story.

Minke leaves Surabaya to continue his education at Betawi and to remain safe. On the boat Minke meets Ter Haar, a former subeditor of *Soerabaiaasch Nieuws*, the colonial paper to which he has previously contributed. Not surprisingly Minke is treated to a monologue on Dutch colonialism that "became increasingly like a pamphlet" (ASB 260, CAN 259):

Didn't you, Tuan, use the name of Max Tollenaar to invoke the work of Multatuli, Max Havelaar? From that people would know that Tuan is the spiritual child of Multatuli. Your humanity is strong. Nonetheless, humanity without personal knowledge of life in the Indies could be a lost cause. What is called the modern era, Mr. Tollenaar, is the age of capital's victory. Everyone in the modern era is ruled by big capital, even the education that Tuan followed in H.B.S. was adapted from the needs of capital— not your personal needs, Tuan. Even the newspapers. Everything is arranged by capital: morality, law, truth and knowledge. (ASB 260, CAN 259)

What can be done? Ter Haar confirms that colonizers the world over are worried by what the Filipinos attempted: a rebellion against the Spanish led by educated provocateurs. Coincidentally, Ter Haar has a friend who knew one of the Native leaders, José Rizal, "An adroit poet as well as lover . . . writing poems in Spanish as you do in Dutch. A doctor, Mr. Tollenaar, and you mean to become a doctor. This similarity is perhaps no coincidence" (ASB 265, CAN 264). A specter of comparisons indeed. Just as colonialism predicates modernity so the imagined community gains in productive possibility from being linked to a correspondent on Buru, caught in a meanwhile from which memory attempts a rescue. If Minke is not fully conscious of the suasion of dialectics, Ter Haar at least conveys its principle: "In the long run . . . as the Natives, whatever their nation, increasingly understand European knowledge and science the more they will follow in the footsteps [*jejak*, the very footprints of the next volume] of the Filipino Natives who have tried to free themselves from Europe, whatever the path and means. The Filipino Natives wanted an independent nation just as Japan is now an independent nation, acknowledged by civilized countries all over the world" (ASB 267, CAN 265). Minke asks whether the Indies might be part of this prediction to which Ter Haar replies, "Certainly, but I don't know when" (ASB 267, CAN 266). The antithesis is clear but the outcome has no date, and especially from the vantage point of Buru.

Minke rounds out his text once more with further notes on the Filipino revolution, appropriately embellished: "In my mind's eye I saw an educated Filipino group emerge [in] a war that could not be depicted on the [wayang] puppet stage. It was more fantastic than even I could imagine. They were not led by individuals, but by an oppositional mindset, represented in their organization [the Filipino League]" (ASB 277, CAN 275). He goes on to recount the intervention of the United States, which initially assisted in the defeat of the Spanish only to facilitate a new dependency. The lesson is pointed regarding: "white power that was anywhere equally greedy" (ASB 278, CAN 276).

Just as a legal proceeding was a plot closure device in the first volume, so *Child of All Nations* gets back to the courts to resolve family business. Robert Mellema dies in Los Angeles from syphilis but not before sending Nyai Ontosoroh a long letter explaining the circumstances of her husband's death. While the letter would be crucial in the trial of Fatty (Jan Tantang), Minke reedits it for his novel because "his writing contained too many language errors" (ASB 292, CAN 289), a subtle reminder that even legal evidence is not the stuff of truth in fiction. One considerable legal problem remains, however: the rights of Maurits Mellema to Boerderij Buitenzorg, the issue that ended the first volume. Here again it is treated with melodrama when Mellema turns up to inform Nyai Ontosoroh to pack her bags. Mellema is accused of killing Annalies by taking her away from Minke and her mother. He is also denounced for robbing Nyai Ontosoroh of that which she has worked so hard to maintain. The exchanges intensify and Mellema leaves before he is attacked (he postpones the handover). Thus, the second volume ends much like the first, with Minke and Nyai Ontosoroh consoling each other that at least they fought back. In terms of seriality nothing suggests closure, and the opening frame of the tetralogy provided by Minke looking back remains open at the end of *Child of All Nations*. The decision to fuse the two volumes for initial publication in English had more to do with economies of scale than aesthetics, and marketing the dissident than marking the contours of his project. They do not form a whole but a fragment, albeit one with common identities.

Since in *Footsteps* ("Footprints"), Minke will reflect on the composition of the first two volumes as novels written prior to studying in Batavia, and because there will be a five-year gap before the publication of Pramoedya's *Footsteps*, I want to provide further comment on the logic of composition in the *Quartet*. Prameodya clarified the circumstances of the writing of the *Quartet*, but it is easy to see why, especially in the Suharto years, commentators have made exaggerated claims for the writing process. First, countless reviews place Pramoedya on Buru for fourteen years but, although he was arrested and imprisoned in 1965 (without official charges ever being filed), the "Humanitarian Project" at Buru was not operational until 1969, which is when he arrived.[38] Second, Pramoedya's early years on the island featured a prohibition on writing and reading materials. Max Lane suggests that even possession of paper might receive a punishment up to and including death (TEM 361), and this was when Pramoedya made most use of his oral storytelling skills. Here, however, the record gets a little murky. In *The Mute's Soliloquy* Pramoedya recalls that even in isolation in 1971 he studied German each day, which would suggest that reading and writing matter might be at hand (he makes no mention of a teacher). The breaks in the translated text of the memoir by Willem Samuels only compound the mystery. He translated the entire eight hundred pages in typescript of *The Mute's Soliloquy* but was given carte blanche to edit it for publication (the two-volume version in Bahasa Indonesia is also edited but contains much more historical detail). Samuels's dedication and expertise are not in question here, merely the issue of Pramoedya writing. Pramoedya recalls that in December of 1969 Major Kusno, commander of the penal colony, ordered that workers concentrate on agricultural production. Passages follow—"that month" and then "that same month"—then the narrative records that Major Kusno gave Pramoedya a pen, ink, and a writing pad with "an accompanying letter signed by the major" granting him "the restoration of my right to write" . . . "four years since my imprisonment in 1965" (MS 33–35). Two pages later, Pramoedya's writing tablet was "more than half full" and he wanted to destroy it not out of fear for his life but because he found the writing itself unsatisfactory. Sometime between December 1969 and July 1971 Pramoedya is forced to trade his pen for a bamboo hat and thus he loses his writing instrument. After two years in a "Model Group"—basically special cases who were isolated from the main prison population—Pramoedya begins writing again in July 1973: "I had time to write. Gradually I began to see take shape my former dream of writing a novel about the period of national awakening. I knew that what I wrote would be, at best, notes for a first draft but soon nine writing tablets had been filled" (MS 46). The oral storytelling, then, was concentrated in the two years of isolation with the "Model Group," a fact confirmed by interviews (for instance: "During mass executions of political prisoners, in the isolation cell I told the stories to my friends. During official ceremonies, my fellow isolated friends told the stories to other friends who were not being isolated, and that's how they were spread").[39]

The centrality of orality in the *Buru Quartet* may seem weakened by the timeline intimated here (the dependence on orality extended to two years at the most out of a total of fourteen years of incarceration), but the comparative brevity concentrates Pramoedya's vision and provides a burst of creativity in 1973. When Pramoedya ends both *This Earth of Mankind* and *Child of All Nations* with "Buru. Spoken, 1973. Written, 1975" he invites the interpretation that they had been entirely spoken by 1973 and entirely written by 1975, but this is not entirely the case. As we have already noted, the oral versions provided an outline, not a talking book, and there are enough references to "compiling" by Minke to suggest reordering by Pramoedya and his editor occurred after 1975, and particularly after Pramoedya's release and before the publication of the first two volumes in 1980. Whatever the timeline, the fear of confiscation remained and intensified the aura of emergency that is immanent to the extant text. The nine notebooks are taken from Pramoedya and never returned. He would have to begin yet again.

And begin again he does. In a 1998 appendix to *The Mute's Soliloquy* Pramoedya includes a list of what he wrote on Buru. In addition to the *Quartet* there were three other novels and a play as well as the hundreds of pages that would make up the memoir itself (including letters that Pramoedya wrote to his children not knowing whether he would ever be able to send them). He also worked on an encyclopedia that would essentially rewrite the Netherlands East Indies Encyclopedia. That manuscript was destroyed as well as any material in Pramoedya's possession at the time of his release in 1979. My sense is that some of the material for the encyclopedia became the historical markers found in the tetralogy.[40] Much of what is lost is actually repeated as Pramoedya writes against both official amnesia and the forces of effacement. Pramoedya saw the Buru manuscripts as works in progress that depended on revision and supplementation. Of the novel *Mata Pusaran* ("Whirlpool") he comments on Buru that it: "must be rewritten from the very start. Why? Simply because I obtained a batch of data more reliable than what I previously had access to . . . there is no final word" (MS 76). Visits to the island by religious figures, doctors, and later, reporters, allowed for the smuggling of material in both directions, although how much "data" this yielded is unclear. Nevertheless, quizzed about his works written on the island Pramoedya tells a reporter in 1977 that "I can't say any one of them is actually finished" (MS 334). Asked by another what he will do after he is released Pramoedya says first, "I'll clean up my manuscripts. I have no reference books to do that here" (MS 331). In the international public sphere the dissident writer is always subject to the power of mythologizing, a seductive discourse that romanticizes rebellion—especially rebellion elsewhere—and finds the actual writing read in advance. Even Max Lane, whose efforts in opening Pramoedya to English readers are immense, stokes mythology in his introductory notes ("Pramoedya obtained writing materials and the opportunity to write only in the last few years of his time at Buru" [F 9]). Again, of the ten years that Prameodya was forced to endure the hardships of Buru, he was writing for at least six if not eight of them. And, while his productivity was immense, Pramoedya's literary output was aided by prisoners who took over most of his daily chores (he thanks them more than once) and the introduction of a typewriter (when he trained for journalism Pramoedya learned speed typewriting). The original manuscript from which *The Mute's Soliloquy* was translated was delivered to Samuels in typescript. With the number of references to notepads one must assume the manuscripts were an admixture of hand and typewriting, but how many were "cleaned up" or edited with additions from "reference books" is hard to say. In one interview Pramoedya claims, "I never re-read my own writing" and when asked why adds, "If I reread it, I'll keep rewriting it, and it'll never be finished."[41] The irony is that because so many of Pramoedya's manuscripts were destroyed he essentially had to rewrite the bulk of them. Not all have been reconstructed: *The Girl from the Coast*, for instance, is all that remains of a projected trilogy, two volumes of which were incinerated on that fateful night of October 13, 1965. In the end, the number of years he wrote on Buru is less important than the fact he was driven to keep on writing at all costs, but better to appreciate that resilience and will than the hyperbole that spins well beyond it.

Meanwhile, on Buru, the tetralogy begins again. Max Lane is right to describe *Footsteps* as the "story of a beginning" (F 10). We have mentioned the importance of double time and in volume three this finds Minke, as Lane points out, both beginning anew in Batavia and discovering Indonesia "at its conception." The tone that begins *Footsteps* shifts from that of *This Earth of Mankind* and *Child of All Nations*. If the novel was spoken before 1973 and written by 1975 it does not stay silent about the decade between writing and publication in 1985. The moment of danger in which Pramoedya enacts memory has not passed, but this beginning has the air of more studied reflection. It is as if once Pramoedya worked on the *Sang Pemula* project, detailing the life and historical documents of Tirto, Minke could be rendered more confidently *as* fiction, even though publishing both a biography and a fiction of the same person would inevitably invite comparisons between the two. The coincidence of the projects suggests a logical interaction that does not diminish the achievements of either. "I came here to be victorious, to be big and successful," thinks Minke as he arrives in Betawi (Batavia, now Jakarta). He continues: "You don't want to become modern? You will be dependent on all the forces at work in the world outside" (JL 1, F 15). In case this self-assurance escapes the reader Minke is even more blunt: "I am a modern man. I have freed my mind and body from all ornamentation. . . . I am free! Utterly free. I am bound only by specific things that interest me" (JL 1, F 16). One cannot read these lines without also linking Minke's moment to Pramoedya's. First, with Pramoedya incarcerated on Buru, the New Order has effectively freed him of ornamentations of mind and body. It has stripped him, sometimes literally, and now he is free to write the New Order into oblivion using a discourse of modernity the "New Order" has usurped. Second, however, by late 1979 Pramoedya was under city arrest in Jakarta. He had arrived, like Minke, to triumph for now. Even with the restrictions on his movement and the bans that would begin again on his writing the die was cast: the writer and the writing now sat at the heart of the repressive regime, indomitable.

It is 1901; the new century has dawned and Minke exudes the confidence of studied perception. He has arrived in Betawi to learn medicine. Minke is already known because of his stories in Dutch and this makes it easier to mingle not just with the colonial elite but with those thinkers who challenge its prescriptions. He meets van Kollewijn, who sees Dutch development as a moral corrective to the era of *Cultuurstelsel* (the Culture System or Forced Cultivation) that permitted the peasantry of the Indies to shore up the economy of the Netherlands. If the distance between the Netherlands and the East Indies is collapsing then the latter cannot necessarily depend on the good graces of its new neighbor. Minke is identified as exactly the product of this vexed yet creative proximity and, given Minke's pronouncements above, he finds the fit described by van Kollewijn unnerving.

So, is it possible that an educated Native, a modern Native can produce his own identity? . . . Such an individual identity would also signal that a man and his epoch are at one. . . . Science and knowledge, gentlemen, whatever their extent, do not have an individual identity. The most remarkable machine made by the most remarkable of men does not have an individual identity. Yet the simplest story written can represent individual identity, or even the identity of a nation. (JL 26, F 39)

Minke has not only come into an age, but come of age. This differs from the late-eighteenth- and nineteenth-century novel of education because the social prism cut by colonial relations radically refracts the concept of the modern as it is lived in the colony. Van Kollewijn assumes an unproblematic correspondence, a harmony, not just between personality and the times, but between modern man and its colonial correlative. Minke does not have the status or the knowledge to contradict van Kollewijn's platitudes but Ter Haar takes up the charge admirably. All this talk of freedom and free labor reminds him that Native labor is not "free." Rather than artfully displace the glories of the modern onto Minke, Ter Haar asks van Kollewijn about the practice of *rodi*, guaranteed "free labor" whose proceeds accrue directly to the Dutch but is not recorded as income. Never mind about moral debt, how about paying back some of this fraudulently extracted surplus value? Marie van Zeggelen is also present at the meeting (Holland's first woman parliamentarian) and prods both Kollewijn and his sidekick, General van Heutsz, about the Netherlands' expansionist plans for the East Indies. This only increases the level of discomfort for the colonial apologists in attendance. Finally, Minke is emboldened to use his experience, gathered in Trunodongso's story, and asks: "Thank you, Honorable Member. About this free labor, Honorable Member, is this the same freedom that excludes and expels farmers who do not want to rent their land to the sugar mill?" (JL 34, F 46). The story rejected by his newspaper and that he subsequently destroyed now assumes an active presence in the mind of the colonizer. In Surubaya such confrontations were implied but here, in Betawi, the politics of discourse are rigorous and clear, and this will mean not just opposing the likes of van Kollewijn but maintaining a wariness of Dutch sympathizers like Ter Haar.

Minke's mother comes to visit and she informs him that his enthusiasm for the French Revolution and his cultural airs have changed him: "You've become a black Dutchman dressed as Javanese" (JL 52, F 64). Between colonial authority and Javanese tradition, Minke must cut his own path. Thus, he meets the lover of Khouw Ah Soe, Ang San Mei, who teaches English at a school run by the Tiong Hoa Hwee Koan for overseas Chinese (this political and cultural organization was formed in 1900). As they discuss, in English, the comparative fates of Chinese and Indies women, Minke begins to fall for Mei. Their emotional attachment only builds as he helps her through a bout of malaria and, once more, Minke has an anchor to complement his otherwise wayward mind. Because of language difference (Minke does not know Mandarin Chinese, and Mei does not speak Malay or Javanese) their story features awkward moments of translation but it addresses the role Chinese might play in the future of the nascent nation. The latter is of no small interest to Pramoedya, who had already been imprisoned for speaking out on behalf on Indonesia's Chinese population and whose book *Hoa Kiau di Indonesia* (1960) attacked discriminatory laws against it (this was Pramoedya's first banned book in Indonesia). The book took the form of a series of epistolary essays addressed to "Ch. Hs-Y" (actually Chen Xiaru, a translator who had accompanied Pramoedya on his second trip to China in 1958). There is much speculation on how intimate their relationship became, but intellectually their correspondence was heartfelt and often profound. Even if she was not the basis for Mei, Chen certainly helped shape and complicate Pramoedya's understanding of what is too often thought of in Indonesia as "masalah Cina"—the "Chinese problem." While on a trip to aid in Mei's recuperation they stop at Jepara to meet up with Kartini, which allows for more discussion on comparative modernity and the critical participation of women. Kartini, who remains nameless in this encounter, is described as a freethinker: "this Native was also a modern person" (JL 94, F 102). Like Mei, she is an educator with a democratic spirit and asks her how to reform and popularize education. Mei replies that a large association is the key "with a strength greater than the number of members within it" (JL 97, F 105). Minke, who is translating the exchange, recalls an article he has read: "The gods now are not as generous as they were in our ancestors' time. The modern age has made people take more responsibility for themselves, to take it from the hands of the gods. There was no longer a Deus ex machina like in the ancestors's myths . . . said the article" (JL 97, F 105–6). Except in novelistic fiction, of which this is a pertinent example.

Is Minke more interesting to Pramoedya, or the history that he lived? Certainly the first two decades of the twentieth century are crucial not just for exploring the burgeoning opposition to Dutch colonialism but in following the complex maneuvers of states, colonial and otherwise, throughout Asia. Pramoedya always believed that spice was at the root of colonialism ("the world was colonized by Europe because of Indonesia's spice islands") which, just like his claim that *Max Havelaar* "killed colonialism," is overblown but far from historical fantasy.[42] In Minke's time, the Dutch wanted sugar more than spices but when he mentions the foreign interests mulling the coal station on Sabang Island (Germans, English, French, Russians, and Japanese) one is reminded that colonialism was and is a servant of resource wars and that capital must accumulate by any means necessary. The weakening of the Dutch state was encouraged by anticolonialism in the Indies and by competing powers with an eye on resource extraction and regional hegemony.

When Mei dies from complications associated with a stomach infection, one wonders if Minke's wives must be sacrificed for his image to emerge as national hero, or whether this is a plot-clearing device to focus Minke's attention elsewhere than on the heart of romance? The ideologies of form exist at other levels than that which sutures romantic fulfillment.

That said, when Minke meets Nyai Ontosoroh again she is married to Jean Marais and within the space of a few lines Minke has proposed to his daughter, May, whom Minke knew as a child. Fortunately, May wants an education first so the reader is spared too much tortuous explanation for Minke's spontaneity, if not for their engagement. (There is a similar cloying nature to Minke's brief tryst with Mir, the wife of one of Medan's lawyers, Hendrik, that produces much handwringing over whether the child she has is his. The issue is serious but the emotions feel insincere.)

Meanwhile, on Buru; meanwhile, on Bali. Minke receives a series of letters from Ter Haar on the ongoing resistance to Dutch military incursions that began in 1904. The Balinese do not have the military materiel; but even after the fall of Denpasar, their determination is undiminished. For his part, Minke has been inspired by Mei's constant stress on nationalist organizations and so he sets his sights on helping to form one, a *sarekat*, whose business would be conducted in Malay (the official name is *Sarekat Priyayi*, to hide its populism behind aristocratic interests in the Dutch administration). The fact that Minke is able to persuade big landowners to contribute underlines that the regional rich have a stake in independence, if only to assume the authority now garnered by the Dutch. Not only is the organization legally registered but so is its weekly magazine, *Medan*, and the stage is set for the distribution of potentially anticolonial print. Subscriptions for the journal multiply quickly and soon *Medan* is available in Sumatra, Borneo, the Celebes, and the Moluccas. The activity recounted intensifies as the organization provides legal advice and looks to establish Native schools and hostels independent from the colonial government. Minke's newfound vocation brings him to the attention of the colonial authorities, and they follow his footprints—and those of *Sarekat Priyayi*. Van Heutsz, the governor-general, meets with him (affording Minke his first ride in an automobile) to express his support of both the organization and its journal. He also pledges to help start up a newspaper because Native ignorance cannot build or drive trains. The problem, as van Heutsz sees it, is that education produces questions, of the kind that Minke himself has asked, which do nothing to help him run the colony more efficiently. There is appreciable and critical balance in the tetralogy between how modernity captures Minke's imagination and how it threatens colonial administration. The antimony generates narrative, as if the *Quartet* breaks across the breach opened by the discourse of modernity, now endorsing the formation of the modern person, now castigating him for free thinking. The question that Minke does not ask van Heutsz is the one he always effectively hears: "Colonization and civilization?"[43] The simplicity of Césaire's question belies its complex insinuation in the discourses of colonialism and decolonization. It is form-giving; it traces the contours of the long space, the function of duration in seeking sublation of a historically specific antimony. The narrative extends not to imitate duration but to measure imaginatively what is and is not closed off by this founding contradiction of modernity. Just as the nation idea is divided by this breach, so too individual nations have been split apart in the process of overcoming its logical contradiction.

The narrative does not refrain from its didactive purpose vis-à-vis the power of print. Jean Marais comments in a letter: "You are doing more than the daily publication of a newspaper, you are initiating an awakening. If this is not so then no one would read your paper and it would not survive" (JL 237, F 242). The colonial papers strike back by printing all kinds of attacks, while the wire service limits the international news that *Medan* can print (although this does not stop Minke and his staff copying from international papers). There is also competition in the form of a Javanese organization, *Boedi Oetomo* (BO), that Minke joins. Again, the promise of education would be the secret to its success, this time in Javanese. But the *Sarekat* had failed in its educational mission; only its newspaper remained. In addition, Minke worries about the BO's parochial and elitist nature, not only limiting its independence to Java and Javanese, but also to *priyayi*—not known for their revolutionary fervor on behalf of peasants, for instance. Minke is seeking a greater unifying principle to gird anticolonialism. Islam is suggested and Minke considers this possibility as long as it does not exclude or marginalize "modern learning" (these are not mutually exclusive political or intellectual domains). Each successive meeting seems to sway Minke's notion of a Native movement in a different direction. An Indo or "Mixed Blood" named Douwager declares the answer to be the assertion of one people in the Indies, the Indisch, who no matter what their race are prepared to live and die for the Indies, for an identification that exceeds whatever differences they might otherwise perceive (F 305). This is a classic nation idea pertinent for a geographical area that is multiple in so many ways. But just in case its allure shines too brightly Douwager adds this greater unity should deploy Dutch over Javanese and Malay.

Pramoedya uses distance and duration to measure his difference with Minke's consciousness. In the same way, Douwager's theory is not simply modified by substituting Bahasa Indonesia for Dutch in producing a spirit of *Indisch*, the greater unity linking and consolidating the rich heterogeneity of the archipelago that today represents the fourth-largest population on this earth of mankind. The vacillation in nationalist strategy is constitutive: it is inherent both in the moment of "awakening" and in the ongoing eventness of nation. Pramoedya's exotopy is bound to the same moment as movement—to ongoing eventness—and this can just as easily collapse distance and duration as give them shape as history. There is, however, a specificity at stake in the form where eventness is given. The long space is not a descriptive device for new wine in old bottles, that the content of decolonization is poured into the novel. The process is chronotopic yet does not reveal itself as a literary type or genre; the principles of genre are themselves at stake in the coordinates of postcoloniality. The chronotope of the *Buru Quartet* is an active displacement of the historical because it does not settle accounts with history either side of the moment of decolonization. If Pramoedya believes it is truer than the meticulous records of the Dutch archive or the selective mythologizing of the *Orde Baru* (which for Pramoedya can only mean *Orde Buru*) it is not because it sits *as* history but because it engages with historicity as possibility, a struggle that lives on in decolonization.

However much Pramoedya had the benefit of hindsight, his reflections on Minke's awakenings are chronotopically entwined. This is why it seems as if Pramoedya is either living in Minke's time, or Minke is living in his. Minke meets with the Princess of Kasiruta, who has come to him for help because she is being prevented from returning home from Bandung after completing her studies at primary school. After hearing her story Minke comments, "Everybody says there are only two kinds of exile, five years or forever" (JL 293, F 301). When he relates her plight to another rich friend Haji Moeloek (the author of an anonymous novel on the sugar industry), he replies: "What a boring story. All stories that are not about freedom are boring. It's as if there is no better life in this colony than those of exile. Other people explore the world, laughing, smiling, and joyous. Now here there are people exiled in their own country" (JL 303, F 309). Pramoedya is preparing the ground for *House of Glass*, but surely the internal polemic here is about his own fate? The parallels intensify in the final volume, right down to the document that Minke is supposed to sign to exile himself from the political, but the point is the double time of the tetralogy, its bridge between times. In "My Apologies, in the Name of Experience," Pramoedya refers to the "symptomatic facts" of Sultan Agung's weakness avoided by court poets of the time and subsequently by mainstream Javanese history.[44] It is a suggestive term that also describes the ways in which Prameodya's story is made present in the tetralogy. This is because the project of historical displacement appears to separate Minke's accounts from Pramoedya's own, yet they are part of the same chronotope, a time/space that requires a similar repression.

It is tempting to say this is history's ghost, a doubling and shade crucial to Pheng Cheah's interpretation and a theme prominent in both Anderson's comparatism and Alex Bardsley's commentary on Pramoedya's essay. Since I view the philosophy of the ghost as itself symptomatic of materialist theory's purchase on reality after the collapse of "actually existing socialism" these critiques are apposite and intriguing on a number of levels.[45] The specter is a form of masking, and in "Apologies" Pramoedya invokes this spirit as an extension, a stretching across time, of his own.

Perhaps if earlier I had been educated in a particular discipline, history for example, I might do the research that would answer: why does all this happen and continue to happen? But I am a writer with minimal education, so it is not the materials of history that I examine, but its spirit. This I began with the tetralogy *Bumi Manusia*, particularly working on the currents that ebbed and flowed during the period of Indonesia's National Awakening. And so there came to be a new reality, a literary reality, a downstream reality, whose origin was an upstream reality, that is, a historical reality. A literary reality that contains within it a reorientation and evaluation of civilization and culture, which is precisely not contained in the historical reality. So it is that the literary work is a sort of thesis, an infant that on its own begins to grow in the superstructure of the life of its readers' society. It is the same with new discoveries in every field, that carry society a step forward. ("My Apologies," 4)

Minke, like this literary work, is a kind of thesis who is drawn dialectically from within the moment's antithesis. The only structural problem for the *Quartet* is whether it provides a synthesis its thesis prohibits (like the banks of the Lusi River dissolving their boundaries in making them). The *revenant* returns from the future and is not just the character that will live on in Pangemanann's tortured conscience. And thus it is Pramoedya himself who haunts these references to internal exile, to prohi-

bitions on publication and movement, to otherness that is otherwise held
to be the excess of Dutch projection.

In the novel what saves the exiled princess is marriage to Minke
which, given the fate of his first two wives, is something of a cruel reversal.
Minke's involvement with political and economic organizations can have
similar adverse effects but they are detailed to elaborate the shifting strategies of nationalist ideology. His ongoing argument with Douwager over
the principle of *Indisch* identification is really about the extent to which
individual organizations contribute or not to a united front against the
Dutch. Minke argues trade and Islam are a firmer basis for unity than the
abstraction of *Indisch*.

But Douwager pushes further: "We need to incite an Indies nationalism. We need a political party, not only social or trade organizations.
The Indies have never had a political party. That's what I have meant up
until now" (JL 339, F 343). Pramoedya, in "Apologies," remarks that one
of his chief aims in the tetralogy was to go to the roots of the history of
Indonesia's "nationalist awakening" and this lies in the thickening of such
exchanges. The problem, however, is that while Pramoedya has Minke
cross paths with key historical figures, the concretizing of historical roots
for something as broad as "nationalist awakening" is difficult to convey
in the consciousness of his main protagonist. If Minke's fervent document gathering and transcription makes him an appropriate medium for
recording the increasing momentum of nationalist thought, it is difficult
to expect him at the same time to represent, in himself, the quintessence
of that movement. This is more than a remark on whether Tirto, the historical basis for Minke, is a galvanizing figure like Guevara, or Nehru, or
Sun Yat-sen, or Rizal for that matter (interestingly, all but one trained as
doctors—in *House of Glass* Pangemanann notes that the emancipation
of enlightenment was often stimulated by lawyers but "In Asia awareness was spread that society was sick and must be cured" [RK 62, HG
62]). The limit in individuation is also about the schism between all that
the novel can bring to nation narration and the substance of its historicity. Anderson offers a persuasive theoretical model both for explaining the divide and for bridging it; but it is just as clear in beginning from
Pramoedya's narrative schema, brilliant in its own way, he is bound to for-
malize some of the fragility that necessarily determines the *Buru Quartet*'s
intervention. Buru sharpens Pramoedya's vision, yet the predicament in

nation and nationalism exceeds the specificities of narration Pramoedya employs and this is redolent in Anderson's more recent spectral embrace. Pramoedya had some ghosts of his own to exorcize, particularly those from the Lekra days. The fact, however, that he outlived the abhorrent Suharto regime only partly vindicates the prescience of the tetralogy. The New Order collapsed in 1998 not simply from its crass excesses of power but from the contradictions of a nation wrought by globalization with its attendant themes of debt crisis, currency vulnerability, and capital flight. Eventness as the impress of the future means when we use terms like *colonialism, nation*, and *postcolonialism* they must bear the weight of a ghostly afterlife in neocolonialism, postnation, and transnationalism. The "meanwhile" of Buru finds Minke appropriate but simultaneity is itself appropriated in the time of nation. The form of the novel is stretched: the crisis, however, also stretches the concept beyond the form.

Minke maintains that "One feature of the modern was the emergence of responsible individuals with personal awareness who were not in awe of their superiors" (JL 356, F 359), but events question the neatness of the formula. If the first two volumes sometimes rely on talking heads and the prepared statements of letters and newspaper articles, *Footsteps* garners its momentum from action less dependent on Minke's compilation skills and more on Pramoedya's keen historiographic reading of the period. This is preparing the ground, aesthetically and politically, for the absence of Minke's direct narrative agency in *House of Glass*. Minke's role remains essential to the meaning of the tetralogy, but his decentering problematizes the degree to which the narrative follows the logic of the *Bildungsroman*. Most of the themes that burn brightly by the end of *Footsteps* have more to do with nationalist historiography, and this reflects an urgency of memory less dependent on Minke's scribbling or the speed of Pramoedya's typing. It also suggests a symbiotic relationship between Anderson's understanding of the role of language and print culture and Pramoedya's reading of Tirto against the grain of New (re)Ordering.

Pramoedya's essays of the early 1990s refer explicitly to his reading of Anderson's *Language and Power*; indeed, his use of the word "power" is dependent on Anderson's elaboration.[46] All but one of the essays in *Language and Power* were written and published before the last volume of the tetralogy appeared and even that one was based on an earlier paper and article "directly inspired by Pramoedya Ananta Toer" (LP 13). Six of the eight essays were published before *Footsteps* and four before any part of the *Buru Quartet*. As noted, Anderson's correspondence with Pramoedya began in the 1970s (although Anderson is vague about whether this was during the prison years). Even if their exchanges did not begin until after Pramoedya was released from Buru in 1979, this was six years before the publication of volume three. Pramoedya claims that he does not read his own writing, yet he also argues that he revised his Buru production based on the availability of an archive after his departure from the prison island (certainly the reassembly of his research material helps to write the two volumes on Tirto that he worked on in the early 1980s). Prameodya's inspiration for Anderson is fairly clear, but one wonders whether Anderson's essays on Indonesia played any role in the different narrative strategies of the last two volumes of the tetralogy? Does this matter and why?

Such questions imply a more dialogic reading of the *Buru Quartet*, one that would itself reveal a productive interaction of theory and practice while simultaneously freeing it of the studied reliance on either Minke's *or* Prameodya's worldview. It does not reduce one text to another, but registers dialogic eventness in an "imagined community" of comparatist theory and the writing of emergency. Pramoedya is deeply concerned to free Indonesian identification from the *kampung* of Javanese culture and language, a modernization project simultaneously separating Enlightenment thinking from colonial ideology while prying nationalism loose from Javanese hegemony. Anderson's fieldwork from the 1960s on changes his understanding of the power of language in historicizing change in Indonesia. Pramoedya's readings in modernity and history affect the manner in which he can tell his stories. As Anderson seeks an interpretation "internal to Javanese society and culture" (LP 199) using *Bumi Manusia*, Pramoedya writes one that is only possible through a discordant break with Javanese internality.

Bardsley points out that Pramoedya's reference to *Language and Power* in "My Apologies" is superfluous since he had already acknowledged the force of an indigenized version of ancestral bloodletting revered in the *Mahabarata* in an article as early as 1950, "Gado-gado": "Indonesians are warred upon by the Indonesians themselves . . . and this civil war persists from century to century as well."[47] On the same page in *Footsteps* where he talks of disharmony, Minke bemoans how the *Mahabarata* and *Bharatayuddha* inhibit modernity because they focus on internecine fighting and god-loving in general. Pramoedya's acknowledgment of Anderson in "My

Apologies" is really about the function of power and charisma in Java that would falsify history and keep the populace under the thrall of despots like Sultan Agung and Suharto. Of more interest, however, is Anderson's essay on early nationalist thought, "A Time of Darkness and a Time of Light," in which he discusses the "autobiography" of Soetomo, a member, like Minke (Tirto), of the STOVIA medical school in Batavia and the founder of Budi Utomo (Boedi Oetomo). As a founder of the Indonesian Study Club, the Partai Bangsa Indonesia (Party of the Indonesian Nation), and the Partai Parindra (Great Indonesia Party), Anderson describes Soetomo as "one of the most prominent nationalist leaders of his generation" and "that generation's most enduring political personality" (LP 245). When he first appears in *Footsteps* Minke cannot remember his name and makes it sound as if the success of Budi Utomo had more to do with Minke's paper, *Medan*, than the activist aspirations of Soetomo. Similarly, while both Minke and Soetomo were inspired to organize after a speech by an old Javanese doctor who spoke at the school (Minke does not name him but Soetomo does, Dr. Wahidin Soedirohoesodo), Minke adds that he has also made this suggestion to Soetomo. Anderson notes that Soetomo was the first renowned Indonesian to attempt an autobiography, a well-known text called *Kenang-Kenangan*—a title that could be translated as "Memoirs" but as Anderson points out can also be rendered as "Memories." It is only Pramoedya himself who managed to produce a similar text for and as a life of Tirto (first, by memories as fiction, then through biography as restoration). Soetomo's preface could have been Pramoedya's to the *Buru Quartet*: "The writer's hope is that . . . this book of memories . . . can be used as a means for comparing conditions in the former time [*zaman dahulu*] with the present [*masa sekerang*]" (LP 248). Anderson makes provocative use of the distinction in time and generation indicated by such phrases to complicate the passage from tradition to modernity

Soetomo's separation from his forefathers is located exactly at this conceptual level: that he perceives himself and them encased in different times. Yet the *connection* is at the level of that pluralized perception. Here are signs of a new "watching self," of a distancing between person and culture. It looks very much, too, as if Soetomo is embarking on the construction of an *idea of a tradition*. For what, in the end, is a Tradition, so understood, but a way of making connections in separation, of acknowledging by not repeating? The distinction between *zaman dahulu* and *masa sekarang*, then, is probably less one of historical epochs than of altered states of consciousness. (LP 253, emphasis in original)

Are we not here discussing some of Minke's key disagreements with his parents but also, more important, the modern exotopy that permits Minke's awakening? Anderson sees Soetomo using two distinct versions of time within the same consciousness, and their juxtaposition permits not only Budi Utomo but the idiosyncratic form of Memories. The central section of Soetomo's book is dedicated to the founding of the organization but this sits in contrast with his grandfather's experience of village life, where basic harmony is disrupted by Soetomo's boyish unruliness. For Anderson the effect of harmony exists as sounds, words without signification, that are only "spoiled" by Soetomo's later attempts at explanation. The embeddedness of sound exists for memory, but memory betrayed to an extent by inscription because the eventness of those village sounds must remain largely ineffable to greater signification. Anderson has conveyed a similar sense by not translating; here he links passages by an absent allusion: "[the harmony of village life] emerges in a way that is both typically Javanese and strongly reminiscent of the writing of Indonesia's greatest author, Pramoedya Ananta Toer" (LP 254). Anderson does provide a reference for comparison later (from *Tjerita dari Blora*), but the reader here must reminisce alone. Two points are revealing from Anderson's essay of 1979. First, it seems quite surprising that Tirto, Soetomo's classmate at STOVIA, does not get a mention in this historical account and yet, if Anderson is right about Soetomo's sense of history, the absence of key events and figures is characteristic. Second, it might then seem astounding that Soetomo, or Tomo, gets such short shrift in *Footsteps*, particularly since Anderson notes that May 20, the day when Budi Utomo was founded, is celebrated annually as the day of national awakening in Indonesia. The twist, however, is in the order of time because what Anderson argues as a specific amalgam in Soetomo is also expressed in one of Pramoedya's early short stories. In a determined moment of metonymy, Pramoedya reads Soetomo's double time into Tirto's otherwise modern linearity. I am not suggesting that Pramoedya needed Anderson's thesis to consolidate Minke's awakening, but it is striking that Pramoedya's long space is more inclined to a man who died in imprisonment and obscurity than to a nationalist whose parallel life was already part of Indonesian lore. This is not just a case of the marginal figure providing more fictive potential but of the artist making a history more historical, because consciously double-timed, than the historical record itself. The symbiosis is in Anderson's illumination of history beside itself, comparing the memories of one with the aesthetic reach of another whose storytelling at the time was stretching time/space with the art of memory. Anderson says his essay on Soetomo is his favorite because it is the most "achieved," but I wonder whether its true achievement is that it prefigures the historiographic emergence of Minke as a fictive embodiment of what in Soetomo is only an instinct: "being a good Javanese by becoming a good Indonesian"? (LP 262).

Elements of Minke's life at school seem borrowed from Soetomo's, especially the insults hurled at Javanese by the other students. Recall again that Minke's own name is derogatory ("monkey") although the one that Soetomo hears is *penthol* (idiot or dummy). The roughing up of Native students reminds Soetomo of the excess of privilege and the necessity for justice, lessons of experience that dot the early chapters of *Footsteps*. Anderson ingeniously tracks Soetomo's education as a play on copying. By not copying (cheating), the Native students are behaving like the Dutch—they have copied them; yet their Javanese traditions celebrate imitation (of forefathers, of moral composure). The nationalist solution will be "imitating by not imitating"—a kind of copy that is not one, or the image of a life, Minke's, that may have never been. The solidity of *Footsteps* is achieved more through action punctuated by "live history" than the strained mechanism of note taking and letter pasting. Minke is not just being overtaken by events, but by a conception of history that mediates his consciousness as self-consciousness.

Footsteps ends with incidents typical of a novel in series and of foreshadowing in general. First, there is the appearance of Pangemanann, a Menadonese government official who "admires" Minke's work and is a dab hand at fiction, having written a story himself, "Si Pitung," which he hopes Minke will serialize in his paper. Pangemanann describes the threat of "De Zweep," a gang led by Minke's old nemesis, Robert Suurhof. Sure enough, they attack the offices of *Medan* and Suurhof gives Minke a severe beating. Some of the gang are briefly jailed but Minke's wife, the Princess of Kasiruta, and Minke's friend Sandiman exact full revenge by shooting Suurhof and killing two others. The authorities temporarily close *Medan*, ostensibly as a reaction to the attack, but actually to the paper's serialization of a novel condemning the sugar industry and to Minke's accompanying article. At this point Minke is unaware of Pangemanann"s surveillance. Because of the violence, Minke relinquishes his leadership of the *Sarekat*; he believes that performing propaganda work outside Java and the Indies will both consolidate the movement and ensure his relative safety. Before he can leave, however, he is arrested by Pangemanann and taken away, pointedly, without shoes on his feet.

Footsteps (*jejak langkah*, "footprints in the mire"—shoeless feet will leave footprints in mud) is a novel with *This Earth of Mankind* and *Child of All Nations* as a preface, and *House of Glass* as a conclusion. It relies less on episodes and orality, less on the "outline" of memory, and more on the "details" of the dawn of Indonesian nationalism, an emergence independent of Minke's full apprehension. Pramoedya could have spoken the elements of *Footsteps* on Buru but there is little of the anxious archive about it. The issue is not about preserving a purity in the moment of danger that should pervade its narration; after all, Pramoedya remained under threat, actual and implied, well after his release from Buru. The question falls on the logic of chronotope that in the first two novels conveys both a didacticism and a means of self-preservation (stories told before roll call to lift fellow prisoners' spirits and bolster Pramoedya's endurance). *Footsteps* has some of this quality and something else again, the chronotope of link and legacy. The combination is dialectical and dialogical, eventness as a process that is ongoing between Minke's life and the life of he who inscribes him. The shift is both tonal and formal, from the impress of all that is gone to all that remains: footprints that *have* survived in two directions.

House of Glass is the most difficult of the *Buru Quartet* for it challenges the inevitabilities of national awakening and, simultaneously, Minke's role in that process. Pramoedya has, in the tetralogy, spoken an archive, storytold its outline, disseminated its ethics of responsibility first to those in his cell block, then by retelling to other prisoners on Buru. The first two volumes bear much of this orality and urgency, and the third volume is a more studied elaboration of consciousness inscribed. Together, these three volumes are Minke's trilogy but he does not announce this (he indicates that the first two novels are his in the third). Pangemanann is the one to reveal the extent of Minke's authorship because the novels are now part of *his* files, a framing device eerily at one with the power/knowledge nexus that finds Pramoedya memorizing in jail. For Max Lane the real protagonist is history, that which Pangemanann, the narrator of the final volume, must suppress in order for his creative collaboration with the Dutch to persist. Although his historiography is more nuanced, Bahari arrives at a similar conclusion: "The texts that Pramoedya infiltrates in the Buru tetralogy are both in history (existing in "reality," outside his novels) and about history (used by Dutch colonialism and—by implication—the *Orde Baru* to tell their versions of the 'truth'). They are converted to narration within the frame of memory, and what they recover is history itself."[48] Anderson acknowledges the historical aura, as does Pheng Cheah in *Spectral Nationality*. But given Anderson's specific and illuminating interpretation of Pramoedya's project one should not be surprised that the "real protagonist" has a different name. After noting that no Indonesian reader would believe Pangemanann, a Native raised in France, could be a high-ranking officer in the colonial secret police, Anderson adds: "The file-keeper and file-contaminator of *The Glass House*, who is also the ultimate narrator, is a dystopic prolepsis. But he narrates, and the scope of what he narrates is nothing other than the nation" (SC 338). What holds the *Quartet* together is the possibility of a frame that must exceed it for it to be intelligible. Pramoedya encourages this surplus by making the text a collection of papers in a state archive designed to assure its removal yet preserve its revelation. Much of Pramoedya's own archive was destroyed over the years, but some texts were confiscated and what a collection this must be. The logic of excision is made determinate in what the *Buru Quartet* can mean. All of the loss and possibility of remembrance is concentrated on this conceit. Like the Lusi River, the form of the tetralogy is reconfigured by eventness in time which must, in the exigency of nation, transgress what is given by cognition. Pramoedya is close to Minke in the approximation of reason's need, the desire for narrative freedom, but he is closer still to Pangemanann and the logic of "dystopic prolepsis," for what has time wrought but the flow of colony into penal colony, a tampered archive of utopian liberation from which Pramoedya's own narrative has been cut (and some of Pangemanann's too)? The force of prolepsis for Pramoedya is its direct confrontation with the proleptic paroxysm provided by the New Order. This means not only, like Minke, compiling historical documents, but also, like Pangemanann, insinuating an alternative narrative trajectory in Minke's novels of record. Did Pramoedya know this when he wrote the opening line of the tetralogy "People called me

Minke"? (BM 1, TEM 15). Probably not.[49] The framing device provided by *House of Glass* emerges in the burden of Minke's first-person narration in volume three that finds nationalism much greater than conscious apprehension. The failure of Minke to hold the narrative is not the victory of surveillance and suppression embodied in Pangemanann, but the triumph of memory's instant, the distillation of a chronotopic truth questioning the assumption of the nation as a universal in the modern era. This concept of transnationalism seeks to understand what must be transgressed in the nation form to make decolonization possible.

Pangemanann is a colonial crony, a product of colonialism's desire to make the colonial subject the author of its own subjection. One might expect Pramoedya to be hard on Pangemanann, and Indonesian readers must delight in his impossible position and tortured conscience. Yet this is not the thesis in narrating from his point of view. It is rather to explore the colonial unconscious that must itself be politicized, written, to foreclose the fawning admiration for thoughts European, specifically colonial, and for a kind of mythological continuum displacing agency in the present. Pangemanann is a rigorous observer, but if *House of Glass* is literally his panoptic medium the interest for the reader is in the limits of this way of seeing. When Minke first meets him, he describes Pangemanann as a big man with a cane, well-dressed and well-spoken. Pangemanann praises Minke, but he also extols the virtues of the colonizer's humanitarian instincts and the "ethical" policy the Dutch pursue to maintain their colony. This allows Pramoedya the narrative device of historical detachment that Pangemanann pursues to rationalize his collaboration.

Minke may be loosely based on Tirto, but Pangemanann is pure invention and, like any Native informant, a rich resource of fantastic projection and irony. Thus, when he is given the task of "handling" Minke he retells his story as if Minke himself had written it, but in the third person:

What must I do to him? He is neither a criminal nor a rebel. He is only an educated Native who loved his country and homeland too much, who tried to cultivate his people, who tried to uphold justice in his life, for his people on this earth of the Indies, for all peoples on this earth of mankind. He was completely in the right, and I not only took sides with him but I was also among his most sincere admirers. (RK 6, HG 6)

Pangemanann has at least the first two volumes of the quartet in mind when he avers, "His writings . . . . left the impression of a person who was restless, uncertain, feeling his way, and rather confused, immersed in a flow of disparate European thought, all of which he received piecemeal" (RK 6, HG 7). Yet this close attention to Minke's work and image also contains a hint of erotic hero worship: "He had smooth skin like a langsat fruit, a well-maintained mustache, thick and black and tapered at each end . . . . By Native standards he was handsome, strong, and appealing, especially to women . . . . He took confident steps without hesitation towards greatness . . . . Secretly I honored him" (RK 6–7, HG 7–8). Out of honor, Pangemanann gets Suurhof to frighten Minke (he also suggests murder), which is the premise behind the incident leading to the Princess taking potshots in the previous volume (it is Pangemanann who arranges to have the Princess present in the hope that Suurhof might die with Minke). The plan fails and this is why the administration resorts to Minke's exile, on Ambon.

Pangemanann's rise within the colonial bureaucracy may stretch credulity but is largely unremarkable, save for the intensity of his opportunism and unrelenting belief that "The face of European ethics must remain clean" (RK 46, HG 46). As Pramoedya constructs a double time that makes present Pangemanann's world of *"surveiller et punir"* Pangemanann himself elicits a double consciousness. Nationalism in the Indies was blocked not only by a deep-seated recalcitrance in local culture but the logical consequences of modernity itself. A colonial theorist, a lawyer called Meneer (Mr.) K warns the Dutch regime that a "second Philippines" is quite possible in the Indies because "colonial problems in Asia are closely connected, like one chain link to another" (RK 48–49, HG 49). As an educated Native, Pangemanann wonders about the "strange ideals" of Minke that must be curbed or shaped to colonial ends. Being a self-described instrument of this power, however, makes Pangemanann ill as collaboration assumes the tenor of affliction: his body revolts against his conflicted consciousness of "principle" and "livelihood" (RK 55, HG 55). Part of his cure is writing, as if he might explain himself to his wife by writing out what he calls his "two-faced" nature. This device allows Pangemanann's notes to be more personal and reflective than his surveillance, and yet both can exist simultaneously as a colonial record. It is a commonplace now to examine the parameters of subaltern expression within the texture of colonial discourse; but what Pramoedya attempts by contrast is to refract counterdiscourse not just through Pangemanann's self-reflection on his plight, but through the unconscious in his colonial encounters. It is a tension inexpressible in Minke but wonderfully suited to Pangemanann's collaboration.

The strength of Pangemanann's narrative exists in Pramoedya's ability to reveal the ambivalent and destructive allegiance of the colonized subject and to convey his own plight, recolonized on Buru. That Pangemanann hopes his notes will be read by his family—like Pramoedya writing letters to his children that he is forbidden to send—is the fold of the quartet, a crease in the teleology of the modern in which its chronotope is, for a moment, synchronic and synchronized, decades apart and yet of the same instant. The prisoners of Buru are forced to build their own prison; in their roads and houses and fields they map the very conditions of their incarceration. Yet in becoming the eyes of the colonizer Pangemanann is no less complicit in his own imprisonment: the "house of glass" that is his panopticon is also what surrounds him. Like Minke, Pramoedya writes in internal exile but, like Pangemanann, it is writing that sees enough to doubt its own possibility as archive.[50] The glass house seems to have no walls but both Pramoedya and his fifty-year-old counterpart (Pramoedya is the same age as Pangemanann when he drafts this novel) know they have been built, for every second confirms the fact. In one of his "undelivered" letters to his children Pramoedya notes the "Revolution of 1945" "represents emancipation: the opening of a new room in the house of humanity, expansion of a new building block in humanitarian development" (MS 256), and yet this house has "bars" behind which sits the writer, awaiting extinction. Like Pangemanann, Pramoedya sees everything, but from a particular position: "Whatever one's opinion, in the final denouement the question of death is determined by how and from what angle it is viewed. The answer thus depends on both the kind of lens one uses, and the kind of material it is made from" (MS 74). The long space materializes in the medium of perception, in that which is immanent to ways of seeing.

Ironically, the master of the glass house moves into Minke's old domicile in Buitenzorg. Pangemanann has been given the task of elaborating whether conditions are ripe for Natives to emulate the Filipino insurrection, keeping in mind this revolution was itself usurped. The Dutch fear nationalism in the East Indies enough to encourage an "ethical" policy of collaboration. Yet the real threat of nationalism is not from armed insurgency but the ground that it prepares for further foreign machination.

Pangemanann's charge is to maximize the art of pacification while studying the region for signs of predatory imperial competition. Pangemanann does not have the benefit of Pramoedya's hindsight, but these long hours and passages with Pangemanann in the state archives (supplemented by strategic subscriptions to foreign papers and journals) is a lesson to Pramoedya's projected readers: Indonesia today is a part of this narrative.

In Minke we witness his interpretation of power and knowledge as seeds of organization. He not only assembles the discourse of modernity but resembles it as an embodiment of a corresponding will to organize, in the *Sarekat* that becomes SDI. In Pangemanann we follow a counterlogic, reactionary to the extent that it wishes to head off the consequences of "awakening." Yet, Pangemanann's extralocality facilitates a metacommentary placing narration at the heart of possibility: "From the writing I was able to see how the writer's thoughts and feelings were constructed, his desires, his tendencies, his dreams, his stupidity and lack of intelligence, his knowledge, and all of this was constituted as one, as if tied together by clear glass threads. Each piece of writing was a special world, floating between the world of reality and the world of dreams" (RK 103, HG 102). This is not Pramoedya's view, but it measures the dreamy projections of Javanese nostalgia for the heyday of its kingdoms before the fall of the Majapahit in 1478 against the harsh manifestation of the gulag that is a consequence of such hypostatization. More than this, however, *House of Glass* reveals the author pondering the servants of state repression as they themselves assess the archive they have purloined, or banned, or otherwise erased from the public sphere. We read Pangemanann reading Minke as if the New Order (and as an intimation of transnationalism, we) were trying to read Pramoedya.

There were as many as 123 notebooks. They were all full of Minke's bad handwriting, much of it scratched out. These books were tied together in several bundles. They were all written in Dutch. The first of these was apparently a story that had already been published in Malay in Medan and was entitled "Nyai Permana" [A number of concubines]. I put that bundle aside. I had already read that in Malay and it will not answer my questions. The second bundle was entitled This Earth of Mankind, the third Child of All Nations, the fourth Footsteps [Footprints—*Jejak Langkah*]. One day I might write about these texts. (RK 117–18, HG 117)

Pangemanann's reflections permit a recapitulation of the first three novels. They also serve to corroborate Minke's narration through the state's repetition of facts offered in the earlier volumes. Minke's ordering scrambles the chronology in the tetralogy because his method of assembly includes dreams and imaginings. Pangemanann's approach is more meticulous and yet, because history in his account is about the unfolding of events within different movements that may or may not directly touch upon Minke's record, it is no more truthful or straightforward. Bahari concludes that Pramoedya seeks only to make history provisional and contingent. The crux of the narrative falls to a hermeneutics of dissent that proposes meanings.[51] This is resonant of Gadamer or Ricoeur but does not necessarily make fiction better history even as it repeats the familiar refrain of fiction as history and vice versa. It is easy for fiction to derail Dutch rule in history; just have Pangemanann emphasize accuracy and ethics, then have him trundle off to the whorehouse or lie constantly to himself about his motives. This is what fiction does: put flesh on facts and they begin to walk in all directions. Yet this is hardly a rejection of history. While colonialism could fudge the difference between history and historiography the colonized are compelled to fight that conflation in the name of "all that is gone" from their history. Historical novels can be extremely powerful narratives but they are novels about history not *as* history. Pramoedya venerates Tirto by fictionalizing him in the tetralogy, then by writing a biography that includes an array of supporting documentary material. These are very different projects but one has the effect of dialogically legitimizing the historical claims of the other. The problem with Bahari's term "w/righting history" is that hermeneutics is naturally inclined to favor writing over "righting" which leaves "right history" a nonstarter. Bahari's approach, however, confirms Pramoedya's own interest in history and its spirit, a road that leads in the direction not of Gadamer but of Hegel.

Hegel provides a progressivist paradigm of self-consciousness, both contingently historical and logically imperative that in *Bildung* are arrayed into a unity. This enables an objective analysis of the subjective, or Spirit, that becomes a logical function of universality in self-consciousness. The temptation would be to view Pangemanann's disinterested pursuit of reason's needs as Hegelian "reasonableness" while Minke is imbued with a spirituality at one with culture, or *Bildung*, and acts through consciousness as ethical substance. The novel is as fickle with philosophy as it is with history, but from Goethe on, the *Bildungsroman* can be read as the Hegelian

subgenre par excellence. Pheng Cheah, pointedly, finds Pramoedya seeming most Hegelian in his book on Tirto in which Pramoedya argues for
Indonesia's national awakening as a consciousness formed through the
"negation" of Dutch colonialism. I tend to think, however, that the work
on Tirto is read back into his fictional counterpart, from *Footsteps* on. For
Pramoedya history remains dynamic: "as a person and a writer who shares
in bearing the burden of change, I look at it according to national criteria. The era of Soekarno and the Trisakti doctrine was nothing but a sort
of thesis. The New Order, an antithesis. Therefore, for me, it is something
that in fact cannot be written about yet, a process that cannot yet be written as literature, that does not yet constitute a national process in its totality, because it is in fact still heading for its synthesis."[52] The Hegelian
aspect is that the synthesis is presumed; the materialist concern is that the
novel cannot preempt this process as a totality before history itself has rendered it as such. Yet if Pramoedya offers Hegelian dialectics it is because
"literary reality" does not passively sit by waiting for unity to align itself.
The novel puts contradictions into play so literary reality might stimulate
what is intrinsic to historical change: it is history's spirit rather than its
record.

While studying nationalism Pangemanann is sent further papers
written by Minke, probably provided involuntarily. Again, one cannot
but think of Pramoedya as Pangemanann muses on Minke's plight: "He
had the right to write anything he wished, maybe a memoir, maybe a
confession. He had the right" (RK 161, HG 161). In the midst of asserting his support, Pangemanann has a vision of Minke appear before him:
old, poorly dressed, and in slippers. Pheng Cheah makes much of such
haunting for it not only demonstrates the depth of Pangemanann's torn
consciousness but a kind of structural spectrality in the nation narrative.
Cheah calls this "spectral promise," and it is appropriate to the themes of
causality in Pramoedya's writing since the fear of inscription itself chases
the New Order all over Indonesia during Suharto's rule. What does one
do with a malevolent spirit? Speak to it? Write to it? In November 1973,
Pramoedya receives a letter from Suharto. Like Pangemanann who, if not
written at this point, is beginning to materialize, Suharto is compelled to
address Pramoedya, whose absence haunts national consciousness: "For
every person a mistake in judgment is common, but that must of course
be followed by its logical consequence, that being: 'Honesty, courage, and

the ability to rediscover the true and accepted road'" (MS 62). Suharto's letter is an extraordinary document for here the national leader addresses the victim of his repression as if the latter had a choice in the matter. If every person makes mistakes in judgment is the path to Buru measured only by an inability to repent, and when was that opportunity offered? Pramoedya, along with many of his fellow inmates, was never given the chance to answer charges because none were formally leveled (this formula is not the monopoly of repressive postcolonial regimes). Just to underline Pramoedya's identification with Minke he notes in his response to Suharto: "the mark that I leave behind, the traces of my footsteps, are there to be judged by anyone" (MS 63). Pramoedya is polite, as anyone who has witnessed the expiration of other prisoners on a regular basis would be, but reminds his fellow "Native" that the "logical consequence" of his detention, even if it means death, ensures an afterlife that can be envisioned. This may not constitute a right, yet it is an indelible trace. Or, as Pangemanann puts it: "Although he [Minke] failed as a doctor, he succeeded in establishing an empire, and opening up development. And all of modern Natives' activities will follow along in his footsteps" (RK 143, HG 143).

Two versions of time seem to clash in these exchanges. For the Dutch colony, time is the condition of assimilation, the sublation of pastness into a mythic shell that simultaneously preserves epic traditions while leaving the eruption of colonial modernity undisturbed. The long space Pramoedya articulates, however, is a chronotope ardently specifying place in time so that any simultaneity must attend to concreteness. This requires understanding the production of ghosts in the present, including himself during his lifetime (Bardsley describes Pramoedya as a "particularly prominent ghost").[53] The slaughter of Indonesian communists and sympathizers by the New Order produced an emblematic absence as presence and this is not an allegory in *House of Glass*: it is the very substance of its narrative voice. What is being hailed in Pangemanann's panoptic paranoia is the impossibility of negating material presence. The chronotope makes time/space take on flesh, albeit of an ethereal kind. The problem of colonization is a problem in decolonization: what spirits must be settled to facilitate a break from dehumanization? Pangemanann's house is haunted and so is Suharto's Indonesia. For every facade of national spirit there is a meanwhile, on Buru: a spirit of the other providing both shame and shade to nation.

As Minke notes, exile can be five years or for life (Pramoedya is on the cusp between the two as he writes the tetralogy), and Pangemanann pays close attention to Minke's correspondence from Ambon as the nationalist looks forward to resuming his leadership role upon release. Pangemanann imagines himself engaging Minke in an explanation of his plight, and the narrative addresses him in the second person. Rifling through his texts, Pangemanann answers questions that have not been posed to him, and again one thinks of Suharto who has heard of complaints but responds as if they were directed to him individually, and by Pramoedya. The use of the second person conjures Minke in his absence and hails Prameodya in his current predicament: "That your efforts from the beginning were affected by heavy punishment was a mistake. As time passes the Indies will increasingly get used to exile" (RK 175, HG 175). These passages are examples of "double-voiced discourse" (PDP 185–99), a dialogic interaction of two distinct voices within the same utterance usually directed toward the same semantic object.[54] Bakhtin elaborates several forms of such discourse, but here we see a model of the author's intention refracted through the narration of a character whose worldview cannot but clash with that of the writer. Furthermore, Pangemanann's text is not just double-voiced, but is a double interpellation: he hails Minke while Pramoedya invokes him to speak truth to the power he (Pangemanann) represents. Pramoedya provocatively links this to his chronotope, the double time that binds "meanwhile, on Buru" to "meanwhile, on Ambon" so that Pangemanann's commentary on Minke's trilogy imagines a critique of Pramoedya's quartet with a sideward and simultaneous glance at Pramoedya's own reading. Such doubling in the final form of the tetralogy took some timely detours to complete. Because the long space is the distillation of material it does not simply stretch the time/space of its content— the surface markers of plot or character or conflict—but the nature of the project extends the conditions and the tone of the author's engagement. Thus, seriality is also a function of dilemma: how can one capture the eventness in being of decolonization when that process exceeds the event of its inscription? The long space demands a time that is not its equal, a duration that cannot in fact be represented as it is and is therefore refracted yet condensed, dispersed yet contained, by a frame that impels further narrative. At the center of *House of Glass* Pangemanann, with Pramoedya by his side, looks back in time yet also into the eyes of Suharto.

I returned to studying the texts of Raden Mas Minke. I got the impression, that accept for Ny[a]i Permana, the manuscripts were linked one to another. Between This Earth of Mankind and Child All Nations on the one hand, and Footsteps on the other, I discovered a schism. I had not decided whether they were all parts of an autobiographical series or not. For the time being I considered them as a series of interesting stories, with all their drawbacks and advantages. I would set aside a specific time to compare them with reality as well as official documents. In fact, what I've written is because of the influence of these texts, and I have no hesitation in admitting it.

Reading these as stories, the first text more often reflected the process of modernisation in the nature of thinking among the indigenous people at the beginning of this century. The world of thoughts of indigenous people and the world of European thoughts met in this story, either by exploding in a clash or by accommodating each other. (RK 176–77, HG 176)

Pangemanann continues that the manuscripts' autobiographical content was ultimately inconsequential because Minke is a medium for modernity. No longer bound by nature he acts as a free individual and is affected by all of the products of that new consciousness. Pangemanann's recapitulation of the first three volumes is simultaneously Pramoedya's reaccentuation, as if the storyteller must condense the tale, with all of its episodes, to strengthen its meaning and sustain its author. Pangemanann says that in the trilogy Minke is "an intellectual witness to the events of his era" (RK 193, HG 193) and again one is reminded of Pramoedya whose testimony hovers on the brink of oblivion. For much of his life Pramoedya's writing was read by his enemies whose bans tried to prevent it reaching its intended readers and interlocutors. While that situation largely eased after the fall of Suharto, the readers themselves have changed so that the lessons of Pramoedya's stories are in the process of a new reaccentuation. They are documents of a past that is present still in what Indonesia can become.

Yet as part of this eventness, the *Buru Quartet* is more than an unquiet ghost inviting specters of comparison. The disjunction that brings Pangemanann to the fore in the final volume is neither the triumph of print capitalism nor the Andersonian analogy between nation form and novel in which empty homogenous time is instantiated. Its meanwhile is indeed symptomatic, for Pangemanann peruses Minke's papers as the latter struggles away in exile toward death, and this is a parallel as displacement. The analogic concept that links novel and nation in Anderson's thesis is its weakest aspect not because it is benign, but because it permits a kind of studied amateurism by experts at either end of the analogy who can claim that their specific research is, using the term "imagined community," the equivalent of another.

Pangemanann lives the contradictions of his affiliation in almost every word. *House of Glass* is, at this level, a novel of conscience whose content is the measure of belief between colony and a form of identification that as yet has no name. The "action" of the novel is a version of Minke's action focusing on reading and interpretation. One reads of Minke as already read and the drama for the reader emerges in the stark difference between this reading and Pangemanann's. The emergency of memory is less prominent, as is the staccato didacticism, yet there remains the urgent appeal to a reader who must arrive without guarantees (Rizal, as Anderson points out, addresses his readers in *Noli me tangere* as "friend or enemy" and the novel pivots on this ambiguity).[55] If there is a pathos in the first two volumes that Minke's account may never reach a Native reader, in the final volume Pramoedya offers an alternative, the state functionary whose powers of admiration are only matched by his duty-bound malevolence. You confiscate my writing, says Pramoedya, but such is the power of my discourse that in reading it your spirit will be broken not mine. And for the Indonesian readers who clamored for the first two volumes in 1980 before they were banned the following year, *House of Glass* demonstrates that power *of* displacement and *as* displacement. They read too that Minke's voice of awakening is irrepressible just like Pramoedya's, but the truth in the parallel lies in writing more than its analogy for nationalist consciousness. The form of the novel does not describe a nation; its chronotope is a space of enunciation, a heuristic device about the process of nation and its grounds of intelligibility. Commenting on Franco Moretti's use of Anderson's thesis, Jonathan Culler comments:

What we seem to find is that the more interested one becomes in the way in which particular sorts of novels, with their plots and their imagined worlds, might advance, sustain, or legitimate the operations of nation-building, the richer and more detailed one's arguments about novel and nation become, but at the cost of losing that general claim about the novelistic organization of time that was alleged to be the condition of possibility of imagining a nation. The more detailed the critical accounts of novels and their possible effects, the less powerful and encompassing the general theory of the novel.[56]

The slippage from Anderson's analysis of the novel for nation to the more dubious claim that novelistic imaginings "make" nations by representing them is a particular function of the suppression of decolonizing logic. Moretti invokes the example of the *conte philosophique* to mark the novel's insufficiency, but it is decolonization that substantiates this material disjunction because it takes up the site of the novel as one contested modernity among others.[57] That a novel is a condition of possibility for imagining "something like a nation" (Culler) is at once the promise of liberation and the dilemma of its form. Just as decolonizing nationalists did not wait on the novel for urgent intervention so postcolonial states do not sit in earnest for a novel that offers a nation in their own image. The importance of the long space rests on its dialogicity, not its capacity for analogue. The problem of form is at its most acute when likeness cannot do the work of materialization. This is where the agency of *el demonio de las comparaciones* (that Anderson borrows and translates from Rizal as the "specter of comparisons") can problematize the space of analogy.

Pangemanann tries to square the free association encouraged by the Dutch in their "ethical" policy with their requests to clamp down on individual organizations who are exercising such freedom. He argues Boedi Oetomo and the Association of Government Priyayi have helped to diffuse opposition to other less palatable aspects of colonial rule by intimating a level of autonomy in decisions about education and local disputes. Siti Soendari, however, is more threatening because she sees organizational activity as not only lifting women's social status but challenging Dutch *and* traditional versions of the social simultaneously. There is also the thorny issue of Dutch radicals' involvement in East Indies politics. Pangemanann discusses the work of Sneevliet, who broadly dismisses Boedi Oetomo for pandering to the Dutch while ostensibly embracing Native concerns. The critique reads as an extension of Pramoedya's and underlines once more the focus on Minke's alternative vision, however it is imagined beyond Tirto.

Tirto was a journalist and Pangemanann remarks on journalism's deep importance to Native consciousness. While no one should doubt the impact of print culture on the circulation of ideas in general, its precise effect is difficult to gauge. Beyond suppositions about the meaning of circulation and the profiles of readers, Pangemanann is left with his own speculation about which forms of Native identification it might stimulate. The importance of writing as recording is a theme throughout the tetralogy and one that touches Pangemanann personally (his involvement with a prostitute is set down in her notebook and he is blackmailed by a police officer because of it). This, combined with the various attempts to establish a Native educational infrastructure, constitute the main alternatives to the Dutch colonial episteme. Pangemanann interests Pramoedya because he shares Minke's worldliness and tries to surmise consequences based on his reading. It is the proof of Anderson's "meanwhile" but not wholly the substance of a "meanwhile" structured by imprisonment and torture. Indeed, most of the final volume is chillingly dispassionate, as if Minke, like Pramoedya, is to be noted, filed, and left largely silent alongside the earlier texts. It is only in the final section, when Pangemanann meets Minke in Surabaya on his return from exile, that Pangemanann finds himself marginalized within his own capacity to narrate (pointedly, this would be Pramoedya's first port of call after his return from Buru).

Minke is in a difficult situation, financially, because of the seizure of his property and assets; politically, because his exile has removed him from the main currents of Native resistance in Java (Ambon, coincidentally, is the island adjacent to Buru); and legally, because the Dutch, through Pangemanann, require a signed statement certifying his withdrawal from activism. Minke has been shorn of those attributes that constitute him as a fully socialized human subject before the colonial state; small wonder the conditions of adjudication fall to the rhetoric of ghosts and haunting. This attests to the efficacy of Pramoedya having Pangemanann take up the position of narration because he excludes Minke in his own name: "Yes, in exile you could do no more than recall and reflect on the time that has passed, and thus this past seemed closer. As a former police commissioner I could understand that. Inmates forever gossiping about their problems as if they had no present or future. I could understand" (RK 297, HG 298). The long space is not just a mark of duration but a logic of cartographic intimacy doubled by memory's time of the now. Its seriality is bound by a specificity that does not set aesthetics against a verifying outside but is honed by the powerful and often taboo imbrication of the two. The eventual present of all that is made new as past is closer to the dialectics of a freeze frame, a momentary homeostasis of Benjaminian messianism shot through with material contradiction.

And so we find Pangemanann and Minke sitting together in a taxi, one awed by his comparative insignificance, the other cowed by state repression. Pangemanann tries to befriend him as a fellow Native schooled by Europeans to question that which Europe has made in its image. The road they travel is now asphalt, as if this covered the cost of colonization.[58] These are remarkable passages in which Pangemanann refers back to the earlier volumes as he seeks confirmation for their veracity and his "reading" of Minke. One thinks of Pramoedya telling this story to his fellow prisoners with the possibility of their knowing response that Pangemanann's references fall short of understanding. Yet one also imagines Pramoedya reconstituting a long space refracting the ban on the first two volumes while chiding the *New Order* for its hermeneutic deficiencies. It is strongly affirmative in its eventness by hailing the past as constitutive in the present.

Pangemanann seeks Minke's signature to guarantee his political neutralization. Buru inmates are asked to sign two statements before they are released: one that promises not to disseminate Marxist-Leninism or otherwise upset the order of the state (this includes seeking legal recourse for wrongful imprisonment); the other promising that, despite overwhelming evidence to the contrary, prisoners had not suffered torture and forced labor. Indonesia, under Suharto, adds another negation to Pangemanann's by imploring its victims to deny the substance of their victimhood. The banality of authoritarianism is never in doubt: statements to the contrary are not just sinister but cynical. The dialogic interaction continues, as if *The Mute's Soliloquy* were reading the *Buru Quartet* and vice versa. The journalists who finally gain access to Buru at the moment of its disassembly elicit confirmations of Pramoedya's beliefs. Unrepentant he states:

Just as politics cannot be separated from life, life cannot be separated from politics. People who consider themselves to be nonpolitical are no different; they've already been assimilated with the current political views—they just don't feel it anymore. This is normal. Throughout history, almost all literary works have been political. People must broaden their understanding and accept the fact that politics, not political parties, is tied in with anything and everything that is related to power. As long as man is a social animal, he will participate in political activity. [And here the dialogism cuts also in the direction of *Imagined Communities*] Showing respect for the flag, singing the national anthem, and paying taxes are political statements. (MS 333)

Meanwhile, in *House of Glass*, Minke interjects:

Everything is connected to politics! Everything runs on organization. Do you gentlemen think the illiterate farmers who only hoe do not interfere in politics? As soon as they hand over a small part of their production to the government of the village as tax, they have engaged in politics, because they have confirmed and acknowledged government authority. (RK 313, HG 313)

Minke does not sign the document and dies not long after from illness. Pangemanann continues to address Minke in the second person, as that spectral presence of nation engaged by Cheah. His mind is now overcome by thoughts of death, as if his heartbeat had been all along in rhythm with Minke's. In a symptomatic flourish, the tetralogy ends not with Pangemanann's death but with the surrendering of the archive that is the *Buru Quartet* to Sanikem (Nyai Ontosoroh). This is appropriate for a number of reasons. As an orphan, Pangemanann understands well the special bond that Minke, the child of all nations, has with his adoptive mother (even if this is not legally affirmed). *House of Glass* has been dedicated to explaining the substance of that bond since Minke cannot articulate it himself. Sanikem, now Madame Le Boucq, lives in France and the shifting of the archive beyond what is extant in the East Indies both allegorizes the portent of colonial libraries and describes an arc of the long space in the international public sphere; what the text says to Indonesians is also predicated on its ability to arrive from a constitutive outside when the state polices eventness from within. But finally, the text returning to Ontosoroh is not a convenient closure to a sprawling work of some fifteen hundred pages. If Anderson is right that nation pivots on an axiomatic meanwhile permitting imagination a quintessentially modern purchase on community, the novel is not its equal but its question. The form demands an impossible capacity to cognize a process ongoing as if from the outside. It asks not for an understanding of its analogy but for a dialogic struggle with its duration. The awakening to nation is the sunrise of memory over slumber but cannot guarantee a form for that eventness, even as the novel diligently attends to it. Benjamin uses the term dialectical image to mark the moment of modernity and it stretches well beyond the shorthand of our meanwhile:

It's not that what is past casts its light on what is present, or what is present its light on what is past; rather, image is that wherein what has been comes together in a flash with the now to form a constellation. In other words, image is dialectics at a standstill. For while the relation of the present to the past is a purely temporal, continuous one, the relation what-has-been to the now is dialectical: is not progression but image, suddenly emergent. Only dialectical images are genuine images (that is, not archaic); and the place where one encounters them is language. Awakening.[59]

This Quartet Which Is Not One

Puis des clameurs, puis un tumulte.
—Eugène Fromentin, *Une année dans le Sahel*

Assia Djebar's Algerian Quartet is not yet complete. Over two decades in the making, Djebar's tetralogy still conjures its final volume (one of the working titles is "The Tears of St. Augustine" ["les larmes de Saint Augustin"]), which is not just a sign of Djebar's intense working of form but also symptomatic of her profound engagement with writing as history—a process that finds history writing the space of form as a receding horizon.[1] Given that the first volume of the Quartet appeared in 1985 and Djebar was "deep into the third novel" in 1988 (the third volume was eventually published in 1995, the second in 1987), the period necessitated for the fourth volume is noticeably protracted. As her bibliography shows, Djebar has written many other books during this period, all of which directly affect the contours, real and imagined, of the Quartet (one of them, *La femme sans sepulture*, was begun in 1981 and put aside for twenty years before being completed).[2] Djebar's aesthetic is a scriptible voice in the space of silence, a complex troping on history that explores writing as a feminist intervention against what history determines as unutterable.[3] It is not a single voice, however much it appears to encapsulate her oeuvre in general, because the approach decenters a monadic consciousness that would represent Algerian woman as unproblematically identifiable; indeed, Djebar often begins her novels from a position in which representational aesthetics suppresses in advance the woman's story. This presents a continuing dilemma for Djebar as she writes the ultimate volume of her tetralogy; but clearly it pinpoints an ongoing crisis in reception and reading (and, of course, translation), for the project has been so long in the offing that criticism tends to finish the Quartet for her, projecting its formal completion and speculating each new book is the volume the form intends (*Far from Medina* and *Algerian White* are the usual suspects, but other texts can be indirectly linked in this way).[4] Such desire is not outside the present project the original premise of which was founded on the inspiration Djebar's writing provides: how to articulate the postcolony beyond the deleterious prescriptions of the colonial episteme? In what language? In what form? The alternative strategy is no less suspect, which is to argue historical texture measures the Algerian Quartet's incompleteness; it is a tetralogy whose very principles of narration subtend the possibility of completion, even with the addition of a fourth volume. Indeed, the paradox of enclosure will weigh on the following argument, as it does on Djebar's metaphor of the great house in her writing whose labyrinthine, mauresque, hybrid architecture is best exampled by the Alhambra.[5] If there is value to the hermeneutics of the fragment, it is because it relies on Djebar's understanding of the quartet as a specific form itself, which depends, paradoxically, on fancy as that which overreaches its borders (the correlative here lies in classical music and a tradition of composition, the fantasia, around which Djebar further complicates her aesthetic).[6] Finished or not, the Quartet is form under erasure, identification under threat, a moment of Benjaminian danger that does not distill memory so much as question the possibility of its inscription, an interrogative force that Djebar calls a "pulsion memorielle."[7] In Djebar's writing one witnesses an entropy in the laws of form themselves; so as I herald the emergence of a quartet that has yet to be, I will simultaneously argue in the future anterior that this, therefore, will not have been a tetralogy. The long space does find a home in trilogies and tetralogies but marks their insufficiencies as more than convenient formal failures: it is an effulgence of conditional limits on codes of expressivity, on what might give substance to narration itself. As with Farah and Pramoedya, nation is at stake, albeit imaginary and imagined in ways that question available formulae, and like Harris, the language of form is being stretched to breaking. But Djebar compounds the problems of inscription by taking the exilic as the sign of form's asphyxiating strictures, and yet that existential margin is the very space where what is left to writing might be laid down, bloodied by fighting the *longue durée* of colonial lore. While the inevitability of the fourth volume is assumed, no assurance governs what form these new modes of addressivity might take. This is the other project in which Djebar's *kalaam* (*qalam* or pen in Arabic) is engaged.

There is a studied intricacy in Djebar's intervention: positively in the knowledge of imperial French deracinated from colonial subjugation to Algerian statehood; and more negatively in Djebar's connection to academic institutions (now New York University but previously Louisiana State University) that can leaden utterance with a reflexivity mediated by scholarly exchange—particularly now, when institutionalized French is so concerned to wrap the francophonic with precious inclusivity. Djebar does not render narration for academic consumption; but when we consider the formal attributes of vexed affiliation this also extends to academic discourse which for Djebar, as a history teacher and Islamic scholar, is more than a vague abstraction. If one ponders Djebar's consummate skill in articulating Algerian sensibilities (in Algeria and its diaspora), she is one of the Maghreb's greatest writers (and preeminent among those who emerged in the second half of the twentieth century—Mohammed Dib, Kateb Yacine, Abdelkebir Khatibi, Leila Sebbar, Tahar Ben Jelloun, Rachid Boujedra, to name a few from this rich constellation).[8] Djebar has been famous in the Maghreb from the publication of her first novel, *La soif* (1957), but critical response in the West should also be noted, especially since the appearance of the pivotal collection, *Femmes d'Alger dans leur appartement* (1980—subsequently translated into English as *Women of Algiers in Their Apartment* in 1992) and intensively from the 1990s on.[9] How might this inflect the writer's perception of her project? The example of Djebar reconfigures the "subject" of world literature and particularizes the long space as both an index of my project for an adequate critical framework regarding extended transnational fiction and as a writer's public domain. Djebar finds herself so proximate to academic discourse she comes close to ironizing and not simply introjecting it. In a response to Clarisse Zimra (who, along with Anne Donadey and Mildred Mortimer, has provided crucial openings both to anglophone and francophone critiques of Djebar alike)[10] Djebar notes, "Undoubtedly—and as you have yourself told me many times—*Women of Algiers* is key to the rest of my corpus."[11] Is it because Djebar has been informed so many times that *Women of Algiers* is the linchpin of her work that she is now convinced of that observation or is she quietly congratulating the critic for acknowledging what she believes, that the mix of fact and fiction, voice and memory, image and gaze, history and autobiography that characterizes the *Women of Algiers* collection sets up the challenge in understanding her writing before and since and particularly in meeting the aesthetic and political provenance of the Algerian Quartet?

Djebar's "Postface" to *Women of Algiers* has been called "a major theoretical intervention" so one might be forgiven for seeing the hermeneutical power not only in Djebar's provocative epigraphs (tracked in Donadey's
Recasting Postcolonialism) but also where Djebar herself articulates interpretive principles *as criticism*.[12] Few have taken Djebar's own pronouncements as part of the formal achievement in the Algerian Quartet, even if
these form a blueprint on the ineffable or, to borrow from Djebar's original
title for *Far from Medina*, "silence sur soie" (a silence on silk, but also the
homonym, "silence sur soi," a silence on the self). All inscription, whether
on paper, screens, or veils, is silent and is a silent witness to those eyes that
pore over it. Silence is not the lack of words but their plenitude as text. The
political problem is who speaks them—who speaks and who is spoken for
in the conflictual realm of the uttered and the unutterable? We can ask
"What does the veil say?" (What does it mean?); it speaks without a voice
and this is the quality of silence on silk but also silence "about" a veil of
silk, the suppression of dialogue around its logic of signification where a
woman's voice is meant to be, meant to mean. There is pain and horror
written into silent silk, which has seen violence perpetrated in the maintenance of silence in women's history, Algerian history, and versions of Islamic history, all of which are key concerns of Djebar's writing. Djebar
has often alluded to the blood of writing which maintains its connection
to the violence of history.[13] Here we are concerned to trace four constitutive elements in that regard: transcription, translation, transcoding, and
transformation. But do not trust this math because, like Isma and Hajila
from *A Sister*, there is a doubling up and oblique division ("the sultana
has a double/is one within two" [*Ombre Sultane*, 104]) just as four volumes
might be three in the scheme of things. The "trans" is both a mnemonic
device and a condition of possibility, something remembered from a writing yet to be, from a form as yet unenunciated.

Certain truths overdetermine the body of texts making up the quartet, the blood that makes words, the silence that makes voice, as if for all
the anamnesis that recalls history through imagination (a postcolonial
practice of writing explored by Francoise Lionnet and Anne Donadey)
history's immediacy is deeply frangible in the moment of writing.[14] What
stays Djebar's hand in the act of writing the Algerian Quartet is the massacre of students protesting bread prices in Algiers in October 1988 and
the civil war that began after the national election of December 1991 (the

election was annulled when it became clear that the FIS [Islamic Salvation Front] would emerge victorious with 188 of the 430 seats at stake in the first round). Djebar understands well the violence of colonialism but nothing can prepare one for the violence of the postcolony, especially when galvanized economically and socially by ethnic, religious, and geographic difference. When the government fires on its own people, or when the murder of unarmed civilians becomes the tactic of choice whether pro- or antigovernment, the complex contradictions of colonization's shadow are intensified and place great weight on the substance of identification. What does it mean to be Algerian when that subject is divided against itself, and violently, in so many ways? Does the crisis of the postcolony press the terms of allegiance? Should the Islamists hold sway? Should the Berbers assert their autonomy through a separate state? Should the secular socialists give up their dream of redistribution for privatization, particularly of the profitable gas and oil industries? Should anyone question that the French arms the same military that fought against them in the war of independence? And what of Saudi Arabian funding of Wahabi-based political parties who at different times have been assisted in their endeavors by the beneficent ministrations of the CIA? Is Algeria's Law of Civil Harmony (1999) sufficient to quell the machinations at work from such a multitude of interests? Djebar has never been able to call the war against the French a "revolution" because it did not revolutionize the extant conditions of Algerian women and did not end the paradigm of subservience that colonialism (but not colonialism alone) helped to propagate. What 1988 and the continuing threat of civil war underline is not the luxury of writing but writing's emergency. How can one contemplate the reflexive desire to recreate the past as speaking still when the present is so bound to murderous conflagration? Djebar has opined that "Narration must not tell the story but interrupt it: that is to say, suspend it, surprise it at all costs."[15] The same is true of history in relation to form. Thus, the form of the quartet cannot be Algeria or, if it is Algeria then no quartet will be found. No revolution without transformation.

Djebar links the form of fiction to the sociopolitical realities of the Algerian state: "I wish to specify here I have *never* used the term *revolution*, even at the time when it was flooding and drowning every discourse, public or private . . . *this* is what I understand by the term *form*, a certain kind of rigor and precision in one's thinking. That's what I intended for

La soif; that's what I came back to with *Ombre sultane*. You might call it an ethic."[16] There is a much discussed break in Djebar's published writing (from 1962 when she took up a position teaching history at the University of Algiers through most of the 1970s), which culminates in a turn to film and to the stunning achievements of *La Nouba des femmes du Mont Chenoua* (1978) and *La Zerda ou les chants de l'oubli* (shot in 1979).[17] The work in cinema does not stop Djebar's passion for writing but rearticulates it: "Film gave my writing a vision; French became my camera" (*Women* 174). Like "voicing," these are metaphors but are "rigorous" and "precise": when one wants to displace the gaze of Delacroix (whose painting gives Djebar's *Women of Algiers* its title) and other Orientalists, writing as a "stolen glance" is not just appropriate but vital. Yet the use of "form" here as an ethic is as provocative as it is confounding. There is an ethics of writing wherever answerability is at stake but this does not necessarily secrete form, at least not with the "rigor and precision" Djebar suggests. Part of the challenge in the Algerian Quartet (to be) is not to confuse Djebar's ethics of form with *a* form, the quartet, that undoes the neatness of such a connection, especially in light of the historical crisis alluded to above. The long space is a means to span the historically specific contexts of postcolonial narration via a sedimented duration that putatively exceeds them. The device becomes form at the moment when the writer herself seeks to express the historical disjunction of postcolonialism as extended narrative, as a chronotope that is neither one person's experience of decolonization nor even a group's, but is a narrative of the process of change itself. Form is not a metaphor of questioning but its constitutive possibility.

If the Quartet is already written it is because Djebar constantly writes and rewrites her stories, reinflecting earlier tales in the present and borrowing freely from her historical research and film production notebooks or diaries. As in a musical quartet, a fantasia, the art comes down to arrangement and the careful, while fanciful, use of sound, tone, and transcription. The process is also exacting in the manner of poetry: it conveys the manner in which the women's story can be told, spoken, and seen. Women are both actors and witnesses in the Quartet as if the narratives are a demonstration of agency and recording. Djebar does not fill in the gaps of French colonial history and the adventures of Eugene Fromentin, Matterer, or Barchou. Colonial history is what it is: it is not to be filled in but engulfed, and thus Djebar floods its murderous objectivity with subjective excess and imagined interlocutors from the capture of Algiers in 1830 to the strife of the present day. That Djebar's alternative history is written in French has provoked a predictable response: if Algeria's break from France is not revolutionary the radicalism that would deploy the language of the colonizer is not unquestionable either. The use of French does not betray decolonization, at least not by fiat, because Djebar begins narration from within the schism that colonialism rends in language (which, in Algeria, also means a break between Berber, Djebar's ancestral language, and Arabic, the language of her home). One should not have to list again the great number of francophone writers of North Africa who have dialogized the consonance of French with France but what is the philosophical register of this difference? Derrida, the Algerian, suggests: "We only ever speak one language . . . we never speak only one language."[18] Language is an injunction that one lives within. An individual language can be chosen or learned but the principle to which Derrida alludes is *of* language and thus provides an aporia when applied to *one* language (the occasion for Derrida's formulation is an intellectual exchange with Abdelkebir Khatibi for whom deconstruction in the Mahgreb is a material condition of scarcity that stands in bleak contrast to its generally extravagant excess in Western theory).[19] It is always important to ask why a postcolonial writer uses a colonial language, but what happens to a language of empire when it is subject to refraction by difference? Francophone, like anglophone, is not a monopoly of postcolonies: it continues the work of decolonization in the former empire's heart. The question has already moved beyond rationalization to the more interesting level of material contradiction.

That Djebar begins *L'amour* with such contradiction is symptomatic of her deep interest in the problem of language for identification. The young Arab girl is led to French school by the hand of her father (himself a schoolteacher), and immediately the *mise en scene* of postcoloniality and the structural/poststructural is engaged. If it is the framing device for a certain philosophy of writing, then it is also an opening to parentheses that cannot be closed by regulative form. Paradoxically, the entry into French knows no interclusion; it cannot block difference not just because of faith in the wily signifier but because its materialization preexists the event of Djebar's writing. The intricate compositional layers of *L'amour*—three parts with three overlapping interlocutors (the French colonial archive, Algerian women's oral testimonies, and fragments of Djebar's autobiography), each part further subdivided (the third in particular by "movements" that emphasize the musical leitmotif of *fantasia*)—are a writerly challenge to the order of history and to the reliance on postcolonial narrative as a mimetic content awaiting the eager gaze of those convinced Algerian inscrutability requires "unveiling." Like Glissant's Martinique, or Harris's Guyana, Djebar's Algeria maintains a right to opacity, although for different reasons, politically and aesthetically.[20]

Because Djebar writes in French, her position within the text is *intercessive* (a term she has used to describe the influence of French painters but also her colonial interlocutors): she resists the notion that she or her writing somehow stand for Algerian women.[21] It is a dangerous gambit because such complex affiliation can be misread as evasive: the writer ultimately places her faith in her writing as writing and however much *l'ecrit* sounds like *les cris* the women of the text are still disembodied by discourse. This misconstrues the way Djebar transcribes: she takes proximity with her Algerian sisters as a condition of collapsing inside and outside and therefore challenges masculinist discourses of seclusion. It is also a body politics, "To read this writing I must bend over backwards, plunge my face into shadows, scrutinize the vaulted rock or chalk, let the timeless whispers rise up, bloodied geology" (*L'amour*, 58). Distance is duration of another kind, not condescending separation. Transcription is narration across writing itself. We still have the writing of oral narratives, particularly those of the *porteuses de feu*, women warriors in the Algerian War of Independence (stories that Djebar sets down in the region of her native Cherchell), but this is not a truth in writing because Djebar does not accurately reproduce the words of the "fire carriers." If Djebar disturbs the archive by reimagining the moment of its record this also cancels through the scene of her note taking as women tell their stories about the war with France ("France" here is the French army). The disturbance of language is enough to set the form in motion.

The first two sections of *L'amour* find Djebar oscillating wildly between autobiographical fragments and colonial narration. She names her sources (except herself who, like other characters, has a double) and locates historical documents and the order of time to which they pay obeisance. One key example of troubling the archive is the manner in which Djebar takes up the position of Pelissier in recording the French occupation from the 1830s on. Pelissier's deeds are alarming but they are delivered in the style of the ardent researcher who exposes documents to the light of day. It is June 1845 in Algeria and Colonel Pelissier has orders to mop up regional tribal resistance. His Arab collaborators show off their horsemanship by performing a *fantasia* but it is fire that performs the work of suppression. On June 19 Pelissier orders that fires be lit outside the caves of the recalcitrant Ouled Riah tribe and by the following day at least fifteen hundred men, women, and children have been burned to death or asphyxiated. Similar massacres are perpetrated elsewhere in Algeria during the French "pacification" campaign (yet resistance continued even after the French claimed the process was complete). Djebar plays on Pelissier's compulsion, which is not so much about guilt but writing itself. She quotes Lieutenant-Colonel Canrobert bemoaning that Pelissier "gave in his report an eloquent and realistic—much too realistic—description of the Arabs' suffering" (*Fantasia*, 75). Djebar thanks Pelissier for his record because it allows her, and in French no less, to constitute a shroud of death upon which she will write, to link the past with the present as a constitutive, although not necessarily chronological, process. Djebar treats the record of Pelissier's barbarism as an open text that is simultaneously a palimpsest with "other" inscriptions resting beneath (*Fantasia*, 79). The trope of the palimpsest is extremely powerful in postcolonial narration where it typifies how colonial discourse has written over the conditions and experiences of the colonized and contains a text that is simultaneously its counternarrative.[22] The weakness of the device is not just its archaism (colonial archives have not had much use for medieval parchment) but that it suggests the true story can be scratched at and revealed as already composed. Certainly this is not the tendency in Gerard Genette's interpretation, who elaborates the term as an instance of narrative transfocalization, but Bakhtinian double voicing does not prioritize one inscription over another in this way.[23] Djebar's achievement in transcription is actually closer to a reverse palimpsest: she writes in French "beneath" French to deracinate its origins while appearing to write over it with the authority of correction. True, Marx and Engels ascribe a negative connotation to the reverse palimpsest in the *Communist Manifesto* by suggesting that German socialists adopted French antibourgeois rhetoric without acknowledging its difference from the specificity of their own class conflict.[24] Here it is a more proactive and destabilizing strategy. Djebar adopts the style of the impassioned recorder the better to intercede with "the charred passion of my ancestors" (*Fantasia*, 97). Like Pelissier, Djebar is an "intercesseure," but one dedicated to fire of a different sort, the heat of matrilineal narration and the spark of a collectivity not always "Algerian" and never innocently "French" with its masculinist "flickering flames of successive fires" (*Fantasia*, 46).

Transcription for Djebar, as several commentators and Djebar have pointed out, is also an act of anamnesis; she is transported along an axis of eventness to relive not just her own life but the lives of others at key moments in history. Like Pelissier, she is a scribe who does more than witness; her own passion for the scriptible is always at stake. The mode of transcription entails, as Djebar underlines above, an ethic, a commitment suffusing her work with a plurality of surfaces, as if the palimpsest trumps priority with polyphony, with "I"s that bleed into one another. Like Fanon, Djebar is always questioning, but for her this means transcription is also reinscription and rearticulation. This reveals the continuing struggle to wrest silence from the unwritten, whether in the look of one of Delacroix's odalisques or in the spaces where patriarchy offers asphyxiation. Transcribing archives demystifies them. The key to transcription is Djebar's vexed relationship to French. Time after time in the three volumes of the Quartet she draws attention to the opening created between the voices of Algerian women and Djebar's French in representing them. This space is not just the contact zone of colonial encounters theoretically elaborated by Mary Louise Pratt, but a chronotope in which an encounter does not find the space of Algeria chronological.[25] Thus, in the third section of *Fantasia* the "recorded" voices of women resonate as if in the battle of Algiers in the nineteenth, not twentieth, century, and are transcriptions from interviews Djebar conducted with relatives from her tribe for the film *La Nouba*. Interestingly, one senses the interviewer from the film, Lila (another Djebarian double), in the novel but the Chenouan women resist rearticulation even as they challenge the pained solemnity of the colonial discourse preceding them. Part Three begins with two epigraphs, one from the Algerian St. Augustine and the other from a note by Beethoven, "quasi una fantasia," the significance of which is not to be found in the noun so much as the Latin conjunction: seemingly, almost, but not. The question of semblance here is axiomatic, for what seems like fantasia in fact resists such taxonomy (just like Beethoven's musical correlative, although Djebar wants to reproduce the effect of alternating contrasts in Beethoven's sonatas). Djebar's transcription resides in the "almost," textures the "seemingly," but does not assume identity. It is more than ambivalence: Djebar resists the mimetic because this is language as projection; likeness opens itself into objecthood and even tribal metonymy cannot escape its reach. Strategic noncoincidence has its pitfalls so the text proceeds as a layered confession, a testimonial in which the voice of one speaker tends to merge or overlap the voice of another (hence a certain appropriateness in palimpsest as polyphony rather than parchment).

The first voice of the section is the narrative "I" who, at seventeen, struggles to cry out, to vomit, the "macabre residue of a former century" (*Fantasia*, 115). It is as if the narrator carries within her this submerged absence as presence, as if the organs of her body are themselves an archive: the difference between affiliation with place and affiliation with movement through space. Djebar suggests (most pointedly in "Anamnesis")[26] that the hand is the most provocative link between the act of writing and the body to be inscribed (hence the importance of the severed hand that Fromentin finds) and thus, while the writing itself is not the equivalent of the anticolonial agencies of her sister rebels, it too resists in an archive of sound, place, and body. The narrator's recollection is quickly followed by the first of the voices, Cherifa, whose testimonial describes the machinations of the French army in attempting to separate the mountain tribespeople, removing as many as possible to the plains where they can be policed more easily. The mountains and caves present a tactical nightmare for the French, who are subject to hit-and-run attacks by the *maquis*. Cherifa's younger brother, Ahmed, however, is shot dead and she narrowly escapes an onslaught. The realism is stark and gritty but then Djebar modulates its tone with a subsequent section in the third person that picks up on Cherifa's account and amplifies its meaning for transcription. By altering the angle of address to include an omniscient narrator authorial voice is paradoxically implicated in the event. The effect is like cinematic montage since two perspectives are juxtaposed in the service of a third meaning that is common to both but specific to neither. That the sequence lacks the immediacy of image is overcome by the reflexive capacity of poetic language making the voice a substance for the *Verbe*. The difficulty rests in whether Cherifa's testimony is outweighed by the virtuosity of the poet in Djebar. Cherifa exclaims, "But I saw him fall! Right in front of me!" (*Fantasia*, 121, 122) yet the "clamor" of the narrator speaks perhaps more loudly: "The discordant dirge of inarticulate revolt launches its arabesques into the blue. The lament swells in an upsurge of sound: glissandos passing into vibrato; a stream of emptiness hollows out the air. Barbed wires taut above invisible torments" (*Fantasia*, 123). Such sentences are turned not just to the tenor of voice but also to inscription as sheet music. The meaning is not that the second voice makes the first live, but that twenty years after her brother's death Cherifa's memory is channeled into telling more broadly construed. The compositional rhythm extends into the contrapuntal chords of the auto-biographical "I" whose next utterance takes on the question of strategic silence, both agential and aphasic. The link to Cherifa revolves around the "French," both as language and as an occupying force. This renders the narrator's expressions of love mute yet accentuates her interest in people of her birthplace whose "ancestral warmth" (*Fantasia*, 129) permits speech without possession. The passage between the autobiographical "I" before the War of Independence and the memories of that war some twenty years after in the recollections of "voices" of the tribe, triangulated to some degree by the poetic commentary, does not congeal into a continuum. Even the ironic addition of a "chronology" in the English translation fails to return linearity to the tetralogy. The point of the chronotope is eventness tuned not just to aesthetic anamnesis but to an open concatenation ("At last, voice answers to voice and body can approach body" [*Fantasia*, 129]). If the inscription of memory is anamnesic, the formal implications are proleptic. Unfortunately, history exacts its revenge on such poetics and the vibrancy of *L'amour*'s movements finds vital bloodlines drowned in violent profusion.

The precise alternation in the movements of *L'amour* (autobiographical sketch, transcription of an interview with a woman remembering the resistance to the French, omniscient narration, then more first-person recollections of youth followed by further transcription and a commentary) stands in contrast to the effervescent language, the madness of love (*L'amour fou*) that is itself the fantasia's fancy. It is both writing through the body and composing through rhythm: the sounds of Djebar's birthplace that sing within consciousness and an unconscious desire measured in the otherwise ambivalent space between utterance and silence. We may not be able to speak of a tetralogy (yet) in Djebar's oeuvre as she desires it, but in the movements that structure the third part of *Fantasia* one can read the "silence of writing" as a formal composition (six elements repeated five times then a finale), as a medium of imaginative counterpoint.

The difficulty of Djebar's project will not permit this neatness to remain, as if the immediacy of writing must unravel the studied arrangement of compositional elements. One might proffer such dissolution as an allegory of Third World subjectivity breaking against the terms of modernity's charge, a narrative in which the emergence of a decolonized Algeria is thwarted by the dead weight of formal prescription (nation state or nothingness) and the inability of North African heterogeneity to suffer the rigors of "civilized" culture. This does not exonerate the "represented" but places renewed emphasis on the terms of representation. So, the movements will round *Fantasia*, but Djebar's polyphonic voice does not hold in the contrasting movements of *Vaste est la prison*, where the clamor is a tumult that defies transcription.

The first movement of *L'amour* again picks up Cherifa's story when she is captured and imprisoned by the French. Whether in solitary confinement or on a hunger strike Cherifa maintains a passionate nonrecognition of the French that extends to the French that Djebar uses. If the second testimony is linked to the first by chronology it is punctuated by the personal (Cherifa loses her older brother) and is immediately followed by the sisterly embrace of the narrator marking a contradiction in transcription: the familiar play on strange and foreign that French allows ("Strange little sister who henceforth I inscribe, or that I veil in a foreign language" [*L'amour*, 160; *Fantasia*, 141]) offers the relationship of the stranger to the strange. Thus, what is at stake here is both the real of Cherifa's experience, buried by official discourses about the war, and the impossibility of French transcription. What is actually written comes close to the very embrace (the section is titled "corps enlacés") that French is felt to deny by invoking the capacity to sing ("je voudrais pouvoir chanter" [*L'amour*, 161]) in the space of dispossession. The scriptible voice teeters on oblivion because it addresses the abyss between speech and writing yet has a supplementary resonance in Djebar's work as a reenactment of the incapacity of the colonizer's language to embrace what is extant Algerian speech. This supplement is itself reaccentuated by gender, a category that must sing and sign women's voice by problematizing the neutrality of language. Thus, in a few pages, Djebar stages the intricate dilemmas of her craft, the overlapping and interrogative themes of history, writing, voice, body, woman, home, violence, occupation, separation, and memory: all "embraced" in a language of collective autobiography that yet doubts the capacity of language to be autobiographical, collective or otherwise.

Just as both feminist and postcolonial studies have moved from binary opposites to in-betweenness (hybridity) to dispersal, singularity, and mourning so Djebar's writing increasingly seems to fit this hermeneutical ambivalence. As Djebar problematizes affiliation in writing through her connection to Algeria, its cultures and peoples, her institutional presence has a symptomatic purchase on interpretation, yet this proximity is rarely figured into the critical act. One is left with the paradox that the more Djebar writes of self-effacement, disappearance, silence, absence, and erasure the more she is critically inscribed, traced, figured, and represented as appropriate evidence for the critical techniques she refracts. This is not unique by any means, but it has significant implications for the work of decolonization.

The interpellation of the interpretative informant is no less questionable than that of the native informant, whose supposed access to the truth of the Other has often served a logic of othering that sutures the epistemic superiority of the West and its protocols. Criticism has rightly deconstructed the truths of objecthood found in the "is" of colonialism and postcoloniality. Such an approach is superfluous with Djebar because she writes from within a conditional and articulate decentering. The cautionary note is about Djebar's nuanced ambivalence about identification produced not only in the material relationship to Algeria but also in the discursive regimens of postcolonial critique. The danger in this second-order reflexivity is seeming to discipline the writer for a genuine interest in reframing critical discourse itself. The point would be to apprehend the proximity and imbrication of theory as itself symptomatic of a specific moment of decolonization requiring just these kinds of indivisibility. At the formal level, this exerts a tremendous pressure on the writing of the tetralogy. Decolonization can occur before independence as a material symptom (hence the historical trajectory of the second volume, *L'Ombre Sultane*, that intensifies the juxtaposition we have already noted in the first) but this re-collection is itself a working through of the terms of decolonizing expression. What is specific to the long space is a transnationalism produced by an engagement with the real of colonial history and marks the extended narratives considered in this book differently from the "epicalness" of the novel in general. We might term this a sensitive dependence on the initial conditions of colonialism, a fragility that measures its violent tendency to paroxysm, chaos, and *tumulte*.

The precise movements in Part Three of *Fantasia* stand in contrast to the peripateia of their content. While the transcriptions of the mountain women are realistically conveyed Djebar also establishes new dialogues, new utterance contexts to include the fractured linguistic economies of her youth. The effect is startling because in the sections marked "Voice" Djebar not only provides a written record of those whose lives speak but are not necessarily inscribed (these revolutionary women do not read or write [*Fantasia*, 148]) but a speech genre undermining any attempt to rationalize her narration in French. Her tribespeople do not interrupt the text literally but logically in the subtle movement Djebar constructs. The content of each voice, say Zohra's in the second movement, is clear: it is a record of Algerian women's resistance to French occupation and a transcription of the war of independence. A single "Voice," read alone and aloud, feels unedited and conveys the urgency and passion of a time remembered not as yesterday, but as the very breath on lips:

At first, I owned thirty-one cows. . . . In the end, I didn't have a single one left! The soldiers took the lot!

My farm was burnt down three times. Whenever they came back and found it in good repair, they knew the Brothers had rebuilt the house for us! They brought roofing tiles they'd taken from the colonizers' houses. Once again, the French soldiers destroyed it. Once again, the Brothers brought us tiles from the French houses and gave us shelter again . . . "France" came again. So then we decided to do the cooking in the open air, between walls without a roof or even forest. (*Fantasia*, 149; *L'amour*, 170)

The determination not to allow the French to get their way echoes Djebar's equally practiced resistance to French. If there is irony in the telling of this tale in French it is canceled by the timbre of the transcription and its position with other components of the movement. Just as women like Cherifa and Zohra will never submit to the dictates of French hegemony so Djebar's rendering of their narratives sharply announces that even in French, French (or "France") will not be spared. Yet these glimpses into Algerian resistance work not just as content and in juxtaposition to other voices (the writer, the historian, the autobiographer), but also through repetition and extension.

In the same movement the author as autobiographer recalls family gatherings and tribal rituals. These are woman-centered moments permitting the elders to teach subsequent generations correct practices but also notable stories or riddles; yet, because the younger women themselves do not speak, a question is raised about their reflection on the knowledge conveyed. The narrator notes that the speaking women do not use "I" in telling their stories but nevertheless reveal their inner hurt and fate. Both the young who do not speak and the old who cannot say "I" are united by an absenting of the self, one which allows the narrator's grandmother to berate a sister for an overly emotional outburst. If the colonizer silences women, how much more silence is produced by women's introjection of traditional self-effacing propriety? The energetic engagement of the women resisting colonial incursions is directly contrasted with the "I" narrator in the autobiographical sections whose continual struggle is to find a voice by ventriloquating those of the tribeswomen (the term Djebar uses is *enlacer*, which is to hug or clasp but also to entwine or interlace as if by this juxtaposition a form of *parler femme* may be sutured, a body might be composed). Like stolen tiles, Djebar takes French from the French to rebuild what the French have plundered yet French returns, the French return, to destroy this edifice. The multiple languages of the Maghreb are a reality; for better or worse they are the stuff of conquest, flight, and fancy. The question is not whether French is appropriate but whether the intricacies of the form, the tetralogy's organizational structure, find a freedom in interlacing a narrative bound to flight (the keyword is *fugitif*, which is both the escapee and the ephemeral, the fleeting [*fugitivement*]) or by refuge. The difference is a delicate displacement aesthetically but a more brutal materiality for those who have not escaped the stitched truths of colonialism, patriarchy, fundamentalism, nationalist alibis, and civil war.

Within *Fantasia*, the movements of Part Three are the counterpoint to Parts One and Two, separated by the poetic and musical interlude in italics called "Sistrum" (after the ancient Egyptian percussion instrument). Part Three has its own compositional correlative in the fugue, whose polyphonic structure introduces a main theme or tonic which is then answered by a "voice" that picks up and extends it. The process, repeated, forms an exposition answered with a finale or counterexposition. The root of fugue is flight or fleeing and in musicology is eventually connected to a flight of fancy that brings us back to fantasia. The style is necessarily Baroque genealogically but not absolutely. Interestingly, in its Romantic revival its intricacies were often described as "academic" or studied, but in the twentieth century flight itself implied a compositional freedom well suited to a modernist desire to slip the obligation to content, the dead weight of *Dasein*. Modernity's sister, psychoanalysis, also gives us the fugue state, whose characteristic dissociation is often read to be a refuge from trauma. Djebar is so conscious of all these compositional elements and their tropical inconstancy that technique itself threatens to become the heroine of her art. The voice that answers this theme should not admonish desire, since desire laughs at such adjudication. Far from excluding Djebar in her own name, such displacement finds her skills integral. We call this formal injunction discrepant integrity but only as it places a pause over both the author and critic about *les cris* in *l'écrit*.[27]

Silence or speech, the silence of writing, the silence in speech: all are symptoms of narrative's dance with oblivion, a performance materially and not just serendipitously allied with a North African woman writer stepping among contingent formations of language, gender, and nation. Coming almost halfway through *Fantasia* "Sistrum" or *Sistre* talks back to the rhythmic and sometimes violent point/counterpoint of the education of a young Arabo/Berber woman under French colonialism and the simultaneous yet subsequent conversation with the French colonial archive. Writing and voice are the characters in this dialogic and, rather than summarize their interaction, the final note in *Sistre* is struck by poetic transition and thematic echo. It begins with a long silence lying in the throat (*râler en silence*, to fume, yet *râler* also as to gasp one's final breath). Silence is a source of sound, in this case of interlaced echoes (*sources d'échos entre-croisés*), the very compositional structure of the fugue to follow and a chiasmatic trace that can be found throughout the Quartet so far. More than this, however, silence streams from the throat in phrases of exuberant alliteration and rhyming: "surgeon susurrant sous la langue," "retrouve souffles souillés de soûlerie ancienne." The embodied, erotic language conveys both the sensate aspect of sound from silence and the sensuality of a voice whose liquid tongue conjures appropriate water imagery and the moist sexuality of ecstasy. This is the love in the novel's title (excluded in the English translation), an emotional embrace that takes pleasure in exploring silence for its potential to express, lovingly, that which it otherwise appears to deny, voice: "Soufflerie souffreteuse ou solenelle du temps d'amour, soufriere de quelle attente, fievre des staccato." The art of the prose poet is conjoined with sensual instrumentation (the sistrum could accompany rites of Isis) in a lush linguistic outburst daring French exoticism to gaze covetously.

Many critics have noted the effect of listening to Djebar read her poetry or prose, readings that offer a lilting cadence and subtle use of pauses, but Djebar understands such performances largely fall on deaf ears in Algeria where many of those whom she transcribes, like Cherifa and Zohra, are illiterate and do not speak French (even those who read Arabic have comparatively little access to translations of Djebar's work). If her writing is an extended love letter to the people of her home country, its arrival is as vexed as Djebar's relationship to French: the freedom and the pleasures of French are sent with an indemnity of separation as well as communication. The searing poetry of *Sistre* is only matched by the eloquent silence of linguistic difference, yet this is the reason for instrumentation and its percussive correlative so that even if French is not known its music is expressed. What would the history of Algerian resistance to the French sound like? Perhaps a fugue that permits fancy, but if Djebar's Quartet so far is any indication it would have to be both polyphonic and dissonant; it would have to embrace the music of the mountains as well as the coast and rely on the power of memory, of silence in history, and of creation ("création chaque nuit" like Scheherazade [*L'amour*, 125]). Certainly it would be the space of voices, if not harmony.

If *Sistre* is the counterexposition to Parts One and Two of *Fantasia* then *Tzarl-rit* represents the flourish that ties Part Three to the rest of the book since it concludes the five movements that precede it. The musical motifs remain, as does the striking emphasis on transcription, here interpreted not as writing over but as writing under and through. Like the voice that the "I" narrator cannot remember of her long-departed paternal grandmother, the reverse palimpsest creates in the space of whispers, a woman's space where voices do not so much confirm presence as trace, a verbal edge between women as they remember history as an alternative archive. In "Tzarl-rit" recollection is multiply represented, although not altogether representable, which is the point in using two epigraphs from Arabic-French dictionaries that attempt to render the cry specific to "tzarl-rit" (is it of women's joy or misfortune?). The narrator first recalls a woman named Pauline, a schoolteacher who fought for her ideals in the 1848 revolution and for her troubles was deported to Algeria in 1852. She is there for only four months but during this time writes feverish letters to friends and family, some of which record the lives of Algerian women she meets. The narrator sees a comrade in letters, joined by a French vocabulary, *enlacées*, entwined

(*L'amour*, 250; *Fantasia*, 223). As with the paradox of French that weighs down Algerian expressivity, this kindred voice frees the narrator (to write but also to move, since, as Djebar points out, the body is also a woman's language).

The second compositional element of the finale is a reflection on Eugene Fromentin, another French "visitor" to Algeria, an artist who falls in love with the light he finds there (Djebar had previously considered the "intoxicated gaze" of Delacroix in *Women of Algiers*). Like Pauline, a contemporary, he writes of the Algeria he sees and similarly refracts the trace of Algerian women—in this case the dying words of Haoua, who has been kicked in the face by the horse of a rejected lover who is performing in a Fantasia. The historian notes, "Can no love-story ever be invoked in these regions except by its tragic consequences?" (*Fantasia*, 225). Djebar registers both a "murmur in the margin" and Fromentin's own fantasia, a love for Haoua that leads to an ex-lover's revenge. We have, then, two records of French occupation in two forms of solidarity. The first, delivered in French correspondence, is the work of a revolutionary in exile; the second, the diary entry of an artist whose passion extends rather than curtails local suffering. What is the "true tragedy" of the fantasia, the historian asks? Is it, as is suggested in Fromentin's words "the gesture of a victory in flight," the paradox of a successful "charge" that ends with horses withdrawing, or of a passion that ends in death? Fromentin loves Algerian light. The mimetic faculty of colonialism seeks to take this light by freezing time and, from this perspective, decolonization extends time and thus releases a light (narrative?) denied. Just as Djebar runs two historical records side by side yet within one another, so we are confronted with the difficulty of two tropes in dialogic struggle: one whose fulcrum is vision and visual representation (*the* most prominent logic of Orientalism); the other whose sense perception is aural, dissonant yet syncopated, freely styled yet formally distinct. The fantasia carries the weight of synesthesia (*L'amour* excerpts Delacroix's "Excercice des Marocains" on its cover and the rhythmic imagination of Beethoven or Messiaen within). Both senses are mixed agonistically as if they might throw into relief the sensate barbarism invasion entails (again, the two meanings of fantasia as warlike horsemanship and European classical music). What unites these senses is ultimately the kinetic, the movement that grounds a movement, the very energy that orders the text yet threatens to pull it apart. This too is a trope and it can manifest itself in a startling image, like the severed hand that Fromentin picks up then discards in the wake of a French massacre, a hand that the autobiographical "I" seizes, the hand of a murdered and mutilated Algerian woman now holding the pen of the long space, a kinesis bound to the condition of stolen time and occupied space.

The last compositional element of the finale embraces the other two by grasping the hand of inscription (the dead hand like the unheard screams of those in burning caves can write, can be rendered scriptible, for this is the other side of dialogism, the speech genre of the impossible). The autobiographical "I" speaks of nomad memory and an interrupted voice (the severed sound elucidated in the last part of *Women of Algiers*). Here it is rendered provocative by Djebar's deep reflection on the difference between her speech and writing, overdetermined by the oral and written in Algerian history, the schisms between Arabic, Berber, and French, and a refiguring of the passage from the imaginary to the symbolic as both a feminist and postcolonial problematic. The "I" in her metacommentary is interpreted by critics as ontologically secure or "veiled" beyond the ambivalence veiling connotes. The "veiled" "I" travels the "four corners" of Algeria as if wrapped by the silence that follows funeral lamentations (*Fantasia*, 226). This does not conclude the novel but is a means to open up further concerns of memory, of wounds, of the haunting of butchered tribes, and especially of the fate of Algerian women who dare to stand up (*dressée libre*) who she, the narrator, hears even now deathlike in the triumphant cry of the fantasia. It is a remarkable set of passages dedicated to affect not as mourning but as an aesthetic compulsion caught between joy and misfortune.[28] Because this simultaneously negotiates the fraught space of nation and belonging via a language of decolonization *and* deracination Djebar finds her narrative poised on the abyss of form. If she can fuse the past to the present she cannot, as a historian or novelist, assemble the present that presses on her mode of apprehension. She thus opens up a fantastic dialogue with history, utterances that speak through official narratives, but then finds new and formidable interlocutors who demand space in her writing. These voices, unknown and unheard in her original project, will come to dominate the Quartet and crucially redefine the urgency of form in its articulation.

To transcribe is already to transform in the sense that Djebar's versions of history and of voices is always a form apart from both official

French history and women speaking in the mountains of Chenoua. Yet the act of transcription needs to be kept distinct in order to mark writing itself as an intervention when summoned to identification. In *Fantasia*, and to a great extent in *Sister*, transcription is disruptive, but it is a disturbance in which Djebar's is an active participant. Self-presencing in these two novels is ardent as various speaking subjects take up the story of Algerian women denied transcription even as women themselves are omnipresent storytellers. But anamnesis, self-presencing in the process of articulating a present in a past (with a strong tendency to chiasmus, as Zimra argues) works best as a project of making history new.[29] Its relationship to the present is more problematic because the past allows perspective on what history confers and no such vision surveys immediacy; when time is so tactile its touch is pervasive. At the end of *Sister* the narrator, signaled by italics, notes "the present congeals around us" (*Sister*, 160) but not enough to guarantee apprehension. Taken as individual genres, the historical novel, the novel of the present, and the novel of the future exercise stock conventions; it is only in their admixtures that they bring to crisis genres, if not the form that founds them. Djebar meets this challenge but this cannot diminish the dilemma of time's effect on the form of narration. If we argue postcolonial writing is an emergent formation, an historically specific narration not precipitate but in the process of condensation, then the problem of form refracts something of what Raymond Williams once described as a "structure of feeling."[30]

The concept of the long space can be productively linked to the structure of feeling as "the edge of semantic availability,"[31] to the notion that form in formation struggles against what is both dominant and residual. I invoke structure of feeling here to make the point that the extended narrative of decolonization is a formation in solution whose precise terms of historical distillation must come from a future further from this process *in situ*. The long space is a structure of feeling only to the extent that its provisionality is a consequence of its process in time, which also describes both the arc of its counterhegemonic discourse and its will-to-hegemony in the progressive sense. If such terms are rendered superfluous this might also mark the end of emergence for the form when categories themselves can be more rigorously consigned.

The Quartet thus far is highly structured; its compositional elements organize its narratological surfaces in a very methodical manner. Yet the tetralogy is also suffused with imaginative affiliation and identification that call into question framing devices as just another nefarious construct of seclusion, division, and ordered hierarchy. This tension is highly indicative of a structure of feeling challenging the strictures of dominant orders of experience and expression without becoming merely an amorphous commentary with little or no purchase on the actual orders of culture that obtain. Djebar does not alight upon a formula for this conflict but productively explores a logic of engagement with it. Similarly, structure of feeling is not analogical as such but dialogical, which allows one to ponder form as preformation rather than preformed.[32]

The second volume is begun before the first but is finished two years after it and both books inexorably seep into one another. The commingling is significant on its own terms but here I want to consider the paradoxical structure of the tetralogy (structure, as in "the mutual relation of constituent parts or elements of a whole as defining its particular nature")[33] in relation to the ambivalence introduced in the third volume, *Vaste est la prison* (*So Vast the Prison*)—the book that, metonymically, might stand in for the problem of form in the long space as a whole. *Vaste* is the most determined text in terms of self-presencing while simultaneously the most telescopic historically (it records and rewrites figures of antiquity). If *Fantasia* shows Djebar deftly moving between at least two historical narratives (the French invasion of 1830 and the war of independence begun in the 1950s), in *So Vast* Djebar finds a third narrative interrupting this negotiation. *So Vast* is consistent with both earlier volumes because it is punctuated by an ardent autobiographical voice, yet it is of a different tenor; indeed, it is more a vehicle in the poetic sense. The narrative "I" is the catalyst of Djebar's "free form" and is most attuned to both the musical correlative and the performative *jouissance* of the fantasia as event. It acts as a symbiotic link between the other elements, binding the historical through a figure at once embedded in the genealogy the voices compose. (This is both aesthetic and literal, since Djebar reveals in *So Vast* [330–31] that she is a great granddaughter of Malek el-Berkani, a key figure in the anticolonial rebellion of 1871.) The interruptive and interrogative voice— one prevalent in contemporaneous works such as *Far from Medina* or *The White of Algeria*—carries with it an alternative urgency that stirs memory in emergency (the Benjaminian present as past) as it threatens to cancel in advance the significance of Djebar's immense historical engagement.

With the government massacre of November 1988 in Algiers and the out-
break of civil war after the canceled elections of December 1991, Djebar's
exilic voice becomes more poignant yet also more removed, as if the Algerian history she had painstakingly articulated now demanded recasting
from within the logic of its turmoil. Derrida's Algerian roots help him to
understand the depth of paradox in linguistic signs and its attendant effect on meaning; Djebar's Algerianness teaches her history's purchase on
the substance of form. The nation is a quartet and it is never a quartet. The
form offers a certain perfection aesthetically and socially but defies the
writer who would engage it. The crisis, which is also a crisis of form, must
be transcoded, not because it stands as enigmatically obtuse but because it
interpellates the art of nation as more than record, more than description,
more indeed than accumulation. Djebar begins to doubt her historical
skills for this assumes a being for Algeria that the present roundly contradicts. Pramoedya's narration of nation was girded by a belief in a consonance of form with modernity: architectonically, the nation was to be
made and the perquisites of the tetralogy met that demand. Yet, while one
must appreciate his efforts under the most extreme conditions imaginable,
the steadfastness of the nation's relationship to modernity is less durable
and opens out the imperatives of form to a whole host of pressing concerns: the legacies of colonialism, interdependence on a world scale, the
geopolitics of hegemony, parasitical capital as paranational, and the movement of people as nation negation. Pramoedya wrote nation in defiance
of Indonesia's repetition in difference. Djebar, by contrast, writes against
France's Algeria then wonders if indeed this is the only Algeria possible:
French Algeria, Algeria in French, all else is palimpsest, nomad, veil, and
extravagantly disputed. French Algeria is Algeria from the outside and in
that exotopy both a clarity and the articulation of form is possible. How
far, indeed, is the distance between Fromentin's love of Algerian light and
the heartrending inscription of Algerian white?

Ostensibly, *Vaste est la prison* is structured by writing as silence, erasure, and blood. The third part of the novel borrows from the same source
as the corresponding part in *L'amour*: the research, interviews, and transcriptions Djebar conducted for her first film, *La Nouba*. At this level,
Vaste is consistent with the sharply felt interplay of autobiography and
identification characterizing the Quartet in the early to mid 1980s. Yet
the opening of the novel greatly intensifies Djebar's sense that writing (in

French) reveals a self copresent with the self's oblivion. Such creative entropy can be registered in a number of salient contemporary discourses, but the profundity of Djebar's text lies in its poetic embrace of the conditions that would seek its erasure, as if by taking on the enormity of historical sublation itself the life-affirming power of language is renewed, steeled for the present, like Jugurtha's heroic resistance to Rome in the past. This passion of remembrance figures memory as the living plight of desire. It is a zeal shared with other Algerian writers—Augustine, Kateb Yacine, Franz Fanon, and Jacques Derrida—but none of them has Djebar's ability to discern not just the love in languages with death's proximity, but what silence must say in the space between words as well as within them. Djebar asks whether death, another "silent companion" (*So Vast*, 13) must necessarily speak within redemption? Djebar extends narration as that which collapses interval (the space between) and thus taunts the present with its overtures of effacement, obliteration, and assassination. Djebar takes the principles of embodiment that she has honed so carefully in her other fiction and dares the present to inscribe it rather than mutilate it. This is not some glib masochism in the face of violent victimization (particularly of women) across Algeria. It is an indominatable spirit preexisting the civil war and is evoked among the said and the non-said of the book's characters. It is the silence of writing as translation (a translation from silence) and underlines a specific untranslatability in Djebar's Algeria, if not in Algeria per se.[34]

Djebar's "I" conveys the concreteness of such voicing by contemplating the years of being a silent companion in the *hammam* as other women occasionally mentioned *l'e'dou*, an Arabic word for enemy here signifying husbands of various stripes. When an older woman uses the word the narrator considers its valence, a spoken secret in a woman's space that, once written, assumes another domain where translation may be visible, transparent, and legibility itself becomes a liability. The narrator wants to tear the shroud from death but inscription cannot escape the indemnity she invokes, as if writing allows the enemy to do the work of death. The first part of *So Vast* cheats death through passion, through the sensuality of language in all of its vibrancy. "The threat of imminent disaster" (*So Vast*, 22) is forestalled by an unconditional love of life and a similarly unreserved love affair (with a young man, "L'Aimé," the Beloved). In a touching series of encounters, the narrator works through what is a precondition of love, its wonderful irrationality. No one doubts the subjective temporality and spatiality of love, especially in its spontaneous emergence and florid energy. Falling in love with the enemy has occurred before (a love that remains, in French) but this "forbidden gaze" of the Beloved eloquently turns into passionate apprehension. Thus, just as Djebar abrogates the terms of French for Algerian identification, her narrator challenges social convention despite the violence of its consequences (the wife is beaten but this cannot beat love). To love for oneself is also speaking for oneself and a violent culture of suppression attacks both in the name of order. Here the reverie of love is more empowering and the passages devoted to this freedom through dancing (the body, like words, in flight) are poignant and inspiring. Beneath an aura of seclusion the kinetic becomes subversive. In an interview Djebar recalls her mother admonished her not to use the "I" in talking of herself or otherwise use it anonymously.[35] That tension suffuses the narrator's emotional attachment and yet in each movement of the body, in each glance, in each embrace, the self fights anonymity for selfhood. This may be a metonymic self whose meaning lies in the assertion of Algerian womanhood beyond the logic of silence in the deleterious sense, but an internal polemic emerges through a gathering of voices across the surfaces of Djebar's writing in general and not in the deeply personal experience of love. Djebar does not seek to speak for Algerian women but articulate a counterdiscourse. An appropriate device might be to trace affiliation in which Djebar's being and absence refuses representational claims for a kind of signifying intimacy. This lies at the heart of her long space, writing as a kind of territorial engagement, "une sorte de proche éloignement."[36] It is a difficult point yet one that differentiates between the love linked to fantasia in the first novel of the Quartet and the ability to express love through the "I" in the third. In *Fantasia* surreptitious love letters in French are more about language than the impact of desire on the speaking subject; in *So Vast* love takes hold of language by affirming the emotive over the linguistic.

The language of love is always a translation, the reverie of its dancing body always transcription. It is less a retreat from horror, the orgy of violence unleashed in 1988, but a necessary refuge of self (the fugue of "I") taking pleasure in the fearless exploration of love. In *So Vast* love is transcoded, the passionate "I" confounds thought and precipitates a measure of guilt for the feminist, the daughter, the wife, the historian, the writer in flight. I use transcoding to interrupt the sliding across often redolent in discourses of transcription and translation. Transcoding is a troubling supplement that prepares the ground of transformation yet focuses on concepts rather than praxis itself.[37] Thus, love is not a displacement for history, nor is it the real self subject to that palimpsestic revelation. Instead it is an illicit love, itself a passage of vexed affiliation in a space that *is* but cannot *be* except as a resource of hope, a desire that returns from the future, the release ("délivrance") inscribed in the novel's Berber/French epigraph. The transcoding of love stirs the narrator to question the meaning of her matrilineal inheritance—the power, for instance, of her grandmother's knowledge—just as it causes her to reflect on the weight of patriarchal lore. Among all of Djebar love stories, it is the one that begins most from within the heart not the head, from within the texture of affect rather than in the symphonic weave of the composer, diligently arranging the sonality of fragments.

The counterpoint is first measured in a return to history and its narration otherwise (the counterpoint to the actual violence of 1988 is *Loin de Médine*, a reimagination of the time of Mohammed the Prophet and particularly of his daughter, Fatima, as a "veritable Antigone").[38] Alongside a heartfelt narrative of love and passion Djebar provides a contrasting exploration on transcription by invoking the bilingual stele of Dougga. This double script is epitomized by Jugurtha, a Numidian king who gave the Romans something other than a welcoming dance or display of flowers when they sought to expand their empire across North Africa. Jugurtha is fascinating in his own right and provided a rebellious touchstone to Algerian anticolonialism in the twentieth century.[39] For her part, Djebar is equally curious about Thomas D'Arcos, who is so intoxicated with trade and cultural life in North Africa he becomes, in his sixties, a Muslim. In the 1630s he undertakes an archaeological expedition in Tunis, among the ruins of Dougga, and there finds a stele with two languages inscribed upon it. One language is Phoenician; the other he cannot even guess but he transcribes it and his findings will end up in a Vatican archive. Two hundred years later, a Count Borgia also transcribes the bilingual texts of Dougga, especially those seen on an impressive mausoleum (the stele traditionally marks a grave). Djebar's tone here is reminiscent of her descriptions of Fromentin: she delights in Western exoticism not just to mock its feverish excesses but to mine its History for contraindications of Berber narrative and

an extended instance of biculturalism. Even the architecture of the mausoleum arrays distinct differences in style ("Hellenistic inspiration and oriental archaism" [*So Vast*, 133]), although not with the spectacular arrangement
of space one finds in the mauresque "great house." Djebar records a brief
appearance of Delacroix and again connects the text to *Women of Algiers in
Their Apartment*; then it is quickly on to Sir Granville Temple, who arrives
in Algiers in July 1832, just after Delacroix leaves. Temple, too, will copy
down the bilingual script on the mausoleum and is inspired enough to return to North Africa in 1837 with a Danish friend, Falbe. And so it goes.
Accompanying the French army they witness the siege of Constantine and
the attempt to vanquish the bey Ahmed and his forces, providing commentaries on another sordid chapter of French colonialism. Eventually, a
British consul, Thomas Reade, will have the stele torn from its foundations
and taken to the British Museum. A transcription in Rome, an artefact in
London, a French occupation: the coordinates of not only a stolen glance,
but a stolen history are being drawn, a pronounced parallax of optical de-
lusions and more.[40]

Djebar's fiction problematizes the normative separation of History
from a history that is felt, lived, experienced as a present. It is no coincidence this part of *So Vast* draws on the records of white European men because it is a reflection and refraction on the madcap desire of Orientalism
and masculinism. Djebar ventriloquizes their narration while subimpos-
ing (a reverse palimpsest) the ground of Algerian history and narration.
The strange or foreign writing ("écriture étrange") uses *tifinagh*, a script
voiced and preserved in Berber, a language with many multilingual adher-
ents (Jugurtha, Augustine, Djebar) whose monuments may be displaced
but whose space of enunciation remains in the trace, an architectonic of
interaction. The stele bears this double inscription, literally in the twin-
ning of contrasting alphabets and figuratively in its juxtaposition with
autobiographical excerpts and further transcriptions of "les femmes arable" recounting resistance. The stele is a fetish of Western desire but also
signals its abyss, for its possession does not protect its secret but guarantees transcoding, an effacement that cannot in fact erase or, to use one of
Djebar's more prominent metaphors, a blood that cannot dry. Commentators find the concept of intertext appropriate for Djebar because there is
an insistence on interdependence in the literary and a kind of Kristevan
penchant for Freudian transposition.[41] The story of the stele is a history

of "échos souterrain" but also a transposition of meanings not just between the two texts it carries but between those inscriptions and Djebar's. Djebar dialogizes the materiality of its moment with the discerning eye of an historian and the passionate ear of an interested interlocutor. Transcoding is thus the alignment of historical trajectories and their intercession. Djebar's own writing is not a version of the stele's bilingual array although it clearly iterates such interlingual possibilities. If Djebar mimics the form of the stele it is through the arrangement of complementary texts whose movements "speak" in a space between monument and ruin, inscription and erasure, reflection and eruptive violence, testimony outside the mausoleum and the deathly silence inside. The history recorded in the second part of *So Vast the Prison* writes against the record from which it draws but not as metalepsis. It is interested more in dissemination, what Djebar describes as the polygamous possibilities of Polybe's historicity (the exiled Greek historian who writes of the violence at Carthage and Corinth).[42]

Djebar ends this section with first-person commentary on the Berber princess, Tin Hinan, buried in Abalessa four centuries after Jugurtha's resistance to the Romans and four centuries before the Berber queen la Kahina's resistance to the Arabs. The *tifinagh* inscriptions in her tomb are in fact older than those on the stele and thus she symbolizes not just a link among her Berber revolutionaries but a kind of embeddedness that predates them and lives on still in the desert, in the belly of Africa ("le ventre d'Afrique" [*Vaste*, 164]). Djebar imagines Tin Hinan fleeing with this "secret writing" to preserve it. There is a double movement in Tin Hinan's position for history and thus in the substance of the language she carries with her into eternity. In Djebar's writing, this is the difference between identity and identification, between the substance of the subject that prods objectification (whether obelisk or odalisque the logic is the same) and an imaginative affiliation questioning the stark parameters of a nationalism that at first inspires righteous resistance, but then sublates this spirit by closing off the dialogue of the long space using truncated mythological alibis and state-mandated amnesia. Algerian identification is, like Tin Hinan's necropolis, exorbitant: it is within the putative borders bequeathed by modernity and colonialism but necessarily beyond the logic of their prescriptions. This "beyond," however, must itself be radically particularized, lest its outsideness or exotopy be cathected to an all too predictable critical discourse on cosmopolitan circulation and the comparative "pleasures" of exile.[43] True, Djebar romanticizes her affiliation with her sisters of the Hoggar mountains, but this hardly does justice to her deep commitment to the people of Algeria and to the freedom of its women in particular. For the writer, the historian, and the filmmaker, the "beyond" signals an insufficiency in form, a failure of attributes if not attribution. This is the place where form must always find its initiation but here Djebar resists the notion of form as discovery, the new place "outside," which for postcoloniality is but the novel revelation of colonialism. Neither does she follow modernism's insistence on taboo as a means to pry open narrative discourse and reconnect writing itself with a long space sundered by invasion and conquest. The conditional limits on form are exposed by the writer's confrontation with context which, for Djebar, over-determines the Algerian Quartet. The "beyond" here is a transcription of breath, of voice, the invocation of the lost or erased as never lost or erased (rather than exhume Tin Hinan one should exhale her), and a transcoding of the meaning of history for fiction. Finally, the "beyond" is, like Tin Hinan's experience, fugitive and fleeting ("fugitivement") and this both keeps Djebar writing but preserves a certain impasse in form for which no amount of musical composition will provide sufficient raiment. The long third part of the novel (which is half its length) offers considerable insight on the difficulty of a form-giving process that denies one.

If "A Silent Desire" revisits the transcriptive mode of Part Three of *Fantasia* and uses Djebar's experiences and notes from the making of *La Nouba*, she quickly establishes the process of recording is as much at stake as the stories of the women she interviews. In the first shot she describes, a man in a wheelchair is unable to enter the room where his wife lays asleep because of the steps before him, so he watches and silent desire is drawn across his face. It is an important moment because the camera can help to rethink the place of woman relative to man in Algerian society and this perspective helps Djebar to deobjectify, see otherwise, in her writing, in her French. In *La Nouba* the filmmaker is represented by Lila, who has returned to Cherchell (Djebar's birthplace) in the Chenoua mountains to interview members of her ancestral tribe, those who participated in the resistance to French colonialism. Lila's husband, Ali, is mute and paralyzed after a riding accident, a fact that makes the redrawing of the opening shot in the novel still more interesting. Now it is "la nouba," the turn of the women, to tell their stories and, as we have noted, this is the rationale behind the symphonic form in the round of speaking women. This section is entwined with the tales of Jugurtha and Tin Hinan because it features women of Berber descent who preserve a linguistic embeddedness otherwise inscribed and buried for so long.

Yet the opening shot is doubly prefaced, not just by the fictive filmmaker but by the framing device of the writer who, in a brief but poignant interlude, links the fugitive spirit of Tin Hinan to Zoraide, an Algerian woman whose exploits are recorded in Cervantes's *Don Quixote* then reimagined, voiced, by Djebar. This persistent framing (which continues in the use of epigraphs, different fonts, and shifts from first to third person) is a fugitive aesthetic of metaphor and meaning that will not be silenced, erased, or otherwise submerged in what Algeria represents. If she captures "La nouba" in French (and Djebar doubts she can) it remains released in the impossibility of adequate framing and paradoxically lives on because of it. Like the stele at Dougga, Djebar cannot prevent transcription, transcoding, and translation from being stolen for this is not just the nature of language but the specific risk of transnational territorialization. If the subaltern cannot speak she is spoken; yet if the Algerian woman writes she is written over. Criticism, after all, makes palimpsests so why not revel in the art of subscript? Djebar's language of form, in contrast to Harris, offers the contamination of colonialism as an intriguing prison. The principle of the fugitive slips the fetish of possession, seclusion, and the various veils of patriarchal reverie (perhaps the English translation of *Vaste* using a photograph of faceless veiled women bowed in prayer on its cover is ironic once more).[44]

The authorial interlude, "Fugitive without knowing it," connects Djebar's agency to Zoraide's via the historical links of the women in Djebar's community to those of Andalusia. Djebar thus records the expulsion of Moriscos from Cervantes's Spain to the northern Maghreb, fugitives who brought with them Islam and the keys to their houses in Cordoba and Grenada. Generations later Djebar's mother inherits elements of this history and cultural displacement. She knows their embroidery, their Arabic-Andalusian dialect and, most of all, their music that, like the Mauresque house, is crisscrossed by the mingling of cultures and peoples. The mother wrote down the *noubas* of Andalusia in Arabic to preserve their poetry and music, although these manuscripts are later destroyed by the French for fear they represented a secret nationalism (in effect, they do—so secret that no nation can in fact embody them). The mother mourns this loss not because she cannot remember the songs but because she had written them and now, speaking French, she is no longer so certain in her Arabic script (the severed hand, once more). Djebar writes in French to deny this end of women's writing, this felt erasure of a legacy. The "I" narrator claims to write in her mother's shadow, a daughter who is captive to her mother's status and thus another fugitive in language, another woman in flight. Djebar's "I" uses the phrase "fugitive without knowing it" (*So Vast*, 176; "Fugitive et ne le sachant pas" [*Vaste*, 172]), a difficult formulation since from everything we have argued Djebar hardly seems unconscious of the flight she describes. But her warning is about knowing fugitive sensibility too well; that it succeeds by being experienced "fugitivement" (fleetingly) as a permanent condition occasionally glimpsed (like that first shot). For the North African woman writer positioning necessitates just this pause about consciousness as a completed project within postcoloniality and decolonization. The matrilineal inspiration itself comes with doubt for the *noubas* do not sound the same on the page, or on film for that matter, and certainly not the same way in Paris or New York as they might do in Cherchell. The historical telescoping of Djebar's Quartet so far offers the long space as a form of duration in flight, the fleeting stretched to the horizon historically and geographically. Curiously, the authorial "I" does not record the poetry of the *noubas* (although one could claim that Djebar has come close to reproducing their rhythms and tones in her own poetry). This could be an acknowledgment of the difference between novel and song but might also mean the mother's shadow is not all encompassing. Thus we move from one frame to another but only to find that the parerga do not in fact enclose.[45] This is the point both in reversing the palimpsest and the gaze: the woman looks back through a slit, the veil, the camera eye, at those who assume objectification, concealment. The shadow women (and the woman in shadow) are looking, all five hundred million (*So Vast*, 179). And they are moving. The first movement describes the visit of a mother to her son who is being held captive in France for "criminal association" with the Algerian resistance. It echoes the tale just related by the author of her mother's visit to see her son in a French jail, and Djebar is careful to measure its intensity directly, without recourse to questions of language or the deep structures of history. Despite being separated for so long, the mother has traveled to be with her son. These are vignettes, yet they are also cinematic, visual, and in "Arable Woman II" Djebar lets the emotive angle of address mingle with the position of the camera, the documentary "eye."

For some, this *mise en scene* would be enough but Djebar disturbs its acknowledgment, daring the reader to take the view of the film crew that the director is too "intellectual" (*So Vast*, 204) or that for the first time it is a woman who directs (who is "le patron" [*Vaste*, 199]). Such interruptions are pronounced (sharper still in the English translation where the interior monologue is italicized) but they come close to being dulled by indulgence, as if the reflexive might miss the opportunity for purity in sound or image. On the one hand, it is perfectly in keeping with the politics of Djebar's writing that the personal should declare its participation in the utterance; on the other, a complementary politics of postcolonial difference finds an excruciating dead end in identity and articulates therefore a discrepant identification (or "dissidentification") taking pride in the power of disturbance (as interval, pause, lacuna). Fragments too are bits of identity and provide little solace from the power that identifies. Perhaps this preempts the desire to speak beyond the fragments, to talk intimately with a community that has had enough of interruption, but in general it places special emphasis on a logic of reading. The power of identification is greater than its sum in identity. The process of affiliation is key: it draws time and space and the frames that link them: "Only later will I try to see the inner gaze, the essence, the structures, what takes flight under matter" (*So Vast*, 206).

And so the spirit of the fugitive is measured in the present and/or a recent past. The sharp eye of the filmmaker is juxtaposed with the direct narration of the women of Chenoua, each shot and each vignette modulating each other to stave off solipsism and documentary objectivity. The grandmother, Fatima (Djebar's original name) is given away at the age of fourteen by her father to Soliman, whose age could be anywhere from sixty-two to one hundred! The custom assures patriarchal order, the exchange of "property" (the father gains one of Soliman's daughters) and plenty of offspring. The granddaughter (a week after ending her first marriage) imagines her grandmother on her wedding night, perhaps hoping for a bride thief but resigned to the grey face that will stare at hers. Soliman is rich, but no amount of wealth can assuage this captivity. Djebar reminds us Fatima's silence is not defeat and she can communicate much by not speaking (as in *Women of Algiers*, the women will signal from their balconies). Soliman soon passes on and Fatima, rather than wait on her inheritance, goes back with her daughter to the mountains. In the director's commentary Djebar echoes the sentiments of the previous section, and especially the feeling for this space called "home," which is also a space of creation, an everyday space ("espace quotidien" [*Vaste*, 220]). Djebar suggests the director remakes herself by rediscovering the "original form" (*So Vast*, 228) of the film, which lies precisely in daily proximity not detachment. The director marks this presence by acknowledging the nearness of a local woman who cannot be filmed (the man who would give permission is unavailable), a young mother who she calls "Madonna," to further taunt us with the discourse of objecthood. Madonna's existence out of the frame speaks to the production of meaning within it: she has the "grace to secretly question it" (*So Vast*, 228). Here the interior monologue is deliberately conflated; the director's consciousness is inhabited by another, of the woman who does not speak yet says "Si je décidais" ("If I decided" [*So Vast*, 229). If Madonna entered the field of vision, the very logic of seeing in the film would be called into question and what is seen is suffused with her power to make it so. It is small wonder that Djebar has been compared to Trinh T. Minha (and indeed they have spoken together) for she too pivots the image on the cusp of woman's power to obliterate it.[46]

The third movement picks up on Fatima's story to extend the matrilineal genealogy to her youngest daughter, Bahia, who in turn will become the mother of Isma (the "I" narrator) and fill in other elements of the family tree (complicated by Fatima's three marriages). Typhoid strikes and Cherifa, the eldest sister, dies. Cherifa in particular had taken good care of Bahia, and as the women of the community mourn Cherifa's passing they also worry for her six-year old sister, more alone than ever. As the lamentation continues Cherifa's cousin, also from the mountains, speaks in Berber to the city dwellers and gives the novel its title: "Vast is the prison crushing me/From where will you come for me, deliverance?" (*Vaste*, 243). Where indeed. It is a powerful moment rendered more so by the makeup of the gathering, women together free to speak and to comment at will, and by the sharply drawn differences in language between both city and classical Arabic and mountain Berber. The scene is also charged by being written in French, a French that, like the Berber, may have to be translated for many of those present. French is not the deliverance describing this drama. But whereas the Berber is written into the text ("Meqqwer lhebs iy inyan"), the Arabic, even the classical Arabic verse, is translated: it is French first and defiantly so. Here is a riposte to Arabization in contemporary Algeria since the verse and commentaries are in French even as they are stripped of what makes them Arabic. One must be careful here, since Djebar has been outspoken about a concomitant desire to Arabize French.[47] A further point reminds us of those Orientalist scholars who were for a long time flummoxed by the stele at Dougga: the lack of translatability becomes the cause of their desire. What would it mean to Djebar's readers to leave this text untranslated? Would this not be a sign of the postcolonial in a colonial language? Djebar writes under French to disturb its powers of history, and perhaps Arabic is overwritten to say the same thing. But the translation of Berber in Djebar's Quartet remains silent until this point when its powers of description are rendered palpable by inscription.

This is no small matter in North African politics, and the inclusion of Latinized Berber in Djebar's text only accentuates the issue. Neo-Tifinagh, although still struggling for acceptance as an official orthography (it has been recognized by the Moroccan government, for instance) has a much closer relationship to the stele at Dougga (and the Toureg women who are literate in a variant of this form) than the Romanized version which, with obvious irony, has become entrenched in Algeria, especially within the Kabylie-Berber movement (whose riots in 2001, while not as serious as those of 1988, were an intensification of ethnic tension). Conversely, Arabized Berber has all but disappeared in Algeria even as Arabic itself continues to dominate everyday life. Simply put, it is not inevitable that the Berbers of North Africa preserved Tifinagh so it should suffer the convenience or deliverance of a Latin orthography. Perhaps the solution would be to have the French carry the Arabic and Berber equally but that is no more innocent than Djebar's choice. And if transcription is always translation then here it is a prison considerably more vast than the statement itself.

For a year after her sister's death Bahia does not speak as if, by not crying, the words had dried up within her. But life begins again and soon enough, at eighteen, Bahia has her first child, Isma, who the Berber midwife declares will be a nomad, a traveler. Then, her second child, a boy, dies at six months, and with him she seems to bury language itself, or at least Berber, an "autism" as it is called that describes her grief. The text moves within and around these cycles of birth and death, of personal tragedy and unvanquished hope. With each turn it is the filmmaker's detachment that is separated off leaving her to sink deeper into the rhythms of the community. The chapter divisions are notational devices, moments of homeostasis that are artificial against a backbeat of matrilineal endurance and support. The gaze of the filmmaker and her crew is not averted but it cannot merely "take" either. The director concludes that "The camera must measure the silence of my pupils" (*So Vast*, 256; *Vaste*, 251), a process in which the familiarities of the perspectival become aspectival; that is, reflect back on the technology of the gaze itself.[48] Djebar applies this question of cinema to writing and, while it does not bring her back to the *kalaam* (the pen) once more (because her hiatus from writing actually included much writing), it provides her with an appropriate mode of address.

In the fourth movement the narrator remembers herself as a little girl during the Second World War. The French, bombed in their homeland, were also being bombed in their colonies by the Germans, an age-old contest now with considerably different consequences. The Algerians huddle with the *pieds-noirs* in trenches and in this moment of danger and dangerous proximity, the child senses a change in the community's self-identification. Nervously, her mother had spoken in French to a Frenchwoman and, while she worries whether she spoke correctly, a colonial vector has been curved in its assumed teleology. The difference is underlined by a subsequent incident when a French family takes shelter in our narrator's house and are guests of Arab hospitality. The narrator wakes to see the French in her midst and, in a powerful moment of *méconnaissance*, wonders whether she is now the daughter of a French family. The child is on a border (but which one, she asks?), in a space where France and French are no longer outside but are coordinates in her identification. Exotopy does not mean absorption of the other; otherness itself remains axiomatic.[49] This is fiction and we should all be such philosophical three-year-olds, but there is little that is fanciful in the supposition which has its material basis in an indigenous encounter with a colonial other. Of her "awakening" the narrator comments: "This other awakening, the only one from my early childhood that unexpectedly remains as the most vivid, but oblique, in a movement seeking its fragile equilibrium" [*So Vast*, 269; *Vaste*, 264]). It is not the only thesis that holds the narrative together, but it does grasp the principle elements of Djebar's composition: memory, language, consciousness, and motion.

Do the narrator's reflections merge with the stories of arable women or do they remain distinct in their syncopation, the gentle alternation of memory and place? Isma's recollections proceed from a present to a past that then moves chronologically and by themselves bear the spirit of a certain *Bildung*. The film disrupts this identification by representing a present bound to the living recollection of a collective past. The film has assigned roles: it is a film about women but as a form of projection simultaneously questions what may be projected by the director and the narrator. If Isma is precocious in youth, she is also divided and circumspect. There is a certain level of embarrassment in these pages, as if Isma should apologize for reading the Koran and Michaux, even though Djebar has created her to dissipate such self-consciousness. In event, the figures who emerge do so by folding back on the self if not themselves. Djebar often uses the language of cinema to do this and because of its discourse ("Who is the camera?" *So Vast*, 308), she is able to understand flight, what escapes, as a logic of image and text. This means imagining in the space of silence so that a peasant girl, Zohra, who watches the action (Zohra, Djebar's second prenom) can enunciate a hope beyond it.

In the sixth movement the tempo changes again, signaled by the use of subtitles breaking up the text into smaller components and by different roles within the same woman. The narrative has almost imperceptibly returned to the first part, in which Isma's love gets her beaten by her husband. We are now with Isma being consoled and supported in her subsequent divorce. Meanwhile, she is ready to present her research as a "semi-documentary" called "Arable Women" (Isma has an ear for punning). Isma also relates that, ironically, after having recorded so many births (and the effect on women's mortality because of them) she cannot have children herself and the narrative moves back in time once more as she relives the adoption of her daughter. In the years following the war of independence there were many orphans available for adoption and, although the process was hardly simple, Isma has a good chance. And then Isma thinks of her daughter at the age of twenty in 1988. History has quickened and its blood now is fresh and flowing freely. Isma's daughter is in Algiers that autumn when the bread riots are put down, and Isma flies from France to join her. Djebar herself was already well into writing this novel before the crisis and joins her daughter in Algiers when the riots erupt so history and autobiography catch up with her tetralogy.[50]

Djebar has called on the past for the present but now finds the latter authoring her history. As noted, this will lead to half a dozen other works, initially to *Loin de Medine* but also to the elegiac *Le blanc d'Algérie* and the essay collection, *Ces voix qui m'assiegent*. *So Vast* is also stuttered by the election debacle of late 1991. When Clarisse Zimra interviews Djebar in 1992, Algeria's President had just been assassinated and the country was quickly spiraling into chaos and civil war. Djebar refers to "polishing the final pages," but one should not be surprised that another three years would elapse before the novel saw publication. While the effect of October 1988 is clear, the impact of the war is harder to gauge on either the form or content of *So Vast*, except toward its end. The references to filmmaking are largely to Djebar's completed production, and this follows through to the last day of location shooting in the section marked "Arable Woman VII." The seventh and final movement, however, "Shadows of Separation" is different. As Isma notes the death of the respected Sidi, her uncle, she asks herself what reason lies behind this acknowledgment. Her answer is, in part, because Sidi represented a segment of society who, even if they did not openly fight the French, outlasted them. If these ordinary Algerians were more isolated after independence, it was because the nationalists had become strangers to them. Djebar wants to embrace the Sidis of the community rather than contemplate the murdered and the murderers. Yet at this point the narrative gives up on its autobiographical surrogate as if the conceit that has structured the text for so long can no longer bear the weight of the architectonic in which its characters move. Suddenly, the fugitive in the narrator explodes within her. She wants to run away, erase herself and her text, and this means separating from the "sakina" (serenity) promised by Isma's earlier love. Isma, "the name," one of several taken by Djebar (that includes "Djebar"), drops away and no longer offers its protective fiction. Whether one agrees with the way Djebar divides masculine and feminine in Algeria, in this section one appreciates the dilemma her polyphonic lineage now represents. None of her criticism of the Orientalists and the stele stealers is blunted, but the genealogical richness that built the story cannot be a more authentic Algerianness than the identification threatening to tear the country apart. And so the movements turn to dirges and the voice rethinks an earlier invocation of "severed sound" in dreams of self-mutilation.

Jugurtha is recalled, both his spirit of resistance and his death in incarceration. Yet a touchstone that might spark deliverance and release only accentuates the news that accompanies it: the murder of Djebar's friend, M'Hamed Boukhobza, in June 1993. Boukhobza, a sociologist, is seen as too closely tied to a government that, after the canceled elections, is of dubious mandate. The FIS (Islamic Salvation Front) and sympathizers with it and the AIG (Armed Islamic Group) were the likely culprits, but the manner of Boukhobza's death, a kind of ritualistic bleeding of the heart, shocks Djebar to the core. It is one of many deaths that Djebar will attempt to write out (*Algerian White* focuses directly on Boukhobza and two other murdered friends, Mahfoud Boucebi and Abdelkader Alloula, in a manner closest, emotionally and chronologically, to the denouement of *So Vast*). The historian valiantly hails Jugurtha as he watches the commemoration of Masinissa, he whose exploits are celebrated bilingually on the stele. Djebar imagines his bravery and intelligence, but also his reticence, his implacability. Eventually, imprisoned in Rome, the hegemon will teach him a lesson (he is "le premier Lumumba d'Afrique"), but with the blood of her friends not dry Djebar seeks communion in the long space with a Berber warrior who speaks even now to what cannot be erased, written over, or in the case of the stele, stolen by the West: the idea that apprehending the prison initiates the process of its sublation. It is an extraordinary moment in Djebar's fiction because she takes all that she has learned from the women of Chenoua and writes back to an Algeria (an Algerian) that is present. Thus, Jugurtha uses the same incantation enunciated at Cherifa's death, and who is to say which is more immediate in this chronotope? Djebar takes vastness and deploys it to mean what is shared. The vastness of the prison as chronotope is then shrunk in direct proportion to its recognition: the imprisonment can be individuated, personalized, while the logic of incarceration can be generalized, socialized. This is what strikes Djebar, "malgré la distance du temps" (*Vaste*, 334—"despite the distance of time" [*So Vast*, 345]). The distance of time, what the long space inscribes, is an aesthetic injunction on what history has otherwise sundered.

Djebar adds a word to Jugurtha's lament, *Tasraft* (trap), which is his fate but also his meaning for Rome. His is a shadow, as Djebar calls it, cast over the present as the dead return, indiscriminately: "Their desire haunts us, we women. For too long each of us has been held in our bodies or, like me, too often without a voice. As my hand methodically runs across these notebooks my voice is patiently drawn from me, or rather, and this is something I barely understand, the sound of my heart is torn from me"

(*So Vast*, 346; *Vaste*, 335). The latter evokes the fate of Boukhobza but critically links it to a necessity for voice. There is an urgency here for Djebar as a writer, as a woman, and as an Algerian that galvanizes the end of the novel even as it clearly speeds beyond it. As Anne Donadey has noted, although the novel finishes with a "fourth" part, its basic structure follows that of *Fantasia*.[51] The additional section provides a catharsis in crisis but could be interpreted to end the Quartet as is. I am not suggesting that the elaborate architectonic of the tetralogy has been rendered superfluous by the greater need to voice at all: the point is the long space is dedicated to exigency so even when a narrative is not based in the present the instant of decolonization is stretched. This is a logic bound by a desire for renegotiation of time and space after or against empire, including the unfinished business of preexistent or persistent patriarchy. If this desire does not exactly take up the *kalaam* (*qalam*) in the way that Djebar seizes the pen, it is nevertheless a ghost that cannot be exorcized without the danger of returning to silence, reassuming a smaller space of utterance, writing more easily "heard" by those for whom a protracted engagement would be to take such culture too seriously, as an equal.

In the last passage before Part Four, Djebar recalls a nightmare in which a nasty phlegm clings to her palate and stifles her. In her dream she uses a knife to operate on herself, to cut out the thick paste smothering her voice, despite the blood and the danger of voicelessness. She describes the procedure as both an amputation and a childbirth ("enfantement") and it is a very writerly dream. Amputation can mean to cut down or trim a text and "enfantement" can refer to the birth of a work. Djebar views this mouth as a channel for ancestral voices, but even more, it continually expels "the suffering of others, those shrouded or hidden before me" (*So Vast*, 350; *Vaste*, 339). The operation is continuous because the voicing must not stop. If the weight of history is inordinate in Djebar's writing, the ethical demand is even greater. "I do not cry, I am the cry" (*So Vast*, 350) is a sentiment as appreciable as it is daring. Here writing is stretched to its limit not just by the attempt to embody, but by a present that refuses writing, disavows any and all transcription of its eventness, of the scene of its erasure ("ecrasement"). If we might claim a second caesura in Djebar's writing, despite profound evidence to the contrary, it is based upon another order of proximity, the present, as violence, to her. The words are in profusion, but they do not necessarily find the form in which the mauresque of the Quartet was precipitate. The fourth volume can no more complete that edifice or movement than Algerians today can hold fast to the same promise of nation that drove France from their door. The integrity of decolonization remains but not the assumption of an appropriate framework to sustain it.

The structure of both the first and third volumes of the Algerian Quartet offer four parts but properly embrace three (the final ambivalence in structure questions what is proper to the form). Historically, if not allegorically, this is an interpretive clue to the project of the Quartet, which takes on a task greater than the neatness of fours or threes and finds an alibi of form interrogated by the force of Djebar's sociopolitical commitment. If the initial conditions of the Quartet feature transcription, translation, and transcoding, then all three are reworked or transformed according to a different agenda articulating a certain impossibility in their respective claims. Exotopy, at this level, is the mark of a constitutive outside defying aesthetic will and formal consistency. While this is a truism of any artistic act, it does not absolve criticism from specifying the conditions of each one, the better to understand the logic of creation for all, each in their eventness, each in their genre of apprehension. If the structure of the long space is only conveniently a trilogy or tetralogy (because its chronotope is bound to a temporospatial logic that does not "make" primarily in threes or fours, or decades, or national borders), this does not negate the meaning of such divisions but places special emphasis on their modes. It is not the utility of form that Djebar is after but its rhythm, its pulsion in the cultural unconscious of national belonging and community. The writer of the long space may well espouse nationalism, because of its strategic lever in the work of decolonization, but as a writer she cannot accept the notion of nation *or* novel on such terms if they are irreconcilable with the break from colonization desired. For Djebar the task of writing out Algeria (and writing out of Algeria) produces a complex imbrication of styles, times, voices, and images that simultaneously write under Algeria, breaking through the narrative surfaces of its otherwise blank (*blanc*) certitude. Yet the same historical and feminist impulses to transform what is legible in Algeria as "composed" also pull at the composition of the Quartet as the present of Algeria writes back in a bloody script of war and conflagration. *Fantasia* predicts this possibility (which is why, despite its urgency, *So Vast* may be read with it consistently); but again, for

Djebar the condition of the present is located in a distant past for which her imagination offers corruscating immediacy.

In the second volume, *Ombre Sultane* (a title in which the Sultana's shadow makes her also the shadow of a Sultana, or a Sultan's bride, an ambiguity that disappears into *A Sister to Scheherazade* in the English translation), Djebar imagines Algerian women by investigating the relationship of women and Islam within women's relationships. While other North African writers have attempted this, most notably Nawal el Saadawi (whose *Woman at Point Zero* Djebar cotranslated into French) Djebar brings to the project her flair for historical scholarship that, coupled with her constant picking away at figures of French as French, provides a disjunction simultaneously profound and paratactic.[52] The erudition lies in Djebar's engagement with indisputability in the story of women and Islam (the first text to interrupt Djebar's Quartet is *Far From Medina*, which fictionalizes the thirty-year period after Mohammed's death); the parataxis concerns the seriality of the narrative, histories placed side by side without linear time as a bridge (this is a problematic figure of a figure, since strictly speaking parataxis refers to sentence elements without subordination or conjunction). Much of the aesthetic and political power of Djebar's writing comes from the ability to collapse the epic distance of Islamic history as it reflects on, or shadows, women's participation in it. Djebar positions herself as a secular critic and for some that may be sufficient to dismiss her attention. Her engagement, however profane or fictive, is interested in the lived substance of Islamicism for Algerian women, not in choosing between religion and the mundane.

Parataxis allows us to understand the sharp doubling of women in *Ombre Sultane*—a mother and daughter, two wives, two sisters—all of whom are linked thematically, particularly through the voice, without conjunction. The doubling in each instance is a measure of dialogic reciprocity that finds Djebar stretching and compressing elements of history according to matrilineal time. Several critics have noted this solidarity binds women to a common quest, the sublation of the harem literally and figuratively in the political unconscious of North African women.[53] The harem is a paradoxical space facilitating friendships otherwise denied in public fora (another space that Djebar highlights toward the end of the novel is the *hammam* which is the first space of *So Vast*). Doubling and paradox inform the mode of parataxis because, whatever the power of patriarchy to suppress, the women's relationships exist synchronically as a complement without succession. Indeed, it is in connecting the logic of space for women and Islam to simultaneity that Djebar charts an original chronotope, one both linguistically multiple (Arabized French, transcribed dialect, poetic syntax, mimicry) and extraordinarily embedded. "Tzarl-rit" captures this paradox in voice but its spatial dimension is often given over to the veil. There is no word in English that can carry the force of veiling and voicing; it is, like the silence of silk, an expression of the power in the untranslatable itself.

In *Sister*, Isma is portrayed as a liberated Algerian woman bent on raising the consciousness of her traditional, secluded, and passive sister, Hajila. Isma is a shade of Djebar's autobiographical voice we have tracked in *So Vast* and is a fictional foil, a test of rebellious spirit at its most personal. Yet what is revealed in the juxtaposition of the "I" narrative (Isma's) and the "you" narrative (Hajila's) is the extent to which Hajila's suppression throws light on Isma's, despite her "European" education and Western dress. Thus, Isma gives Hajila the key to her apartment so she may come and go as she pleases in contrast to her domestic situation (where her husband is a conservative brute who beats her for not asking permission to leave); yet, by thinking more about her freedom, Isma comes to understand patriarchy is a little more tenacious than the power exercised through the veil and seclusion. Indeed, Isma comes to regard her own liberation as contingent on Hajila's, a classic revolutionary rhetoric that cannot see individual freedom without common good. Both Isma and Hajila must be expressed simultaneously, an act of coparticipation and reciprocity, as *nashiz* (rebellious women) if the promise for women in the time of the Prophet is to be realized in the present. Djebar, who once wanted to be an architect, is fascinated by the ordering of space, by the ways in which the subject can be subjected by spatial restrictions. The prison is vast for the women of her narratives because it is not restricted to prison. Djebar emphasizes movement to counteract the prescriptions of internment on the one hand, but also meeting places, like the hammam and the balcony, on the other, where voice can do the work of movement. Moments of movement alone, however, are not sufficient to countermand the logic of seclusion that is literally built into the social. The solidarity of the pairs in *Sister*, then, is symptomatic of a more general desire to make liberation beyond individual volition and this in turn constructs the narrative.

There are other pairings in the novel, the sultane and her shadow, and the writer with her language, French, that might also be thought of as confounding the efficacy of a monadic consciousness. Is such simultaneity representable or translatable and what form is distilled in that attempt? While *So Vast* does follow *Sister* in obvious ways (the fate of Isma, for instance, is clearly rethought in volume three of the tetralogy), *Sister* is a central text in addressing the logic of form seen in the other volumes. If the books can be read as separate novels, *Ombre Sultane* argues most strongly for their cumulative effect, for their form beyond division. No other novel among those this project has considered takes on the burden of form for all of the others in quite this way, but just as important signals an abyss for that very ambition. As Donadey has cogently revealed, the epigraphs in the Quartet are the clearest sign of a project framework.[54] Yet the logic of form also proceeds in the transcoordination of enunciation, chronotopes of voice, that signal connections not predicated on the colonial episteme. If each element of *Ombre*'s duos situates a consciousness, its significance only "appears" in correlation to another, in the movement between these instances of voice. The difficulty is in tracking the relation rather than the extant voice whose transcription is usually named or signed by person as position (first, second, third). At the end of *So Vast* Djebar asks Algeria what it should be called because its civil war has exploded its nominative being. It is a marvelous rhetorical device, but it also draws attention to an insufficiency in the name as a condition, as a relation of identification. It is because the formal requirement is in relation that the Quartet cannot equal nation in naming it. Form asks the question of nation, to which the novel struggles to reply. In the mode of relation rests an artful catechresis, a creative misnaming, that is itself a category crisis (in naming, in subjectivity, in the structure of time/space). The error in postcolonial nationhood is necessary to the truth that is its overcoming of colonialism, not the falsehood of postcolonies pitched against the truths of nation sanctioned by imperial domain. For our exilic writers with their exotopic imagination this might seem an aesthetic compulsion, but it is bound to the political relation that is the postcolony.

For Djebar, the pairings of *Ombre Sultane* are symptomatic of complex difference, whether in gender, class, region, dialect, or language. The logic of "trans," of crossing, links Isma and Hajila in their experience of space and subjective apprehension (Isma's "I" is not more authentic than the use of "you" or "tu" of Hajila). We see moments of merging in the voices but the idea is not principally oneness or a dissolution into wholeness. Isma suggests that by addressing Hajila she is causing her to exist ("Comme si, en vérité, je te créais" *Ombre*, 91 [*Sister*, 82]) and this is a powerful injunction. On the one hand, it reminds us of a certain ideological movement, interpellation, that ceaselessly attempts to hail a subject and position it in the same moment; on the other hand, Isma invokes interpellation's unconscious, the subject's ghostly surrogate, the shadow or shade (*ombre*) of its very possibility. Hajila is her sister in the shadow of her husband (like the *sultane*, Scheherazade, to hers) but is also the shadow of her sister, Isma, and Hajila's presence haunts the substance of Isma's freedom. We have come across this phantomatic presencing before. Here, Djebar emphasizes its meaning for a necessary impossibility in language permitting form to appear. For Isma, the failure of words simultaneously signals the dissipation of herself in the present and the emergence of Hajila in her consciousness ("ta forme s'impose" *Ombre*, 91 [*Sister*, 82]). Similarly, Scheherazade understands that only by acknowledging Dinarzade, her sister, beneath the bed will she be able to continue spinning tales for the Sultan of Baghdad and defer violent retribution. Such interdependency is a measure of Djebar's belief in the mode of feminist solidarism required to transform gender relations, but the social emphasis is almost always accompanied by a belief in writing's coparticipation:

The thirty years that have passed since my first novel have not changed identity, whether this is paper, a passport, membership of blood and soil.

    After thirty years, however, let me state this: I present myself first as a writer, as a novelist, as if the act of writing each day, alone to the point of asceticism, has come to alter the weight of this membership. Because identity is not only that of papers or of blood, but also of language. And if it seems that language is, as they say so often, a "means of communication," it is for me especially, as a writer, a "means of transformation" in the way that I practice writing as exploration. (*Ces voix qui ma'assiégent*, 42)

    For most writers such a declaration is a practiced idealism, one that is appreciable in its earnestness if not in its political effect. Yet, for postcoloniality, the continuing work of decolonization, it has often fallen to writers to explain how transformation also proceeds in the act of writing itself. In *Ombre Sultane* Djebar emphasizes a polemic that is common to the other volumes: the transcription of oral tales is always already a transformation, but not one that guarantees the perspicacity of writing in relation to speech. Instead, it draws attention to the logic of transformation as ambivalently poised (like the Sultana Scheherazade's nightly tales) so that the novel itself is bound to historical necessity, to fathom speech, extant, lost, barely audible, otherwise unspoken. Like Scheherazade, we want Isma to succeed in her independence and thus inspire Hajila's, but in the pair the shadow or shade assumes a material force in order for the story to be told. For most critics, the means of transformation in Djebar's writing is the mixing of genres and forms (history, autobiography, testimony, dialogue, music, song, memory), but they rarely ponder if Djebar's hybridized narration itself constitutes a propositional form in its own right. In the means of transformation the nature of the transformation is itself articulated.

Yet each "trans" we explore—transcription, translation, transcoding, and transformation—no more confirm a formula of form than Djebar's term "quatuor Algerienne." Indeed, each term comes with a shadow in another, or at least this is the process that *Sister* foregrounds. In a provocative and far-reaching discussion of the Moroccan writer Abdelkebir Khatibi, Réda Bensmaïa analyzes how his *Le livre du sang* disorients Orientalism in the reverie of a double language unique in its present but predicated on a past form, the mystical epic Hikayat.[55] If the latter has a rule it is the suspension of difference (between narrator, hero, author, narratee, and so on). This is paratactic narration as a decentering chronotope (whereby time/space relations are reordered to the point where order itself is questioned). As Bensmaïa points out, Khatibi is attacking the "haunted thinking" of Arabs (EN 140) whose fascination with mystical narrative conspires with an Orientalism all too willing to gaze upon such fantasia. Djebar is aware of this haunting, which for Khatibi inspires the taunting exorcism of "Never another Scheherazade" (EN 139—in a book called *Ombres japonais*), but Djebar sees the principle of the ghost as enabling because it permits an extension of woman beyond objecthood. It is not the content of the tale that provides a touchstone in *Sister* but the eventness of narration, the shared spaces of women's enunciation. Thus, Djebar joins with Khatibi in the injunction "Never another Scheherazade" but writes beneath it "Always an Other Scheherazade" (a reverse palimpsest that also appears in the Beur trilogy, *Shérazade* by Leïla Sebbar).[56]

Djebar marks this imperative as impossibility in a number of ways. She recalls the iconic storytelling of Scheherazade to elaborate telling as sisterly resistance. Djebar eschews both classical Arabic for this narration or any popular equivalent as similarly ingrained with traditions of gender hierarchy; but then, just as forcefully, she Arabizes French to say that Algerian feminist expression does not ultimately pivot on a choice between contaminated languages. Khatibi's answer to troubled postcolonial narration is *bi-langue*, a "langue de l'autre" that does not choose an extant language but writes one from the impossibility of absolute choice. If Khatibi, as Bensmaïa argues, makes French fearful by introducing the untranslatable as always translated, then Djebar's politics of language stresses a maternal immediacy in the moment of translated untranslatability, in which the untranslatable is neither the lack of equivalence or artful fusion but the absence of an originary lexicon of voice among the women of her writing that could decide, "This is translatable; this is not." French occupation produced a territory of languages, as Djebar puts it (*Ces voix*, 46); but because of Algeria's assertion of autonomous linguistic space, French hegemony could not secure borders and this axiom of colonial logic (the paradigmatic failure of apprehension) finds dispossession itself dispossessed, or reterritorialized. Rather than let the languages decide, or their powerful arbiters, Djebar employs something of Khatibi's "third ear" (the ear of the Other, the capacity to hear silence on silk) so that whispers in one story (those of Scheherazade and Dinarzade) resonate in others (those of Isma and Hajila). The structural elements in the other novels are here in *Sister* (the musical correlatives, the historical keys, the involution of public and private space, women's voicing as specifically embodied, etc.) but perhaps it stands alone in naming the agency of the writing process around these elements. Djebar could not have known that the shadows and shades that she "unearths" in *Sister* (139) would become the throng of death that ends *So Vast* but she understood early on in the Quartet how this might come about. "The present congeals around us" (*Sister*, 160) and in that stasis a promise and menace hangs over a form adequate to its inscription.

This imbricates the fate of woman and Algeria: the movement of the former is cast against the dynamic dystopia predicated in the latter. For Djebar, the chronotopic contradictions between the two are confirmed both by the brutalities of the civil war in which women have been raped, mutilated, and murdered but by the long space itself, whose coordinates trace the persistence of historically-specific inequities and atrocities across an otherwise unspoken archive in Algerian being. Just as the pairings in

Sister are not binary oppositions, so woman and Algeria are not categori-
cally incommensurate: they measure the substance of form in the apparent untranslatability between them. Indeed, when Djebar, or others, say
that Algeria is untranslated or untranslatable it means only that the time
of overcoming such contradiction is set as a task (*traduire* as the becoming
of form, not the assumption of a form, or genre, like the novel), a process
demonstrably not completed by raising a flag of independence. That duty
is not Djebar's alone: translation increasingly becomes the art of collective
reciprocity for which the gestures of the nation state too often represent
a galling impediment. What remains untranslatable is liberation more
broadly construed in the passage from colonialism to postcolonialism.

No state that has thrown off the yoke of colonial dominion, however, warrants the genre of blame that the West, coincidentally and particularly, has fostered. Edward Said eloquently warned against the politics
of blaming the victims yet few would deny it still informs commentary on
postcolonial upheaval and crisis, even down to the finger-wagging about
the term postcolonial itself. Djebar is not outside these political ironies
because she has so ardently addressed their meaning for Algeria and the
Maghreb. She is also a postcolonial intellectual, a migrant, an exile, and
a cosmopolitan whose Arabo-Berber roots provide her with a unique positioning and exotopy. Bensmaïa has analyzed the situation of Algerian
intellectuals in light of the civil war that has a deep resonance in our discussion of the Quartet. Using Slavoj Žižek's pithy reading of the enigma
of Slovenian socialism (which for Žižek is always bound to a Lacanian
Aufhebung), Bensmaïa proposes a model of power and the intellectual in
Algeria that features a "quadruple contradiction" and "quadruple constraint": "four contradictory . . . and totally irreconcilable 'injunctions.'"[57]
Thus, the FIS asks those in power (and intellectuals) to declare their mal-
feasance and illegitimacy in ruling Algeria; the government, the military
and the FLN demand that the FIS admit their atrocities, their alien fa-
naticism, and the misadventure in winning the election of 1991; the first
two are then required by the excluded, the middle classes, to confess to
their equally moribund and destructive tendencies; finally, the equally excluded, the intellectuals, have sought an agency they themselves have been
declined yet have been forced (typically to the point of murder and assassination) to declare it is their activism, nevertheless, that is the primary
cause of Algeria's implosion. As Bensmaïa points out, from the time of

independence Algeria did not foster a productive role for intellectuals either within the institutions of government or within the discursive logic of a public sphere. We thus have in Bensmaïa's intriguing thesis the semblance of "four contradictory injunctions" that are in fact three with the fourth founded on a missing, or shadow, agency not corresponding to the power base materially inflected in the others. Writers, the supreme mediators among the intelligentsia, are called upon (a fifth injunction?) to meet their agential absence: "the writers will take on the task of creating a *space of the possible* in their works, a space where everything that cannot be realized here and now can on the other hand at least be offered to thought (as possible)" (Bensmaïa, "Vanishing," 12, emphasis in original). These sentiments reveal the concrete contradiction of nation and writer in postcoloniality. What is given to one as a political injunction to build in the detritus of colonialism cannot aspire to the space of possibility in the aesthetic act that no more realizes extant states than those states perform the cultural as a simple determinant. Where these acts are linked is in the injunction as an impossibility, not as an underlying cause or effect, but as a constitutive demand of form-making between nation and writer. To that degree, the intimation of a misaligned or missing agency is at once apt and troubling.

Djebar's Algerian Quartet speaks to the space of the possible where quadruple contradictions are three. The first injunction says that not only does French colonial history elide the barbarism perpetrated in its name (and persistent in "Nostalgeria" to this day) but knows that it does so, a consciousness if not conscience Djebar cannily revises in listening to the archive. The second injunction relates to the first via transcription, which is to say that the space of amnesia is subjected to a countermand in anamnesis, one that performs another impossibility in the reverse palimpsest or, to use a (mixed) metaphor closer to Djebar's writing (*La femme sans sepulture* in particular), a tapestry unstitched beneath its tableaux by the severed hands and sounds of those women memory cannot lay to rest. The third injunction demands transcoding, a paradigm cleaving to the contradictions of language sharply accentuated by colonialism in the Maghreb and scandalously deploys French to explore this *logique metisses*. All of which leads to the fourth injunction, the part that cannot square, the contradiction that cannot perform the work of the others but instead exists to shadow their substance, to challenge the rule of form that would exclude it. Here seethes the impossible opposition of woman and nation, forwarding the claims of the former in so many ways, rights, space, voice, gaze, while reading the latter as an identity formation suffused with proscriptions against the same, as if its phenomenological presence for writing could only mean prohibition, silence, violence, death. The idea is not to turn a tetralogy into a trilogy, but to emphasize the force of form in Djebar's writing does not admit such neat parameters. The effulgence of form in the Algerian Quartet must lie elsewhere than in its putative four volumes in what writing gives to nation that the nation cannot give to itself: a time/space commensurate with the break from (colonial) subjugation.

Notes

1. *Jalan Raya Pos* (*De Groote Postweg*) [*The Great Post Road*], dir. Bernie Ijdis (The Netherlands: Pieter van Huystee Films, 1996). Although the camera work and editing in this documentary are rudimentary, in general the pacing and use of silence (principally Pramoedya's) are strongly evocative of Pramoedya's situation at the time—a period in which Suharto's rule, though waning, hangs over Pramoedya's sense of narration. Just prior to the sequence described, Pramoedya refers directly to his problems with writer's block (the phrase in Bahasa Indonesia is in English) and the scene ends with a close-up of the fire I describe. As a whole the film interweaves biographical moments of this kind with a pointed voice-over by Pramoedya that ponders the colonial and postcolonial meanings of the Great Post Road itself. I would like to thank Chris GoGwilt of Fordham University for initially bringing this film to my attention.

2. This phrase, "earthly world," appears in the title of Auerbach's 1928 monograph, *Dante als Dichter der irdischen Welt*; but as Edward Said notes in his introduction to a new edition of *Mimesis*, the phrase is rendered as "secular world" in Manheim's 1961 translation. The use of "secular" is not unfounded but de-emphasizes the materiality implied in Auerbach's reading.

3. Wilson Harris, "Quetzalcoatl and the Smoking Mirror: Reflections on Originality and Tradition," in *Wilson Harris: The Unfinished Genesis of the Imagination*, ed. Andrew Bundy (London/New York: Routledge, 1999) p. 194.

4. See Fredric Jameson, "The End of Temporality," *Critical Inquiry* 29 (summer 2003): 695–718. Jameson suggests that modernism begins in the interstices of two temporalities, the time lived between agricultural and urban life—a comparatist conception of "deep time" (699) unavailable, and therefore symptomatic, of a certain postmodern flatness or inability in depth perception. I would not claim that the long space replays this paradigm of comparative temporality, yet it is striking that the extended form of postcolonial writing addresses precisely the conflict of perception wrought by the conventions of the colonial episteme.

5. Jameson, "The End of Temporality," 700. It has to be said that, despite Jameson's claims to the contrary, this position exists as a statement rather than as

a fully engaged explanation both in this essay and in other instances where the "Third World" or the decolonizing South are addressed.

6. Mikhail Bakhtin, "Forms of Time and of the Chronotope in The Novel," in Mikhail Bakhtin, *The Dialogic Imagination*, ed. Michael Holquist, trans. Caryl Emerson and Michael Holquist (Austin: University of Texas Press, 1981), p. 250. Bakhtin's point appears in his "Concluding Remarks" written in 1973, some thirty-five years after the initial theorization in the essay itself.

7. In part this is a Bakhtinian insistence on *being* as always already *co-being* and, significantly, as the process of the event of being. *Sobytie* can simply be "event" in Russian, but for Bakhtin it was ineluctably linked to being itself as an event. Bakhtin will stress the uniqueness of event as that which grants being its distinctiveness, but I tend to maintain the everyday use within the philosophical principle so that *eventness* accentuates *event* as being-in-the-world. This is an event, therefore, not just of philosophical substance, but of the coordinates of co-being as time and space. Postcolonial being as event thickens in the apprehension of its chronotopes with the caveat that the aim is not the assumption of being but an understanding of the processes by which it may be subsumed, overreached.

8. See Henri Lefebvre, *The Production of Space*, trans. Donald Nicholson-Smith (London: Blackwell, 1991), p. 110. Although the current project is a very long way from being Lefebvrean, I am attempting, nevertheless, to connect an aesthetic process of form to the production of "social space" that is postcoloniality.

9. Johann Wolfgang von Goethe, "On World Literature," in *The Collected Works (Volume Three): Essays on Art and Literature*, ed. John Gearey., trans. Ellen von Nardroff and Ernest H. von Nardroff (Princeton: Princeton University Press, 1986), p. 224.

10. Franco Moretti, "Conjectures on World Literature," *New Left Review* 1 (Jan/Feb 2000): 54–68. Moretti's initial article provoked a spirited response from a number of quarters and is perhaps best represented by the collection *Debating World Literature*, ed. Christopher Prendergast (London: Verso, 2004). It is on the basis of Moretti's "conjectures" that he embarks upon a wild excursion into literary modeling in a series of articles that became the basis of the book, *Graphs, Maps, Trees* (London: Verso, 2005).

11. Moretti, "Conjectures," in Prendergast, *Debating*, p. 162.

12. Ernest Renan, "What Is a Nation?" trans. Martin Thom, in *Nation and Narration*, ed. Homi Bhabha (New York: Routledge, 1990) p. 11. Transnationalism differs from postnationalism to this degree: that going through or across nation maintains a sensitivity to the strategic and liberatory possibilities of nation where a more global sense of common responsibility and community has yet to take hold outside of economic hegemony. This may require thinking at the edge of or outside the limits of nation as convention. See, for instance, Reda Bensmaia, *Experimental Nations: Or, The Invention of the Maghreb* (Princeton: Princeton University Press, 2003).

13. Assia Djebar, "Anamnesis in the Language of Writing," trans. Anne Donadey and Christi Merrill, *Studies in Twentieth Century Literature* 23:1 (1999): 177–89.

14. See Etienne Balibar, "The Nation Form," in *Race, Nation, Class: Ambiguous Identities*, eds. Etienne Balibar and Immanuel Wallerstein, trans. Chris Turner (New York: Verso, 1991), pp. 86–106.

15. David Damrosch, *What Is World Literature?* (Princeton: Princeton University Press, 2003), p. 1. (WWL 1)

16. Franco Moretti, "More Conjectures," *New Left Review* 20 (March/April 2003): 9.

17. See Edward W. Said, "The Public Role of Writers and Intellectuals," *The Nation* (September 17/24, 2001): 36. This essay appeared the week of 9/11 and has been largely overlooked because of the pall associated with that event. I would suggest, however, that its analysis of intellectual responsibility as a transnational imperative has gained in prescience, and much of what I offer here is in the spirit if not the letter of Said's example.

18. Assia Djebar, "RAÏS, BENTALHA . . . Un an après" ("RAÏS, BENTALHA. . . . A year later"), trans. Marjolijn de Jager, *Research in African Literatures* 30:3 (fall 1999): 12. Djebar's poignant dirge reflects upon a massacre in Algeria in 1997. The emphasis is both on the trauma of that moment and a certain irreducibility in its apprehension. For me it is the specificity indicated that stretches the form of time in postcoloniality.

19. See Gayatri Chakravorty Spivak, "The Rani of Sirmur," in *Europe and Its Others: Proceedings of the Essex Conference on the Sociology of Literature, July 1984*, vol. 1, eds. Francis Barker et al. (Colchester, U.K.: University of Essex Press, 1985), p. 133. Note that the assumption concerns the availability of land to be written upon rather than a legibility in which culture already exists (so that in effect, if not in reality, the land is always already written). The later application of this reading to Heidegger can be found in Gayatri Chakravorty Spivak, *A Critique of Postcolonial Reason* (Cambridge, Mass.: Harvard University Press, 1997), pp. 428–29. The assumption of a blank space available for inscription is also part of what Assia Djebar means by "le blanc d'Algerie" or the White of Algeria.

20. See Frantz Fanon, *Black Skin, White Masks*, trans. Charles Lam Markmann (New York: Grove Press, 1967), especially Chapter One. Obviously, Fanon's relationship to Sartre's ideas are complex, but it is symptomatic of Fanon's desire to de-essentialize decolonization that he questions the assumptions of Sartre's schema.

21. See Arif Dirlik, "The Postcolonial Aura: Third World Criticism in the Age of Global Capitalism," in *Dangerous Liaisons*, eds. Anne McClintock et al. (Minneapolis: University of Minnesota Press, 1997), pp. 501–28.

22. Lefebvre, *Production of Space*, 116.

23. Raymond Williams, *The Long Revolution*, rev. ed. (London: Pelican, 1965).

24. Edward Said, *Orientalism* (New York: Vintage, 1978), p. 14. Said continues, "Even one or two pages on 'the uses of Empire' in *The Long Revolution* tells us more about nineteenth century cultural richness than many volumes of hermetic textual analyses." Those who have followed Said, particularly in the United States, have tended to downplay the importance of Said's creative dialogue with Williams. As Said imagines his project in *Orientalism*, he seeks "a better understanding of the way cultural domination has operated. If this stimulates a new kind of dealing with the Orient, indeed if it eliminates the 'Orient' and 'Occident' altogether, then we shall have advanced a little in the process of what Raymond Williams has called the 'unlearning' of 'the inherent dominant mode.'" *The Long Space* cleaves to this genealogy.

25. Raymond Williams, *Culture and Society 1780–1950* (Harmondsworth: Penguin, 1961), p. 321.

26. See Raymond Williams, *Border Country* (London: Chatto and Windus, 1960); *Second Generation* (London: Chatto and Windus, 1965); and *The Fight for Manod* (London: Chatto and Windus, 1979).

27. See Gauri Viswanathan, "Raymond Williams and British Colonialism," in *Cultural Materialism: On Raymond Williams*, ed. Christopher Prendergast (Minneapolis: University of Minnesota Press, 1995), pp. 188–210. Viswanathan's account is a crucial corrective to any theoretical approach that would assume unproblematically the mantle of Williams's cultural materialism. Viswanathan ends her essay with the quip "there is, after all, no view like the one from the *other* country" (208) by which she means India. One wonders if the critique remains the same once one substitutes one country for another, say, Wales?

28. This goes beyond writing over the word "society" with "imperialism," although an entire critical framework may be enjoined around that point. See Edward Said, *Culture and Imperialism* (New York: Vintage, 1993).

29. See Aijaz Ahmad, *In Theory* (London: Verso, 1993).

30. Edward W. Said, "Introduction to the Fiftieth Anniversary Edition," in *Mimesis*, by Erich Auerbach, trans. Willard R. Trask (Princeton: Princeton University Press, 2003), p. xvi.

31. Aamir Mufti has usefully suggested "critical secularism," a paradigm of "unbelief" for this position. See Aamir Mufti, "Critical Secularism: A Reintroduction for Perilous Times," *boundary 2* 31:2 (summer 2004): 1–9.

32. Edward Said, *The World, The Text, and the Critic* (Cambridge, Mass.: Harvard University Press, 1983), p. 166.

33. Neil Larsen, *Determinations* (New York: Verso, 2001), p. 54.

34. See Etienne Balibar and Immanuel Wallerstein, *Race, Nation, Class: Ambiguous Identities*, trans. Chris Turner (New York: Verso, 1991); and Etienne Balibar, *We, the People of Europe?* trans. James Swenson (Princeton: Princeton University Press, 2004), p. 17.

35. Etienne Balibar, "Ambiguous Identities," *Politics and the Other Scene*, trans. Chris Turner (New York: Verso, 2002), p. 66.

36. Benedict Anderson, *Imagined Communities* (New York: Verso, 1983); *Language and Power: Exploring Political Cultures in Indonesia* (Ithaca, N.Y.: Cornell University Press, 1990); and *The Spectre of Comparisons* (New York: Verso, 1998). Although not conceived as such, I view these works as a trilogy on the fictions of nation.

37. Harry Harootunian, "Ghostly Comparisons: Anderson's Telescope," *Diacritics* 29:4 (winter 1999): 137.

38. Pheng Cheah, "Grounds of Comparison," *Diacritics* 29:4 (winter 1999): 3–18. Cheah is building around Anderson's notion of the grammar of nationalism elaborated in the introduction to *The Spectre of Comparisons* and in Part One of the same book. It should be noted that the slippage between the grammar of nationalism (as an ideology) and the grammar of nations (as an institutional syntax) is not innocent and reclaims some of Balibar's insights on structural imperatives in a phenomenological key.

39. Anderson, *Spectre*, 229. As more than one commentator has pointed out, the phrase Anderson borrows from José Rizal is "el demonio de las comparaciones," which yields a devil even more than a ghost.

40. Pheng Cheah, "Grounds of Comparison," 11–12. One of the reasons that Anderson does not depend on the Max Lane translation of Pramoedya's *Buru Quartet* is that key terms, such as the world of comparison (*alam perbandingan* [also the nature of comparison]), are missing from the text. Cheah follows this suspicion by using his own translations (while acknowledging their debt to Anderson). In the world of comparison, however, this can lead to confusion since Cheah quotes from the Hasta Mitra version of the text (according to pagination—this is the Jakarta publication I will use) but always references the Wira Karya version (the difference between the Bahasa Indonesia and Malay version is not great, but substantial enough for the latter to carry a glossary). The problem is confounded by Cheah using the Australian publication of Lane's translation whereas the "world" edition used for "comparison" is very different in pagination. This does not detract from Cheah's theorization, which in *Spectral Nationality* is substantial, but it underlines that the grounds of comparison are very much dependent on a methodology of translation (that includes its system of referencing) and this can be ghostly, or devilish, in its own way.

41. Pramoedya Ananta Toer, "Dia Yang Menjerah" in *Cerita dari Blora* (Jakarta: Balai Pustaka, 1952). Here, as elsewhere, Anderson uses his own translation, but see also Pramoedya Ananta Toer, *All That Is Gone*, trans. Willem Samuels (New York: Hyperion, 2004). "Dia yang menjerah" can be translated as "She who gave up" as Anderson does, or "She who surrendered." Interestingly, Samuels favors a word that downplays the role of resignation: "Acceptance." The differences between Anderson's translation (*Spectres*, 40–41) and Samuels's (*All*, 153–154) are

pronounced and depend on contrasting translation strategies. Anderson favors a translation aimed at Southeast Asian scholars whereas Samuels's technique inserts the explanation necessary for a wider readership (*Pesindo*, for example, is described as a socialist party and the new vision of Ies [Is in Anderson's translation] is a socialist future) yet drops corresponding elements that Anderson would find crucial, including the fact that Is assembles a new identity in the form of serialization.

42. See Partha Chatterjee, "Anderson's Utopia," *Diacritics* 29:4 (winter 1999): 128–34. Chatterjee might have drawn attention to another glaring difficulty in Anderson's penchant for the literary: the emphasis on the novel occludes the role of other forms of cultural expressivity in nationness. The part played by poetry in the formation of India as a nation must be considered more decisive than the impact of novels. For my part I wish to explore the questions raised by a certain logic of form rather than provide a prescription for form, or form as a prescription.

43. Antonio Negri, *Time For Revolution*, trans. Matteo Mandarini (New York: Continuum, 2003), p. 112.

44. See Anne McClintock, "The Angel of Progress: Pitfalls of the Term 'Postcolonialism,'" in *Colonial Discourse and Postcolonial Theory*, eds. Patrick Williams and Laura Chrisman (New York: Columbia University Press, 1994), pp. 291–304.

45. See Homi Bhabha, *The Location of Culture* (New York: Routledge, 1994).

46. See Jonathan Culler, "Anderson and the Novel," *Diacritics* 29:4 (winter 1999): 20–39.

47. Culler is referring specifically to Moretti's *Atlas of the European Novel, 1800–1900* (London: Verso, 1998).

48. See Pierre Bourdieu, *Distinction*, trans. Richard Nice (Cambridge: Harvard University Press, 1984).

49. Immanuel Wallerstein, *The Modern World System* (Three Volumes) (New York: Academic Press, 1974/1980/1988). Without belaboring the point, here is another trilogy that necessitates extension as critique, and what is true of an understanding of capitalism is a provocative injunction for postcolonialism.

50. See, for instance, Franco Moretti, *The Way of the World*, trans. Albert Spragia (New York: Verso, 2000); and *Modern Epic*, trans. Quintin Hoare (New York: Verso, 1996).

51. For Prendergast and Apter, see Prendergast, *Debating*; for Arac, see Jonathan Arac, "Anglo-Globalism?" *New Left Review* 16 (July/August 2002): 35–45.

52. Franco Moretti, *Atlas of the European Novel 1800–1900* (New York: Verso, 1998).

53. Mikhail Bakhtin, *The Problem of Speech Genres and Other Late Essays*, trans. Vern W. McGee, eds. Caryl Emerson and Michael Holquist (Austin: University of Texas Press, 1986), p. 42 .

54. See Bakhtin, *Dialogic*, 136.

55. Achilles Mbembe, *On the Postcolony*, trans. A. M. Berrett et al. (Berkeley: University of California Press, 2001), p. 196; hereafter abbreviated as OP.

56. Jonathan Arac, "Anglo-Globalism?" *New Left Review* 16 (July/August 2002): 35–45.

57. See Emily Apter, *The Translation Zone* (Princeton: Princeton University Press, 2006), especially Chapter Three.

58. I had originally planned to include both Farah's *Blood in the Sun* trilogy and his earlier *Variations on the Theme of an African Dictatorship* trilogy but the analysis of the latter and its relationship to the former must await another occasion. That Farah has begun a third trilogy both illuminates my thoughts on seriality in decolonization and problematizes any specific project. Similarly, I began the chapter on Harris with a mind to encompassing both *The Guyana Quartet* and the *Carnival Trilogy*, but the structure of chronotope in the latter is complex enough to require a separate study. The original version of this introduction also included readings of Achebe, Mahfouz, and Galeano, but their analysis must now await another occasion.

CHAPTER 2

1. Martin Heidegger, "The Origin of the Work of Art," in *Poetry, Language, Thought*, trans. Albert Hofstadter (New York: Harper and Row, 1971), p. 36.

2. Although Harris would surely appreciate Derrida's wordplay, it is the nature of the politics of language in history that is at issue here. See Jacques Derrida, "White Mythology: Metaphor in the Text of Philosophy," in *Margins of Philosophy*, trans. Alan Bass (Chicago: University of Chicago Press, 1984), pp. 207–92.

3. I have argued this case for Glissant in particular. See Peter Hitchcock, "Antillanité and the Art of Resistance," *Research in African Literatures* 27:2 (summer 1996): 33–50.

4. The cross-cultural for Harris is much more than the oft-berated cultural politics of recognition associated with institutional multiculturalism. Harris sees modernism as modernity's autocritique, but one that founders on its understanding of sedimented myth and its unspoken correspondences. For Harris, as for Glissant, a major exception is William Faulkner, whose imaginative grasp of space and place creatively links the American South to the South, a major nexus of Caribbean and South American consciousness. See Wilson Harris, *The Womb of Space* (Westport: Greenwood Press, 1983). See also Edouard Glissant, *Faulkner, Mississippi*, trans. Barbara Lewis and Thomas C. Spear (New York: Farrar, Strauss, and Giroux, 1999).

5. Harris's critical language is as effervescent as his fiction and is highly recommended. See Wilson Harris, *The Womb of Space* (Westport: Greenwood Press, 1983), p. xvi.

6. The secondary material on Harris is voluminous, with individual books of criticism available in places where Harris's own writing often is not. The most complete and up-to-date bibliography is maintained by Hena Maes-Jelinek, whose

dedication and explication of Harris's work is both exemplary and visionary in a different key. In addition to Maes-Jelinek's monograph on Harris, *Wilson Harris* (Boston: Twayne, 1982) and over fifty articles, she has edited two excellent collections on Harris: *Wilson Harris: The Uncompromising Imagination* (Mundelstrup: Dangaroo Press, 1991), and (with Benedict Ledente) *Theatre of the Arts: Wilson Harris and the Caribbean* (Amsterdam/New York: Rodopi, 2002). Maes-Jelinek's book for Twayne includes a useful biography. For a pertinent autobiographical exploration, see Wilson Harris, "Wilson Harris, An Autobiographical Essay," in *Contemporary Authors Autobiography Series*, vol. 16 (Detroit: Gale Research, 1992), pp. 121–37. Also published in Joyce Adler, *Exploring the Palace of the Peacock: Essays on Wilson Harris*, ed. Irving Adler (Mona, Jamaica: University of West Indies Press, 2003), pp. viii–xxxiv. For Maes-Jelinek on the insufficiency of theory, see Hena Maes-Jelinek, "'Latent Cross-Culturalities': Wilson Harris's and Wole Soyinka's Creative Alternative to Theory," *European Journal of English Studies* 2:1 (April 1998): 39–40.

7. See, for instance, "Interview with Wilson Harris" by Kerry Johnson, *The Journal of Caribbean Literatures* I:1 (spring 1997): 83–95.

8. This presents its own alibi, unfortunately, because as Andrew Bundy points out, Harris has been at work on one enormous dream book and one can only work against it by taking it on whole, which is certainly not my intention here. See Andrew Bundy, ed., *Wilson Harris: The Unfinished Genesis of the Imagination* (London/New York: Routledge, 1999).

9. The negative connotations of "survey" are legion in the institutionalization of colonialism. It is fitting, therefore, that Harris's profession in his twenties teaches him the opposite. Harris's "sudden eruption of consciousness" (Harris, "Wilson Harris," 128) transforms his worldview, and he emerges from the jungle in the 1940s with a new sense of wonder and oneness that is immediately perceptible in his contributions to the Guyanese literary journal *Kyk-over-al*. Note that here I will use "Guyana" even when referring to what was British Guiana in Harris's history before independence.

10. Mikhail Bakhtin, *The Dialogic Imagination*, ed. Michael Holquist, trans. Caryl Emerson and Michael Holquist (Austin: University of Texas Press, 1981), p. 14.

11. Wilson Harris, "Quetzalcoatl and the Smoking Mirror: Reflections on Originality and Tradition," in *Wilson Harris: The Unfinished Genesis of the Imagination*, ed. Andrew Bundy (London/New York: Routledge, 1999) p. 187 (emphasis in original). Further references to this text will be noted as Q followed by page number.

12. Wilson Harris, *The Carnival Trilogy*, (London: Faber and Faber, 1993), p. 37. The trilogy is composed of: *Carnival* (London: Faber and Faber, 1985); *The Infinite Rehearsal* (London: Faber and Faber, 1987); and *The Four Banks of the River of Space* (London: Faber and Faber, 1990). Originally it had been my intention to read the trilogy and quartet together as a truth in the form of allegory (especially

in relation to realism), but now I believe that Harris's conception of "carnival" offers an allegory of form that requires discussion in its own right.

13. Wilson Harris's *The Guyana Quartet* is available in several editions. The tetralogy was originally published by Faber and Faber of London as four separate volumes: *The Palace of the Peacock* (1960), *The Far Journey of Oudin* (1961), *The Whole Armour* (1962), and *The Secret Ladder* (1963). The edition to which I will refer is Wilson Harris, *The Guyana Quartet* (London: Faber and Faber, 1985), which contains Harris's "Note on the Genesis of *The Guyana Quartet*" written the previous year (the volume will be noted in the text as GQ followed by page number).

14. Strictly speaking, this is not a distinction that Goethe draws upon since the subject of his essay is epic and dramatic poetry, but Bakhtin finds the principle of difference itself illuminating of the novel's prescience. Goethe's essay, which may well have been cowritten with Schiller, is "Über epische und dramatische Dichtung" in J. W. Goethe, *Sämtliche Werke*, vol. 36 (Stuttgart and Berlin: Jubiläums-Ausgabe, 1902–1907), Pp. 149–52. The essay is edited and translated in J. W. Goethe, *The Collected Works: Essays on Art and Literature*, vol. 3, ed. John Gearey, trans. Ellen von Nardroff and Ernest H. von Nardroff (Princeton: Princeton University Press, 1994), pp. 192–94.

15. See, Wilson Harris, "Tradition and the West Indian Novel," in *Tradition, the Writer, and Society* (London: New Beacon, 1967), p. 37. Again, Bakhtin views the effulgence of the novel as itself a sign of epic exhaustion; Harris, on the other hand, takes T. S. Eliot's position that the epic is distant only because of contemporary imaginative constrictions. Subsequent references will be noted in the text as TWS followed by page number.

16. See C.L.R. James's appendix to *Tradition, The Writer, and Society*, pp. 69–75. James writes that he does not know who Harris has been reading but he finds parallels in Heidegger's views on language as the "openness of the existent." James sends Harris some of Heidegger's writing and Harris replies that he agrees with him. James continues the connection in C.L.R. James, *Wilson Harris: A Philosophical Approach* (St Augustine/Port of Spain: Extra-Mural Department, University of the West Indies, General Public Lecture Series: West Indian Literature 1, 1965). In particular, he considers *Dasein* in relation to *The Secret Ladder*, the last volume of the quartet. James's point pivots on the meaning of existentialism for Caribbean writing, one that is not novel but is relatively unexplored in relation to Harris and his literary production of the 1950s and 1960s. If the terms of existentialism have less purchase today, they nevertheless have a deep resonance in African-Caribbean writing in the moment of decolonization.

17. Wilson Harris, *Jonestown* (London: Faber and Faber, 1996), p. 5.

18. For Paget Henry's approach to Harris see, in particular: "Wilson Harris and Caribbean Philosophical Anthropology," *The CLR James Journal* 7:1 (winter 1999–2000): 104–41 (the entire issue is dedicated to discussion of Harris); "Wilson

Harris and Caribbean Poeticism," in *Caliban's Reason: Introducing Afro-Caribbean Philosophy* (New York: Routledge, 2000), pp. 90–114; and "Framing the Political: Self and Politics in Wilson Harris," *Journal of Caribbean Literatures* 2:1–3 (spring 2000): 82–95.

19. Guyana itself has a unique history in the understanding of colonialism, particularly since its postcolonial formation has largely been based on the ethnic and racial divisions between its Afro-Guyanese and Indo-Guyanese populations initially represented by the figures of Forbes Burnham and Cheddi Jagan, respectively. The machination of the British government in this schism is particularly noteworthy. See, for instance, Henry B. Jeffrey, *Guyana: Politics, Economics, and Society: Beyond the Burnham Era* (London: F. Pinter, 1986); Ralph R. Premdas, *Ethnic Conflict and Development: the Case of Guyana* (Aldershot: Avebury, 1995); Kean Gibson, *The Cycle of Racial Oppression in Guyana* (New York: United Press of America, 2003); Reynold Burrowes, *The Wild Coast: An Account of Politics in Guyana* (Cambridge, Mass.: Schenkman, 1984); and Chaitram Singh, *Guyana: Politics in a Plantation Society* (New York: Praeger, 1988). For a general if hardly impartial reading of Guyana, see Ovid Abrams, *Metegee: The History and Culture of Guyana* (New York: Ashanti Books, 1998).

20. The latter narrative is recounted in Alan Riach, "The Presence of Actual Angels: The Fractal Poetics of Wilson Harris," *Callaloo*, 18:1 (winter 1995): 34–44. The occasion was the University of Cambridge Smuts Memorial Fund Commonwealth Lecture in October, 1990. Riach notes that Harris quipped that Aunt Alicia had graciously provided him with the title for his lecture, "The Fabric of the Imagination," that she left behind on a scrap of paper. The substance of this lecture has since been published as, Wilson Harris, "The Fabric of the Imagination" in *The Radical Imagination*. Note that an identically titled lecture appeared earlier the same year in *Third World Quarterly*, 12:1 (January 1990): 175–186; reprinted in Anna Rutherford, ed., *From Commonwealth to Post-Colonial* (Mundelstrup: Dangaroo Press, 1992), pp. 18–29. Apparently, Aunt Alicia is a mischievous reader of *Third World Quarterly*. Personally, I am taken with this fantastic intervention for it allows Harris at Cambridge to answer Alicia's plea that he should speak out of his "vulnerability," a feeling at one with the intimidating aura of a former heart of imperial learning.

21. See, in particular, Peter Hitchcock, *Imaginary States* (Champaign/Urbana: University of Illinois Press, 2003).

22. Carpentier's critical statements often constitute a round assault on his own fiction including, most obviously, *The Lost Steps*, trans. Harriet de Onis (Minneapolis: University of Minnesota Press, 2001). For an account that carefully links Carpentier's jungle sojourns to those of Harris, see Antonio Benitez-Rojo, *The Repeating Island*, trans. James E. Maraniss (Durham, N.C.: Duke University Press, 1992), pp. 177–98.

23. See, Benitez-Rojo, *The Repeating Island*, particularly the Introduction and Part Three. Subsequent references will be noted in the text as RI followed by page number.

24. See D. Graham Burnett, *Masters of All They Surveyed: Exploration, Geography, and a British El Dorado* (Chicago: University of Chicago Press, 2000).

25. Michael Swan, *The Marches of El Dorado* (Boston: Beacon Press, 1958).

26. Richard Schomburgk, *Travels in British Guiana 1840–1844*, trans. Walter Roth (Georgetown, Guyana: Daily Chronicle, 1922).

27. Walter E. Roth, *An Inquiry into the Animism and Folk-lore of the Guiana Indians*, 30th Annual Report of the Bureau of American Ethnology, 1908–1909 (Washington: Smithsonian Institute, 1915).

28. Roth also translated the work of Richard's older brother who was also engaged in the exploration of Guiana. See Robert H. Schomburgk, *Travels in British Guiana and on the Orinoco During the Years 1835–1839*, trans. Walter Roth (Georgetown, Guyana: Argosy, 1931).

29. I mention this to underline two important components of reading Harris. The first element does not insist that we disregard myth but place the author himself firmly within its scope of storytelling. Second, these historical materials, particularly those that create the El Dorado fantasy, are never less than symptomatic of the colonial episteme and should be seriously considered for their "revision" in postcoloniality. As for what this says of Harris's self-making, he is free to believe that he imagined the Carib bone-flute before reading about it in the appendix to Swan's book when he was a writer in residence at the University of Toronto in 1970. For an article that investigates the Roth connection while accepting Harris's explanation, see Russell McDougall, "Walter Roth, Wilson Harris, and a Caribbean/Postcolonial Theory of Modernism," *University of Toronto Quarterly* 67:2 (spring 1998): 567–92.

30. Schomburgk, quoted in Burnett, 28.

31. See Hena Maes-Jelinek, "The Myth of El Dorado in the Caribbean Novel," *Journal of Commonwealth Literature*, 6:1 (June 1971): 113–28; Andrew Bundy, "El Dorado and the Grail Legend: A Memorandum on Twinship in 'Body of Civilisation,'" *Journal of Caribbean Literatures*, 2:1–3 (spring 2000): 31–34; Antonio Benitez-Rojo, *The Repeating Island*, trans. James E. Maraniss (Durham, N.C.: Duke University Press, 1992), pp. 177–98; and Barbara J. Webb, *Myth and History in Caribbean Fiction: Alejo Carpentier, Wilson Harris, and Edouard Glissant* (Amherst: University of Massachusetts Press, 1992).

32. See D. Graham Burnett, *Masters of All They Surveyed: Exploration, Geography, and a British El Dorado* (Chicago: University of Chicago Press, 2000).

33. See Gregory Shaw, "Art and Dialectic in the Work of Wilson Harris," *New Left Review* 153 (September/October 1985): 121–28.

34. See Fredric Jameson, "Third-World Literature in the Era of Multinational Capitalism," *Social Text* 15 (1986): 65–88. I agree with Imre Szeman that Jameson's

position has often been misread and has become a veritable whipping post for postcolonial positions that seek to expunge Marxist and materialist categories from their approaches. Nevertheless, it is Jameson himself who begins with a "sweeping hypothesis" and proceeds to integrate "Third-World Literature" by means of this generalization. The actual argument, as Szeman points out, lies elsewhere in understanding the logic of globalization itself, but the opening gambit remains a strategic error vis-à-vis theorizing beyond the Western proscenium. See Imre Szeman, *Zones of Instability* (Baltimore: Johns Hopkins University Press, 2003), especially Chapter One.

35. Aijaz Ahmad's vigorous response to Jameson is almost as well-known as Jameson's original argument and forms a centerpiece in his *In Theory: Class, Nations, Literatures* (New York: Verso, 1992, p. 97).

36. Tung-pin Lu, *The Secret of the Golden Flower: A Chinese Book of Life*, trans. Richard Wilhelm with a commentary by C. G. Jung [Eng. trans. Cary F. Baynes] (New York : Harcourt, Brace, 1938). The "secret" in *The Secret Ladder* and the "far journey" in *The Far Journey of Oudin* are both Jungian, but do more than cite mystical "Oriental" texts. For Harris, the archetype suspends in advance any recourse to Western knowledge as foundational. See, for instance, Harris's comments on Jung in "Merlin and Parsifal" in *Wilson Harris: The Unfinished Genesis of the Imagination*, pp. 58–66.

37. See Wilson Harris, "A Talk on the Subjective Imagination" in *Explorations: A Selection of Talks and Articles 1966–1981*, ed. with an introduction by Hena Maes-Jelinek (Mundelstrup: Dangaroo Press, 1981).

38. Jeremy Poynting, "Half Dialectical, Half Metaphysical: *The Far Journey of Oudin*," in *The Literate Imagination: Essays on the Novels of Wilson Harris*, ed. Michael Gilkes (London: Macmillan, 1989), pp. 103–28.

39. See, for instance, "Creoleness: The Crossroads of a Civilization?" in *Wilson Harris: The Unfinished Genesis of the Imagination*, pp. 237–47. One could also cite the evidence of Harris's own hybridity.

40. See, for instance, Glyne A. Griffith, "Metaphysics and Materialism: Wilson Harris and V. S. Naipaul," *Deconstructiong, Imperialism, and the West Indian Novel* (Kingston: University of the West Indies, 1996), pp. 53–81.

41. Chaitram Singh, *Guyana: Politics in a Plantation Society* (New York: Praeger, 1988). Although Singh's account is clearly "interested," his general characterization is a feature of studies of Guyana since independence.

42. "Creoleness," 239.

43. Stephanos Stephanides, "Victory Over Time in the *Kali Puja* and in Wilson Harris's *The Far Journey of Oudin*," in *The Literate Imagination: Essays on the Novels of Wilson Harris*, ed. Michael Gilkes (London: Macmillan, 1989), p. 134.

44. As Craig Brandist notes, another key difference between Bakhtin and Buber on dialogue is the latter's investment in the aura of mysticism, precisely

what would attract Harris's sensibility. Craig Brandist, *The Bakhtin Circle* (London: Pluto Press, 2002).

45. Hena Maes-Jelinek, *Wilson Harris* (Boston: Twayne, 1982), p. 17.

46. Wilson Harris, "Creoleness," in *Wilson Harris: The Unfinished Genesis of the Imagination*, ed. Andrew Bundy (London/New York: Routledge, 1999), p. 241.

47. Wilson Harris, "Literacy and the Imagination," in *Wilson Harris: The Unfinished Genesis of the Imagination*, ed. Andrew Bundy (London/New York: Routledge, 1999), p. 82.

48. Spivak's approach is not only to identify the international division of literacy and its consequences for national and global power but to encourage a form of literacy in transnationalism as a means to address the theoretical limitations in postcolonial thought. See Gayatri Chakravorty Spivak, *A Critique of Postcolonial Reason* (Cambridge, Mass.: Harvard University Press, 1997), especially the section on "Culture."

49. For more on this position, see Maryse Condé and Madeleine Cottenet-Hage, eds., *Penser la créolité* (Paris: Éditions Karthala, 1995).

50. In Harris's various revisions of the quartet we should note a switch from Abram to Abraham (GQ 249) from the two-volume edition (22).

51. Theodor W. Adorno, *Hegel: Three Studies*, trans. Shierry Weber (Boston: M.I.T. Press, 1993), p. 6, see also p. 121.

52. Theodor W. Adorno, *Aesthetic Theory*, trans. and ed. Robert Hullot-Kentor (Minnesota: University of Minnesota Press, 1997), p. 115.

53. Charles H. Rowell, "An Interview with Wilson Harris," *Callaloo*, 18:1 (winter 1995): 194.

54. Hena Maes-Jelinek, *Wilson Harris* (Boston: Twayne, 1982), p. 36.

55. See R. S. Crane, "The Concept of Plot," in *The Theory of the Novel*, ed. Philip Stevick (New York: Free Press, 1967), pp. 141–45.

56. Robert Carr, "The New Man in the Jungle: Chaos, Community and the Margins of the Nation-State," *Callaloo*, 18:1 (winter 1995): 133–56.

57. See Wilson Harris, "Interior of the Novel: Amerindian/European/African Relations," in *National Identity*, ed. K. L. Goodwin (London: Heinemann, 1970); reprinted in Wilson Harris, *Explorations: A Selection of Talks and Articles 1966–1981*, ed. with an introduction by Hena Maes-Jelinek (Mundelstrup: Dangaroo Press, 1981).

58. Wilson Harris, "Profiles of Myth and the New World" in Bundy, ed., 207.

59. The attribution of this quote remains something of a mystery—Harris does not recall his source (based on my exchanges with Hena Maes-Jelinek) and a definitive text has yet to emerge.

60. See John Macmurray, *The Self as Agent* (New York: Harper, 1957) (Gifford Lectures, University of Glasgow, 1953, vol. 1 of *The Form of the Personal*); and *Persons in Relation* (London: Faber and Faber, 1961) (Gifford Lectures, University of Glasgow, 1954, vol. 2 of *The Form of the Personal*).

61. Hena Maes-Jelinek, *Wilson Harris* (Boston: Twayne, 1982), p. 1. As such, the term is more a way of reading both Harris and Bakhtin than it is a constitutive conceptual key in their own theorizations.

62. This extends even to their placement: in the Faber two-volume collection of *The Whole Armour* and *The Secret Ladder*, the Blake, Mayer, and Macmurray epigraphs appear before *The Whole Armour* rather than *The Secret Ladder*. This could have been an editing oversight, a measure of Harrisian revision, or an element of the arbitrary in their constellation.

63. See Paget Henry, "Wilson Harris and Caribbean Poeticism," in *Caliban's Reason: Introducing Afro-Caribbean Philosophy* (New York: Routledge, 2000), 90–114.

64. Harris's aesthetic principles seem to trump in advance this possibility. For instance, if, as Sandra Drake maintains, everything for Harris contains the possibility of a *zemi*, an Arawak animistic belief in the play of forces across all objects—humans to rocks and waterfalls—then the novel itself must necessarily remain an impoverished index of such forces, since it cannot be them at the same time as it measures them. See Sandra E. Drake, *Wilson Harris and the Modern Tradition: A New Architecture of the World* (Westport, Conn.: Greenwood Press, 1986), pp. 174–75.

65. For this Buber connection see Louis James, "Fenwick's Log: Reading 'The Text of Landscape,'" in *Theatre of the Arts: Wilson Harris and the Caribbean*, eds. Hena Maes-Jelinek and Bénédicte Ledent (Amsterdam: Rodopi, 2002), pp. 103–9.

CHAPTER 3

1. For overviews of Farah's career in writing to date, see Derek Wright, *The Novels of Nuruddin Farah* (Bayreuth, Germany: Breitinger, 1994; 2nd ed., 2004); and Patricia Alden and Louis Tremaine, *Nuruddin Farah* (New York: Twain, 1999). The special issue of *World Literature Today* (autumn 1998) 72:4, celebrating Farah's receipt of the Neustadt Prize, is also an important background resource, as is Derek Wright's excellently edited collection, *Emerging Perspectives on Nuruddin Farah* (Trenton, N.J.: Africa World Press, 2004). Wright's monograph, like his articles, tends to be more incisive, although the second edition is preferable since the first covers Farah's work only up to *Gifts*. If Farah's characterizations tend toward types, it is partly because the Western reader seems bound to look for them. The first trilogy, *Variations on the Theme of an African Dictatorship* is composed of: *Sweet and Sour Milk* (London: Allison and Busby, 1979); *Sardines* (London: Allison and Busby, 1981); and *Close Sesame* (London: Allison and Busby, 1983). The second trilogy and the subject of this chapter, *The Blood in the Sun* is comprised of: *Maps* (New York: Penguin, 1986; hereafter, M followed by page number); *Gifts* (New York: Penguin, 1993; hereafter, G followed by page number); and *Secrets* (New York: Penguin, 1998); hereafter referred to as S followed by the page number.

2. Rhonda Cobham provides a critical approach to this issue in her article, "Misgendering the Nation: African Nationalist Fictions and Nuruddin Farah's

Maps" in *Nationalism and Sexualities*, eds. Andrew Parker, Mary Russo, Doris Summer, and Patricia Yaeger (New York: Routledge, 1992), pp. 42–59.

3. Two topics remain crucial to the analysis of postcoloniality that the aforementioned Parker et al. collection only begins to address: the role of gender and sexuality in the formation and subsequent adumbration of the postcolonial state, and the link between this and the often hostile accounts of exile and cosmopolitanism in postcolonial writing. For pertinent references to the latter, see the chapter on Pramoedya. For creative and critical assessments of the former see, for instance, Sangeeta Ray, *En-Gendering India: Woman and Nation in Colonial and Postcolonial Narratives* (Durham, N.C.: Duke University Press, 2000); Anne McClintock, Aamir Mufti, and Ella Shohat, eds., *Dangerous Liaisons: Gender, Nation, and Postcolonial Perspectives* (Minneapolis: University of Minnesota Press, 1997); and Elaine H. Kim and Norma Alarcon, eds., *Writing Self Writing Nation* (Berkeley, Calif.: Third Woman Press, 1994). For an overview of the fraught politics of gender and nation, see Lois A. West, ed., *Feminist Nationalism* (New York: Routledge, 1997).

4. First among these is Derek Wright, "Nations as Fictions: Postmodernism in the Novels of Nuruddin Farah." *Critique* 38 (1997): 205–20. See also Charles Sugnet, "Nuruddin Farah's *Maps*: Deterritorialization and 'The Postmodern,'" *World Literature Today* 72:4 (autumn 1998): 739–47. Sugnet argues that Farah's postmodern stylistics are primarily a product of an affinity for the postmodern experience of the exilic as deterritorialization. Certainly both Wright and Sugnet pick up on key components of Farah's approach to writing. The epistemic implications of postmodernism's reach, however, remain largely untheorized.

5. The position is outlined in Mikhail Bakhtin, *Toward a Philosophy of the Act*, eds. Vadim Liapunov and Michael Holquist, trans. Vadim Liapunov (Austin: University of Texas Press, 1993). See also, Mikhail Bakhtin, *Art and Answerability*, eds. Michael Holquist and Vadim Liapunov, trans. Vadim Liapunov (Austin: University of Texas Press, 1990); hereafter abbreviated as AA; and M. M. Bakhtin, *Problems in Dostoevsky's Poetics*, trans. Caryl Emerson (Minneapolis: University of Minnesota Press, 1984); hereafter abbreviated as PDP. That outsideness operates in several sometimes *contradictory* registers in part measures Bakhtin's ambivalence about its philosophical sources. It is also, however, a symptom of its multiple valence within discourses of the other, whether Bakhtin is considering the distance between "author" and "hero" or between the subject and its conditions of subjectivity. For his part, Todorov remains largely faithful to the aesthetic coordinates of Bakhtin's investigation. See Tzvetan Todorov, *Mikhail Bakhtin: The Dialogical Principle,* trans. Wlad Godzich (Minneapolis: University of Minnesota, 1984). The substance of my formulation is initially forwarded in Peter Hitchcock, "Exotopy and Feminist Critique," in *Bakhtin: Carnival and Other Subjects*, ed. David Shepherd (Amsterdam: Rodopi Press, 1993), pp. 194–209.

6. Nuruddin Farah, *Yesterday, Tomorrow: Voices from the Somali Diaspora* (London: Cassell, 2000), p. 48. This book is itself a testament to a material if not materialist negotiation of outsideness for the Somali diaspora.

7. Quoted in William Riggan, "Nuruddin Farah's Indelible Country of the Imagination," *World Literature Today* 72:4 (autumn 1998): 700.

8. See Nuruddin Farah, "Bastards of Empire," *Transition* 65 (1995): 28.

9. Kwame Anthony Appiah, "For Nuruddin Farah," *World Literature Today* 72:4 (autumn 1998): 703.

10. In addition to Cobham's intervention cited above, see also: Amina H. Adan, "Women and Words," *Ufahamu: Journal of the African Activist Association* 10:3 (1981): 115–42; Hilarie Kelly, "A Somali Tragedy of Political and Sexual Confusion: A Critical Analysis of Nuruddin Farah's *Maps*," *Ufahamu: Journal of the African Activist Association* 16:2 (1988): 21–37; and Derek Wright, "Requiems for Revolutions: Race-Sex Archetypes in Two African Novels," *Modern Fiction Studies* 35:1 (1989): 55–68.

11. Farah's novel of 2003 is called *Links* and features an epigraph from Freud on the link as a double life. *Links* is the first of a new trilogy (the second volume is *Knots*) that refracts Farah's experience of return to Somalia as one not just of confrontation with the conditions of a failed state but as a failure of imagination that is not the monopoly of Somalis themselves. These "links" are both a political and aesthetic challenge.

12. The territorial disputes over the Ogaden region are long-standing, but actual hegemony was greatly influenced by the competing agendas of the United States and the Soviet Union during the Cold War. This geopolitical overlay still produces sharply partisan critique, but other political interests (African, nationalist, and so on) are superceding this aura. See, for instance, Helen Chapin Metz, ed., *Somalia* (Washington D.C.: Federal Research Division, 1993); Jamil Abdalla Mubarak, *From Bad Policy to Chaos in Somalia: How an Economy Fell Apart* (New York: Praeger, 1996); Ali Jimali Ahmed, ed., *The Invention of Somalia* (Lawrenceville, N.J.: Red Sea Press, 1995); and I. M. Lewis, *A Modern History of Somalia*, 4th ed. (Athens: Ohio University Press, 2003).

13. Derek Wright, "Parenting the Nation: Some Observations on Nuruddin Farah's *Maps*," *College Literature* 19:3 (October 1992): 177.

14. Nuruddin Farah, "Why I Write," *Third World Quarterly* 10 (1988): 1597.

15. Hilarie Kelly, "A Somali Tragedy of Political and Sexual Confusion: A Critical Analysis of Nuruddin Farah's *Maps*," *Ufahamu: Journal of the African Activist Association* 16:2 (1988): 21–37.

16. Compare, for instance, Derek Wright, "Parenting the Nation: Some Observations on Nuruddin Farah's *Maps*," *College Literature* 19:3 (1992): 176–84, and 20:1 (1993): 76–83 with Derek Wright, "Nations as Fictions: Postmodernism in the Novels of Nuruddin Farah," *Critique* 38 (1997): 205–20. The latter has not only absorbed the substance of the former, but recast its genealogy according to postmodern stylistics. To be fair, Wright does maintain that it would be "perverse" to claim Farah as a "thoroughgoing postmodernist" ("Nations," 194); but while this suitably admits the notion of a productive mixed parentage, it also suspends the

postcolonial question of postmodernity that is often framed around the question of history, family, or otherwise.

17. Nuruddin Farah, "Wretched Life," interview with Patricia Morris, *Africa Events* (Sept. 1986): 54.

18. See Wright, "Parenting."

19. Farah's epigraphs are never innocent, so when Francesca Kazan says of *Maps*, "There are no whites in this textual world," one might at least consider the reach of their insinuation. See Francesca Kazan, "Recalling the Other Third World: Nuruddin Farah's *Maps*," *Novel* 26:3 (spring 1993): 253–68. If epigraphs (in Farah, Harris, and Djebar) appear to coddle a certain cultural esteem (which, after all, is a basic meaning of the epigraph), their authority is ambivalently positioned.

20. A pertinent if brief survey of Somali cultural traditions can be found in Kathryne S. Loughran et al., eds., *Somalia in Word and Image* (Washington, D.C.: Foundation for Cross-Cultural Understanding, 1986). Poetry, in particular, occupies a strong cultural position in Somali life. See, for instance, B. W. Andrzejewski and I. M. Lewis, *Somali Poetry: An Introduction* (Oxford: Clarendon Press, 1964). Even Siyad Barre used "court" poets to sing his praises in the popular press, and more so when opponents used slightly more barbed words both in newspapers and in BBC radio broadcasts across Somalia (the latter, separate from state-run radio, gave greater latitude to criticism while permitting the British to exercise an ideological presence in Somali daily life).

21. Nuruddin Farah, "A Country in Exile," *Transition* 57 (1992): 4.

22. Mikhail Bakhtin, *Art and Answerability*, eds. Michael Holquist and Vadim Liapunov, trans. Vadim Liapunov (Austin: University of Texas Press, 1990): 81–87.

23. See Achille Mbembe, *On the Postcolony*, trans. A. M. Berrett et al. (Berkeley: University of California Press, 2001).

24. Related but alternative assessments can be found in Tim Woods, "Giving and Receiving: Nuruddin Farah's *Gifts*, or, the Postcolonial Logic of Third World Aid," *Journal of Commonwealth Literature* 38:1 (March 2004): 91–112; and Francis Ngaboh-Smart, "Dimensions of Gift-Giving in Nuruddin Farah's *Gifts*," *Research in African Literatures*, 27:4 (1996): 144–58.

25. See Jacques Derrida, *Given Time: 1. Counterfeit Money*, trans. Peggy Kamuf. (Chicago: University of Chicago Press, 1992), p. 12. Subsequent references will be noted in the text as GT followed by page number.

26. This sorry tale is recorded over and over again. See, for instance, Howard P.Lehman, *Indebted Development* (New York: St.Martin's Press, 1993); Paul Vallely, *Bad Samaritans* (New York: Orbis Books, 1990); and Helen O'Neill, *Third World Debt* (New York: Frank Cass, 1990). While debt forgiveness has elicited both sincerity and posturing in equal measure, the problem of systemic indebtedness and postcolonial delinking has been complicated more recently by the specter of First World debt, specifically that of the United States. All four countries invoked in my primary case studies in this book have been judged either failed or weak states

in the international public sphere, and in two examples, Algeria and Indonesia, this seems to have helped rather than hindered further oil and gas exploitation. Nevertheless, the fact that three of these states are strongly Islamic has precipitated renewed attention on the nexus of state failure and "fundamentalist terror." It is unclear at present what gift, if any, this might constitute.

27. Sydney Pollack's 1985 film won seven Oscars including Best Picture and Best Director. Full of lush photography and dry-cleaned safari duds, it was a basic star vehicle for Meryl Streep and Robert Redford. Isak Dinesen's book, however, was quite different in tone and outlook even if Baroness Karen Blixen (her real name) could not help exoticizing Kenya if not her coffee plantation. Mentioning *Out of Africa* dates Farah's book since Dinesen's memoir was basically out of memory by the time the film went to video. Isak Dinesen, *Out of Africa* (New York: Modern Library, 1992).

28. See Marcel Mauss, *The Gift: The Form and Reason for Exchange in Archaic Societies*, trans. W. D. Halls (London: Routledge, 1990).

29. Much of this position is outlined in Mikhail Bakhtin, *Toward a Philosophy of the Act*, trans. Vadim Liapunov (Austin: University of Texas Press, 1993). The key Russian word is *sobytie*, which combines being, event, and the "co-" of cooperation (*so*). Despite the uniqueness of the term, however, its philosophical roots lie elsewhere in the works of Scheler, Brentano, and Cohen. For this narrative, see Craig Brandist, *The Bakhtin Circle* (London: Pluto, 2002), especially Chapter Two.

30. Nuruddin Farah, "Celebrating Differences: The 1998 Neustadt Lecture," *World Literature Today* 72:4 (autumn 1998): 709.

31. Homi Bhabha, *The Location of Culture* (Newc York: Routledge, 1994), p. 191.

32. The novel "Tallow Waa Talee Ma" was not completed.

33. During his exile Farah has lived in Italy, Germany, Britain, the United States, Uganda, Sudan, Ethiopia, Gambia, Nigeria, and South Africa. Appiah notes that "Nuruddin Farah has been thrown out by more African countries than most people have visited." Kwame Anthony Appiah, "For Nuruddin Farah," *World Literature Today* 72:4 (autumn 1998): 704. And yet he has remained African in his identification and in his location for much of his life. While Farah has contended that "distance distills" (Nuruddin Farah, "A Country in Exile," *Transition* 57 (1992): 5), this distance has been calibrated by ardent proximity.

34. See V. N. Voloshinov, *Marxism and the Philosophy of Language*, trans. Ladislav Matejka and I. R. Titunik (Cambridge, Mass.: Harvard University Press, 1986).

35. An excellent appraisal of the shared theoretical concerns of Bakhtin and Lukács can be found in Galin Tihanov, *The Master and the Slave*, (Oxford: Oxford University Press, 2000).

36. See J. M. Bernstein, *The Philosophy of the Novel* (Minneapolis: University of Minnesota Press, 1984), especially Chapter Three.

37. See Georges Bataille, *The Accursed Share*, vol. 1, trans. Robert Hurley (New York: Zone Books, 1991).

38. See Mbembe, *On the Postcolony*, especially Chapter Three on the "Aesthetics of Vulgarity." This essay also marks Mbembe's albeit brief embrace of Bakhtinian concepts.

39. Neal Ascherson, "On the Edge of Catastrophe," *New York Review of Books* 46:4 (March 4, 1999): 19.

40. Anne Ursu, "Secrets," *Rain Taxi Review of Books* 3:2 (Summer 1998, 10): 27.

41. Francis Ngaboh-Smart, "*Secrets* and a New Civic Consciousness," *Research in African Literatures* 31:1 (spring 2000): 129 .

42. See Gayatri Chakravorty Spivak, *A Critique of Postcolonial Reason* (Cambridge, Mass.: Harvard University Press, 1997). Spivak's aim is clearly to mark a necessity for literacy in transnationalism itself, one that would link the various cultural contours of postcoloniality to the international division of labor.

43. See Jacques Derrida, *The Gift of Death*, trans. David Wills (Chicago: University of Chicago Press, 1995). One expects this book to be a sequel to *Given Time* but, although it shares a concern to elaborate the paradox of the gift, it is built around a different conceptual key, that of ethics. Subsequent references will be noted as GD in the text followed by the page number.

44. Confirmed in conversation with Nuruddin Farah, Cape Town, South Africa, November 2004. "Words" is much too bland a title given the specific nature of words that Farah has in mind. Nevertheless, there is a certain resignation in this title that remains in spirit in the novel as published.

45. Said S. Samatar, "Are There Secrets in *Secrets*?" *Research in African Literatures* 31:2 (spring 2000): 137–42.

46. See Moretti's preface to the new edition of Franco Moretti, *The Way of the World*, trans. Albert Sbragia (New York: Verso, 2000), p. v.

47. The most exuberant review of *Secrets* as a taboo-breaking sexcapade is by Michael Eldridge, who cockily summarizes: "The whole thing seems to boil down, in short, to 'sperm-and-blood.'" See Michael Eldridge, "Out of the Closet, *World Literature Today* 72:4 (autumn 1998): 767–75.

48. See Jacqueline Bardolph, "Brothers and Sisters in Nuruddin Farah's Two Trilogies," *World Literature Today* 72:4 (autumn 1998): 727–32. Alden and Tremaine add: "The iconic figure in the second trilogy is the orphan; the central concern is building identity within newly conceived social relationships that nurture the freedom of all. The situation of Farah's characters, engaged in the delicate negotiation of autonomy and relationship, has resonance at the level of the nation. Their fragility as orphans is paralleled in the evident fragility of the nation, a parallel Farah made explicit in an interview in 1992, the year he completed the first draft of *Secrets*: 'The central theme of the second trilogy . . . is that in all of [the three novels] a baby boy is either found or lost. Now, imagine: an African Islamic society in

which babies are abandoned. . . . The whole thing is apocalyptic. . . . Society is an orphaned baby, parentless, with no wise elder to guide it." Patrica Alden and Louis Tremaine, "Reinventing Family in the Second Trilogy of Nuruddin Farah," *World Literature Today* 72:4 (autumn 1998): 765. The interview can be found in Feroza Jussawalla and Reed Way Dasenbrock, *Interviews with Writers of the Post-Colonial World* (Jackson: University Press of Mississippi, 1992), pp. 42–62.

49. See Aimé Césaire, *Discourse on Colonialism*, trans. Joan Pinkham (New York: Monthly Review Press, 1972), p. 68.

50. Wilson Harris, *Tradition, the Writer, and Society* (London: Beacon, 1967), pp. 46–47.

51. See, for instance, Ian Adam, "Nuruddin Farah and James Joyce: Some Issues of Intertextuality," *World Literature Written in English* 24 (1984): 34–43; and Simon Gikandi, "Nuruddin Farah and Postcolonial Textuality," *World Literature Today* 72:3 (autumn 1998): 753–59.

CHAPTER 4

1. Here, as before, I will refer principally to the second edition of *Imagined Communities*. See Benedict Anderson, *Imagined Communities* (London: Verso, 1991), pp. 22–26. Subsequent references will be noted in the text as IC. On *Jetztzeit*, an inspiration for this use of time, see Walter Benjamin, *Illuminations*, trans. Harry Zohn, ed. Hannah Arendt (New York: Schocken, 1969), pp. 261–64. The singularity of Anderson's position rests not on his understanding of Benjamin alone, but on the conceptual link he makes with Auerbach and the exegesis of Augustine in *Mimesis* from which Anderson quotes. The section carries the subheading "Apprehensions of time" and indicates a simultaneous interest in perception and foreboding that I will argue is constitutive of Pramoedya's historicism. As for "meanwhile," Anderson doubts its significance in the realm of Messianic time and thus *Jetztzeit* is modernity's pause, especially here where nation formation is concerned. At this level, my use of "meanwhile" continually flags a logic of displacement rather than endorses it.

2. There is one other example of an untranslated passage in *Imagined Communities,* and it appears in the same chapter, although it is in French and it is not included for its sonality.

3. See Peter Hitchcock, *Dialogics of the Oppressed* (Minneapolis: University of Minnesota Press, 1993), especially the final chapter.

4. "Things Vanished" is available in a new English translation as "All That Is Gone" in the collection of the same name: Pramoedya Ananta Toer, *All That Is Gone*, trans. Willem Samuels (New York: Hyperion East, 2004), pp. 1–30; abbreviated as ATIG. Several of Pramoedya's early stories are autobiographical, but see also the memoir *The Mute's Soliloquy*, trans. Willem Samuels (New York: Hyperion East, 1999); abbreviated as MS. Pramoedya is often described as self-educated,

but this omits the strong influence of his mother's storytelling (much more so than his father's career as a teacher/headmaster). Like much of Pramoedya's life, this remains to be adequately elaborated. The website maintained by Alex Bardsley dedicated to matters Pramoedyan is a useful resource, as is the basic outline provided by Contemporary Authors Online from Gale. The research of Andreas Teeuw is indispensable. See Andreas Teeuw, *Pramoedya Ananta Toer: de verbeelding van Indonesië* (Breda, Nederland: De Geus, 1993). This text is also available in Bahasa Indonesia: see Andreas Teeuw, *Citra Manusi Indonesia dalam karya sastra Pramoedya Ananta Toer* (Jakarta: Pustaka Jaya, 1997). Some of this material will be summarized below.

5. "Things Vanished," trans. with commentary by James Siegel, in *Glyph: Johns Hopkins Textual Studies* (Baltimore: Johns Hopkins University Press, 1977), p. 97.

6. Pramoedya achieves something very similar in his novel *The Fugitive* that, as Anderson points out, recalls the structure of *wayang*, Japanese shadowplay, in the midst of canceling it through contemporary themes. Benedict R. Anderson, "Review of *The Fugitive*, by Pramoedya Ananta Toer," *World Literature Today* 65:2 (spring 1991): 367. See also, Pramoedya Ananta Toer, *The Fugitive*, trans. Willem Samuels (New York: William Morrow, 1990). Samuels makes a similar point in his "Note to the Reader."

7. Here I am attempting to triangulate Lukács's *The Theory of the Novel* with Bakhtin and Benjamin around the concept of time's narration. See Georg Lukács, *The Theory of the Novel: A Historico-Philosophical Essay on the Forms of Great Epic Literature*, trans. Anna Bostock (Cambridge, Mass.: MIT Press, 1971); hereafter, TN. Lukács argues that only the novel "includes real time—Bergson's *durée*—among its constitutive principles" (TN 121). Duration in the epic is not "real time" but a chronotopic adjunct, or "adventure time" to borrow from Bakhtin that effectively abolishes time. Bakhtin and Benjamin were close readers of Lukács (it is said that Bakhtin began a translation of *The Theory of the Novel*), as the following may indicate:

> Everything that happens may be meaningless, fragmentary and sad, but it is always irradiated by hope or memory. And hope here is not an abstract artifact, isolated from life, spoilt and shop-worn as the result of its defeat by life: it is a part of life; it tries to conquer life by embracing and adorning it, yet is repulsed by life again and again. And memory transforms the continual struggle into a process which is full of mystery and interest and yet is tied with indestructible threads to the present, the unexplained instant. Duration advances upon that instant and passes on, but the wealth of duration which the instant momentarily dams and holds still in a flash of conscious contemplation is such that it enriches even what is over and done with: it even puts the full value of lived experience on events which, at the time, passed by unnoticed. . . . Herein lies the essentially epic quality of memory. (TN 126)

Postcoloniality is the name of hope in duration, in persistence. It cannot be sublated merely by announcing endless exception. It must be approached as a problem of time itself. For the most sustained and persuasive analysis of Lukács's provocation for Bakhtin, see Galin Tihanov, *The Master and the Slave* (Oxford: Oxford University Press, 2000). A significant reappraisal of Lukács's *The Theory of the Novel* can be found in J. M. Bernstein, *The Philosophy of the Novel* (Minneapolis: University of Minnesota Press, 1984). Finally, I am also struck by the concept-metaphor of time that Lukács uses: "Thus it is that time becomes the carrier of the sublime epic poetry of the novel: it has become inexorably existent, and no one can any longer swim against the unmistakable direction of its current nor regulate its unforeseeable course with the dams of *a priori* concepts" (TN 123–24). Here the form-giving of time and the Lusi River are conjoined.

8. All translations from the *Buru Quartet* are my own unless otherwise noted. See *Bumi Manusia* (Jakarta: Hasta Mitra, 1980), abbreviated as BM; *Anak Semua Bangsa* (Jakarta: Hasta Mitra, 1980), abbreviated as ASB; *Jejak Langkah* (Jakarta: Hasta Mitra, 1985), abbreviated as JL; and *Rumah Kaca* (Jakarta: Hasta Mitra, 1988), abbreviated as RK. Pramoedya's publisher in Malaysia, Wira Karya, has also published a significant edition of the *Buru* tetralogy that is for the most part identical to the Jakarta text, although it does carry a glossary of terms that indicate key cultural differences between Bahasa Indonesia and the Malay of Malaysia. The primary translation in English is the American Morrow/Penguin version. See Pramoedya Ananta Toer, *This Earth of Mankind*, trans. Max Lane (New York: Penguin, 1991), abbreviated as TEM; *Child of All Nations*, trans. Max Lane (New York: Penguin, 1991), abbreviated as CAN; *Footsteps*, trans. Max Lane (New York: Penguin, 1990), abbreviated as F; and *House of Glass*, trans. Max Lane (New York: Penguin, 1992), abbreviated as HG. There are significant debates about the translation strategies involved in producing the English-language texts, some of which I will address in due course. Quotations from the *Buru Quartet* will include both the Hasta Mitra and Penguin page references.

9. The theoretical and political pitfalls between nation and narration have been sharply debated, as have relevant discussions that challenge nation as a conditional limit. A good starting place is Homi Bhabha, ed., *Nation and Narration* (New York: Routledge, 1990). For a while countercritique took the form of a reconfigured cosmopolitanism. See, for instance, Pheng Cheah and Bruce Robbins, eds., *Cosmopolitics: Thinking and Feeling Beyond the Nation* (Minneapolis: University of Minnesota Press, 1998). For doubts about the political efficacy of this move, see, for instance, Timothy Brennan, *At Home in the World: Cosmopolitanism Now* (Cambridge, Mass.: Harvard University Press, 1997).

10. Ernest Renan, "What Is a Nation?" trans. Martin Thom, in *Nation and Narration*, ed. Homi Bhabha (New York: Routledge, 1990), p. 11.

11. The novel, as a significant cultural artifact, speaks to the problem of nation on any number of levels (evident in my prior comments), but the latter must primarily

be held as an issue of political institution whose answer involves social narration more broadly construed, broader still than the adjudication of an individual nation.

12. Pramoedya published a biography of Tirto in 1985, the research and writing of which partly ran in parallel with his fictional representation. See Pramoedya Ananta Toer, *Sang pemula dan karya-karya non-fiksi (jurnalistik), fiksi (cerpen/ novel) R. M. Tirto Adhi Soerjo* (Jakarta: Hasta Mitra, 1985).

13. "Imagined community" is a term that now has a separate life from its early theorization. Interestingly, Anderson's perception of his book's intervention (recounted in the preface to the second edition) itself has the air of the novelistic: "It seemed better, therefore, to leave it largely as an 'unrestored' period piece, with its own characteristic style, silhouette, and mood" (IC xii).

14. See Benedict Anderson, *The Spectre of Comparisons: Nationalism, Southeast Asia and the World* (London: Verso, 1998). [SC]

15. José Rizal (1861–96) was a key figure in the development of Filipino nationalism (Rizal, for his efforts, was executed by the Spanish colonial government). While Pramoedya, both in his fiction and in his correspondence with Anderson, provides an initial model for key components of the "imagined community," it is Rizal who has increasingly become for Anderson the embodiment of the concept's historical force. There are several reasons for Anderson's altered focus. First, Rizal lives a history that in his own context Pramoedya fictionalizes. Second, Anderson did not have the access to archives in Indonesia that he had in the Philippines. Third, I believe there is a riddle in the production of the *Buru Quartet* that was not solved in Pramoedya's lifetime (in large part because of the vagaries of extant manuscript and editing techniques). The attention to Rizal intensifies in *The Spectre of Comparisons* and has expanded further still in a series of essays (a triptych, suggests Anderson) in the *New Left Review*. See Benedict Anderson, "Nitroglycerine in the Pomegranate," *New Left Review* 27 (May/June 2004): 99–118); "In the World-Shadow of Bismarck and Nobel," *New Left Review* 28 (July/August 2004): 85–129; and "Jupiter Hill," *New Left Review* 29 (September/October 2004): 91–120, now collected with other essays as *Under Three Flags* (New York: Verso, 2005). Since I perceive a certain seriality in my own project, Rizal's diptych (*Noli Me Tangere* and *El Filibusterismo*) is more than relevant since it bears critically on the long space, one that includes Anderson's extensions. When faced with the realization that the translation of Rizal that he used was poor ("fascinatingly corrupt" [IC xiii]), Anderson reimagined *Imagined Communities*—the translation in question is José Rizal, *Noli Me Tangere,* trans. Leon Ma. Guerrero (London: Longman, 1961)—by learning Spanish in order to consult the Rizal archive in Manila's Instituto Nacional de Historia. The point would now be to reimagine it again from a position that takes into account not just Anderson's revisions but the logic of seriality itself as a postcolonial provenance.

16. Pramoedya Ananta Toer, *Tjerita dari Djakarta* (also *Cerita dari Jakarta*) (Jakarta: Grafica, 1963). The English edition is Pramoedya Ananta Toer, *Tales from*

Djakarta, trans. Nusantara Translation Group with an introduction by Benedict Anderson (Jakarta: Equinox, 2000), hereafter TFD. The Nusantara Translation Group is described as an association of graduate students in the Department of South and Southeast Asian Studies at the University of California, Berkeley. This form of collective endeavor is crucial both to the future of postcolonial studies and to the concept of "world literature" itself.

17. See Benedict R. O'G. Anderson, "Sembah-Sumpah," in *Language and Power* (Ithaca: Cornell University Press, 1990), 194–237; hereafter, LP. In a far-ranging argument Anderson shows how Javanese, and Javanese literature, function as a form of ghost in the identification processes of Bahasa Indonesia. The formalities and hierarchies intrinsic to Javanese socialization do not disappear in the use of Bahasa Indonesia but exist in dialogic tension so that moments of *sembah* (a respectful gesture of obeisance) are often answered, particularly in Pramoedya's fiction, with the swearing available to Bahasa Indonesia. It should be noted, respectfully, that the passage from *This Earth of Mankind* that Anderson uses to open his argument includes several versions of swearing (*kursi*) but not *sumpah* as such (the passage ends with *menyumpah*, another synonym for swearing [*Bumi manusia*, 109]), although the force of his polemic remains clear. One final point: "the Honored Lord" to which Minke refers in the passage will, a few lines later, be revealed as his father, which adds another significant dimension to the exchange.

18. In addition to Anderson's *Language and Power*, the following works elucidate this critical period in Indonesian history: J. D. Legge, *Indonesia* (Sydney: Prentice Hall of Australia, 1980); Leslie Palmier, ed., *Understanding Indonesia* (Aldershot: Gower, 1985); Robert Cribb and Colin Brown, *Modern Indonesia* (London: Longman, 1995); Daniel S. Lev and Ruth McVey, eds., *Making Indonesia: Essays on Modern Indonesia in Honor of George McT. Kahin* (Ithaca, N.Y.: Cornell Southeast Asia Program Publications, 1996); B. B. Herring et al., *New-Order-Indonesia: Five Essays* (Townsville, Queensland: Centre for Southeast Asian Studies, James Cook University of North Queensland, 1988); and Virginia Hooker and Howard Dick, eds., *Culture and Society in New Order Indonesia* (Kuala Lumpur and New York: Oxford University Press, 1993.)

19. Brathwaite uses Nation language as a means to express identity through place and/or environment, a logic that links the islands of the Caribbean without erasing their specificity or their historical links with Africa. See Kamau Brathwaite, *History of the Voice: The Development of Nation Language in Anglophone Caribbean Poetry* (London: New Beacon, 1984).

20. See Pheng Cheah, *Spectral Nationality* (New York: Columbia University Press, 2003).

21. See Multatuli (Eduard Douwes Dekker), *Max Havelaar; or, the Coffee Auctions of the Dutch Trading Company*, trans. Roy Edwards (New York: Penguin, 1967). See also Pramoedya Ananta Toer, "The Book That Killed Colonialism,"

New York Times Magazine (April 18, 1999): 112–14. The latter forms part of a special issue dedicated to the turn of the millennium. While Pramoedya's claims for *Max Havelaar* are hyperbolic, the debates that followed Multatuli's publication certainly represent a watershed in the fight against Dutch colonialism in Indonesia.

22. This error in judgment calls into question Pramoedya's understanding of the nationalist ideology in play and its consequences for free speech. Pramoedya's work for Lekra is all the more remarkable because at the same time that he was questioning the ideological correctness of his fellow artists he was supporting the rights of Indonesia's large Chinese migrant population, a solidarity rewarded by a year in jail.

23. For more on Pramoedya's sense of the period, see *The Mute's Soliloquy* and Pramoedya Ananta Toer, "Maaf, di atas Nama Pengalaman" ("My Apologies in the Name of Experience"), trans. Alex G. Bardsley, www.radix.net/bardsley/apolog.html.

24. See Clifford Geertz, "Java Jive," *New Republic*, 214:17 (April 22, 1996): 31–35.

25. This contention is recorded by Chris GoGwilt. See Chris GoGwilt, "Pramoedya's Fiction and History: An Interview with Indonesian Novelist Pramoedya Ananta Toer," *Yale Journal of Criticism* 9:1 (1996): 147–64. Because of Resink's friendship and intellectual influence on Pramoedya (and the fact that Pramoedya dedicates the first two volumes of the *Buru Quartet* to him) his comments are always instructive. Although Nyai Ontosoroh is crucial to the development of Minke's worldview, her own presence in the tetralogy is sometimes muted.

26. See Matthew Rothschild, "Pramoedya Ananta Toer," *Progressive* 63:10 (October 1999): 31–33.

27. See Walter Benjamin, "Theses on the Philosophy of History," *Illuminations*, trans. Harry Zohn, ed. Hannah Arendt (New York: Schocken, 1969), p. 255.

28. The thesis novel often takes the form of a didactic approach to a specific social or political problem. It attempts in no small way to reveal social shortcomings, but the power of its voice depends not just on the perspicacity of its critique but on the social position of the novelist herself and the nature of crisis. If postcoloniality embraces the thesis novel, it is less clear that the postcolonial novelist can assume an unqualified reader base for such didacticism or how crisis mediates this relationship. Pramoedya's model is often Steinbeck, particularly *The Grapes of Wrath* (Pramoedya also translated *Of Mice and Men* into Bahasa Indonesia), and this reveals Pramoedya's commitment in writing and its asynchronicity.

29. GoGwilt, 58.

30. See Takashi Shiraishi, "Reading Pramoedya Ananta Toer's *Sang Pemula* [The Pioneer]," *Indonesia* 44 (October 1987): 129–139. Shiraishi's own contribution to an understanding of Indonesia's *Bildung* can be found in Takashi Shiraishi, *An Age in Motion: Popular Radicalism in Java, 1912–1926* (Ithaca, N.Y.: Cornell University Press, 1990).

31. Cheah, 275.

32. Paul Ricoeur, "Narrative Time," *Critical Inquiry* 7:1 (autumn 1980): 180.

33. See Razif Bahari, "Remembering History, W/Righting History: Piecing the Past in Pramoedya Ananta Toer's Buru Tetralogy," *Indonesia* 75 (April 2003): 61–90.

34. Raden Adjeng Kartini was the daughter of an aristocrat from Jepara. She was one of the first native women in the East Indies to receive a Western education. Pramoedya's earlier research on Kartini was published as: Pramoedya Ananta Toer, *Panggil aku Kartini saja* (Jakarta: Nusantara, 1962).

35. Pramoedya edited a collection of Malay fiction—*Tempo Doeloe: antologi sastra pra-Indonesia* (Jakarta: Hasta Mitra, 1982)—that included two stories by Kommer.

36. J. M. Bernstein, *The Philosophy of the Novel* (Minneapolis: University of Minnesota Press, 1984), p. 133, hereafter noted as PN followed by the page number.

37. M. M. Bakhtin, *The Dialogic Imagination*, ed. Michael Holquist, trans. Emerson and Holquist (Austin: University of Texas Press, 1981), p. 94.

38. For those who doubt the cynicism of Suharto, the description of the Buru penal colony as "humanitarian" might give one pause. The pulling and stretching of Pramoedya's Buru days and which ones were dedicated to orality were in evidence again in 1999 with the tour linked to the English publication of *The Mute's Soliloquy*. The mainstream reviews available on Bardsley's website are fairly consistent in this tendency.

39. Matthew Rothschild, "Pramoedya Ananta Toer," *Progressive* 63:10 (October 1999): 32.

40. I agree with Bahari that Pramoedya in the *Quartet* attempts to prove the efficacy of social realism he advocated in his literary criticism, yet I would add that the actual history deployed often interrupts the narrative through sometimes awkward asides and contrived scenes of historical recollection.

41. Rothschild, "Pramoedya Ananta Toer," 32.

42. Pramoedya Ananta Toer, "The Book That Killed Colonialism," *New York Times Magazine* (April 18, 1999): 112.

43. Aimé Césaire, *Discourse on Colonialism*, 32.

44. Pramoedya Ananta Toer, "Maaf, di atas Nama Pengalaman" ("My Apologies in the Name of Experience"), trans. Alex G. Bardsley, www.radix.net/bardsley/apolog.html. Bardsley's "Afterword" and notes are particularly useful in situating this text and the internal polemic of Pramoedya's historical references.

45. There is a fateful consonance between the production of spectral tropology and the end of the Second World experiment that could not but affect the terms and disciplinary understanding of postcolonialism. My position is outlined in "Of Ghosts" in *Oscillate Wildly: Space, Body, and Spirit of Millennial Materialism* (Minneapolis: University of Minnesota Press, 1999).

46. Both "My Apologies in the Name of Experience" and "Literature, Censorship and the State: To What Extent Is a Novel Dangerous?" for instance, hinge upon a historical sense of power in Javanese tradition much indebted to Anderson's

"The Idea of Power in Javanese Culture," from *Language and Power*. Indeed, Anderson is acknowledged in the first essay in this regard.

47. Pramoedya, "Gado-gado," *Pertjikan Revolusi* (Djakarta: Gapura, 1950), p. 31. Quoted in Bardsley's notes to "My Apologies" (see note 46 above).

48. See Razif Bahari, *Indonesia* 75 (April 2003): 72.

49. One is reminded of Melville's opening of *Moby Dick*, "Call me Ishmael," where again the force of identification is precisely that which will be challenged by the more tortuous course of narration itself. As Pramoedya imagines Minke, it is unclear at that moment he was simultaneously imagining Pangemanann reading the line.

50. Given the fragility of Pramoedya's archive we should note the difference between this and that founded by the colonizing desire of commandment. If the archive attempts to instantiate an authority in its commencement (*arche* as foundation), it combines a will to preserve with one to forget strategically. See also Jacques Derrida, *Archive Fever: A Freudian Impression*, trans. Eric Prenowitz (Chicago: University of Chicago Press, 1996).

51. See Razif Bahari, *Indonesia* 75 (April 2003): 61–90. The propositional faith of hermeneutics is not necessarily to be disparaged. Yet if we take the emergency of writing itself seriously in the articulation of postcolonial difference even the gesture to meaning alone may see a luxury.

52. See Pramoedya Ananta Toer, "Maaf, di atas Nama Pengalaman" ("My Apologies in the Name of Experience"), trans. Alex G. Bardsley, www.radix.net/bardsley/apolog.html.

53. See Bardsley's notes and "Afterword" to "My Apologies."

54. See, in particular, M. M. Bakhtin, *Problems in Dostoevsky's Poetics*, trans. Caryl Emerson (Minneapolis: University of Minnesota Press, 1984).

55. Anderson notes in *Spectre of Comparisons* that Rizal wrote in Spanish, even though only 3 percent of his countrypeople understood it, because his fiction was meant as much for his enemies as his friends.

56. See Jonathan Culler, "Anderson and the Novel," *Diacritics* 29:4 (Winter 1999): 25.

57. See Franco Moretti, *Atlas of the European Novel, 1800–1900* (London: Verso, 1998). As Culler notes, Moretti does at least consider the fictionalizing fulcrum of the novel's representation of nation, yet it is just as noteworthy that Moretti then proceeds to conjure a cartographic correlative for this urge.

58. This is not a minor detail since Pramoedya understands the significance of roads in the network that colonialism represents. Indeed, the documentary of Pramoedya, *Jalan Raya Pos* (*De Groote Postweg*) "The Great Post Road," is premised on this fact. Bernie Ijdis, dir., *Jalan Raya Pos*, The Netherlands, 1996.

59. Walter Benjamin, *The Arcades Project*, trans. Howard Eiland and Kevin McLaughlin (Cambridge, Mass.: Harvard University Press, 1999), p. 462.

CHAPTER 5

1. In many ways, Djebar evinces the most developed sense of what extension in dynamic place can mean for the transnationalism of the postcolonial novel. There can be no doubt that the appearance of the final volume would permit a full and revised account of the complex aesthetic and political processes of Djebar's narrative. The present attempt seeks to register the significant elements of the story she has built and its implications for an understanding of a logic of form in decolonization.

2. See Clarisse Zimra, "'When the Past Answers Our Present': Assia Djebar Talks about *Loin de Médine*," *Callaloo* 16: 1 (winter 1993): 116–31. The first three volumes of the Algerian Quartet are: Assia Djebar, *L'Amour, la fantasia* (Paris: Jean Lattès, 1985), translated as *Fantasia: An Algerian Cavalcade*, trans. Dorothy S. Blair (London: Quartet Books, 1989); Assia Djebar, *Ombre Sultane* (Paris: Jean Lattès, 1987), translated as *A Sister to Scheherazade*, trans. Dorothy S. Blair (London: Quartet Books, 1987); Assia Djebar, *Vaste est la prison* (Paris: Albin Michel, 1995), translated as *So Vast the Prison*, trans. Betsy Wing (New York: Seven Stories, 1999). Other works since *Vaste est la prison* include: *Le blanc de l'Algérie* (Paris: Albin Michel, 1995), translated as *Algerian White*, trans. David Kelley and Marjolijn De Jager (New York: Seven Stories Press, 2001); *Les nuits de Strasbourg* (Paris: Actes Sud, 1997); *Oran, langue morte* (Paris: Sud, 1997); *Ces voix qui m'assiegent: en marge de ma francophonie* (Paris: Albin Michel, 1999); and *La femme sans sepulture* (Paris: Albin Michel, 2002). Clearly, the question is not writer's block but the relationship of history and its formal expression. All translations are mine unless the English translation is otherwise indicated.

3. See Peter Hitchcock, "The Scriptible Voice and the Space of Silence: Assia Djebar's Algeria," *Bucknell Review*, special issue: "Bakhtin and the Nation," 43:2 (2000): 134–49; and "The White of Algeria; or, The Paroxysms of the Postcolony" in Peter Hitchcock, *Imaginary States: Studies in Cultural Transnationalism* (Urbana: University of Illinois Press, 2003), pp. 92–117.

4. See Assia Djebar, *Loin de Medine* (Paris: Albin Michel, 1991), translated as *Far from Madina*, trans. Dorothy Blair (London: Quartet Books, 1993), and *Le blanc de l'Algérie*. Both books are redolent with Djebar's historical sensibility and imaginative reworking, but they exist in the margins of the Quartet rather than embrace the core of its formal procedures. For a careful reading of *Loin* that includes an interview with Assia Djebar, see Clarisse Zimra, "'When the Past Answers the Present,'" *Callaloo* 16:1 (1993): 116–31. Djebar is clear that this book is a different but related project to the Quartet. The urge to enlist another work to complete the Quartet was intensified with *Le blanc de l'Algérie,* but although it can be productively linked to the Quartet (especially the third volume) its elegiac mode performs a more pressing role in coming to terms with the personal losses of the civil war. By generalizing the themes of Djebar's work, *Les nuits, Oran,* and *La*

femme cannot help but speak to the project of the Quartet, yet this can be as much as a distraction as it is a revelation of the formal injunction the Quartet represents.

5. The formal structure of the grand house in Moorish architecture plays a pertinent role among the compositional elements of Djebar's oeuvre. As Clarisse Zimra points out, in interviews and in talks Djebar has used this structural analogy to describe the project of the tetralogy. See Clarisse Zimra, "Mapping Memory: Architectural Metaphors in Djebar's Unfinished Quartet," *Esprit Créateur*, 43:1 (spring 2003): 58–68. Other spatial motifs central to Djebar's understanding of women's space include the apartment, the balcony, and the hammam. The mausoleum and the stele are also structural remains that mark memory and a living force in history.

6. Not surprisingly, fantasia for Djebar conjures several connotations simultaneously. It can invoke a display of Arab horseback riding skills and a classical musical composition (that emerges, like colonialism, in Europe from the sixteenth century) in which form is subject to "fancy."

7. See Assia Djebar, "Le Discours de Francfort," *Etudes* 3953 (September 2001): 235–46.

8. The difficulty with arraying writers in this way is not the false regionalism it implies but the fulcrum of colonialism on which such emergence appears to pivot.

9. Critical works on Djebar (including books, articles, reviews, and dissertations) number in the hundreds. The recent period marks not only Djebar's return to writing but, in the same space of apprehension, the effulgence of postcolonial and feminist cultural critique and a concomitant intensification of crisis in postcolonial states, of which Algeria's civil war has been a pressing example. I do not argue that Djebar's writing has been amenable in any opportune manner but that it traces the very proximity of crisis in which academia's own claims to knowledge are precipitate.

10. In addition to works already mentioned, Zimra's publications on Djebar include: "Comment peut-on être musulmane?" *Notre Librairie: Revue du Livre: Afrique, Caraïbes, Océan Indien* 118 (July–Sept. 1994): 57–63; "Disorienting the Subject in Djebar's *L'amour, la fantasia*," *Yale French Studies* 87 (1995): 149–70; and "Writing Woman: The Novels of Assia Djebar," *Substance* 21:3 (1992): 68–84. Mildred Mortimer's work on Djebar includes: *Assia Djebar* (Philadelphia: CELFAN Monographs, 1988); *Journeys Through the French African Novel* (London: Heinemann, 1990), pp. 147–64; "Assia Djebar's Algerian Quartet: A Study in Fragmented Autobiography," *Research in African Literatures* 28:2 (summer 1997): 102–17; "Parole et écriture dans *Ombre sultane*," in *Francophonie plurielle*, eds. Ginette Adamson and Jean-Marc Gouanvic (Quebec, PQ: Hurtubise HMH, 1995), pp. 15–20; and "Reappropriating the Gaze in Assia Djebar's Fiction and Film," in *Maghrebian Mosaic: A Literature in Transition*, ed. Mildred Mortimer (Boulder, CO: Rienner, 2000), pp. 213–28. Anne Donadey's research on Djebar has produced: *Recasting Postcolonialism: Women Writing Between Worlds* (Portsmouth, N.H.: Heinemann,

2001); "Between Amnesia and Anamnesis: Re-Membering the Fractures of Colonial History," *Studies in Twentieth Century Literature*, 23:1 (winter 1999): 111–16; "'Elle a rallumé le vif du passé': L'Ecriture-palimpseste d'Assia Djebar," in *Postcolonialisme et Autobiographie: Albert Memmi, Assia Djebar, Daniel Maximin*, eds. Alfred Hornung and Ernstpeter Ruhe (Amsterdam: Rodopi, 1998), pp. 101–15; and "Francophone Women Writers and Postcolonial Theory," in *Francophone Postcolonial Studies: A Critical Introduction*, eds. Charles Forsdick and David Murphy (London: Arnold, 2003), pp. 202–10.

11. Clarisse Zimra, "When the Past Answers the Present," *Callaloo* 16:1 (1993): 116–31.

12. See "Afterword" by Clarisse Zimra in Assia Djebar, *Women of Algiers in Their Apartment*, trans. Marjolijn de Jager (Charlottesville: University Press of Virginia, 1992).

13. There is a certain violence in the revelation of content that Djebar answers with violent metaphors (thus, the hand at the end of the first volume of the quartet is a severed one, like the severed head in Djebar's short story "La femme en morceaux" from the collection *Oran, langue mort*). The aim of writing is not the restoration of woman through content but the transformation of her apprehension through writing itself.

14. See Anne Donadey, "Between Amnesia and Anamnesis: Re-Membering the Fractures of Colonial History," *Studies in Twentieth Century Literature* 23:1 (winter 1999): 111–16; and Francoise Lionnet, *Autobiographical Voices: Race, Gender, Self Portraiture*, (Ithaca, N.Y.: Cornell University Press, 1989). Djebar uses the term in the same issue of *STCL*. The mode of memory is crucial to understanding both the writing of the self in women's history and postcolonial interruptions of the archive.

15. "La narration ne doit pas raconter l'histoire mais l'interrompre: c'est a dire, la suspendre, la surprendre a tout prix." See Clarisse Zimra, "Sounding Off the Absent Body: Intertextual Resonances in 'La femme qui pleure' and 'La femme en morceaux,'" *Research in African Literatures* 30:3 (fall 1999): 108. The quote is from Zimra's transcription and translation of her notes from an exchange between Assia Djebar and Trinh Minh-ha at Louisiana State University in March 1998.

16. Quoted from an interview not available in the French edition of Assia Djebar's *Femmes d'Alger dans leur appartement*. See "Afterword" by Clarisse Zimra in Assia Djebar, *Women of Algiers in Their Apartment*, trans. Marjolijn de Jager (Charlottesville: University Press of Virginia, 1992), p. 179.

17. Assia Djebar, director, *La Nouba des Femmes du Mont Chenoua*, 1978; and *Zerda ou les Chants de l'oubli*, 1982.

18. Jacques Derrida, *Monolingualism of the Other; or, The Prosthesis of Origin*, trans. Patrick Mensah (Stanford: Stanford University Press, 1998), p. 7.

19. Abdelkebir Khatibi's conversation with deconstruction if not Derrida has been long-standing. See, for instance, *Amour bilingue* (Saint-Clement-la-Rivière: Fata Morgana, 1983); and *Maghreb pluriel* (Paris: Denoël, 1983).

20. For an extensive critique on this point in relation to Glissant, see Peter Hitchcock, "Antillanité and the Art of Resistance," *Research in African Literatures* 27:2 (summer 1996): 33–50.

21. Clarisse Zimra has provided a useful exegesis on this point. See Clarisse Zimra, "Dis/orienting the Subject in *L'amour, la fantasia*," *Yale French Studies* 87 (1995): 149–70.

22. Anne Donadey, in particular, has explored the conceptual range of palimpsest vis-à-vis Djebar. See Anne Donadey, "The Multilingual Strategies of Postcolonial Literature: Assia Djebar's Algerian Palimpsest," *World Literature Today* 74:1 (winter 2000): 27–36.

23. Gerard Genette, *Palimpsests: Literature in the Second Degree*, trans. Channa Newman and Claude Doubinsky (Lincoln: University of Nebraska Press, 1998), p. 285.

24. Karl Marx and Friedrich Engels, *The Communist Manifesto* (New York: Verso, 1998), p. 67.

25. See Mary Louise Pratt, "Arts of the Contact Zone," *Profession* 91 (1991): 33–40.

26. Assia Djebar, "Anamnesis in the Language of Writing," trans. Anne Donadey and Christi Merrill, *Studies in Twentieth Century Literature* 23:1 (1999): 177–89.

27. Several authors have explored the importance of this homonym for Djebar's oeuvre. See, for instance, Mildred Mortimer, *Journeys Through the French African Novel* (London: Heinemann, 1990), pp. 147–64.

28. Clearly Djebar mourns, as *Algerian White* movingly demonstrates, yet I would argue that this is less in the service of some postcolonial melancholia than it is in reconceptualizing the space of utterance itself and its formal perquisites. It recognizes the politics of affect but does not let go of its corollary in effect. Instead of eliding one for the other or placing them in a dubious binary Djebar takes affect/effect as a condition of the materially sensate, a moment of possibility when the senses "become directly in their practice theoreticians" as Marx puts it. See Karl Marx, "Economic and Philosophical Manuscripts," in *The Marx/Engels Reader*, ed. Robert C. Tucker (New York: Norton, 1978), p. 87.

29. Clarisse Zimra, "Mapping Memory: Architectural Metaphors in Djebar's Unfinished Quartet," *Esprit Créateur* 43:1 (spring 2003): 58–68. The link between chiasmus and "chassé croisé" as an architectural form, as Zimra points out, provides the quartet with a certain structural integrity, but it is the weight of Djebar's alternative history that this structure cannot quite bear, and thus my emphasis on extension and conjunction.

30. I have invoked Williams's use of structure of feeling in the introduction. He first uses it in the third section of *The Long Revolution*. See Raymond Williams, *The Long Revolution*, rev. ed. (London: Pelican, 1965). A notoriously slippery term redolent of affect/effect, structure of feeling was never adequately elaborated by Williams himself. See, for instance, Raymond Williams, *Politics and Letters* (New York: Schocken, 1979), pp. 156–165.

31. Raymond Williams, *Marxism and Literature* (Oxford: Oxford University Press, 1976), p. 134.

32. While the notion that the structure of Djebar's Quartet is punctured by feeling is too neat, we nevertheless witness a profound interrogation of the relationship between its formal and historical components that are hard to resolve at the level of authorial consciousness. It is this imaginative edge that pushes Djebar's Quartet beyond the principle of completion even as it may assume four volumes. My chapter title invokes Luce Irigaray's trenchant analysis of woman's sexuality, *Ce sexe qui n'en est pas un* (1977), translated as *This Sex Which Is Not One*. I use this not just as a counter to the structuralism and masculinism often redolent in the will to form in literary history, but as a way to understand Djebar's generic excess and her resistance to what is proper to French and to literary engagement. For more on the specificity of Djebar as a "feminist-in-decolonization" (that also deploys Irigaray) see Gayatri Spivak, "Acting Bits/Identity Talk," *Critical Inquiry* 18 (summer 1992): 770–803. See also Luce Irigaray, *This Sex Which Is Not One*, trans. Catherine Porter (Ithaca, N.Y.: Cornell University Press, 1985).

33. Raymond Williams, *Keywords*, 2nd ed. (New York: Oxford University Press, 1984), p. 301.

34. This is the subject of a special issue of *Parallax* 4:2 (April–June 1998). "Translating 'Algeria'" is linked to a historical crisis in which the powers of translation themselves are called into question. Emily Apter's essay, "'Untranslatable' Algeria" (47–59) argues that while methods of translation must be questioned the greater danger is to leave Algeria "untranslated," whited-out in the international public sphere.

35. See "Afterword" by Clarisse Zimra in Assia Djebar, *Women of Algiers in Their Apartment*, trans. Marjolijn de Jager (Charlottesville: University Press of Virginia, 1992).

36. Assia Djebar, "Le Discours de Francfort," *Etudes* 3953 (September 2001): 239.

37. Two elements of transcoding are at work here. The first continues the problematic connection between transcoding and translation taken up by Gayatri Spivak, "Acting Bits/Identity Talk," *Critical Inquiry* 18 (Summer 1992): 770–803. The second redeploys the concept as it is used by Deleuze and Guattari. See Gilles Deleuze and Felix Guattari, *A Thousand Plateaus*, trans. and foreword by Brian Massumi (Minneapolis: University of Minnesota Press, 1987), pp. 314–15.

38. Djebar, "Discours," 244. Djebar makes the same claim in her "Preface" to "Filles D'Ismaël." See Assia Djebar, "Préface pour Filles d'Ismaël dans le vent et la tempête," *Etudes Littéraires*, 33:3 (autumn 2001): 29–49.

39. For a biographical sketch of Jugurtha, King of Numidia 118–106 B.C., see Phillip Chiviges Naylor and Alf Andrew Heggoy, *Historical Dictionary of Algeria* (Metuchen, N.J.: Scarecrow Press, 1994), pp. 239–40.

40. Here I mean to invoke the central trope of Kojin Karatani's extraordinary reading of Kant and Marx: Kojin Karatani, *Transcritique*, trans. Sabu Kohso (Cambridge, Mass.: M.I.T. Press, 2003). In the figure of the parallax Karatani finds a way to address an impossible point of view through philosophy's concern for

introspection as a mirror. Kant's mode in the *Critique of Pure Reason*, according to Karatani, is the "attempt to introduce an objectivity (qua otherness) that is totally alien to the conventional space of introspection = mirror." (2) The "pronounced parallax" that Kant invokes in his early work is an optical illusion to ward off an optical delusion. By shattering reflection as truth, Karatani is able to negotiate the truths of otherwise impermissible extensions, Kant to Marx, and so on. Slavoj Žižek has recently taken up this provocation in his own inimitable style. See Slavoj Žižek, *The Parallax View* (Cambridge, Mass.: M.I.T. Press, 2006).

41. See, for instance, Clarisse Zimra, "Sounding Off the Absent Body: Intertextual Resonances in 'La femme qui pleure' and 'La femme en morceaux,'" *Research in African Literatures* 30:3 (fall 1999): 108–24. See also Anne Donadey, *Recasting Postcolonialism* (Portsmouth, N.H.: Heinemann, 2001).

42. Polybe is nourished by simultaneous downfalls, "chutes concomitantes" [*Vaste*, 158]), and the aesthetic charge of emergency, that the writing of history is writing first of all ("l'écriture d'histoire est écriture d'abord" [*Vaste* 159]).

43. For an article that addresses the discrepant cosmopolitanism in Djebar's exile, see H. Adlai Murdoch, "Rewriting Writing: Identity, Exile and Renewal in Assia Djebar's *L'Amour, la fantasia*," *Yale French Studies* 83 (1993): 71–92. I have taken exile here as also the burden of institutional filiation.

44. To be fair, Djebar's *Le blanc de l'Algérie* also features veiled Muslim women on the cover, and the veil in France has had an even more vexed recent history. Because of Djebar's sensitivity to the power of images in orientalism one must assume a desire for displacement in this representation.

45. Here I borrow from Derrida on mischievous margins and frames. See Jacques Derrida, *The Truth in Painting*, trans. Geoffrey Bennington and Ian McCleod (Chicago: University of Chicago Press, 1987).

46. See, in particular, Trinh T. Minh-ha, *Woman Native Other* (Bloomington: Indiana University Press, 1989).

47. As noted by Donadey. See Anne Donadey, "The Multilingual Strategies of Postcolonial Literature: Assia Djebar's Algerian Palimpsest," *World Literature Today* 74:1 (winter 2000): 27–36.

48. The perspectival refers to what is given within the frame that can be seen. The aspectival refers to that which enables the possibility of this vision in the logic of the cinematic apparatus itself.

49. I have explored this Bakhtinian notion in several ways. See, for instance, Peter Hitchcock, "Exotopy and Feminist Critique" in *Bakhtin: Carnival and Other Subjects*, ed. David Shepherd (Amsterdam: Rodopi Press, 1993), pp. 194–209.

50. As Djebar explains in her interview with Zimra. See Clarisse Zimra, "'When the Past Answers the Present,'" *Callaloo* 16:1 (1993): 116–31.

51. Donadey, *Recasting*, 92.

52. Naoual El Saadoui, *Ferdaous: une voix en enfer*, trans. Assia Djebar and Assia Trabelsi (Paris: Éditions des femmes, 1981). Djebar also wrote a preface to the work (7–25).

53. See, for instance, Mildred Mortimer, "Assia Djebar's Algerian Quartet: A Study in Fragmented Autobiography," *Research in African Literatures* 28:2 (summer 1997): 102–17.

54. See Donadey, *Recasting*. See also John Erickson, "Translating the Untranslated: Djebar's '*Le blanc de l'Algérie*,'" *Research in African Literatures* 30:3 (fall 1999): 95–106.

55. See Reda Bensmaia, *Experimental Nations: Or, The Invention of the Maghreb* (Princeton: Princeton University Press, 2003).

56. The trilogy consists of Leïla Sebbar, *Shérazade, 17 ans, brune, frisée, les yeux verts* (Paris: Stock, 1982); *Les Carnets de Shérazade* (Paris: Stock, 1985); and *Le Fou de Shérazade* (Paris: Stock, 1991).

57. Reda Bensmaia, "The Vanished Mediators: on the Nature of Violence in Algeria," *Parallax* 7 (April–June 1998): 6.

Index

Cultural Memory | *in the Present*

István Rév, *Retroactive Justice: Prehistory of Post-Communism*

Paola Marrati, *Genesis and Trace: Derrida Reading Husserl and Heidegger*

Krzysztof Ziarek, *The Force of Art*

Marie-José Mondzain, *Image, Icon, Economy: The Byzantine Origins of the Contemporary Imaginary*

Cecilia Sjöholm, *The Antigone Complex: Ethics and the Invention of Feminine Desire*

Jacques Derrida and Elisabeth Roudinesco, *For What Tomorrow . . . : A Dialogue*

Elisabeth Weber, *Questioning Judaism: Interviews by Elisabeth Weber*

Jacques Derrida and Catherine Malabou, *Counterpath: Traveling with Jacques Derrida*

Martin Seel, *Aesthetics of Appearing*

Nanette Salomon, *Shifting Priorities: Gender and Genre in Seventeenth-Century Dutch Painting*

Jacob Taubes, *The Political Theology of Paul*

Jean-Luc Marion, *The Crossing of the Visible*

Eric Michaud, *The Cult of Art in Nazi Germany*

Anne Freadman, *The Machinery of Talk: Charles Peirce and the Sign Hypothesis*

Stanley Cavell, *Emerson's Transcendental Etudes*

Stuart McLean, *The Event and Its Terrors: Ireland, Famine, Modernity*

Beate Rössler, ed., *Privacies: Philosophical Evaluations*

Bernard Faure, *Double Exposure: Cutting Across Buddhist and Western Discourses*

Alessia Ricciardi, *The Ends of Mourning: Psychoanalysis, Literature, Film*

Alain Badiou, *Saint Paul: The Foundation of Universalism*

Gil Anidjar, *The Jew, the Arab: A History of the Enemy*

Jonathan Culler and Kevin Lamb, eds., *Just Being Difficult? Academic Writing in the Public Arena*

Jean-Luc Nancy, *A Finite Thinking*, edited by Simon Sparks

Theodor W. Adorno, *Can One Live after Auschwitz? A Philosophical Reader*, edited by Rolf Tiedemann

Patricia Pisters, *The Matrix of Visual Culture: Working with Deleuze in Film Theory*

Andreas Huyssen, *Present Pasts: Urban Palimpsests and the Politics of Memory*

Talal Asad, *Formations of the Secular: Christianity, Islam, Modernity*

Dorothea von Mücke, *The Rise of the Fantastic Tale*

Marc Redfield, *The Politics of Aesthetics: Nationalism, Gender, Romanticism*

Emmanuel Levinas, *On Escape*

Dan Zahavi, *Husserl's Phenomenology*

Rodolphe Gasché, *The Idea of Form: Rethinking Kant's Aesthetics*

Michael Naas, *Taking on the Tradition: Jacques Derrida and the Legacies of Deconstruction*

Herlinde Pauer-Studer, ed., *Constructions of Practical Reason:
Interviews on Moral and Political Philosophy*

Jean-Luc Marion, *Being Given That: Toward a Phenomenology of Givenness*

Theodor W. Adorno and Max Horkheimer, *Dialectic of Enlightenment*

Ian Balfour, *The Rhetoric of Romantic Prophecy*

Martin Stokhof, *World and Life as One: Ethics and Ontology
in Wittgenstein's Early Thought*

Gianni Vattimo, *Nietzsche: An Introduction*

Jacques Derrida, *Negotiations: Interventions and Interviews, 1971-1998*,
ed. Elizabeth Rottenberg

Brett Levinson, *The Ends of Literature: The Latin American
"Boom" in the Neoliberal Marketplace*

Timothy J. Reiss, *Against Autonomy: Cultural Instruments,
Mutualities, and the Fictive Imagination*

Hent de Vries and Samuel Weber, eds., *Religion and Media*

Niklas Luhmann, *Theories of Distinction: Re-Describing the
Descriptions of Modernity*, ed. and introd. William Rasch

Johannes Fabian, *Anthropology with an Attitude: Critical Essays*

Michel Henry, *I Am the Truth: Toward a Philosophy of Christianity*

Gil Anidjar, *"Our Place in Al-Andalus": Kabbalah, Philosophy,
Literature in Arab-Jewish Letters*

Hélène Cixous and Jacques Derrida, *Veils*

F. R. Ankersmit, *Historical Representation*

F. R. Ankersmit, *Political Representation*

Elissa Marder, *Dead Time: Temporal Disorders in the
Wake of Modernity (Baudelaire and Flaubert)*

Reinhart Koselleck, *The Practice of Conceptual History:
Timing History, Spacing Concepts*

Niklas Luhmann, *The Reality of the Mass Media*

Hubert Damisch, *A Theory of /Cloud/: Toward a History of Painting*

Jean-Luc Nancy, *The Speculative Remark: (One of Hegel's bon mots)*

Jean-François Lyotard, *Soundproof Room: Malraux's Anti-Aesthetics*

Jan Pato<hac>cka, *Plato and Europe*

Hubert Damisch, *Skyline: The Narcissistic City*

Isabel Hoving, *In Praise of New Travelers: Reading Caribbean Migrant Women Writers*

Richard Rand, ed., *Futures: Of Jacques Derrida*

William Rasch, *Niklas Luhmann's Modernity: The Paradoxes of Differentiation*

Jacques Derrida and Anne Dufourmantelle, *Of Hospitality*